Contemporary Post Keynesian Analysis

CONTEMPORARY POST KEYNESIAN ANALYSIS

Edited by L. Randall Wray and Mathew Forstater

This volume collects a number of papers presented at the 7th International Post Keynesian Summer School and Workshop during the summer of 2002 at the University of Missouri–Kansas City. Major topics covered include: perspectives on current economic policy; Post Keynesian approaches to monetary theory and policy; economic development, growth and inflation; Kaleckian perspectives on distribution; economic methodology; and history of heterdox economic theory. Contributors include: Eckhard Hein, Hassan Bougrine, Robert Parenteau, Stephanie Bell, Claudio Sardoni, Thomas Swanke, Etelberto Ortiz, Arturo Huerta, Rumen Gechev, Alcino Camara and Matias Vernengo, Harry Bloch and David Sapsford, Jerry Courvisanos and Bart Verspagen, A. Laramie, D. Mair, and P.J. Reynolds, Richard Arena, James Juniper, Paul Downward and Andrew Mearman, Claude Gnos, Antonio Macedo e Silva, and Dimitri Uzunidis and Blandine Laperche.

Contemporary Post Keynesian Analysis

Edited by

L. Randall Wray

University of Missouri–Kansas City, USA

Mathew Forstater

University of Missouri–Kansas City, USA

Edward Elgar

Cheltenham, UK • Northampton, MA, USA

Publishing by
Edward Elgar Publishing Limited
Glensanda House
Montpellier Parade
Cheltenham
Glos GL50 1UA
UK

Edward Elgar Publishing, Inc.
136 West Street
Suite 202
Northampton
Massachusetts 01060
USA

A catalogue record for this book
is available from the British Library

Library of Congress Cataloguing in Publication Data
International Post Keynesian Workshop (7th : 2002 : University of Missouri, Kansas City)
Contemporary post Keynesian analysis / edited by L. Randall Wray, Mathew Forstater.
p. cm.
"This volume collects a number of papers presented at the 7th International Post Keynesian Summer School and Workshop during the summer of 2002 at the University of Missouri, Kansas City."
Includes bibliographical references.
1. Monetary policy. 2. Inflation (Finance). 3. Economic development. 4. Keynesian economics. 5. Economics. I. Wray, L. Randall, 1953- II. Forstater, Mathew, 1961- III. Title.

HG230.3.I58 2002
330.I5'6--dc22

2004050637

ISBN 1 84376 460 1

Typeset by Manton Typesetters, Louth, Lincolnshire, UK
Printed and bound in Great Britain by MPG Books Ltd, Bodmin, Cornwall

Contents

List of contributors vii
Preface ix

PART I POST KEYNESIAN PERSPECTIVES ON CURRENT ECONOMIC POLICY

1 Wage bargaining and monetary policy in the EMU: a post Keynesian perspective 3
Eckhard Hein
2 Public debt and private wealth 24
Hassan Bougrine
3 Exploring the economics of euphoria: using post Keynesian tools to understand the US bubble and its aftermath 44
Robert W. Parenteau

PART II POST KEYNESIAN APPROACHES TO MONETARY THEORY AND POLICY

4 Money in the time of the Internet: electronic money and its effects 69
Claudio Sardoni
5 Understanding the implications of money being a social convention 84
Thomas A. Swanke
6 Demand management and the monetary system: do currency boards and currency unions spell the end for Keynesian policy? 100
Stephanie A. Bell

PART III POST KEYNESIAN CONTRIBUTIONS ON DEVELOPMENT, GROWTH AND INFLATION

7 Stability conditions for a small open economy 121
Etelberto Ortiz
8 Mexico: strong currency and weak economy 139
Arturo Huerta

9 Economic policy of sustainable development in the countries of transition towards a market economy 157
Rumen V. Gechev
10 Allied, German and Latin perspectives on inflation 172
Alcino Câmara and Matias Vernengo

PART IV KALECKIAN PERSPECTIVES ON GROWTH, INFLATION AND DISTRIBUTION

11 Commodity prices and the dynamics of inflation in Australia 187
Harry Bloch and David Sapsford
12 Innovation and investment in capitalist economies, 1870–2000: Kaleckian dynamics and evolutionary life cycles 205
Jerry Courvisanos and Bart Verspagen
13 Kalecki's theory of income distribution: the answer to a maiden's prayer? 227
Anthony J. Laramie, Douglas Mair and Peter J. Reynolds

PART V METHODOLOGY

14 On the relation between individual and collective beliefs: a comparison between Keynes's and Hayek's economic theories 249
Richard Arena
15 A Keynesian critique of recent applications of risk-sensitive control theory in macroeconomics 267
James Juniper
16 Presenting 'demi-regularities' of pricing behaviour: the need for triangulation 285
Paul Downward and Andrew Mearman

PART VI ISSUES IN THE HISTORY OF THOUGHT

17 Analysing and fighting recession with reference to Keynes 301
Claude Gnos
18 From Say's law to Keynes, from Keynes to Walras's law: some ironies in the history of economic thought 310
Antonio Carlos Macedo e Silva
19 Power of the firm and new mercantilism: an analysis based on Joan Robinson's thought 333
Dimitri Uzunidis and Blandine Laperche

Index 349

Contributors

Richard Arena is Professor at LATAPSES in Universite de Nice, Sophia-Antipolis, Valbonne, France.

Stephanie A. Bell is Assistant Professor of Economics at University of Missouri–Kansas City, Kansas City, Missouri, USA.

Harry Bloch is Professor of Economics at Curtin University of Technology, Perth, Australia.

Hassan Bougrine is Associate Professor at the School of Business Administration of Al Akhawayn University, Ifrane, Morocco and Associate Professor of Economics at Laurentian University, Sudbury, Canada.

Alcino Câmara is Dean of the Law and Economics Center in Federal University of Rio de Janeiro, Rio de Janeiro, Brazil.

Jerry Courvisanos is Senior Lecturer in Innovation and Entrepreneurship at the School of Business in University of Ballarat, Ballarat, Australia.

Paul Downward is Professor of Economics at Staffordshire University, Stoke on Trent, United Kingdom.

Mathew B. Forstater is Associate Professor of Economics at University of Missouri–Kansas City, Kansas City, Missouri, USA

Rumen V. Gechev is Professor of Economics and Business at Galen University, San Ignacio, Belize.

Claude Gnos is Professor at the Centre d'Etudes Monétaires et Financières – LATEC-CNRS in Université de Bourgogne Pôle d'Economie et de Gestion, Dijon, France.

Eckhard Hein is Senior Researcher in Macroeconomics at WSI in der Hans Böeckler Stiftung, Düsseldorf, Germany.

Arturo Huerta is Professor at the Economic Faculty of National University of Mexico in Mexico City, México.

James Juniper is Lecturer at the School of Policy in University of Newcastle, Callaghan, Australia.

Blandine Laperche is Assistant Professor in Economics and Director of the team 'Firms and Innovation' (Lab.RII) at the Université du Littoral Côte d'Opale, Dunkerque, France.

Anthony J. Laramie is Professor of Economics at Merrimack College, North Andover, Massachusetts, USA.

Antonio Carlos Macedo e Silva is Assistant Professor at the Institute of Economics of University of Campinas, São Paulo, Brazil.

Douglas Mair is Professor at the School of Management and Languages in Heriot-Watt University, Edinburgh, UK.

Andrew Mearman is Senior Lecturer in Economics at University of the West of England, Bristol, UK.

Etelberto Ortiz is Professor of Economics at Universidad Autónoma Metropolitana – Xochimilco, Mexico City, México.

Robert W. Parenteau, CFA is Economic Strategist at Dresdner RCM Global Investors, San Francisco, California, USA.

Peter J. Reynolds is Professor of Economics at the Staffordshire Business School of University of Staffordshire, Stoke on Trent, UK.

David Sapsford is Edward Gonner Professor of Applied Economics and Chairman of the Economics Division at University of Liverpool Management School, Liverpool, UK.

Claudio Sardoni is Professor of Economics at University of Rome 'La Sapienza', Rome, Italy.

Thomas A. Swanke is Assistant Professor of Economics at Chadron State College, Chadron, Nebraska, USA.

Dimitri Uzunidis is Professor of Economics and Director of the research unit 'Redéploiement Industriel et Innovation' (Lab.RII) at Université du Littoral Côte d'Opale, Dunkerque, France.

Matias Vernengo is Assistant Professor of Economics at University of Utah, Salt Lake City, Utah, USA.

Bart Verspagen is Professor at the Eindhoven Centre for Innovation Studies in Eindhoven University of Technology, Eindhoven, The Netherlands.

L. Randall Wray is Professor of Economics at University of Missouri–Kansas City, Kansas City, Missouri, USA.

Preface

In the 1970s it became obvious to many non-mainstream economists that graduate students at universities around the world were rarely, if ever, exposed to Keynes's 'general theory' macro analysis, the underlying Marshallian micro-theory and its Sraffian critique and the developments that had taken place since Keynes's and Sraffa's major works, or even to an analysis of the logical difficulties of applying the mainstream models of classical or neoclassical synthesis Keynesianism to real world problems.

Three economists – two Italian and one American living in Italy – decided something had to be done to expose graduate students and young assistant professors of economics to these important, but neglected by most university economics departments, aspects of economic analysis. Otherwise, the areas of knowledge that had been created and developed in Cambridge would be lost to the profession – to the detriment of the entire free world.

The three – Sergio Parrinello, Pierangelo Garagnani and Jan Kregel – obtained funding to start a summer school and conference to occur each year for 10 to 14 days in Italy at the end of August. The Students in this 'school' would be assistant professors and graduate students from around the world. Their travel expenses, hotel accommodation and meals would be subsidized. The attraction for the students would be exposure to challenging new and different ideas, and to obtain a subsidized two-week holiday in Italy. The faculty was composed of professors from various universities in Europe, the USA, Canada and so on, linked to the Cambridge tradition.

A preparatory conference organized by the trio was held in Udine in Italy in the late 1970s. In the following years till the mid-1980s the Europa Hotel with its own private 'beach' on the Adriatic (just outside Trieste, Italy) served as the location for what became known as the 'Trieste Summer School'. Since the Europa Hotel was also a training hotel for chefs, sumptuous and delicious meals (and wine) were added delights for those attending. A tremendous *esprit de corps* was established among the students and between students and faculty at the school.

Unfortunately, by the mid-1980s the organizing trio were having problems obtaining financing and agreeing on the content for the annual meetings. Accordingly, a second phase of this institution was started in 1988 in Knoxville, Tennessee. In 1986 I had received an appointment as the Holly Chair of

Excellence in Political Economy at the University of Tennessee. As part of my employment agreement, the University agreed to make funds available for summer conference in Knoxville for every other year. Consequently, from 1988 to 2000 almost every other year a one-week post Keynesian conference sponsored by the *Journal of Post Keynesian Economics* and the University of Tennessee was held at the Hilton Hotel in Knoxville, Tennessee. Between 60 and 75 professors and graduate students from as many as 16 countries in Europe, Asia, Australia, New Zealand, Africa, and North and South Americas participated in these biennial Knoxville conferences. A selection of the best papers were published in a conference volume for each biennial meeting. Unfortunately, financial problems at the university made it increasingly difficult to finance the biannual conference and the last Knoxville conference was held in the summer of 2000.

In the summer of 2002, the University of Missouri at Kansas City and the Center for Full Employment and Price Stability began the third phase of this post Keynesian school. In June of 2002, they were able to finance a week-long post Keynesian summer school for graduate students and new assistant professors at the university. The school was followed by a three-day conference at the Marriott Hotel in Kansas City. A selection of the best papers from this 2002 conference is published in this volume.

At the time of writing this Preface, post Keynesians from around the world eagerly look forward to the next post Keynesian summer school and conference to be held in Kansas City in June 2004. So the institution of a post Keynesian school and conference that started in Italy still lives on – and the post Keynesian development of Keynesian 'general theory' continues to be made available to eager young minds searching for real solutions to the real world problems of our twenty-first century global entrepreneurial economy.

Paul Davidson
Editor, *Journal of Post Keynesian Economics*

PART I

Post Keynesian Perspectives on Current Economic Policy

1. Wage bargaining and monetary policy in the EMU: a post Keynesian perspective*

Eckhard Hein

1 INTRODUCTION

Since the introduction of the European Monetary Union (EMU) in 1999 monetary policies for the euro area as a whole have been conducted by the Euro System with the European Central Bank (ECB) at its head. According to the Maastricht Treaty, the ECB's primary goal is price stability. Only when price stability has been achieved ought the ECB to support economic policies of the European Union (EU). In choosing its precise goals and instruments the ECB is independent: it is free to define price stability and to apply the appropriate means to achieve it (Bean, 1998; Bibow, 2002a). This institutional design is based on the conviction that politically, economically and personally independent central banks are the solution to the 'time inconsistency problem' of monetary policy. According to this position, independent central bankers display a higher degree of conservatism concerning price stability and a higher degree of credibility in pursuing low inflation than democratically elected politicians. In this view the latter are prone to use 'surprise inflation' in order to boost employment, which will, however, only increase inflation expectations in the private sector without any long-run real positive effects on employment.[1] Central bank independence is hence viewed to guarantee price stability as a 'free lunch', without real costs in terms of output, employment or growth.[2]

There are, however, major doubts whether time inconsistency should be considered the true cause of inflation and whether the role of independent central banks is adequately assessed in this approach (Bibow, 1999; Forder, 1998). From the perspective of a 'monetary theory of production' originating from J.M. Keynes and elaborated in post Keynesian economics, monetary variables controlled by the central bank determine the real equilibrium of the economic system and, hence, the level of employment.[3] Inflation is not a monetary phenomenon but is mainly caused by conflict over distribution in the private sector. In the face of high inflation caused by incompatible distribution claims, a higher degree of conservatism associated with central bank independence will cause losses of employment, at least in the short run, and will affect income shares and growth in the long run.[4] These losses could be avoided, if distribution conflict and, hence, inflation could be contained by institutional arrangements, that is, incomes policies. These arrangements should aim not only at nominal wage and price restraints in periods of full employment, but also at stable unit wage costs and stable prices in periods of recession in order to avoid devastating macroeconomic effects of debt deflation. That is why especially the degree of wage bargaining co-ordination will be of utmost importance for macroeconomic performance under the condition of independent and conservative central banks, as the research on strategic interaction between central banks and wage bargaining has clarified.[5]

As a starting point for our analysis of monetary policies and wage bargaining during the initial period of EMU we draft a post Keynesian model on the interaction of central banks and wage bargaining in section 2 of this chapter. In section 3 we use the results derived from the theoretical discussion to assess the interaction of monetary policy and wage bargaining in EMU. In section 4 the results are summarized and some conclusions for future economic policies are drawn.

2 MONETARY POLICY AND WAGE BARGAINING: A POST KEYNESIAN VIEW

In order to facilitate the analysis of monetary policies and wage bargaining in EMU we outline a simple post Keynesian model of wage bargaining, inflation and monetary policy which will then be supplemented by some effects of wage-bargaining co-ordination. In an open economy without economic activity by the state, the level of employment in this model is determined by effective demand expected by entrepreneurs, when labour productivity is given or following an exogenous trend. The effect of foreign demand on domestic employment is given by the current account surplus which is determined by the real exchange rate – if we assume the Marshall-Lerner condition to hold – and by the growth differential between domestic and foreign economies. With the propensities to save out of profits exceeding that out of wages and both propensities given, private investment is the main domestic determinant of effective demand. Investment depends positively on the expected profit rate and negatively on the monetary interest rate.

The interest rate in a monetary economy is an exogenous variable for the income generating process and is determined by the central bank, whereas the volumes of credit and money are endogenously given by effective demand financed by credit.[6] With the technical conditions of production given, the expected rate of profit depends on the development of the profit share and of capacity utilization. Capacity utilization reflects the development of aggregate demand. The profit share is determined by firms' mark-up pricing on unit variable costs in incompletely competitive markets, that is, by the mark-up and by the relation of costs of intermediate products to wage costs.

The mark-up is determined by the degree of domestic and foreign competition in the goods market. As the mark-up has to cover the firm's actual and imputed interest payments, the minimum mark-up is also affected by the interest rate. For the same reason, the rate of interest determines the minimum rate of profit on real investment in the long run. In the short run, however, there need not be an immediate positive impact of interest rate variations on the mark-up, the profit share and the profit rate, but we can rather suppose an inverse effect on investment and employment.[7] The short-run effects of interest rate variations on investment may be asymmetric. Permanently rising interest rates will choke investment and, hence, employment at a certain point. Falling interest rates, however, may not be able to stimulate investment and employment, if entrepreneurs' profit expectations are depressed. If changes in the interest rate generated by monetary policy are lasting, mark-up and profit share may change in the same direction, because in the long run, firms can only sustain those production processes which yield the minimum rate of profit determined by the interest rate.[8] Changing mark-ups and income shares, however, have no unique effects on investment and employment. Rising mark-ups mean rising unit profits but also falling consumption demand and perhaps falling export demand, if increasing mark-ups are associated with rising domestic prices and, hence, decreasing international price competitiveness of domestic producers. Therefore, the overall long-run effects of changing interest rates on investment and employment depend on the interest rate elasticity of the mark-up, on the savings propensities out of wages and out of profits, on the elasticities of investment with respect to interest rates, unit costs and capacity utilization, and on the effects exerted through foreign demand.[9]

Having so far sketched the determinants of distribution and aggregate demand in our post Keynesian approach we may now discuss the interaction of wage bargaining and monetary policy. Figure 1.1 displays a 'conflicting claims' model of employment and inflation assuming constant production coefficients.[10]

Although wage bargaining is concerned with money wage rates it is assumed that labour unions intend to achieve a certain real wage rate – and a certain wage share with labour productivity (y) given and anticipated. The labour unions' target real wage rate (w_b^r) depends positively on the volume

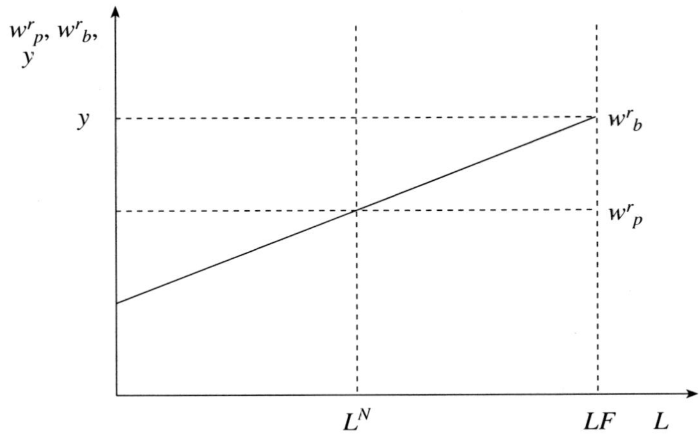

Figure 1.1 Employment and distribution conflict

of employment (L) determined by aggregate demand and, with the working population (LF) given, on the employment rate (L/LF), because unemployment has a negative impact on union bargaining strength:

$$w_b^r = w_b^r\left(\underset{+}{\frac{L}{LF}}, \underset{+}{y}\right). \tag{1.1}$$

At this stage we assume that unions do not consider the macroeconomic effects of their nominal wage demands. There is neither co-ordination between unions in different firms or industries, nor between wage bargaining and monetary policy. Full employment is therefore associated with a union target real wage rate equal to labour productivity (y). Therefore, unemployment has the function to curtail distribution claims of labourers, a view already held by Marx (1867) and Kalecki (1943).

The feasible real wage rate (w_p^r) is given by mark-up pricing of firms. In incomplete markets firms set prices (p) according to a constant mark-up (m) on constant unit variable costs consisting of wage costs and costs for intermediate products which are assumed to be imported:

$$p = (1+m)\left(\frac{w}{y} + \alpha e p_f\right), \tag{1.2}$$

with w for the nominal wage rate, α for the input-output coefficient of imported intermediates, e for the exchange rate and p_f for the price of imported intermediates in foreign currency. The feasible real wage rate given by firms' pricing is therefore determined as:

$$w_p^r = \frac{w}{p}\left(\frac{1}{1+m} - \alpha e\frac{p_f}{p}\right)y. \qquad (1.3)$$

The unions' target real wage and the feasible real wage only coincide by accident. Only if aggregate demand in the goods market generates a volume of employment of L^N, will the distribution claims of domestic firms, domestic labourers and foreign countries be compatible and there will be no acceleration or deceleration of inflation. The rate of unemployment $[(LF - L^N)/LF]$ associated with this volume of employment may therefore be termed the 'non-accelerating-inflation-rate-of-unemployment' (NAIRU). If employment given by effective demand in the goods market exceeds L^N, there will be increasing inflation rates due to escalating conflict. If employment falls short of L^N, inflation rates will be falling and deflation might be the final outcome.

In a model with endogenous money and with investment dominated by expectations related to profitability and aggregate demand, the NAIRU cannot be considered a strong attractor of actual unemployment determined by effective demand in the short run, because there is no 'real balance' effect. Profit expectations and real debt effects on private investment will rather cause cumulative deviation of actual unemployment from the NAIRU.

But accelerating inflation rates originating from incompatible distribution claims will be halted by monetary policies, especially by an independent and conservative central bank aiming at the preservation of nominal wealth and supporting distribution claims of capital. The central bank's policy instrument is the short-term nominal interest rate. Its variations will have lagged effects on the long-term rate in financial markets. Figure 1.2 shows the short-run effects of restrictive monetary policies on employment via effective demand.

As has already been mentioned above, the capacities of the central bank to target inflation are asymmetric. Accelerating inflation can finally be stopped by central banks permanently increasing interest rates, whereas decelerating inflation and deflation cannot be converted by the central bank in either case. Therefore, in our model the NAIRU is only a limit to employment enforced by central banks reacting to conflict inflation. The NAIRU is not the equilibrium rate of unemployment originating from labour market imperfections as in New Keynesian models. In these models either a real balance effect or symmetric reactions and effects of monetary policies have to be assumed in order to neglect long-term effective demand impacts on unemployment and to interpret the NAIRU as the equilibrium rate of unemployment given by supply conditions.[11]

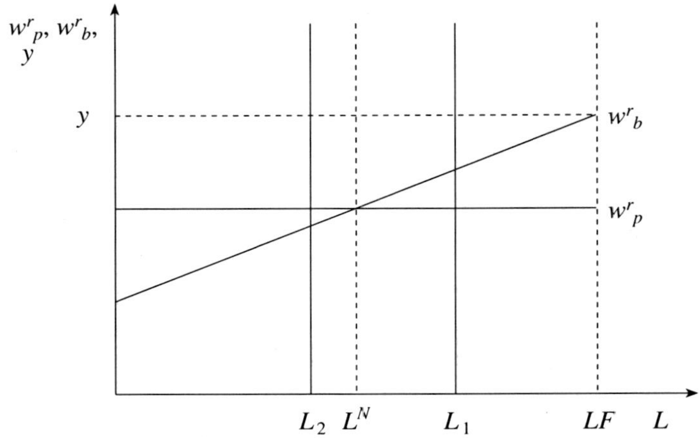

Figure 1.2 Short-run effects of rising interest rates

Although there are no market forces adjusting unemployment to the NAIRU in the short run, there may be some forces making the NAIRU endogenous to the development of effective demand in the long run. At least four channels for the adjustment of the NAIRU to unemployment determined by effective demand can be identified. First, there is the effect of unemployment on effective labour supply. If unemployment persistently exceeds the NAIRU, de-qualification and stigmatization will reduce the number of unemployed competing effectively for jobs, shift the unions' target real wage curve upwards and increase the NAIRU (Layard, Nickell and Jackman, 1991). Second, there is a potential effect of the interest rate on the mark-up. If rising unemployment has been caused by a persistent increase in interest rates, the mark-up may have to increase as well, shifting the feasible real wage curve downwards and adjusting the NAIRU to the actual unemployment rate. This process will be reinforced through a third channel which considers the effects of capital stock growth on productivity growth. Slow investment growth will have a dampening effect on productivity growth and, hence, the feasible real wage rate.[12] A fourth channel considers the effects of slow domestic growth on the exchange rate. If slow domestic growth causes domestic currency depreciation in international financial markets, rising import prices will also contribute to a downward shift of the feasible real wage curve and an increasing NAIRU.[13]

From the endogenous nature of the NAIRU sketched above, it follows that distribution and growth effects of rising interest rates chosen to terminate accelerating inflation in the short run may have adverse effects on inflation in the long run. As a persistent increase in interest rates may cause a higher

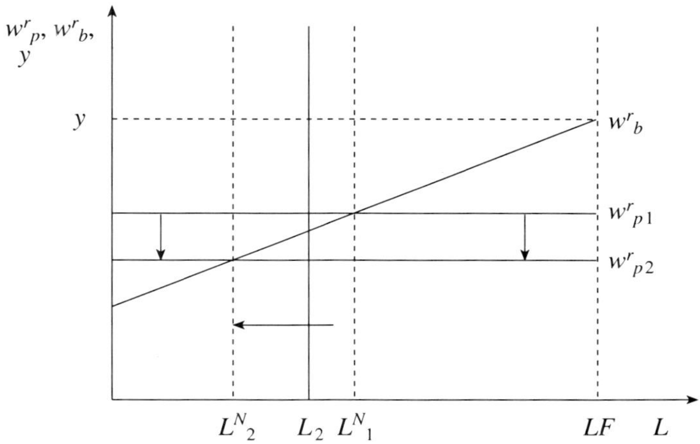

Figure 1.3 Long-run effects of rising interest rates

mark-up, the feasible real wage curve will shift downwards and trigger a higher NAIRU, as shown in Figure 1.3. A negative impact of high interest rates on productivity growth through dampened capital stock growth may also contribute to a rising NAIRU. The same is true, if slow domestic growth causes domestic currency depreciation in international financial markets and, hence, rising costs of imported intermediates. The increase in unemployment generated by the short-run inverse effect of restrictive monetary policies on investment, aggregate demand and output may therefore be insufficient for long-run stability of inflation; the economy will rather be plagued with stagflation. Unemployment will therefore have to increase again through even more restrictive monetary policies in order to reduce inflation. This downward spiral reveals that containing inflation by means of increasing interest rates may not only be harmful for production and employment, but may also be ineffective in achieving stable inflation rates.

In our model, the NAIRU as a short-run limit to employment is affected by the determinants of the feasible real wage, on the one hand, especially by the mark-up and the real exchange rate. On the other hand, it depends on those factors which have an impact on distribution claims of labour unions and their capacities to enforce nominal wage hikes. Given that independent and conservative central banks will prevent unemployment from falling short of the NAIRU, the sustainable degree of employment will be affected by the ability of wage-bargaining institutions to anticipate and internalize the effects of wage hikes on inflation. But the sustainable degree of employment also depends on the actual path of employment and growth on which monetary policies as well as wage bargaining have a major impact.

As recent research on the interaction of independent central banks and wage-bargaining institutions has shown, effectively co-ordinated wage bargaining is able to internalize negative macroeconomic wage externalities (Franzese, 2001a; 2001b; Hein, 2002a). In economies with a high degree of 'effective' wage-bargaining co-ordination, the reduction of inflation rates by independent central banks is accompanied by fewer employment losses than in economies with a low degree of co-ordination. Effective wage-bargaining co-ordination is characterized by a high degree of horizontal bargaining co-ordination between industries (pattern bargaining, state imposed or sponsored co-ordination, intra-associational co-ordination, and so on). In order to solve the implementation problem of collective agreements and to prevent wage dumping or wage drift, effective bargaining co-ordination also has to include a high degree of vertical co-ordination within industries (a high level of union and bargaining agreement coverage, legal enforceability of collective agreements, peace obligations, and so on) (Kittel and Traxler, 2001). The influence of effective co-ordination of wage bargaining on sustainable employment is shown in Figure 1.4.

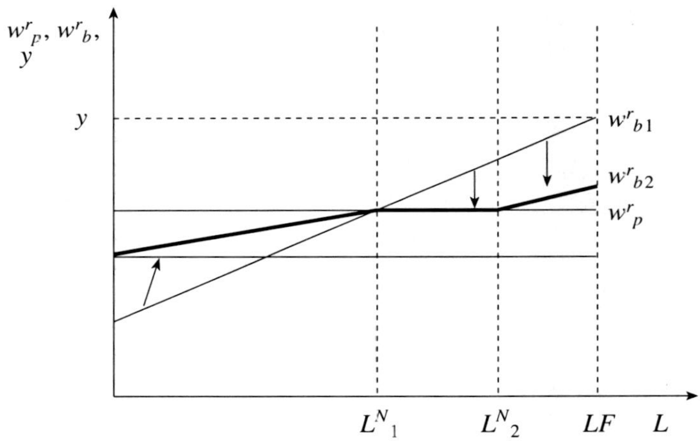

Figure 1.4 Effective co-ordination of wage bargaining

With an increasing degree of effective wage-bargaining co-ordination, the labour unions' target real wage curve shifts from w^r_{b1} to w^r_{b2}. Between L^N_1 and L^N_2 the bargaining parties are able to accept the feasible real wage and to exhaust the scope for distribution taking into account the inflation objective of independent central banks. By means of effectively co-ordinated wage bargaining a constant inflation rate becomes compatible with a range of employment levels. The NAIRU as the short-run limit to employment is no longer unique. Contrary to prevailing propositions, a reduction of the NAIRU can be attained by means of organizing the labour market and co-ordinating the bargaining parties, and does not require decentralization of wage bargaining and deregulation of labour markets. A high degree of effective wage-bargaining co-ordination also has the additional virtue that increasing unemployment will not cause immediate disinflation or deflation with its negative impacts on effective demand and employment. Effective wage-bargaining co-ordination is therefore not only a superior method to contain inflation in an economic upswing, compared to restrictive monetary policies, it is also able to stabilize the economy in an economic downswing.

3 MONETARY POLICIES AND WAGE BARGAINING IN THE EURO AREA SINCE 1999

The transition to the EMU in 1999 has caused major changes in the institutional framework and the interaction between monetary policy and wage bargaining. Under the conditions of an independent and conservative central bank the perspectives for employment and inflation in the euro area depend on the development of wage-bargaining co-ordination, on the one hand, and on the central bank's monetary policies, on the other.[14]

At the start of EMU wage bargaining, systems of member countries differed substantially. Since then systems with a high degree of national co-ordination (Austria, Germany, Finland and the Netherlands) have coexisted with systems of low co-ordination on the national level (France, Italy, Ireland, Portugal and Spain). Under these conditions there have been several attempts by labour unions to co-ordinate wage bargaining across borders.[15] In the Declaration of Doorn (1998), the trade union federations of Germany and the Benelux countries agreed to aim at real wage increases according to productivity growth in order to prevent wage dumping. At the sector level, the European Metalworker Federation (EMF) has been the first to develop concepts of European co-ordination of bargaining demands based on productivity growth rates and inflation. This line has now been followed by most of the European industry federations and by the European Trade Union Confederation (ETUC). Transnational wage-bargaining co-ordination, however, faces serious obstacles, which are rooted in the different national wage-bargaining systems and the different degrees of national co-ordination.

These basic problems are aggravated by some overall trends in the development of wage-bargaining institutions. According to Calmfors (2001), on the one hand, there has been a general trend towards decentralization of wage bargaining since the 1970s because of decentralization of business decisions, stronger international competition and a desire of capital to limit union power.

On the other hand, there has been a tendency towards national social pacts since the 1980s, which aim at nominal wage moderation in order to maintain or improve international price competitiveness of national business under the conditions of slow growth by means of 'competitive corporatism'. Although these two tendencies might contradict each other, they are both detrimental to wage-bargaining co-ordination across EMU countries. Since the introduction of EMU in 1999 the ECB has therefore been faced with uncoordinated wage bargaining across the euro area.

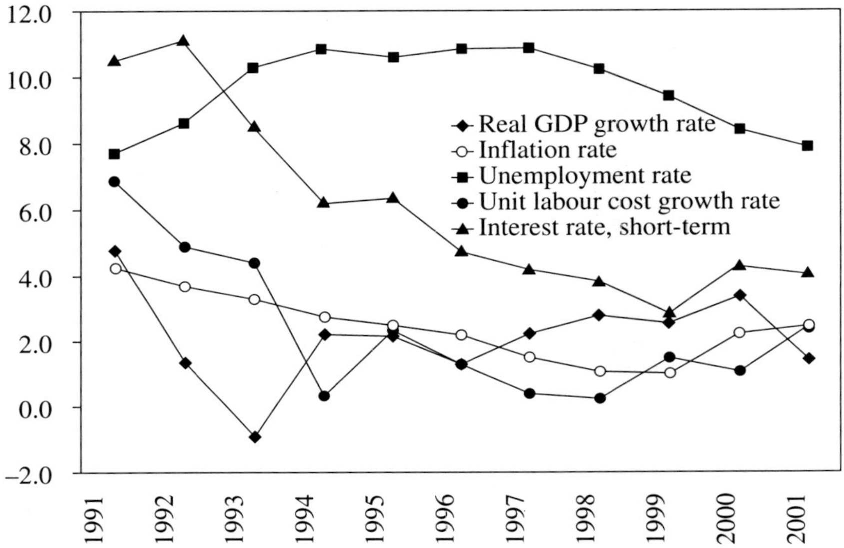

Figure 1.5 Real GDP growth rate, unemployment rate, interest rate, inflation rate and unit labour cost growth in the euro area (EU-12), 1991–2001 (in %)

When the ECB started operations, inflation rates and nominal short-term interest rates in the euro area had come down in the course of the convergence process (Figure 1.5). Nominal unit labour cost growth had also slowed down and had been substantially below consumer price inflation since the mid-1990s. From this it follows, that the wage share in national income had been decreasing during the convergence process. But a high price had to be paid for disinflation and increased profitability through redistribution at the expense of labour: real gross domestic product (GDP) growth slackened and unemployment increased during the first half of the 1990s and remained at a high level during the second half.[16]

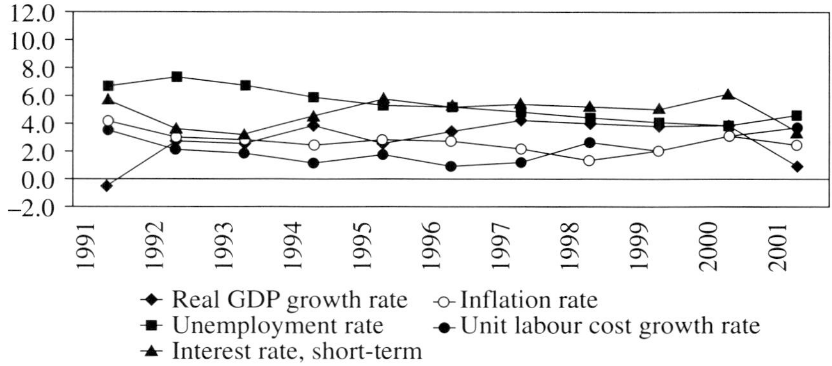

Figure 1.6 *Real GDP growth rate, unemployment rate, interest rate, inflation rate, and unit labour cost growth in the USA, 1991–2001 (in %)*

This weak performance of the countries that were to form the euro area is especially apparent when compared to the performance of the US economy during the 1990s (Figure 1.6). The USA experienced low inflation, which had been decreasing until 1998 and was then increasing until 2000, high real GDP growth rates, especially from the mid-1990s until 2000, and an unemployment rate constantly falling to 4 per cent in 2000. Unit labour cost growth had been below consumer price inflation until 1997 and has approached and finally exceeded the inflation rate since then. The expansive character of the Federal Reserve's monetary strategy accounts for the sustained boom in the second half of the 1990s, when the Fed refrained from monetary contraction although the unemployment rate fell below 6 per cent what was then considered to be the US NAIRU. Nor was the federal funds rate – which has a direct impact on the short-term interest rate displayed in Figure 1.6 – increased when unit labour cost growth began to accelerate in 1998. Only when, in 2000, unit labour cost growth and consumer price inflation exceeded 3 per cent and the stock market price exaggerations had to be confined, did the Fed begin to tighten and, so, contributed to the growth slowdown in 2001. Between November 1999 and May 2000 the federal funds rate was mildly increased by 1.25 percentage points (Figure 1.7). When growth slowed down in 2001 and unemployment began to increase, however, the Fed reacted promptly and decreased the federal funds rate from 6 per cent in January to 1.75 per cent in December, although annual unit labour costs growth continued to rise in 2001.

How has the ECB performed compared with the Fed? Under the conditions of slow European growth, high unemployment, nominal wage restraint and

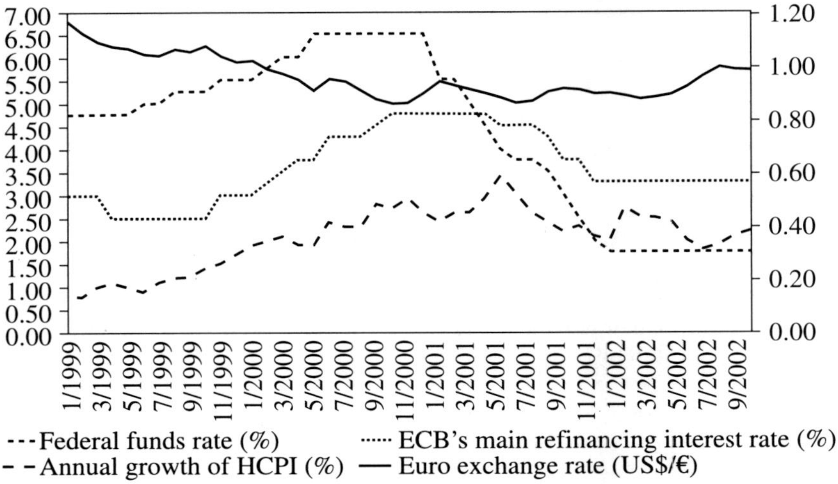

Sources: ECB 1999–2002, Federal Reserve Bank of New York 2002.

Figure 1.7 Federal funds rate, ECB interest rate, euro exchange rate and inflation rate in the euro area (EU-12), 1999–2002

low inflation, the goal and instrument independent ECB defined its primary goal, price stability, to be achieved when annual growth of the Harmonized Consumer Prices Index (HCPI) remains below 2 per cent in the medium term (ECB, 1999). This is quite a restrictive interpretation of price stability, because it undercuts the 3 per cent medium-term inflation record of the former core economy of the European Monetary System (EMS), that is, Germany, (Bibow, 2002a), it neglects that sustained upswings in Organisation for Economic Co-operation and Development (OECD) countries have usually been associated with inflation rates considerably above 2 per cent (Heine and Herr, 2001), and it does not take into account that measured HCPI inflation may exceed true inflation because quality improvements and substitution processes are ignored (Artis, 2002). The potentially restrictive stance of the ECB also becomes clear in its 'two pillar strategy' which consists of a reference value for the growth of M3, on the one hand, and a broadly based assessment of the outlook for future price development and risks to price stability in the euro area as a whole, on the other. The reference value for M3 growth was set at 4.5 per cent and was based on the assumption of a trend decline of velocity of 0.5 to 1 per cent, an inflation rate of 1 to 2 per cent and a trend rate of real GDP growth of 2 to 2.5 per cent. Here it is neither the place to discuss the sensibleness of using monetary quantities as target or reference values for monetary policy – which certainly does not make sense in an endogenous money approach – nor to illuminate the potential inconsistencies which may arise from the simultaneous use of monetary aggregates and inflation prospects as guidelines for monetary policies.[17] Rather, the implications of the assumed low trend rate of real GDP growth underlying the reference value for M3 are of interest in our context. With its modest assumption for potential GDP growth the ECB simply extrapolates the modest growth experience of the 1990s without recognizing that European growth in this period was itself a result of restrictive monetary and fiscal policies. From this a more expansive monetary policy than the one enforced by the Bundesbank on the EMS during the 1990s could not be expected at the very start of EMU. The ECB did not seem to intend 'to give growth a chance' (Bibow, 2002a). The fall in the European NAIRU associated with falling nominal and real interest rates and with increasing competition in goods markets due to greater market transparency could not be expected to be utilized by the ECB in order to promote employment, growth and, hence, a further decline in the NAIRU.

These somewhat pessimistic expectations have been fulfilled by the ECB during the first years. Although in 1999 HCPI growth remained considerably below the ECB target of 2 per cent (Figure 1.7) and annual unit labour cost growth also did not cause any inflation pressure (Figure 1.5), the ECB refused to lower significantly its interest rate on main refinancing operations. The minor reduction of the ECB's key rate from 3 to 2.5 per cent in April was reversed in November under the impression of a continuous decline in the euro exchange rate (Figure 1.7). Gross domestic product growth remained modest and, although employment increased, the potentials for substantial reduction of unemployment were not fully exploited.

In 2000 inflation rates continued to increase and exceeded the ECB's target in the second half of the year. This acceleration of inflation, however, was not fuelled by excessive wage hikes. On the contrary, nominal wage moderation under the conditions of high unemployment, uncoordinated wage bargaining across the euro area and social pacts for wage moderation made unit labour cost growth decline and kept it below the inflation rate. Rising inflation in the euro area was rather caused by import price hikes (crude oil and derivatives) and the continued devaluation of the euro. But although labour unions refrained from demanding compensation for rising consumer prices and although the wage bargainers in Germany – by some perceived to be the European wage-setters – agreed on two-year contracts with moderate nominal wage increases, the ECB rose its key interest rate by 1.75 percentage points from November 1999 to October 2000. With these interest rate hikes the ECB tried to prevent second-round effects of rising consumer price inflation – which labour unions already had abstained from – and attempted to stop the euro decline. But this attempt was in no way successful: the euro exchange rate determined in international financial markets continued to depreciate and the inflation rate accelerated until June 2001 (Figure 1.7) (Arestis et al., 2001; Bibow, 2002a, 2002b). Gross domestic product growth slightly increased because of rising world demand and improved price competitiveness of European exports, and unemployment was reduced but remained at a high level.

The euro area dilemma of nominal wage restraint, tight monetary policies, slow growth, high unemployment, a weak euro and inflation above the ECB's target also dominated in 2001 and during the first few months of 2002. When world economic growth stumbled and the Fed started to lower interest rates in January 2001, as far as 4.25 percentage points by the end of the year, the ECB hesitated until May when the downswing could no longer be ignored and reduced interest rates in four small steps by 1.5 percentage points (Figure 1.7). Harmonized Consumer Prices Index growth, still above the target, did not seem to allow for more expansive policies. But, again, nominal wage growth put no pressure on inflation. Increasing growth of unit labour costs was rather caused by slow productivity growth in a period of economic stagnation. The main causes for rising inflation arose from increasing prices for oil derivatives and rising food prices caused by animal diseases. These exogenous shocks, however, would only cause problems for the stability of the aggregate price level and justify restrictive monetary policies, if relative price changes were to trigger second-round effects of nominal wages, which was not the case in 2001. The rather restrictive ECB reactions were neither conducive to European growth and employment nor to the internal and the external value of the euro: the inflation rate exceeded the ECB's target and the exchange rate continued to deteriorate until 2002 when turmoil in US financial markets and slow growth prospects in the USA made the euro appreciate.

This brief review reveals a profound 'anti-growth bias' (Bibow, 2002a) in the ECB's monetary policies during the first years of operation. The ECB did not follow the Fed's symmetric strategy but focused rather asymmetrically on the short-term outlook of upward price risks without supporting growth and employment whenever the absence of any accelerating inflation risk would have allowed it to. In this sense the ECB followed the Bundesbank's monetary strategy, but under different conditions and therefore with less success than the Bundesbank.[18] Whereas in Germany, as 'a small open economy', the effects of restrictive Bundesbank policies on domestic demand could be partly offset by increasing export surpluses, this compensation was less effective in the euro area as 'a large closed economy' where, moreover, no relief through more expansive fiscal policies could be expected under the conditions of the Amsterdam Stability and Growth Pact.[19]

Dominated by uncoordinated wage bargaining across the EMU and an 'anti-growth bias' in the ECB's monetary policy (together with restrictive fiscal policies dominated by the Stability and Growth Pact) the performance of the euro area has been trapped in a vicious circle. High unemployment and social pacts for international competitiveness have caused nominal wage restraint, which has not been rewarded by the ECB's asymmetric monetary policy (nor by restrictive fiscal policies). Nominal wage restraint and tight monetary policies then have caused slow growth which has been insufficient to reduce actual unemployment substantially and to relieve pressure on nominal wages. High and rising interest rates associated with restrictive monetary policies and the negative effects of slow GDP growth on productivity growth and on the exchange rate have increased the inflation rate and prevented the NAIRU from falling substantially. This has induced asymmetric monetary policies either not to relax or to become even more restrictive. The ECB has so far become a victim of its own strategy.

4 CONCLUSIONS

Starting from the observation that the literature on 'time inconsistency' and 'central bank independence' may neither be able to capture the true causes of inflation in a monetary production economy nor to assess the effects of independent and conservative central banks on inflation, employment, distribution and growth in an adequate way, in this chapter we have outlined a post Keynesian model with endogenous money, in which inflation is mainly caused by conflict over distribution. With labour unions' wage demands propelled by the degree of employment, this model generates a NAIRU as a short-run limit to employment given by distribution conflict and enforced by conservative monetary policies of independent central banks aiming at the preservation of nominal wealth. It is shown that the NAIRU is not a strong attractor for actual unemployment determined by effective demand in the short run, and that in the long run the trend of the NAIRU is influenced by the development of aggregate demand and actual unemployment through different channels. These are the effects of actual unemployment on effective labour supply and, hence, on labour unions' bargaining power. Further, there are the effects of capital stock growth on labour productivity, the effects of the domestic economy's growth prospects on the real exchange rate, and the potential effects of interest rate variations on the mark-up, each of which influences the feasible real wage rate given by mark-up pricing. From this it follows, that restrictive monetary policies will not be effective in containing inflation in the long run. It has finally been shown that effective co-ordination of wage bargaining, that is, successful vertical and horizontal co-ordination, may considerably reduce the NAIRU and may also prevent the economy from sliding into disinflation or deflation whenever effective demand crumbles.

Applying the theoretical considerations to the development of unemployment and inflation in the EMU since 1999, the tendencies of wage-bargaining co-ordination and the ECB's monetary strategy have been discussed. Although there have been several attempts by European labour unions to improve wage-bargaining co-ordination, the trends towards decentralization of bargaining and towards national social pacts for competitiveness have been major obstacles to effective bargaining co-ordination. Faced with uncoordinated wage bargaining across the EMU, the ECB followed an asymmetric strategy in achieving its primary goal – price stability. Although conditions for monetary policies have changed considerably, the ECB imitated the more restrictive Bundesbank strategy rather than the more symmetric and expansive strategy of the Federal Reserve. This meant that the reduction in the European NAIRU made possible by decreasing interest rates and increasing competition in the goods markets could not be exploited by more expansive aggregate demand. Dominated by uncoordinated wage bargaining across EMU and an 'anti-growth bias' in the ECB's monetary policy (and restrictive fiscal policies prescribed by the Stability and Growth Pact), the performance of the euro area was characterized by a vicious circle. High unemployment and social pacts for international competitiveness caused nominal wage restraint, which was not rewarded by the ECB's asymmetric monetary policy. Nominal wage restraint and tight monetary policies then caused slow growth, which fed back on the NAIRU through the effects of low capital stock growth on productivity growth and of modest GDP growth prospects on the exchange rate. Currency depreciation and inflation above the target then induced the ECB either not to relax or to become even more restrictive.

It can finally be concluded that an improved performance of the euro area will only be achieved, if the ECB changes its monetary strategy and abandons its 'anti-growth bias'. More symmetric and hence more expansive monetary policies will be facilitated by the improvement of wage-bargaining co-ordination across the EMU. Co-ordinated wage bargaining, targeting nominal wage improvements determined by national productivity growth and the ECB's inflation target will stabilize the price level whenever employment increases or decreases. The NAIRU will be reduced and deflationary processes will be also prevented. This would allow the ECB to accept responsibility for employment and growth without having to neglect price stability. More expansive fiscal policies will be needed as well, whenever the economy slides into recession. This kind of co-ordinated macroeconomic policy, however, may require major institutional reforms in the euro area.[20]

NOTES

* Revised, shortened and updated version of a paper presented at the Post Keynesian Conference, 29 June–3 July 2002, Center for Full Employment and Price Stability, University of Missouri, Kansas City, USA. An extended version appeared in the *Banca Nazionale del Lavoro Quarterly Review* (Hein, 2002b). I would like to thank the conference participants and an anonymous referee for helpful comments. Remaining errors are, of course, my own.

1. For theoretical foundations see Kydland and Prescott (1977), Barro and Gordon (1983) and Rogoff (1985).
2. The surveys on empirical studies by Eijffinger and de Haan (1996) and Berger, de Haan and Eijffinger (2000) confirm a robust inverse relationship between the index of central bank independence and inflation. However, this does not mean that a causal relationship exists. Low inflation and central bank independence could also be seen as mutual effects of a third factor, that is, inflation aversion in the society as a whole or the dominance of those social groups interested in stable nominal wealth (Epstein, 1992; Posen, 1993; 1998).
3. See Arestis (1996), Davidson (1994) and Lavoie (1992) for comprehensive surveys on post Keynesian approaches to economics.
4. In empirical studies Cornwall and Cornwall (1998) and Posen (1998) have shown that low inflation generated by central bank independence is not a 'free lunch' but is associated with considerable disinflation costs in terms of higher unemployment and slower growth in the short run as well as in the long run.
5. See Franzese (2001a; 2001b) and Hein (2002a) for surveys on theoretical and empirical issues of the interaction between central bank independence and wage bargaining.
6. For the sake of simplicity we assume that the central bank controls the base rate, and that the market rates are determined by mark-ups of commercial banks according to risk and duration of credit. If the mark-ups are constant, the central bank directly affects the market rates of interest in financial markets which are important for investment decisions. On endogenous money in post Keynesian theory see Lavoie (1992, p. 149; 1996), Hewitson (1995) and Moore (1989).
7. As it is shown in Hein (1999) the inverse effects of interest rate variations usually assumed in post Keynesian models need qualification. In order to have an inverse effect of interest rate hikes on investment and capacity utilization, and hence on employment, investment has to be very interest rate elastic and the propensity to save out of interest income has to be quite high.
8. As in post Keynesian models of distribution and growth the rate of profit need not be equal to the rate of interest in equilibrium, rising interest rates may also compress profits of enterprise (Hein, 1999). The empirical results for distribution effects of interest rate variations are generally quite mixed and inconclusive (Argitis and Pitelis, 2001; Hein, and Ochsen, 2003).
9. See Bhaduri and Marglin (1990) for a non-monetary model of distribution and accumulation with different accumulation regimes, Lavoie (1993) and Hein (1999) for monetary extensions of the Bhaduri/Marglin approach and Hein and Ochsen (2003) for an empirical assessment.
10. For 'conflicting claims' models of inflation see Rowthorn (1977), Carlin and Soskice (1990, p. 135), Layard, Nickell and Jackman (1991) and Lavoie (1992, p. 391).
11. See Layard, Nickell and Jackman (1991) as well as Gordon (1997), and for a critique Galbraith (1997) and Sawyer (1997; 1999; 2002) who puts forward an interpretation of the NAIRU as an 'inflation barrier'.
12. See Sawyer (1999; 2002) for a discussion of the effects of productive capacity and productivity growth on the NAIRU. In order to achieve these effects it has to be assumed that labour unions target a certain real wage rate and not a certain wage share.
13. Slow domestic growth imposed by too restrictive monetary policies may cause currency depreciation because assets denominated in domestic currency may be less attractive to

monetary wealth holders due to curtailed prospective returns associated with slow growth prospects (Bibow, 2002a; 2002b).
14. For a more detailed treatment of the potential developments at the start of EMU see Hein (2002a; 2002b).
15. For the differences between national wage bargaining systems at the start of EMU see Traxler (1999). On the state of co-ordination of wage bargaining in the EMU see also Pichelmann (2001) and Schulten (2001; 2002).
16. See Bibow (2001) and Lombard (2000) for a detailed account of the restrictive macroeconomic effects of the EMU convergence process.
17. For a more detailed assessment of the ECB's monetary policies also focusing on internal contradictions and insufficiencies in the monetary strategy see Bibow (2002a; 2002b) as well as Heine and Herr (2001).
18. Bibow (2001) has shown that the asymmetric strategy of the Bundesbank compared to the more symmetric approach of the Federal Reserve accounts for a major part of the growth differential between the USA and Germany in the 1990s.
19. See Hein and Truger (2002) for a more explicit discussion of the role of fiscal policies within the restrictive EMU macroeconomic policy mix.
20. See Arestis, McCauley and Sawyer (2001) for a proposal of an alternative stability pact for the European Union.

REFERENCES

Arestis, P. (1996), 'Post Keynesian economics: towards coherence', *Cambridge Journal of Economics*, **20**, 111–35.

Arestis, P., I.B.F. Mariscal, A. Brown and M.G. Sawyer (2001), 'The causes of euro instability', in P. Arestis, A. Brown and M. Sawyer (eds), *The Euro. Evolution and Prospects*, Cheltenham, UK and Northampton, MA, USA: Edward Elgar, pp. 106–34.

Arestis, P., K. McCauley and M. Sawyer (2001), 'An alternative stability pact for the European Union', *Cambridge Journal of Economics*, **25**, 113–30.

Argitis, G., and C. Pitelis (2001), 'Monetary policy and distribution of income: evidence for the United States and the United Kingdom', *Journal of Post Keynesian Economics*, **23**, 617–38.

Artis, M. (2002), 'The performance of the European Central Bank', *International Review of Applied Economics*, **16**, 19–29.

Barro, R.J., and D.B. Gordon (1983), 'Rules, discretion and reputation in a model of monetary policy', *Journal of Monetary Economics*, **12**, 101–21.

Bean, C. (1998), 'Monetary policy under EMU', *Oxford Review of Economic Policy*, **14** (3), 41–53.

Berger, H., J. de Haan, and S.C.W. Eijffinger (2000), *Central Bank Independence: An Update of Theory and Evidence*, CESifo working paper series, no. 255, Munich.

Bhaduri, A., and S. Marglin, (1990), 'Unemployment and the real wage: the economic basis for contesting political ideologies', *Cambridge Journal of Economics*, **14**, 375–93.

Bibow, J. (1999), *Reflections on the Current Fashion for Central Bank Independence*, Beitraege aus dem Institut für Statistik und Oekonometrie der Universitaet Hamburg, no. 41, Hamburg.

Bibow, J. (2001), 'Making EMU work: some lessons from the 1990s', *International Review of Applied Economics*, **15**, 233–59.

Bibow, J. (2002a), 'The monetary policies of the European Central Bank and the

euro's (mal)performance: a stability-oriented assessment', *International Review of Applied Economics*, **16**, 31–50.
Bibow, J. (2002b), 'The market versus the ECB, and the euro's plunge', *Eastern Economic Journal*, **28**, 45–57.
Calmfors, L. (2001), 'Wages and wage-bargaining institutions in the EMU – a survey of the issues', *Empirica*, **28**, 325–51.
Carlin, W., and D. Soskice (1990), *Macroeconomics and the Wage Bargain: A Modern Approach to Employment, Inflation and the Exchange Rate*, Oxford: Oxford University Press.
Cornwall, J., and W. Cornwall (1998), 'Unemployment costs and inflation targeting', in P. Arestis and M. Sawyer (eds), *The Political Economy of Central Banking*, Cheltenham, UK and Lyme, USA: Edward Elgar, pp. 49–66.
Davidson, P. (1994), *Post Keynesian Macroeconomic Theory*, Aldershot, UK and Brookfield, US: Edward Elgar.
Eijffinger, S., and J. de Haan (1996), *The Political Economy of Central Banking*, Princeton University special papers in international economics, no. 19, May, Princeton, NJ.
Epstein, G.A. (1992), 'Political economy and comparative central banking', *Review of Radical Political Economics*, **24**, 1–30.
European Central Bank (ECB) (1999), 'Die stabilitätsorientierte geldpolitische Strategie des Eurosystems', *Monatsbericht*, January, 43–56.
European Central Bank (ECB) (1999–2002), *Monthly Bulletins*, Frankfurt.
Federal Reserve Bank of New York (2002), 'Historical changes of the Fed fund and discount rate (1971–present', accessed at www.ny.frb.org/pihome/statistics/dlyrates/fedrate.html.
Forder, J. (1998), 'Central bank independence – conceptual clarifications and interim assessment', *Oxford Economic Papers*, **50**, 307–34.
Franzese, R.J. (2001a), 'Institutions and sectoral interactions in monetary policy and wage/price-bargaining', in P.A. Hall and D. Soskice (eds), *Varieties of Capitalism. Institutional Foundations of Comparative Advantage*, Oxford: Oxford University Press, pp. 104–44.
Franzese, R.J. (2001b), 'Strategic interaction of monetary policymakers and wage/price bargainers: a review with implications for the European common-currency area', *Empirica*, **28**, 457–86.
Galbraith, J.K. (1997), 'Time to ditch the NAIRU', *Journal of Economic Perspectives*, **11**, 93–108.
Gordon, R.J. (1997), 'The time-varying NAIRU and its implications for economic policy', *Journal of Economic Perspectives*, **11**, 11–32.
Hein, E. (1999), 'Interest rates, income shares and investment in a Kaleckian model', *Political Economy: Review of Political Economy and Social Sciences*, **5**, 5–22.
Hein, E. (2002a), 'Central bank independence, labour market institutions and the perspectives for inflation and employment in the European Monetary Union', *Political Economy: Review of Political Economy and Social Sciences*, **10**, 37–64.
Hein, E. (2002b), 'Monetary policy and wage bargaining in the EMU: restrictive ECB policies, high unemployment, nominal wage restraint and inflation above the target', *Banca Nazionale del Lavoro Quarterly Review*, **55**, 299–337.
Hein, E., and C. Ochsen (2003), 'Regimes of interest rates, income shares, savings, and investment: a Kaleckian model and empirical estimations for some advanced OECD-economies', *Metroeconomica*, **54** (4), 404–33.
Hein, E., and A. Truger (2002), *European Monetary Union: Nominal Convergence,*

Real Divergence and Slow Growth?, WSI in der Hans Boeckler Stiftung discussion paper no. 107, Düsseldorf.
Heine, M., and H. Herr (2001), *Das Eurosystem: Eine paradigmenorientierte Darstellung und kritische Würdigung der europäischen Geldpolitik*, Berlin: Rosa Luxemburg Stiftung.
Hewitson, G. (1995), 'Post-Keynesian monetary theory: some issues', *Journal of Economic Surveys*, **9**, 285–310.
Kalecki, M. (1943), 'Political aspects of full employment', reprinted in M. Kalecki (1971), *Selected Essays on the Dynamics of the Capitalist Economy*, Cambridge: Cambridge University Press.
Kittel, B., and F. Traxler (2001), 'Lohnverhandlungssysteme und Geldpolitik', *Wirtschaft und Gesellschaft*, **27**, 11–40
Kydland, F.E., and E.C. Prescott (1977), 'Rules rather than discretion: the inconsistency of optimal plans', *Journal of Political Economy*, **85**, 473–92.
Lavoie, M. (1992), *Foundations of Post-Keynesian Economic Analysis*, Aldershot, UK and Brookfield, US: Edward Elgar.
Lavoie, M. (1993), 'A post-classical view of money, interest, growth and distribution', in G. Mongiovi and C. Rühl (eds), *Macroeconomic Theory: Diversity and Convergence*, Cambridge: Cambridge University Press, pp. 3–21.
Lavoie, M. (1996), 'Horizontalism, structuralism, liquidity preference and the principle of increasing risk', *Scottish Journal of Political Economy*, **43**, 275–300.
Layard, R., S. Nickell and R. Jackman (1991), *Unemployment. Macroeconomic Performance and the Labour Market*, Oxford: Oxford University Press.
Lombard, M. (2000), 'Restrictive macroeconomic policies and unemployment in the European Union', *Review of Political Economy*, **12**, 317–32.
Marx, K. (1867), *Das Kapital. Kritik der politischen Ökonomie, Erster Band: Der Produktionsprozeß des Kapitals*, reprinted in Marx-Engels-Werke, Band 23 (1962), Berlin: Dietz.
Moore, B.J. (1989), 'The endogeneity of credit money', *Review of Political Economy*, **1**, 65–93.
Organisation for Economic Co-operation and Development (OECD) (2002), *Economic Outlook*, no. 71, data on CD-ROM, Paris: OECD.
Pichelmann, K. (2001), 'Monitoring wage developments in EMU', *Empirica*, **28**, 353–73.
Posen, A. (1993), 'Why central bank independence does not cause low inflation: there is no institutional fix for politics', in R. O'Brien (ed.), *Finance and the International Economy*, Oxford: Oxford University Press, pp. 41–65.
Posen, A. (1998), 'Central bank independence and disinflationary credibility: a missing link?', *Oxford Economic Papers*, **50**, 335–59.
Rogoff, K. (1985), 'The optimal degree of commitment to an intermediate monetary target', *Quarterly Journal of Economics*, **100**, 1169–89.
Rowthorn, R.E. (1977), 'Conflict, inflation and money', *Cambridge Journal of Economics*, **1**, 215–39.
Sawyer, M. (1997), 'Income distribution, macroeconomic analysis and barriers to full employment', *Journal of Income Distribution*, **7**, 147–60.
Sawyer, M. (1999), 'The NAIRU: a critical appraisal', *International Papers in Political Economy*, **7** (2), 1–39.
Sawyer, M. (2002), 'The NAIRU, aggregate demand and investment', *Metroeconomica*, **53**, 66–94.
Schulten, T. (2001), 'The European Metalworkers' Federation's approach to a Euro-

pean coordination of collective bargaining – experiences, problems and prospects', in T. Schulten and R. Bispinck (eds), *Collective Bargaining Under the Euro. Experiences from the European Metal Industry*, Brussels: European Trade Union Institute, pp. 303–32.

Schulten, T. (2002), 'Europeanisation of collective bargaining: an overview on trade union initiatives for a transnational coordination of collective bargaining policy', WSI in der Hans Boeckler Stiftung discussions paper no. 101, Düsseldorf.

Traxler, F. (1999), 'Wage-setting institutions and European Monetary Union', in G. Huemer, M. Mesch and F. Traxler (eds), *The Role of Employer Associations and Labour Unions in the EMU*, Aldershot: Ashgate, pp. 115–35.

2. Public debt and private wealth*

Hassan Bougrine

INTRODUCTION

Even though economic theory recognizes health, knowledge and education as important elements of human wealth, in popular debates on wealth the general focus is still on the acquisition of physical and financial assets. For instance, the *Webster's Seventh New Collegiate Dictionary* defines wealth as 'the stock of useful goods having economic value in existence at any one time'. This definition reflects the widespread importance of material wealth in the lives of individuals in contemporary (capitalist) societies. Aside from some perverse needs that may be qualified as sheer greed, it is clear that the purpose of seeking to accumulate such wealth is justified by the desire to ensure our well-being throughout our lifetime, as well as that of our offsprings.

The question of why some people are stupendously rich while others are extremely poor has always been at the centre of the debate on social issues. At the heart of the debate is the issue of equal opportunities to acquire wealth. While in aristocracies wealth is concentrated in the hands of a few and passed on to their descendants and heirs, in democratic societies we expect everyone to enjoy the comforts of the good life that wealth provides. In reviewing Tocqueville's (1835 [1966]) work, Robert Goodin (2001, p. 68) summarized what he considers Tocqueville's major distinctions between 'democratic wealth' and 'aristocratic wealth':

> a) whereas aristocratic wealth is inherited, democratic wealth is earned. Democracies offer 'equal opportunities' in ways that aristocracies do not, when it comes to acquiring wealth.
> b) whereas aristocratic wealth is stable, democratic wealth circulates. Democracies offer opportunities for people to 'take it in turn' to be wealthy, in ways that aristocracies do not.
> c) whereas aristocratic wealth gives its holders permanent power in the community, democratic wealth is only a temporary power source. Democracies offer opportunities for people to 'take it in turn' being powerful, depending on their fleeting fortunes, in contrast to aristocracies which vest permanent wealth and hence permanent power in an entrenched elite.

It must be clear from the above distinctions that the notion of 'democratic wealth' cannot be equated with social justice since it accepts the fact that there will always be some who are rich and others who are poor, with the increased probability that some of the poor may one day become rich and vice versa, thus reflecting Tocqueville's (1835 [1966], p. 611) observation that 'the rich daily rise out of the crowd and constantly return thither'. Although the economic situation of some people does improve over time (after graduation, retraining, experience, and so on), this cannot be considered as social mobility in Tocqueville's sense. Tocqueville's claim is certainly exaggerated because, as noted by Galbraith (2000, p. 69) 'single moms don't move from welfare to Forbes 400'. Furthermore, it must also be noted that the mobility that transpires from the notion of 'democratic wealth' is not a result of society's deliberate implementation of the democratic ideals but, rather, a consequence of the increased volatility and instability of market economies. However, recent trends and the current state of income and wealth distribution worldwide (Galbraith, 1998; Galbraith and Kum, 2002; Levy Institute, 1999) indicate that an equitable distribution of wealth can not be achieved through market forces, regardless of the degree of volatility and fluctuations. As Goodin (2001, p. 75) put it 'no realistic amount of randomisation is ever likely to come remotely close to eradicating life-long inequalities owing to people's initial circumstances'. Therefore, 'If we want democratic equality across the whole income distribution, … , random walk is not enough and redistribution through deliberate public interventions is required' (Goodin, 2001, p. 70).

The purpose of this chapter is to show that, contrary to common belief, prosperity and 'democratic wealth' in a capitalist economy depend in a crucial way on greater government intervention. A corollary of this statement is that it is in the private sector's interest (and that of society as a whole) to develop a strong public sector, capable of providing not only law and order (guaranteeing the protection of property rights, and so on) but also, and more importantly, social services and public goods that are essential to growth, prosperity and equality. In the next section, I argue that unfettered inheritance is an impediment to democratization of wealth. In the third section, I show that public sector activity helps the private sector to generate profits and, therefore, to create and accumulate wealth. The fourth section deals with the wealth effects of particular public policies. Some concluding remarks are given in the final section.

GIFTS THAT REALLY COUNT

The distribution of wealth is widely accepted as a good measure of social justice. For this reason, the impact of inter-generational transfers of wealth on its distribution is one of the important issues in the debate about social polarization and wealth inequality in most democratic societies. Although the famous saying according to which, in modern societies, 'wealth never survives three generations' suggests that inheritance is no longer a major source of wealth and social power, there is strong evidence that indicates otherwise. Wealth, in these societies, is not only earned, it is also inherited. In the USA, for instance, bequests of assets have been estimated to account for up to 46 per cent of households' wealth (Kotlikoff and Summers, 1981; Kopczuk and Lupton, 2000). Some studies have found links between inter-generational transfers and the continued racial inequality in the distribution of aggregate wealth (Blau and Graham, 1990; Menchik and Jianakoplos, 1997; Hurst, Luoh and Stafford, 1998; Wolff, 1998). For instance, Darity and Myers (1998) show that 'simultaneous with the rise in general inequality has been a worsening of the relative income position of black families in America' and that there has been a 'widening of the gap between whites and blacks'. Using historical data, Billings and Blee (2000) have shown that today's poverty in the Appalachia region is the result of long-standing social and economic patterns of inequality that favoured the elite families engaged in the timber, mining, oil and gas extraction industries. In a study of wealth distribution in Australia, Badcock (1994, p. 626) concluded that 'the concentration of wealth within the housing market, together with the pattern of housing inheritance, is undoubtedly helping to create a more unequal society'.

Casual observation as well as empirical research indicate that children's educational attainment and their earning capacity are greatly influenced by their parents' wealth and social status. Some studies (see, among others, Solon, 1992; Lam, 1999) have shown that there are inter-generational correlations in educational levels and in occupational earnings. Chiterji and Stafford (2000) find that the differences in asset ownership between African-Americans and other families are explained by differences in ownership patterns, values and knowledge held by the parents and the families. It is also important to note that the size and amount of gifts and inter-generational transfers matter a great deal for the recipient generation since some bequests are insignificant while others allow the beneficiaries to immediately acquire a home or start a business (Loury, 1981; Oliver and Shapiro, 1995). The general conclusion is that inheritance of wealth perpetuates inequality and further polarizes society (Galbraith, 2000; Nissan, 2001). To counteract these negative effects and alleviate poverty, several alternatives have been proposed. They range from inheritance tax (Soros, 2000) to capital grants to young people, a guaranteed job to every person willing and able to work (Mosler, 1998; Wray, 1998) or a guaranteed basic income for all citizens (Janson, 2000).

The advantages and disadvantages of an inheritance tax have been widely discussed in the literature (Shoup, 1966; Feldstein, 2000; Gale and Perozek,

2000; Soros, 2000). To emphasize its supposedly negative effects, opponents of the inheritance tax call it 'death tax' and 'double tax'. They argue that it discourages savings, work, investment and accumulation, all of which are bad for growth and prosperity. Consequently, as Kindleberger (2001, p. 15) observed, 'many want it abolished, though it is paid by only a small per centage of the population'. The main argument for the inheritance tax is that it contributes to creating a meritocratic society in which success depends on talents and qualifications, and not on social status and unearned inheritance. Galbraith (2000, p. 74), for instance, writes 'our children should inherit not a personal fortune but a society in which the reasonable chance to do well in life, to rise and prosper according to merit, is not foreclosed. The estate tax is merely one small, but useful, instrument to that effect'.

Some writers have shown that the inheritance tax alters the gift-giving behaviour to heirs and increases the probability and amount of *inter vivos* transfers and spending, arguing that its elimination would reduce the yearly amount of such transfers by nearly 30 per cent (in the USA). For instance, McGarry (2000, p. 93) maintains that:

> [Estate and gift] taxes increase the cost of transferring wealth to heirs and may therefore make consumption and charitable giving more appealing options for the potential donor. Details of the estate- and gift-tax code [in the USA] also provide strong incentives for gifts to be made at certain times in the donor's life, and to be made to particular recipients. These incentives likely affect the well-being of both donors and recipients and may alter the total amount given over a lifetime.

Others argue that the estate tax has redistributive effects in the sense that it encourages charitable donations (Soros, 2000) or that it constitutes a source of government revenue, which can be used to help the poor (Wolff, 1995; Galbraith, 2000). While I agree that the inheritance tax may encourage social and economic mobility and that it can be used to redistribute wealth, my analysis of the redistributive effects of taxation is fundamentally different from this widely held view. In my opinion, unless the inheritance tax involves dividing physical assets and giving parts thereof to the poor (such as in the case of an agrarian reform, estate and housing, and so on), it cannot have the 'Robin Hood' type of redistributive effects emphasized by others. Referring to the role of taxes in a similar situation, that is, taxes on real assets, Parguez (2000, p. 8) wrote:

> In such an economy, the Robin Hood paradox is true. The State is redistributing the real income it has previously levied by use of sheer force on private agents. The State is behaving like the feudal lords who forced the bondsmen to deliver them a share of their preexisting crops.

However, as shown in Bougrine and Seccareccia (2001), when we are dealing with a monetary economy, which is the case of all modern societies, taxes on monetary and financial transactions do not generate any income for the national government since they are part of a reflux process by which money is being destroyed rather than created. Therefore, taxes cannot possibly be used to redistribute wealth, fund social programs or other projects. For this reason, taxes in general, and the inheritance tax in particular, can only redistribute wealth in the case referred to above and if a progressive taxation system is used to prevent the rich from accumulating so much wealth while at the same time allowing the less wealthy or the poor to accumulate more, so that over time we may achieve a more equal distribution of wealth in society (see the third section below).

If it is generally accepted that societies should seek a democratic governance, not everyone agrees that 'equal opportunities' in the economic realm is a good thing. Some argue that inequality is good for growth and progress. For instance, Bartlett (2000, p. 56) writes:

> the rich perform a public service when they engage in what Thorstein Veblen called 'conspicuous consumption'. They are, in effect, underwriting the cost of bringing new products to market that ultimately become ubiquitous and available to everyone. Since it's not much fun to be rich if everyone can enjoy the same products, the rich aid innovation by pushing the limit of what is possible, encouraging producers to meet their demand in return for large profits. But if the rich perform a valuable social function, must we conclude that they be allowed to pass on their wealth to their descendants and heirs? Does it necessarily follow that the inheritance and estate tax should be abolished?

Bartlett answers both questions in the affirmative, arguing that the estate tax is an infringement on private property, in addition to the familiar disincentive effects mentioned above. However, as pointed out by Galbraith (2000), since Bartlett (2000, p. 58) agrees that '[i]ncome and wealth mobility are unambiguously good because they mitigate inequality' and that 'inheritances are insignificant as a source of major wealth in America', his logical conclusion should have been to support the inheritance tax rather than advocate its abolition.

Bartlett's reference to private property rights and his rejection of public redistributive policies are nothing new. Since the rise of modern capitalism and with the publication of Adam Smith's *Inquiry Into the Nature and Causes of the Wealth of Nations* in 1776, the conventional wisdom has been that the best prescription for prosperity is a free-market economy in which the government acts only as a watchdog, essentially providing law and order but playing no substantial role in economic activity. Although this ideal laissez-faire type of economy *never really existed anywhere*,[1] advocates of free markets like to emphasize the idea that capitalism owes much of its success to 'economic freedom' defined as market supremacy. The basic premise behind such affirmation is that markets are always 'right' and that they ensure economic efficiency, whereas government decisions are inherently inefficient. Even though there is no clear and unambiguous evidence that supports these statements (see Agell, Lindh and Ohlsson, 1997), they are widely used to justify the decisions to curtail public sector activity (less government spending, less taxes, and privatization of public corporations and other services such as education, health and other social programs). As will be shown in the next section, if the short-term effects of such a strategy are damaging to the economy, its long-term effects may threaten the viability of the whole system.

PRIVATE WEALTH AND PUBLIC DEBT

How does public policy affect private wealth? Public policy is typically defined as government intervention in the form of public spending and taxing of private economic activity. Standard theory maintains that taxation is needed to finance government spending and that public deficits arise when such spending exceeds the 'revenues' collected from taxes. It is well known from the literature on public finance that the orthodox theory rejects public deficits (Musgrave and Musgrave, 1989) and opposes any policy that seeks to increase government spending beyond the limits set by 'tax revenues' (Toye, 2000).[2] The basic argument in support of this view is that financing of economic activity (private and public) is constrained by the accumulated savings. Consequently, when the government runs a deficit, it must compete with the private sector for the limited available funds, which leads to an increase in interest rates. Higher interest rates lower private investment but attract foreign capital inflows, which lead to an appreciation of the exchange rate. This, in turn, discourages exports and encourages imports, thus causing a trade deficit. Furthermore, it is argued that when budget deficits are monetized, the result is higher inflation, which leads to a further increase in (cheaper) imported goods and loss of competitiveness. The conclusion is that budget deficits must be avoided because, in addition to all this, they also lead to a higher debt, which jeopardizes the standards of living of future generations.

Several empirical studies have demonstrated that the above conclusions are misleading. For instance, Seccareccia and Sood (2000), using data from six major OECD countries, have shown that the fears of inflation from budget deficits are unfounded. Others have found no causal relationship between budget deficits and trade deficits, thus rejecting the so-called 'twin deficits' idea (see, among others, Blecker, 1992). However, the most damaging criticism to the conclusions of the orthodox model is the one attacking the central premise according to which investment expenditures require the prior existence of a stock of accumulated savings. In the classical world of Adam Smith and others, societies which value thrift and save more will grow rapidly because high savings allow more investment projects to be undertaken. In the Keynesian analysis, high saving rates mean that a smaller portion of income is spent on consumption goods. Low sales, in turn, mean that realized profits would be low and that firms will have to lower their production and, in the process, lay off workers. The resulting unemployment and loss of income further reduce consumption and profits, and force firms to cut down on their investment plans. The higher the saving rate is, the worse the outcome will be. The 'paradox of thrift' may be so severe that it can raise the prospects of bankruptcy for some firms. Contrary to the classical view, in the Keynesian framework investment opportunities depend on the existence of an effective demand that can sustain firms' current and expected profits. Investment precedes saving since the former generates an income, which determines the levels of consumption and saving. Therefore, we conclude that investment (private and public) cannot be constrained by the availability of savings. The question that needs to be addressed then is the following: how is investment, and production in general, financed?

The short answer is that investment expenditures are financed by money. Without money, production cannot take place. The question then becomes: where does money come from and how is it created? Since the objective of this chapter is to study the relationship between private wealth and public debt, it seems appropriate to answer the question by looking at the creation of money in both the private and the public sectors.

In modern capitalist economies, money is created *ex nihilo* via bank credit advances to entrepreneurs who hire labourers in order to produce goods and services for households, as well as capital equipment for inter-firms exchanges. The processes of production and exchange involve transactions that continuously create or destroy money. This process is analysed in detail by the Circuit theory as described in Graziani (1990; 1997), Lavoie (1992) and Parguez and Seccareccia (2000), among others, and is briefly summarized here. At the beginning of the production cycle, one might assume that entrepreneurs have no accumulated savings and no money, but have ideas and plans. Based on their expectations and assessment of market conditions, they decide to produce a given level of output, which will be sold for a given price. However, in order to implement their production plans, they require short-term loans and must, therefore, borrow cash advances from banks, which supply credit based on their own assessment of firms' creditworthiness. This type of finance requirement that depends on the costs of production is referred to in the literature as *initial finance* and is part of the *flux* phase of the monetary circuit.

In the second phase, firms begin recovering the money initially paid out to households (namely, in the form of wages). This is done through the sale of output that was produced during the first stage. The proceeds, which are used to eventually pay back the debt owed to banks, are known as *final finance* and are associated with the *reflux* phase of the monetary circuit. Once the debt is paid back, the reason for the existence of money vanishes. Money is destroyed as the debt is extinguished. If households' propensity to save is nil, firms need not issue any securities since households will have spent their entire wages and salaries in the commodities market, thus ensuring that the monetary circuit is easily closed. However, if households' saving is positive, firms will need to issue new securities in order to capture *more* of the money paid out during the flux phase. If, in addition, households have a preference for liquidity and choose to hold part of their savings in the form of bank deposits, the closure of the monetary circuit becomes somewhat problematic, as shown in Bougrine and Seccareccia (2001, p. 5):

> there is one case in which the closure of the monetary circuit is not possible because of the Keynesian problem of household liquidity preference. In the case where households choose to hold part of their savings in the form of bank deposits, banks would now be forced into a sort of perverse financial 'intermediation' role of re-issuing short-term loans to firms caused by the existence of liquid household deposits withdrawn from the reflux process. Needless to say, this Keynesian problem of insufficient reflux from the private sector to ensure the closure of the monetary circuit would easily disappear if some other sector, particularly the government sector, would incur deficits, by providing the additional liquidity to offset the leakage because of strong household preference for liquidity.

What this means is that, as long as there is some preference for liquidity, firms will not be able to pay back all their loans since their receipts will be less than their initial disbursements. Consequently, when the new cycle begins, firms will need to borrow new loans and the old ones are 'simply rolled over' (see Lavoie, 1992). Since liquidity preference is a major characteristic of modern monetary economies, firms, *as a sector*, are always in deficit because part of their debt will remain unpaid. Moreover, since credit is advanced to firms at the start of each production cycle, thus making the monetary circuit continual, firms will continuously be in debt, especially in a growing economy.[3]

If we now consider the government sector, it should be clear that it is impossible for the government to finance its expenditures by taxes because:

> at the beginning of the fiscal year when the budget is decided and the government starts making actual disbursements, taxes are not yet collected. Moreover, taxes

> cannot be collected at the beginning of the period because incomes on which they are levied have not yet been earned. Therefore, if taxes are to be considered as government's income in any sense at all, then it must be said that they are an income which is contingent on the realization of private agents' income and therefore can only be determined *ex post*. The question that should be asked then is how can we claim that an *ex-post* income is used to finance an *ex-ante* economic activity? This is clearly not possible. In a sense, in accordance with Chartalist theory, money must first be spent before it can be collected in taxes.

If taxes are only collected *ex post* and, therefore, cannot be used to fund an *ex ante* economic activity, how does the government then finance its spending? Wray (1998, p. 75) has answered the question unequivocally by stating that 'government spending is always financed through creation of fiat money'. Indeed, as explained by Bougrine and Seccareccia (2001, p. 10):

> In order for government operations to proceed and incomes to be earned in the public sector, all that is required is that the banking arm of government accepts to honour the cheques issued by its fiscal arm, the Treasury. Since these cheques will then be deposited by the public within the commercial banking system, the government's account at the Central Bank will be debited whereas private agents' accounts at commercial banks will be credited by the same amount.

This is what corresponds to the creation of money and it is in this sense that Lerner (1947) and the Chartalist School speak of money as a 'creature of the state' (see, *inter alia*, Bell, 2001).

It is only at this stage, that is, only after government spending has taken place and incomes have been generated, that the state can exercise its exclusive right to levy taxes. It should not be difficult for the reader to see that the operation of levying taxes is the inverse of the one described above, that is, government spending, which led to the creation of money. Government spending, then, adds to money (made available to the private sector) and taxes subtract from it. The logical conclusion, therefore, is that taxes are destroying an equal amount of money since private agents' accounts at commercial banks are debited and the government's account is credited. It is important to emphasize that while this is happening, that is, the crediting and debiting of the government's account, there is no physical movement or transfer of anything that can resemble a commodity money. Money is truly scriptural. This is why the government cannot amass 'large amounts of money' by collecting higher taxes. The bills and coins which facilitate our daily transactions are only used to represent part of the money or wealth available in private agents' accounts.

What was said about taxes is also true for all receipts by the government from the private sector, be it through selling bonds (or other assets such as public corporations), licences or asking for contributions to social security, unemployment insurance and other programs. None of these 'reflux' operations is needed to finance government spending since the latter has already been financed by the banking department of the government, that is, the Central Bank (see also Bell, 1998). This leads us to the obvious and important conclusion that the government can never be short of funds to pay for any type of domestic expenditure (a job creation program, housing for the poor, and so on) so long as it remains a sovereign nation with its own Central Bank, which is not legally prevented from carrying out the type of transactions described above.[4] Hence, the answer to the question 'where will the government get the money?' becomes evident once we realize that sovereign governments, which are capable of creating money at will, cannot be financially constrained and, as Smithin (2001, p. 9) put it, '[i]f they claim to be, the constraints must be self-imposed.'

A major conclusion that can be drawn from the above discussion is that in order to have a net creation of money, it would be necessary for the government to spend more than it collects in taxes, that is, it must run a budget deficit. Note, however, that a deficit in this sense is nothing more that an *ex post* accounting identity, which has already been paid for (see Parguez and Seccareccia, 2000). This conclusion is derived from an analysis that is framed in the monetary circuit theory but it is perfectly consistent with the neo-Chartalist theory of money, as can be seen from the following statement by Wray (1998, p. 18):

> The government does not 'need' the money in order to spend; rather the public needs the government's money in order to pay taxes. This means that the government can 'buy' whatever is for sale in terms of that money merely by providing that money ... [B]ecause the public will normally wish to hold some extra money, the government will normally have to spend more than it taxes; in other words the normal requirement is for a government deficit.

Therefore, in this framework, public deficits are a source of money (wealth) creation for the private sector. The relationship between a public deficit and its counterpart in the private sector can be clarified further by referring to national accounting. Indeed, as emphasized in Keynesian analysis, if we divide a closed economy into a private sector and a public sector, we must recognize that a deficit (surplus) in the public sector necessarily corresponds to a surplus (deficit) in the private sector. This can be seen easily by manipulating the national income identity for an open economy to get:

$$S - I = (G - T) + (X - M) \tag{2.1}$$

where S stands for saving, I for investment, G for government spending, T for taxes, X for exports and M for imports. Equation 2.1 states that private net saving is equivalent to government deficit plus the balance of payments surplus. It also implies that, for a given position of the balance of payments, any attempt to balance the public budget and/or achieve a surplus will necessarily result in a reduction of the private sector's savings, and hence of its wealth. Moreover, since a public surplus means, by definition, that the government is withdrawing more resources from the private economy than it is injecting in it ($G - T < 0$), government surpluses necessarily lower aggregate demand, which results in lower sales and lower profits for private firms (see also Godley, 2000).

To emphasize the direct relationship between firms' profits and public deficits, we can decompose private sector total savings (S) into households' savings (S_h) and firms' savings or, more precisely, their profits (P), and rearrange equation 2.1 to obtain the familiar Kaleckian profit equation:

$$P = (I - S_h) + (G - T) + (X - M) \tag{2.2}$$

Equation 2.2 clearly indicates that firms' profits are positively affected by investment, government spending, and exports (see Bougrine, 2000; Halevi and Kriesler, 2000; Lavoie, 2000). It is also clear that households' savings, taxes and imports lower business profits. In other words, long-run firms' profits can be sustained by:

- low or negative households' savings (indebtedness)
- a public budget deficit and/or
- an improvement in the balance of payments (BOP).

Since the so-called public deficits, ($G - T > 0$), are clearly a source of profits for firms, we find it ironic that free-market pundits should be advocating a policy based on balanced budgets and/or surpluses. Given the centrality of profit in a market economy, we think it imperative to explore further the role and limitations of each of the three factors mentioned above, as well as the relationship between them.

We have already established that public surpluses, ($G - T < 0$), amount to a net withdrawal of funds from the private sector. This means that in order to compensate for the loss of income previously derived from the government sector, and in order to maintain their spending (consumption) levels, households will be forced to borrow from banks.[5] As indicated by Godley (2000, p. 3), the negative effect of a budget surplus can be offset by an increase in private indebtedness and/or an improvement in the balance of payments. However, after analysing the behaviour of private saving in the USA and other countries, Godley (2000, p. 4) concluded that:

> An increase in private debt relative to income can go on for a long time, but it cannot go on forever because the decisive constraint on borrowing may come not from the extent to which net worth is being mortgaged, but from the extent to which payments of interest and repayments of principal ... can be met out of conventional income. *It is income rather than net worth that is ultimately the criterion of creditworthiness*, since in a crisis it may be impossible for everyone to realize assets simultaneously. (Emphasis added.)

The constraint will indeed become binding since households' income will continuously be eroded by long-term budget surpluses. Furthermore, once households decide to stop borrowing and start saving (or reducing their negative savings), aggregate demand, and consequently production, must fall, thus leading to a recession unless the government reverses the surplus policy and starts increasing its net spending. Therefore, a policy of long-term budget surpluses is not viable because it would force households into unsustainable debt.

Improving the BOP is a possibility that also has it limitations:

1. It can be achieved if a country can use the traditional trade measures (tariffs, quotas, and so on) but we know that none of these measures is permitted under the WTO rules.
2. In a globalized world, it is indeed difficult to exercise with any degree of effectiveness control over capital flows. The situation is particularly problematic for poor developing countries either because they lack the institutions that would allow them to do that or because they are vulnerable to threats from international lenders, including the IMF.
3. A country cannot improve its BOP without negatively affecting its trading partners. So, if the possibility of improving the BOP is feasible for one country, it cannot be feasible for all.

Therefore, the only instrument that remains for improving private sector's wealth is the public deficit. However, one of the declared objectives of the proponents of 'sound finance' and nearly all present-day governments is to 'balance the books' and pay off the public debt. Some economists, including Allan Greenspan, the US Federal Reserve Chairman, have raised the question of what to do with the surplus once the debt has been paid off. Some suggest making it a national savings account (Tyson, 2001), while others think that it may be invested in private assets (Greenspan, 2001; Palley, 2001). This second possibility is paradoxically opposed by some who are at the same time advocating a zero public debt. Their main concern is that it may progressively lead to nationalization of private enterprise, a move that goes against the current trend of globalization, which praises deregulation and privatization of public corporations.[6] From our perspective, the whole discussion about what to do with the surplus is misleading. Rather, what we should be concerned with is the consequences of policies based on budget surpluses.

THE WEALTH EFFECTS OF PUBLIC POLICIES

In the previous section we have seen how taxes and other government receipts are part of a reflux operation that destroys money. Since budget surpluses amount to a net withdrawal of money (wealth) from the private sector, they will necessarily impoverish and depress the economy. Even the most enthusiastic defenders of budget surpluses are now reluctantly recognizing, though not explicitly, that this is indeed the case. Recent examples include the USA, Canada and some European countries where policy-makers are arguing for an increase in government spending and tax cuts to stimulate the economy.

An important component of government spending is interest payment on the debt, which is an income for the rentiers, who in the end are wealthy households who are holding the public debt either directly or through banks and other financial institutions. Since high interest rates increase the rentiers' wealth, it is obvious that these would lobby for a high interest-rate policy. The question that arises then is the following: what causes interest rates to rise and how can we control them?

Orthodox theory does not bother going beyond the simple market forces paradigm and gives the easy answer that interest rates increase automatically when demand for funds exceeds their supply. Some post Keynesians argue that interest rates are exogenously determined and their levels are set by the Central Bank, which can easily manipulate them according to the government's objectives and policies (Moore, 1988; Lavoie, 1992; Smithin, 1996). While this view describes correctly what is common practice in modern economies, there is more to be gained by exploring the mechanisms that actually allow the Central Bank to have such a control over interest rates.

As mentioned earlier, a public deficit increases the net income received by the private sector for the services it provides to the state. When the cheques received by private (individual or corporate) citizens are deposited in their accounts with commercial banks, the balance sheet of the latter is increased by an equal amount on the liabilities side (to the depositors) and on the assets side (since commercial banks now hold government money). It follows that the recipient banks' reserves with the Central Bank will increase. It is well known from the literature on money and banking that such reserves (government money) do not pay interest whereas government bonds do. Since commercial banks are profit-seekers, they do not wish to hold funds that generate no income. Hence, the demand by commercial banks for government bonds increases. However, as explained by Parguez (2000), if the government chooses not to issue any new bonds, the price of the latter would increase and their yield, the interest rate, would fall.[7] Therefore, in the absence of government intervention in the bond market, budget deficits will result in excess reserves in the banking system and therefore cause the overnight rate of interest to fall, whereas surpluses would obviously lead to the opposite result. If the Treasury chooses to issue new bonds, it will acquire, as a counterpart, commercial banks' excess reserves and prevent the overnight rate from falling. Since banks prefer income-earning assets (bonds) to idle reserves and since the Treasury is in a position to set the rate on its new bonds, it follows that the Central Bank can control the interest rate by controlling the issue of bonds.

Now, we must recognize that high interest rates increase the rentiers' wealth at the expense of other groups in society because:

- they lower the value of assets held by households and firms
- they increase the costs paid out by firms and consequently lower their profits, which, in turn, lowers opportunities for expansion and job creation through new investments
- they discourage households from borrowing funds to start new businesses and, therefore, limit the opportunities for them to improve their wealth and well being.

It must be obvious, then, that when a government is pursuing a high interest-rate policy, it must be attempting to protect the *interests* of the rentiers against other groups in society. Such policy clearly leads to an unequal (and undemocratic) distribution of wealth. A low interest-rate policy, on the other hand, favours the interests of ordinary citizens since it gives them access to credit and the opportunity to borrow in order to purchase homes and acquire other valuable assets. Low interest rates spread wealth to a larger portion of society and contribute to the creation of a 'democratic wealth'. In Tocqueville's terminology, we might say that a low interest-rate policy is the distinctive characteristic of democracies since it offers the people 'equal opportunities' to have access to wealth. By contrast, the dominant trend of fiscal orthodoxy, which is based on budget surpluses, serves the immediate interests of the rentier class and, therefore, confers power onto an 'entrenched elite'. Consequently, we conclude that a democratic society should prefer lower interest rates and must, therefore, pursue a public policy that is based on budget deficits, not surpluses.

The view according to which net government spending has positive effects on the private sector is nothing new. Other studies before, some of them using standard neoclassical models, have shown that government spending in the form of public infrastructure increases productivity in the private sector. For instance, Aschauer (1991) and Munnell (1990; 1992), among others, go as far as to argue that the productivity slowdown that characterized most of the industrialized countries since the 1970s, is largely due to the decline of public investment that followed from the conservative policies of spending cuts in order to eliminate budget deficits. Munnell with the assistance of Cook (1990) argue that unequal distribution of public infrastructure contributes to regional disparities if certain areas are neglected. Bougrine (1995) also argues that a well-developed infrastructure attracts more capital investment, which in turn attracts labour and improves employment opportunities. The resulting agglomeration economies have been found to promote higher wages through technical progress, innovation and productivity increases (Bougrine, 1994). Contrary to those living in 'neglected areas', workers who live in regions where such agglomeration economies prevail will undoubtedly benefit from government spending and, therefore, improve their wealth and well-being.

Inequality in access to benefits from government spending does not only follow spacial lines. Social status, age, sex and race are also important characteristics that can cause a bias in allocating government outlays. Studies on gender and racial inequality, for instance, have shown that women and minorities seldom have the same access to government jobs or to benefits from publicly funded services (for example, higher education, subsidies and capital grants, and so on) (see, among others, Peterson, 2001). Therefore, in order to prevent wealth from becoming concentrated in the hands of a few (either because of their location, gender or race, and so on) and in order to make it truly 'democratic' in the sense invoked by Tocqueville (1835 [1966]) and emphasized by Goodin (2001), governments must follow a policy based on public deficits and low interest rates while ensuring that their expenditures are spread evenly across the territory under their jurisdiction.

CONCLUSION

Studies dealing with private wealth and its distribution tend to exaggerate the role of market forces and reject government intervention. The essence of their conclusions is that free, unfettered markets guarantee the best outcome. In this chapter, I have argued that the creation of private wealth and its equal distribution in capitalist societies depend in a crucial way on the implementation of a democratic public policy. In particular, it was shown that public deficits are an important source of wealth for the private sector, which also benefits from the positive effects of low interest rates (with the exception of the rentiers) and a more generous public spending on social programs. The advantages of this policy mix is that it allows more people to have access to equal opportunities to acquire wealth and, in this sense, together with a progressive taxation system, contributes to the creation of a 'democratic wealth'. It was also argued that policies seeking to balance budgets and achieve surpluses have long-term destructive effects on the private sector's wealth and, for this reason, should be rejected even by free-market advocates.

NOTES

* I would like to thank Robert Goodin, Alain Parguez, Warren Mosler, Mario Seccareccia and Randy Wray for their helpful comments and suggestions. Any remaining errors or shortcomings are my sole responsibility.

1. Advanced industrialized countries of Western Europe and North America have historically relied on heavy state intervention for their development over the past 300 years (see Dutt, 1992; Thurow, 1992; Fallows, 1993). Other studies have also shown that recent success stories of the East Asian 'miracle' economies have not been based on free-market ideology but, rather, on the implementation of carefully designed trade and investment policies (see Amsden, 1993; 1996; 1997; Amsden, Kochanowicz and Taylor, 1994; Wade, 1995).
2. Indeed, the basic thinking in these circles is that taxes are the *only legitimate* source of government revenue and that public spending must not exceed the limited 'revenues collected from taxes'. Toye (2000, p. 35), for instance, writes: 'the objective of taxation is, fundamentally, to increase government revenue' and that 'the ability to tax the domestic population is not just another method of financing government expenditure, one among a variety of others. The non-taxation options [that is, borrowing and printing money] for financing are secondary and derivative. Their exploitation requires that the government maintain a sound system of domestic taxation. This is the economic sense in which there is a primacy and a centrality about taxation in the entire armoury of instruments of government finance'.
3. I thank Mario Seccareccia for raising this point.
4. When such legal constraints exist as in the European Monetary Union (EMU), government spending is financed via commercial bank advances (see Marterbauer and Smithin, 2000; 2001; Parguez and Seccareccia, 2000). As stressed by Wray (1998), provincial governments have no power to create money and must therefore rely on taxes and borrowing to finance their expenditures. Smithin (2001, p. 10) points out that this has become the case for those national governments that have 'voluntarily opted for provincial status' in order to become members of the EMU.
5. Households' indebtedness is, therefore, a logical reaction to the (prolonged) policy of budget surpluses. The traditional explanation is that the so-called 'wealth effect' is due to some type of 'wild optimism' that makes people 'feel richer' and therefore would want to borrow more.
6. Even though Greenspan attempts to downplay the fears associated with this scenario when he tells the media that 'the problems of paying off the debt are better than any solution he knows', he is seriously concerned when addressing policy-makers. For instance, in his testimony before the US Senate, he says: 'continuing to run surpluses beyond the point at which we reach zero or near-zero federal debt brings to center the critical longer-term fiscal policy issue of whether the federal government should accumulate large quantities of private … assets', adding that 'This development should factor materially into the policies you [the Senate] and the Administration choose to pursue' (Greenspan, 2001, p. 61).
7. The same result would also occur when commercial banks with excess reserves attempt to lend these in the funds market (see Wray, 1998, p. 86).

REFERENCES

Agell, J., T. Lindh and H. Ohlsson (1997), 'Growth and the public sector: a critical review essay', *European Journal of Political Economy*, **13**, 33–52.

Amsden, A. (1993), 'Trade policy and economic performance in South Korea', in M.R. Agosin and D. Tussie (eds), *Trade and Growth: New Dilemmas in Trade Policy*, New York: St. Martin's Press, pp. 187–214.

Amsden, A. (1996), 'A strategic policy approach to government intervention in late industrialization', in A. Solimano (ed.), *Road Maps to Prosperity: Essays on Growth and Development*, Ann Arbor, MI: University of Michigan Press, pp. 119–41.

Amsden, A. (1997), 'South Korea: enterprising groups and entrepreneurial government', in A. Chandler, F. Amatori and T. Hikino (eds), *Big Business and the Wealth of Nations*, Cambridge: Cambridge University Press, pp. 336–67.

Amsden, A., J. Kochanowicz and L. Taylor (1994), *The Market Meets its Match: Restructuring the Economies of Eastern Europe*, Cambridge, MA: Harvard University Press.

Aschauer, D.A. (1991), *Public Investment and Private Sector Growth*, Washington, DC: Economic Policy Institute.

Badcock, B. (1994), 'Snakes or ladders': the housing market and wealth distribution in Australia', *International Journal of Urban and Regional Research*, **10** (10), 609–27.

Bartlett, B. (2000), 'Death, wealth and taxes', *Public Interest* (141), 55–68.

Bell, S. (1998), 'Can taxes and bonds finance government spending?', Jerome Levy Economics Institute working paper no. 244, July.

Bell, S. (2001), 'The role of the state and the hierarchy of money', *Cambridge Journal of Economics*, **25** (2), 149–63.

Billings, D.B., and K.M. Blee (2000), *The Road to Poverty: The Making of Wealth and Hardship in Appalachia*, Cambridge and New York: Cambridge University Press.

Blau, F., and J.W. Graham (1990), 'Black-white differences in wealth and asset composition', *Quarterly Journal of Economics*, **105** (2), 321–39.

Blecker, R.A. (1992), *Beyond the Twin Deficit: A Trade Strategy for the 1990s*, Armonk, NY: M.E. Sharpe.

Bougrine, H. (1994), 'Capital accumulation, output growth and disparities in labour productivity among Canadian regions', *International Review of Applied Economics*, **8** (3), 283–90.

Bougrine, H. (1995), 'Imperfect competition and the new theory of international trade', in R. Moncarz (ed.), *International Trade and the New Economic Order*, Oxford: Pergamon and Elsever Science, pp. 25–31.

Bougrine, H. (2000), 'Fiscal policy and the current crisis: are budget deficits a cause, a consequence or a remedy?', in H. Bougrine (ed.), *The Economics of Public Spending: Debts, Deficits and Economic Performance*, Cheltenham, UK and Northampton, MA, USA: Edward Elgar, pp. 6–29.

Bougrine, H., and M. Seccareccia (2001), 'The monetary role of taxes in the national economy', paper presented at the Canadian Economics Association meeting, Montreal, Canada, June.

Chiterji, N.S., and F. Stafford (2000), 'Asset ownership across generations', Jerome Levy Economics Institute working paper no. 314.

Darity, W.A., and S.L. Myers (1998), *Persistent Disparities*, Cheltenham, UK and Lyme, USA: Edward Elgar.

Dutt, A.K. (1992), 'The origins of uneven development: the Indian subcontinent', *American Economic Review Papers and Proceedings*, **82** (2), 146–50.
Fallows, J. (1993), 'How the world works', *Atlantic Monthly*, **272** (6), 60–74.
Feldstein, M. (2000), 'Kill the death tax now', *Wall Street Journal*, 14 July, p. A14.
Galbraith, J.K. (1998), 'Inequality and unemployment: an analysis across time and countries', in S. Sharma (ed.), *John Maynard Keynes: Keynesianism into the Twenty-first Century*, Cheltenham, UK and Northampton, MA, USA: Edward Elgar, pp. 152–93.
Galbraith, J.K. (2000), 'The burden of wealth', *Public Interest* (141), 68–74.
Galbraith, J.K., and H. Kum (2002), 'Inequality and economic growth: data comparisons and econometric tests', University of Texas at Austin working paper no. 21, Austin, TX.
Gale, W.G., and M. Perozek (2000), 'Do estate taxes reduce saving?', in W.G. Gale, J.R. Hines and J.B. Slemrod (eds), *Rethinking Estate and Gift Taxation*, Washington, DC: Brookings Institution.
Godley, W. (2000), 'Drowning in debt', *Policy Note*, no. 2000/6, Jerome Levy Economics Institute, accessed at www.levy.org/docs/pn/00–6.html.
Goodin, R.E. (2001), 'Democratic wealth, democratic welfare: is flux enough?', *New Political Economy*, **6** (1), 67–79.
Graziani, A. (1990), 'The theory of the monetary circuit', *Economies et sociétés*, **24** (6), 7–36.
Graziani, A. (1997), 'The Marxist theory of money', *International Journal of Political Economy*, **27** (2), pp. 26–50.
Greenspan, A. (2001), 'Testimony of Federal Reserve officials', *Federal Reserve Bulletin*, **87** (3), pp. 61–65.
Halevi, J., and P. Kriesler (2000), 'On the limitations of fiscal policy: a radical Kaleckian view', in H. Bougrine (ed.), *The Economics of Public Spending: Debts, Deficits and Economic Performance*, Cheltenham, UK and Northampton, MA, USA: Edward Elgar, pp. 135–49.
Hurst, E., M.C. Luoh and F. Stafford (1998), 'Wealth dynamics of American families, 1984–1994', *Brookings Papers on Economic Activity*, **0** (1), 267–329.
Janson, P. (2000), 'Basic income and the Swedish welfare state', Lund University Department of Political Science, working paper.
Kindleberger, C. P. (2001), 'Investing with death in mind', *Financial Times*, 16 July, p. 15.
Kopczuk, W., and J. Lupton (2000), 'To leave or not to leave: an empirical investigation of the distribution of bequest motives', manuscript, Department of Economics, University of Michigan.
Kotlikoff, L., and L. Summers (1981), 'The role of intergenerational transfers in aggregate capital accumulation', *Journal of Political Economy*, **89** (4), pp. 706–32.
Lam, D. (1999), 'Generating extreme inequality: schooling, earnings, and intergenerational transmission of human capital in South Africa and Brazil', University of Michigan Population Studies Center at the Institute for Social Research, research report 99–439.
Lavoie, M. (1992), *Foundations of Post-Keynesian Economic Analysis*, Aldershot, UK and Brookfield, USA: Edward Elgar.
Lavoie, M. (2000), 'Government deficits in simple Kaleckian models', in H. Bougrine (ed.), *The Economics of Public Spending: Debts, Deficits and Economic Performance*, Cheltenham, UK and Northampton, MA, USA: Edward Elgar, pp. 122–34.

Lerner, A.P. (1947), 'Money as a creature of the state', *American Economic Review, Papers and Proceedings*, **37**(2) (May), 312–17.

Levy Institute (1999), *The Macrodynamics of Inequality in the Industrialized and Developing Countries*, Annadale-on-Hudson, NY: Jerome Levy Economics Institute.

Loury, G.C. (1981), 'Intergenerational transfers and the distribution of earnings', *Econometrica*, **49** (4), 843–67.

Marterbauer, M., and J. Smithin (2000), 'Fiscal policy in the small open economy within the framework of monetary union', WIFO working paper 137, Vienna, November.

Marterbauer, M., and J. Smithin (2001), 'The balanced-budget multiplier for the small open economy in a currency union, or for a province in a federal state', paper presented at the conference on *Post Keynesian Economics: Theory and Policy*, University of Notre Dame, South Bend, IN, May.

McGarry, K. (2000), 'Inter vivos transfers or bequests? Estate taxes and the timing of parental giving', *Tax Policy and the Economy* (14), 93–122.

Menchik, P.L., and N.A. Jianakoplos (1997), 'Black-white wealth inequality: is inheritance the reason?', *Economic Inquiry*, **35** (2), 428–42.

Moore, B. (1988), *Horizontalists and Verticalists: The Macroeconomics of Credit Money*, Cambridge: Cambridge University Press.

Mosler, W. (1998), 'Full employment and price stability', *Journal of Post Keynesian Economics*, **20** (2), 167–82.

Munnell, A. (1990), 'Why has productivity declined? Productivity and public investment', *New England Economic Review*, Federal Reserve Bank of Boston (January/February), 3–22.

Munnell, A. (1992), 'Infrastructure investment and economic growth', *Journal of Economic Perspectives*, **6**, 189–98.

Munnell, A., and L.M. Cook (1990), 'How does public infrastructure affect regional economic performance?', *New England Economic Review*, (September/October), 11–32.

Musgrave, R.A., and P.B. Musgrave (1989), *Public Finance in Theory and Practice*, New York: McGraw-Hill.

Nissan, D. (2001), 'Use inheritance tax to give a fair chance to all', *New Statesman*, **130**, (4526), 34.

Oliver, M., and T. Shapiro (1995), *Black Wealth/White Wealth: A New Perspective on Racial Inequality*, New York: Routledge.

Palley, T. (2001), 'The case against budget surpluses: why government debt is good and moderate budget deficits are needed in a growing economy', paper presented at the Canadian Economics Association meetings, Montreal, Canada, June.

Parguez, A. (2000), 'A monetary theory of the public finance', paper presented at the Fifth Post Keynesian Workshop on Post Keynesian Economics for the 21st Century, Knoxville, Tennessee, June.

Parguez, A., and M. Seccareccia (2000), 'The credit theory of money: the monetary circuit approach', in J. Smithin (ed.), *What is Money?*, London and New York: Routledge, pp. 101–23.

Peterson, J. (2001), 'The policy relevance of institutional economics', *Journal of Economic Issues*, **35** (1), 173–84.

Seccareccia, M., and A. Sood (2000), 'Government debt monetization and inflation: a somewhat jaundiced view', in H. Bougrine (ed.), *The Economics of Public Spend-*

ing: Debts, Deficits and Economic Performance, Cheltenham, UK and Northampton, MA, USA: Edward Elgar, 122–34.
Shoup, C.S. (1966), *Federal Estate and Gift Taxation*, Washington, DC: Brookings Institution.
Smithin, J.N. (1996), *Macroeconomic Policy and the Future of Capitalism: The Revenge of the Rentiers and the Threat to Prosperity*, Cheltenham, UK and Brookfield, USA: Edward Elgar.
Smithin, J. (2001), 'Can we afford to pay for social programs?' paper presented at the Canadian Economics Association meeting, Montreal, Canada, June.
Solon, G. (1992), 'Intergenerational income mobility in the United States', *American Economic Review*, **82** (3), 393–408.
Soros, G. (2000), 'No, keep it alive to help the needy', *Wall Street Journal*, 14 July, p. A14.
Thurow, L. (1992), *Head to Head: The Coming Economic Battle Among Japan, Europe and America*, New York: William Morrow.
Tocqueville, A. (1835 [1966]), *Democracy in America*, vol. 2, New York: Harper and Row.
Toye, J. (2000), 'Fiscal crisis and fiscal reform in developing countries', *Cambridge Journal of Economics*, **24**, 21–44.
Tyson, L.D. (2001), 'The surplus? Make it a National Savings Account', *Business Week*, 19 February, p. 26.
Wade, R. (1995), 'Resolving the state-market dilemma in East Asia', in H.J. Chang and R. Rowthorn (eds), *The Role of the State in Economic Change*, Oxford: Oxford University Press, pp. 114–36.
Wolff, E. (1995), *Top Heavy: A Study of the Increasing Inequality of Wealth in America*, New York: Twentieth Century Fund.
Wolff, E. (1998), 'Recent trends in the size distribution of household wealth', *Journal of Economic Perspectives*, **12** (3), 131–50.
Wray, R. (1998), *Understanding Modern Money*, Cheltenham, UK and Lyme, USA: Edward Elgar.

3. Exploring the economics of euphoria: using post Keynesian tools to understand the US bubble and its aftermath

Robert W. Parenteau

INTRODUCTION

During periods of prolonged economic growth and robust financial asset returns, an economics of euphoria, as the late Hy Minsky described it, can be described. Rising asset prices can act as an accelerant on investment spending and as a depressant on the household saving rate. These shifts can fuel boom conditions in the economy, further validating an asset price appreciation. A self-amplifying feedback loop is introduced, taking portfolio positions and economic behavior far from a sustainable path. Private sector deficit spending is encouraged by asset price appreciation. Eventually, private deficit spending leads to a private debt build-up, which in turn can bring the economy to a state of what Minsky termed financial fragility.

However, under certain conditions, the emergence of the financial fragility in the later stages of asset bubbles can be thwarted. In a private closed economy, any attempt by businesses to deficit spend on capital equipment due to an equity bubble can be frustrated as household savings fall in response to the asset bubble. Rising profits, via the Keynes/Kalecki profit equation, result as investment spending increases exceed household savings increases. This improves the internal funds available for firms to service their debt, thereby reducing their financial fragility.

By moving to the more realistic setting of an open economy with a government sector, financial fragility conditions become less likely to be thwarted. A private sector debt build-up will tend to arise during an asset bubble in an economy with a high income elasticity of import demand and some degree of automatic fiscal stabilizers. If policy-makers mistakenly pursue currency appreciation and fiscal restraint during such a bubble, profits can become even more elusive. As private sector deficit spending persists with a rising fiscal surplus and a falling trade balance, external debt builds up. Households and firms become susceptible to explosive private debt trap dynamics. Once the bubble bursts, traditional policy responses become much less effective because of this emergent financial fragility.

In order to investigate the recent US equity bubble, three relatively simple tools will be used to reintegrate financial and macroeconomic dynamics along post Keynesian lines.[1] The first tool is the Keynes/Kalecki profit equation: it will be used to understand why the investment boom accompanying the financial mania was eventually met with a falling rather than a rising profit share. The second tool is the financial balance equation: it will help identify how changes in expenditure plans inspired by the financial mania led to a surge in private sector debt loads, especially when combined with misguided policy moves. The third tool is a more conventional debt trap equation, here adapted to the US non-financial corporate sector: it will expose the unsustainability of asset bubble driven growth, while also indicating how dangerous Fisher style debt-deflation dynamics which frustrate normal policy responses can be unleashed in a post-bubble environment.

Before employing these analytical tools, three points of contact between the equity bubble and the economy need briefly to be introduced. There are reasons to believe the equity bubble boosted the propensity of firms to invest in capital equipment, reduced the propensity of households to save and altered the preferences of foreign investors for US dollar denominated assets. Through these points of contact, financial market conditions influenced economic outcomes.

For example, equity prices can reflect a number of the elements driving investment spending, including the cost of capital and expected profit rates. Keynes, in his *Treatise on Money* (Keynes, 1953), operated along these lines in devising what Minsky would revive as the two-price model of investment spending. Keynes introduced an arbitrage condition between the spot demand price of the existing stock of capital, found in financial market prices of corporate liabilities, and the flow supply price of newly produced capital equipment, found in product market spot prices or orders. Keynes (1964, p. 151) explained this approach as follows:

> But the daily revaluations of the Stock Exchange, though they are primarily made to facilitate transfers of old investments between one individual and another, inevitably exert a decisive influence on the rate of current investment. For there is no sense in building up a new enterprise at a cost greater than that at which a similar existing enterprise can be purchased; whilst there is an inducement to spend on a new project what may seem an extravagant sum, if it can be floated off on the Stock Exchange at an immediate profit.

Minsky also made this arbitrage condition a key element in his financial theory of investment, which in turn provided the basis for his investment theory of the business cycle. Minsky (1986, p. 186) wrote, 'In a corporate capitalist economy with a stock exchange, the market valuation of a firm's capital assets and market position substitutes for the price of capital assets'. Minsky further noted, 'Whenever the price of capital assets exceeds the cost of investment, an implicit capital gain is realized at the moment an investment project is fully assimilated to the stock of capital assets. Such capital gains serve as a lure that induced investment activity' (ibid., p. 214).

As clear as the logic of Keynes's two-price theory may be, econometric investigations of the power of this model, proxied by tests of various types of *q* ratios, have not proven particularly encouraging (Morck, Shleifer and Vishney, 1990). However, considering the increasingly widespread use of stock options as an integral part of the management compensation, it is entirely plausible that equity prices played a larger than usual role in perpetuating the investment spending boom of the 1990s. For example, capacity utilization actually fell for most of the second half of the 1990s (Figure 3.1), yet the investment share of GDP in inflation-adjusted terms rose to a new post-war high during this same period – not what would be expected from accelerator, bottleneck or normal capacity based capital spending models. Nor was the low cost of equity capital (introduced by surging equity prices) an element in the capital spending boom, as shares were net repurchased, not net issued, by the corporate sector at a record pace during the bubble years. Any serious explanation of the investment boom, then, must at least in part

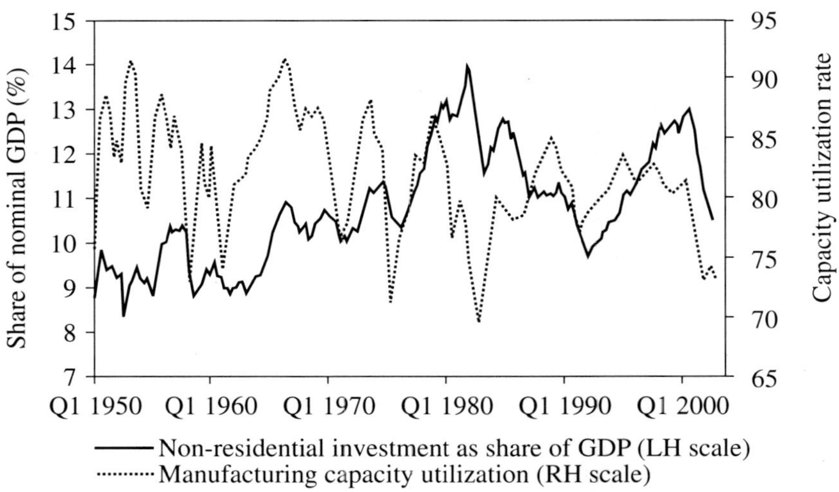

Figure 3.1 A late 1990s investment boom despite falling capacity utilization

turn to the growing relevance of the arbitrage condition highlighted in the Keynes/Minsky two-price theory as corporate managers increasingly gained ownership in firms.

Household saving preferences, Keynes argued, are primarily a function of the level of income. Keynes held to a 'fundamental psychological law' whereby households are 'disposed, as a rule and on the average, to increase their consumption as their income increases, but not by as much as the increase in their income' (Keynes, 1964, p. 96). Keynes, however, was also willing to allow a role for changes in the value of household wealth. As he noted in the *Treatise* (Keynes, 1953, vol. 2, p. 197)

> Who can doubt that a man is more likely to buy a new motor car if his investments have doubled in money value during the past year than if they have been halved? He feels far less necessity or obligation to save out of his normal income, and his whole standard of expenditure is raised.

In the *General Theory* discussion on the trade cycle, Keynes introduced an important interaction between a shift in his marginal efficiency of capital schedule, as initiated by a sharp fall in equity prices, and a shift in the propensity to consume. Keynes (1964, p. 319) observed,

> Now, on the class who take an active interest in their Stock Exchange investments, especially if they are employing borrowed funds, this naturally exerts a more depressing influence. These people are, perhaps, even more influenced in their readiness to spend by rises and falls in the value of their investments than by the state of their income. With a 'stock-minded' public, as in the United States today, a rising stock market may be an almost essential condition of a satisfactory propensity to consume … .

Two empirical observations suggest Keynes's mention of these wealth effects was not entirely misplaced. First, the gross household saving rate has not consistently risen in the post-war period. Starting in 1982 (about the same time as the equity bull market began), the gross household saving rate has fallen, most recently to levels last seen in the Great Depression.[2] Second, changes in household net worth (scaled by disposable personal income) display an inverse correlation with the rate of gross household saving out of disposable personal income, as displayed in Figure 3.2. Wealth increases from asset price appreciation appear to be treated as a substitute for saving out of household income flows.[3]

The third point of contact between the equity bubble and the real economy can be found in the foreign exchange market and its influence on the balance of trade. Early advocates of flexible exchange rates espoused the view that trade imbalances would be more likely to self-correct if currencies were free to float. Hidden beneath this self-correcting theme found in the flexible

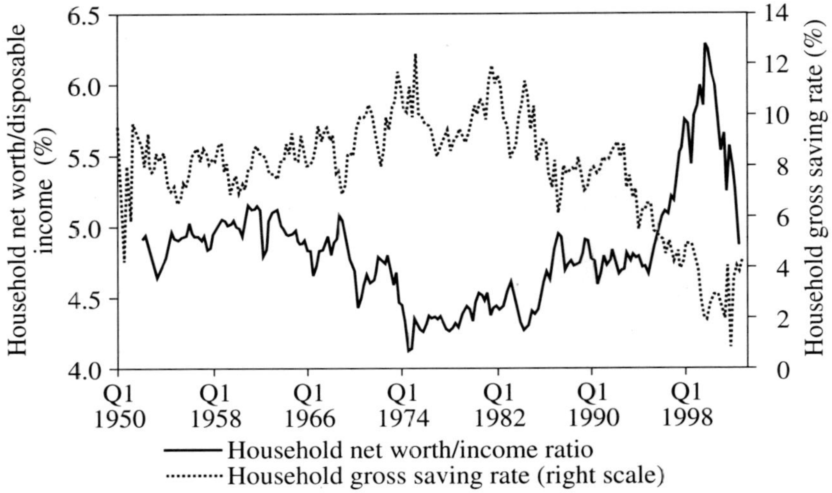

Figure 3.2 The wealth effect on household saving

exchange trade argument was an implicit assumption that trade or current account flows would dominate capital flows. As capital controls were dissolved in the 1980s and 1990s, capital flows became a more influential element in exchange rate determination.

To see why this could reduce the self-correcting properties of flexible exchange rate, consider what happens when an increase in expected profitability induces a higher investment level. This produces a shift out in the IS curve against, for simplicity's sake, a fixed LM curve. At the resulting higher income level, the current account balance decays. With the resulting higher interest rate level, foreign investors should be more attracted to US debt instruments. Improved profit expectations should also encourage a higher desired share of US equities in foreign portfolios. Taken together, these portfolio preference shifts operating on stocks of wealth are likely to swamp any changes in the net flow supply of dollars offered with the falling trade balance. The dollar can appreciate on this *ex ante* balance of payments surplus. Foreign investors experience currency gains on top of any capital gains in US financial assets held. Thus, the shift in foreign portfolio preferences can be self-validating through currency effects. The result is dollar appreciation despite a widening current account deficit, which can further undermine the trade balance.

In summary, expectations and behaviors that shape real economic activity are influenced by financial market outcomes. With these three transmission channels between the equity market bubble and the economy in mind, it now becomes possible to explore why the longest business cycle expansion in US history was accompanied by a profit squeeze before turning to the related issues of growing financial imbalances and emergent private debt trap dynamics.

THE MACRO PROFIT EQUATION AND EQUITY BUBBLE DYNAMICS

The Keynes/Kalecki profit equation can offer a useful framework for understanding the influence of equity bubbles on corporate profitability. Keynes appears to have buried this relation on his way from the *Treatise on Money* to the early drafts of the *General Theory*[4], but Kalecki, in his own independent discovery, was able by 1933 to independently build the macro profit equation up from the national income and expenditure identity (Kalecki, 1971, essay 7). In a private closed economy, total income must equal total expenditures. If income can be partitioned into profits and wages, and expenditures can be divided into investment and consumption, then simple algebra reveals the identity:

$$\text{Profits} = \text{Investment} + \text{Consumption} - \text{Wages} \tag{3.1}$$

Assuming no income is distributed to households from corporate profits, then the profit equation can be simplified to:

$$\text{Profits} = \text{Investment} - \text{Household savings} \tag{3.2}$$

Investment expenditures are an injection to the circular flow of income, while household savings are a leakage from this circular flow. Wages paid out to households working in the corporate sector must be recovered by firms through the sale of consumer products to the household sector. Essentially, the more income the household sector manages to save, the less corporations are able to recoup their labor expenses.

When this simple profit relation is combined with the two-price theory of investment, strong recursive dynamics can result. Minsky found the resulting upward instability dynamic especially intriguing. He described this upward instability as follows:

> A deviation of quasi-rents, Q, from what was expected affects not only the way investment impinges upon the balance sheets of firms; it also affects the price level of capital assets. If actual quasi-rents are greater than anticipated, the excess of profits over expected profits will raise Pk (the demand price for capital goods), increasing the gap between the Pk and Pi (the supply price of capital goods) ...

> This situation implies an increase in investment demand relative to the ability of internal finance. Profits in excess of those anticipated therefore increase the demand for investment by improving the flow of internal funds, raising the (implicit) price of capital assets and increasing borrower's willingness to finance externally.
> (Minsky, 1986, p. 194)

This upward instability is made even more powerful if wealth effects influence household savings. However, financial fragility cannot easily arise in this model without a foreign and government sector. Replacing the restrictive assumption of a private closed economy with a more realistic open economy that includes a public sector, the Keynes/Kalecki equation can be expanded as follows:

$$\text{Profits} = \text{Investment} - \text{Household savings} - \text{Fiscal budget balance} + \text{Net exports} \quad (3.3)$$

Once the macro profit equation is expanded to include a government and a foreign sector, and reasonable assumptions are introduced about the behaviour of the fiscal and trade balances during the late expansion phase of the cycle, it becomes possible to show how a profit squeeze can develop endogenously. This endogenous profit squeeze tends to increase the financial fragility of firms as an expansion progresses, thereby disrupting the bullish spiral of equity prices. Increasing financial fragility and faltering equity prices can provide sufficient reason for firms to pull back their investment spending plans, thereby marking the reversal of Minsky's upward instability dynamics. As profits fall short with lower investment spending, the feedback loop spirals downward.

Minsky was aware of these effects on profits, even if he did not always fully sketch them out in various renditions of his model. Minsky (1986, p. 150) wrote:

> Because a balance of trade deficit tends to constrain profits, an economy in which imports react strongly to income – as is now true of the United States – will experience constrained increases in profits when the domestic economy expands. This effect weakens the expansion and increases the investment and government deficit needed to achieve and sustain full employment.

The Keynes/Kalecki profit equation can offer a useful analytical tool for exploring macrodynamics during asset bubbles. By replacing an income-driven household saving model with a wealth-driven model, Minsky's financial fragility dynamics appear to be thwarted. However, once the profit equation is opened up to allow fiscal and trade balance influences as well, an equity bubble inspired private spending boom can still be accompanied by a late expansion profit squeeze, as explored next in more empirical detail.

AN EQUITY BUBBLE WITH A PROFIT SQUEEZE

With this expanded variant of the Keynes/Kalecki profit equation, a richer set of profitability and sector financing dynamics can arise. In an equity bubble led expansion, profits are fed by the rising propensity of firms to invest and the rising propensity of households to consume. In an economy with some degree of automatic stabilizers in fiscal policy, and a high income elasticity of imports, profit growth is dampened by these two leakages from the circular flow. Beyond these endogenous effects, any bias in fiscal policy favoring public debt reduction, and any bias in foreign exchange policy favoring domestic currency appreciation also crimp profits. If these effects are strong enough, they can swamp the private sector spending boom and produce a profit squeeze. This is in fact what we observe in the USA during the second half of the 1990s.

Specifically, on an after tax basis, nonfinancial corporate profits as a share of nominal GDP peaked in 1997 at a 4.2 per cent reported and 4.9 per cent adjusted level (Figure 3.3). Profit margins this high had not been seen since 1980 on a reported basis and 1968 on an adjusted basis. Until the middle of 1997, the bull market inspired surge in the investment share of GDP and the drop in household savings rates swamped the mild deterioration in net exports and the sharp rise in the government fiscal balance, and profitability was supported. From its trough in 1992 to the middle of 1997, the non-residential

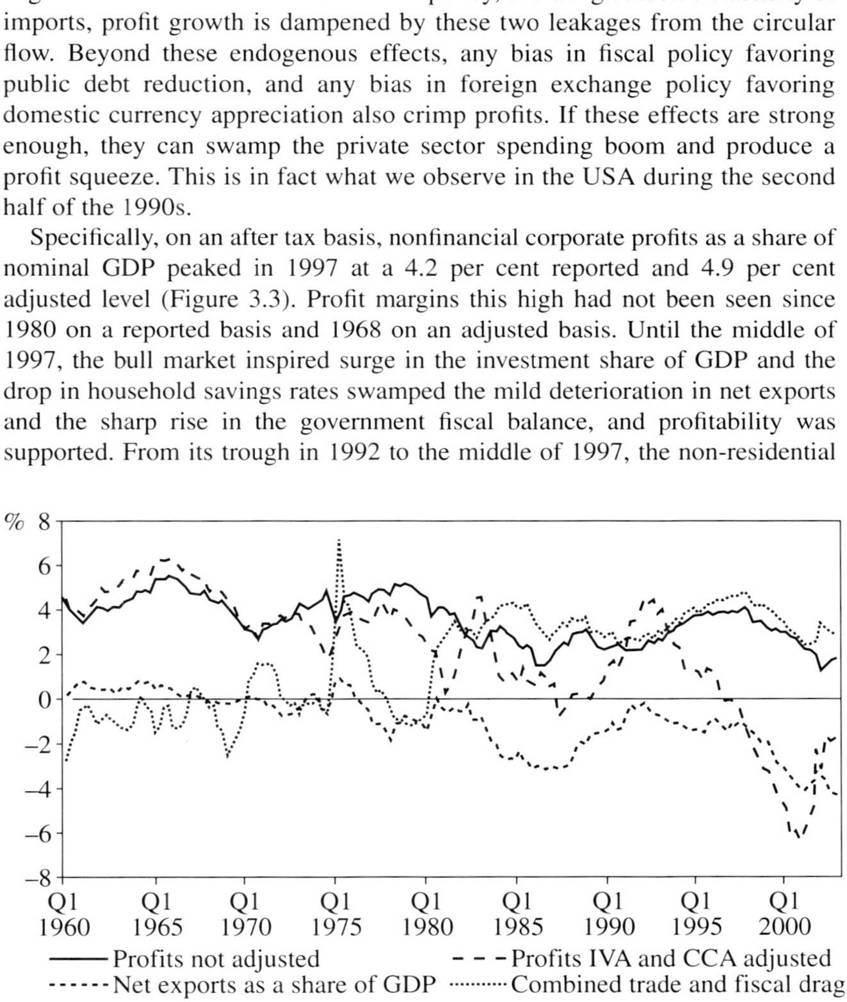

Figure 3.3 After tax non-financial corporate profit share and the fiscal and trade drag

fixed investment share of nominal GDP rose from 9.7 per cent to 12.2 per cent, while household gross savings as a share of nominal GDP fell from 6.7 per cent to 3.3 per cent. Meanwhile, the budget deficit shrank from –5.1 per cent of nominal GDP to –0.5 per cent while net exports fell from –0.6 per cent to –0.9 per cent of nominal GDR Consequently, the private sector spending boom was, up until the middle of 1997, sufficient to overwhelm the profit drags imposed by fiscal rectitude and a weakening trade balance.[5]

As equity prices bubbled higher, corporations lifted the non-residential investment share of nominal GDP to an 18-year high by the third quarter in 2000. Households similarly lowered their gross savings share of nominal GDP down to a low last seen in the Great Depression. That is, the private sector spending boom did not let up after the profit margin peak in 1997. However, at the same time, under the influence of rising US incomes, rising realized capital gains and a rising dollar, the government fiscal balance swung into a 2.4 per cent of nominal GDP surplus while net exports ran deeply into a deficit of 3.9 per cent. With US private income flows being drained off by the fiscal surplus, and siphoned abroad to bolster foreign profits via the trade deficit, US corporate profit margins were squeezed just as the Keynes/Kalecki profit relation would suggest.

In this fashion, the cumulative feedback loop of higher equity prices – higher investment spending – higher profits – higher equity prices which Minsky identified as central to the upward instability of the economy was derailed. Endogenous leakages from the circular flow of income end up dampening realized profits. Exogenous shocks are not required to disrupt this process, nor is an interest rate spike required to break the chain. Minsky's financial fragility theory can thereby be placed on a more generalized footing, and one that is less dependent upon central bank behavior, commercial bank liquidity preferences or the disruption of any one large borrower's capacity to service debt.

One curiosity remains. With profit margins under increasing pressure after 1997 from the rising budget surplus and the deepening trade deficit, why did equity returns continue to soar until early 2000? Why were profit expectations so divorced from reality? By definition, asset bubbles involve some degree of disconnection between reality and perception. Promoting such cognitive dissonance is, of course, greatly in the interest of speculators and financiers. John Kenneth Galbraith has captured this 'vested interest in error that accompanies speculative euphoria' in the following passage: 'The euphoric episode is protected and sustained by the will of those who are involved in order to justify the circumstances that are making them rich. And it is equally protected by the will to ignore, exorcise, or condemn those who express doubts' (Galbraith, 1990, p. 9).

This aspect of asset bubbles corrupts the discovery process investors are supposedly engaged in. The information processing ability of financial markets is corrupted when the providers of financial information face unusually large rewards for distorting financial information. Compensating managers with stock options introduces just such a moral hazard. Plainly put, the very reporting of financial information so central to asset market efficiency was left in the hands of agents incentivized to produce higher stock prices. As Warren Buffet recognized in 1999:

> A significant and growing number of otherwise high-grade managers – CEOs you would be happy to have as spouses for your children or as trustees under your will – have come to the view that it's okay to manipulate earnings to satisfy what they believe are Wall Street's desires. Indeed, many CEO's think this kind of manipulation is not only okay, but actually their duty.
>
> (Cited in Cadette, Levy and Thiruvadanthai, 2001, p. 4)

That earnings standards eroded in a country that prides itself on financial market transparency is no small irony. More alarming is the logical absurdity displayed in long-term earnings expectations provided by Wall Street analysts that arrived by the mid-1990s. By the height of the bubble, S&P 500 long-run earnings forecasts had soared to 18 per cent per year – this despite the nosedive evident in trailing five-year annualized growth of corporate profits as measured in the national income accounts (Figure 3.4).

Even during the booming New Era of the 1990s, S&P 400 revenue growth averaged closer to 4 per cent per year. Disinflation kept nominal top-line growth relatively slow. Assuming that 4 per cent sales growth held indefi-

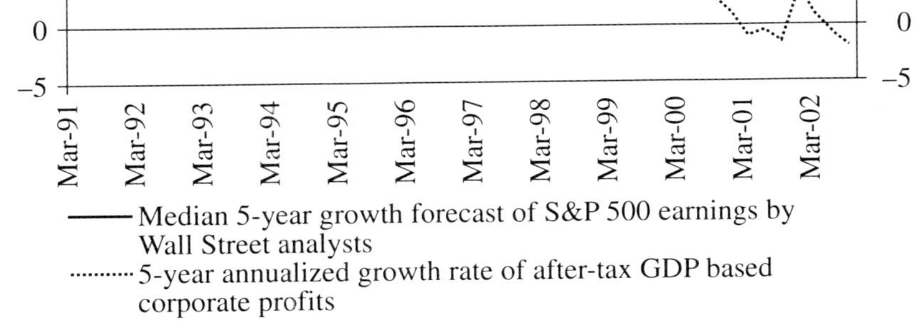

Figure 3.4 What were Wall Street analysts doing?

nitely, 18 per cent long-run profit growth rate implied not just a 'frictionless' economy by 2022, but a thoroughly costless economy as well. Profit margins would reach 100 per cent in two decades under the assumptions asserted by Wall Street analysts.

It is this realpolitik of financial markets that explains the enormous cognitive dissonance surrounding corporate profits during the bubble years. Given the incentives stock options introduced to management, it should come as no surprise that following the bursting of the equity bubble, companies like Enron and JDSU have massively restated their earnings histories, and investors have begun to wonder whether earnings were just a mirage.

THE FINANCIAL BALANCE EQUATION AND THE EQUITY BUBBLE

To understand the financial balance approach, recall that spending by any one sector of the economy need not be constrained by the income earned by that sector in any given accounting period. Deficit spending by one sector will tend to produce income in excess of expenditures in another sector, or net nominal saving. Financial claims issued by the deficit spending sector will end up being held by the net nominal saving sector.[6] The financial balance equation simply requires the net nominal savings of all macro sectors to sum to zero, since in the aggregate, total income must still equal total expenditure, total investment must equal total saving, and for each borrower there must be a lender.

Returning to the expanded profit equation, sector financial balances can be introduced in four easy steps. First, the fiscal budget balance and the net export balance must be moved to a net saving basis. Government investment must be subtracted from the fiscal budget balance on current expenditures to arrive at the government financial balance. Adjustments for net investment income and unilateral transfers must be made to net exports to arrive at the current account balance, which is the inverse of the capital account balance, the relevant foreign financial balance. Second, depreciation must be considered for the capital stock held by firms, households and the government to move the analysis to a cash flow basis. Third, by dividing investment into residential and non-residential (including inventory change) components, the financial balances for the business sector can be isolated from the household sector as follows:

$$\begin{aligned}\text{Profits} - \text{Non-residential investment} = {} & \text{Residential investment} \\ & - \text{Household savings} - \text{Government financial balance} \\ & + \text{Current account balance}\end{aligned} \tag{3.4}$$

As the corporate sector was incentivized during the equity bubble years to put new high-tech equipment in place at a rapid pace despite the profit squeeze, the business sector financial balance eroded. From a peak of 2.4 per cent of nominal GDP in early 1993, the business financial balance decayed steadily until the end of 2000, when it troughed at –4.6 per cent of nominal GDP.[7] This lead to a rising stock of financial liabilities on business balance sheets despite the lesson of 'credit headwinds' earlier in the decade. Total domestic non-financial business debt nearly doubled from $3.7 trillion in 1993 to $7.1 trillion in 2002.[8]

The fourth step required in moving from the macro profit equation to the sector financial balance equation is to shift the household sector items to the left-hand side, consolidating the private sector. The expression now appears as:

$$\text{(Profits – Non-residential investment) + (Household savings – Residential investment) = Current account balance – Government financial balance} \quad (3.5)$$

When household consumption outlays exceed their disposable income, gross savings in the household sector is negative. Earlier, the gross savings rate of the household sector was shown to fall during periods of asset price appreciation. When residential investment expenditures exceed gross savings plus depreciation, the household sector is deficit spending, and net saving for the sector is negative. The household sector financial balance decayed from a peak surplus of 4.4 per cent in late 1992 to a deficit of 2.4 per cent in late 2001 (Figure 3.5).

In order to deficit spend, households must emit liabilities (or sell existing assets), and these liabilities must be accumulated by other sectors that are net saving. Under the influence of the equity bubble, the household sector increased its leverage despite the memory of the distress wrought by the 1980s consumer debt binge. Total household debt also nearly doubled from $4.2 trillion in 1993 to $8.2 trillion in 2002.

Consolidating the business and household sector, the summary financial balance equation appears as follows:

$$\text{Private sector balance = Current account balance – Government financial balance} \quad (3.6)$$

If the propensity of foreigners to spend on exports is low, and if fiscal policy is set to run a surplus, then the private sector will tend toward a path of persistent deficit spending, regardless of the *ex ante* preferences of households and firms. This increases the private debt load over time. In the case of

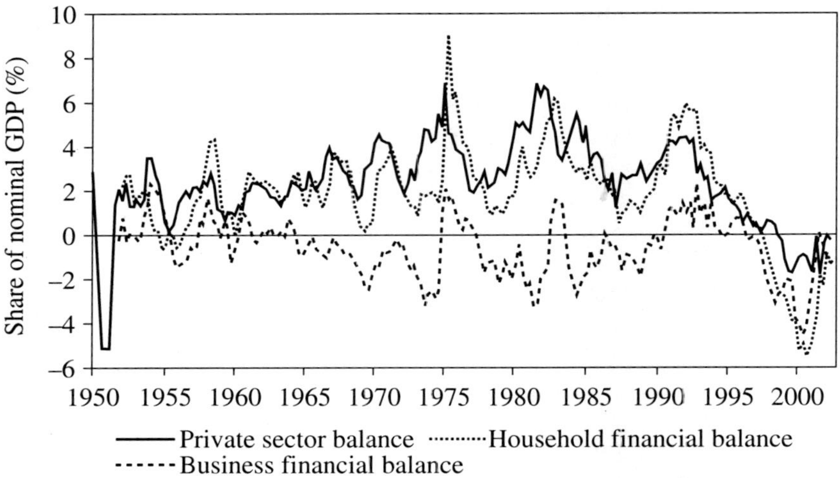

Figure 3.5 *US private sector financial balances*

the USA, the private sector balance dropped from a 5.9 per cent of GDP surplus in the first quarter of 1992 to a deficit of 5.5 per cent of GDP in the third quarter of 2000. Two-thirds of this shift can be accounted for by the swing in the government financial balance from –6.1 per cent to 1.3 per cent of nominal GDP over the same period (Figure 3.6). The remaining one-third is attributable to the decay in the current account from –0.2 per cent to –4.2 per cent of nominal GDP.

To summarize, flow imbalances can lead to balance sheet disequilibria in the private sector, not just the public sector. In fact, the financial balance equation highlights an extraordinary irony of the push toward fiscal surpluses begun early in the Clinton Administration. The rhetoric of fiscal austerity was often couched in thoroughly inappropriate family budget analogies. It was argued that just as any one family cannot keep spending beyond its means without eventually finding itself bankrupt, so too the government budget must be kept within its means. Using the financial balance equation above, a persistent push towards higher fiscal surpluses in a country like the USA with a chronic current account deficit will eventually lead the private sector to bankruptcy. The Rubin Doctrine of ever-rising fiscal surpluses and a strong dollar was perhaps one of the most effective methods for financially destabilizing the private economy that could have been concocted.

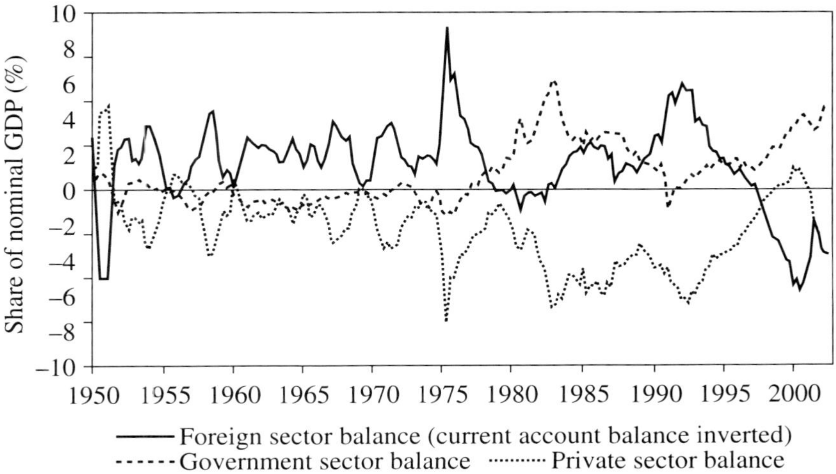

Figure 3.6 *Financial balances by sector net lending must sum to net borrowing*

FROM FINANCIAL IMBALANCES TO PRIVATE DEBT TRAPS

Flow imbalances generated by the push of bubble-induced private deficit spending, and the pull of misguided fiscal and foreign exchange policies, will mount over time in the form of overly leveraged US household and corporate balance sheets on the one hand, and foreign portfolios saturated with financial claims on US assets on the other. What, then, is the limit to this debt dynamic?

A fall in rate of income growth relative to interest rates can trigger a rising debt to income ratio for any deficit spending sector. However, once it becomes apparent to creditors that a sector of the economy is entering an explosive debt path, credit rationing is generally not too far behind. Since income growth depends to a certain extent on net new credit creation, the end result of these debt trap dynamics usually is not explosive debt growth but, rather, a collapse of income growth as credit is rationed. This leads to the invalidation of prior debt claims, and a financial crisis is triggered.

World Bank and International Monetary Fund (IMF) officials have used debt trap equations to monitor risks in developing nations for some time. By the late 1970s, these debt trap equations were also applied to the public sector in developed nations to analyze prolonged fiscal deficit spending.[9] But rarely are debt trap equations examined for the private sector. Given the unprecedented US private sector deficit generated during the equity bubble, this selective application of debt trap equations is wholly inappropriate.

In one of its simpler variants, the debt trap equation can be summarized in discrete time terms as follows:

$$\text{Future debt/Income ratio} = (1 + \text{Interest rate} - \text{Income growth rate}) \times \text{Current debt/Income ratio} - \text{Primary financial balance/Income ratio} \quad (3.7)$$

Since interest expense grows as a function of the interest rate times the existing debt load, and the income growth rate determines how fast the denominator in the debt/income ratio expands, all that is needed is the financial balance excluding interest expense (the primary balance) to determine the future debt/income ratio of any sector.

To apply the debt trap equation to the non-financial corporate sector, several modifications are necessary. First, sector income must be properly defined. Nominal GDP for the non-financial corporate sector is not the appropriate income concept, as employee compensation and net interest expense must be subtracted from this aggregate to arrive at corporate profits. Corporate profits are themselves not sufficient, as they must be placed on a retained cash flow basis to identify the capacity to service debt. Accordingly, dividend and tax payments must be subtracted from corporate profits while depreciation and the inventory valuation adjustment must be added back. Gross after tax interest expense also needs to be added back to this cash flow basis to establish a pre-interest expense cash flow series. Second, an implicit average interest rate series can be constructed using the gross interest expense for the non-financial corporate sector in any one year divided by the non-financial corporate debt level at the end of the prior year. Third, a primary surplus series can be constructed by adding gross after tax interest expense to the non-financial corporate sector financial balance.

With these adaptations in mind, a five year forward simulation can be used to assess the sustainability of the non-financial corporate debt load. The following base case assumptions are made:

- the average interest rate on the outstanding stock of non-financial corporate debt will fall 50 basis points per year for the years 2002–06[10]
- the growth rate of non-financial corporate GDP will migrate back to its post-war average of 7.3 per cent over the period 2002–06
- the growth rate of non-financial corporate cash flow will bear its post-war average relationship to non-financial corporate GDP growth, and migrate steadily back to 8.2 per cent

- the primary financial balance as a share of non-financial corporate cash flow will also bear its normal post-war relationship to non-financial corporate GDP growth, falling steadily back to a 10.3 per cent surplus, just below its post-war average.

With these relatively favorable assumptions in mind, Figure 3.7 shows the debt/cash flow ratio for the non-financial corporate sector results for years 2002–06. The debt to pre-interest expense cash flow ratio surges from a low of 361 per cent in 1997 to a new post-war high of 490 per cent at the peak of the equity bubble. With the above assumptions, the debt load climbs higher to 506 per cent by 2003. By the end of the forecast period, the debt load does fall as the interest rate and cash flow growth rate converge, but it remains near the highs recorded in the previous recession.

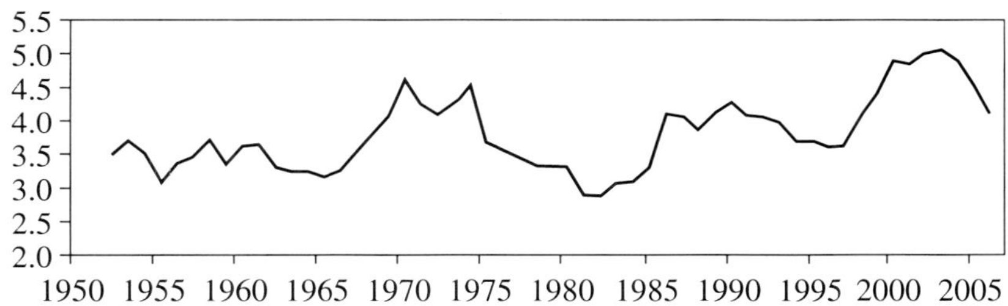

Figure 3.7 Non-financial debt/cash flow + after tax interest expense

In other words, while the debt/cash flow ratio does not display an explosive trajectory given the favorable assumptions above, there is not much room for error. Should corporate bond yields prove downwardly sticky because of elevated levels of default and delinquency, or should rising household saving and a deepening trade deficit dampen non-financial corporate cash flow growth rates, leaving the corporate sector financial balance in deficit, then the debt/cash flow path will prove less manageable. Furthermore, assuming the next recession starts beyond 2006, the debt/cash flow level will still be at a historically high level, leaving little in the way of a margin of safety at the next business cycle peak. Nor has any attempt been made to account for off balance sheet debt which may be forced back on the balance sheet over the forecast horizon.[11] This could occur through the changes in accounting rules already under way regarding special purpose entities, through the increased recognition of underfunded pension liabilities, or through less aggressive or opaque accounting practices by chief finance officers (CFOs) wary of litigation or shareholder scrutiny.

Since the draconian interest rate shock imposed by Volcker, the cash flow growth rate for the nonfinancial corporate sector has tended to remain well below the implicit interest rate on corporate debt. The critical change in the 1990s was that the primary surplus eroded as this sector's financing gap opened up to over $300 billion by 2000. As a consequence, the primary surplus ceased to be large enough to offset the explosive debt dynamics inherent in the difference between the sector's implicit interest rate and the pre-interest expense cash flow growth rate. Unless the business financing gap improves during both future recessions and expansions, or unless corporate debt is entirely refinanced at low nominal interest rates, the corporate sector will remain poised on a dangerous debt path.

Wynne Godley, Bill Martin and others have performed plausible simulations for the private sector debt/income path with similar results. Given the private sector financial imbalances that developed in the bubble years, there does not appear to be an easy way out. More likely, as credit events continually unfold, credit will be quantity rationed to the private sector by increasingly risk-averse lenders. The resulting financial constraint on income growth could very well place the US economy at risk of reproducing Japan's most recent 'lost decade' of debt deflation.

THE DOWNSIDE RISK OF A FISHER STYLE DEBT DEFLATION

Equity bubbles support private sector deficit spending, and sustained deficit spending leads to debt build-ups that leave balance sheet disequilibria in place. When equity bubbles pop, as they may do endogenously when rising fiscal and trade imbalances squeeze profits, private sector flow imbalances will tend to correct. The *ex ante* willingness of households and firms to deficit spend will tend to wither away as asset prices fall. As desired net private saving increases, household and business expenditures will be cut back, and slower income growth will unfold. This pattern is clear over the past 50 years: the private financial balance has tended to improve as share of GDP during periods of weakening nominal GDP growth, and to decay during periods when nominal GDP is accelerating (Figure 3.8).

On average, since the trough in 1950, the private financial balance as a share of GDP has decayed by 3.9 per cent of nominal GDP from the trough to the peak of the post-war business cycles, and improved 3.4 per cent from the peak to the trough. The business sector tends to account for two-thirds of this swing.

Changes in private portfolio preferences also accompany these attempts to redress flow imbalances. As household and corporate net worth declines with

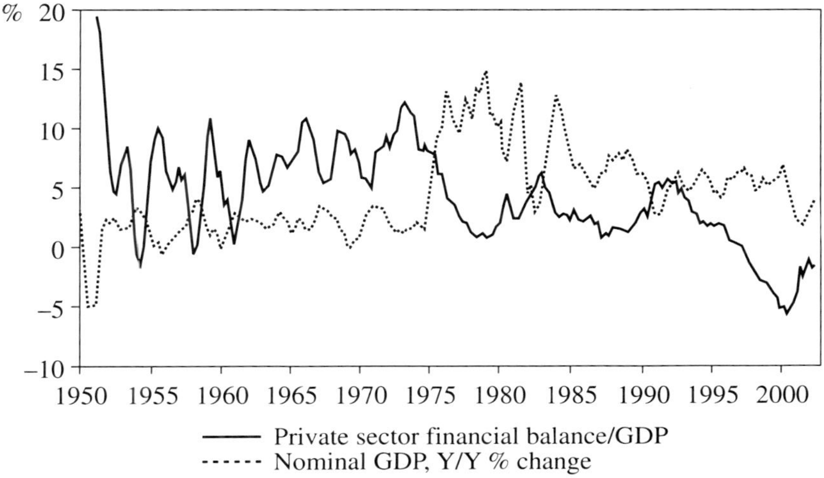

Figure 3.8 US private sector financial balance and economic growth

falling stock prices, the private sector will try to reduce its debt load. Liquid assets will be built up on these same balance sheets. Equity holders may view the disruption of their euphoric return expectations as a reason to reduce the proportion of their portfolios in equities. Creditors will tend to require a higher premium to hold the increasingly risky debt of the private sector. While each wealth owner will try to reduce exposure to the riskiest liabilities issued by the private sector, in the aggregate, since someone must hold the outstanding debt, asset prices will need to fall further until all existing assets are willingly held. Of course, if expectations of financial asset returns are at all formed adaptively, this is an invitation to disaster.

These private portfolio and spending responses to a burst asset bubble can introduce one of the greatest threats to capitalist economies, namely debt deflation. As Irving Fisher described in his seminal 1933 article, just as the economy can be susceptible to a certain upward instability as asset price advances encourage higher spending preferences, so too can a vicious cycle be unleashed when falling asset prices lead to less deficit spending and a lower preference for debt (Fisher, 1933). Fisher noticed that a recursive process of falling loans, falling product prices, rising currency demand, falling deposits, falling product prices and further credit revulsion could take hold, leaving behind a perverse rise in real interest rates as economic activity collapsed.

Minsky carried this strand forward by combining Fisher's insights with Keynes's framework. Minsky argued a break in asset prices would tend to damage investment spending enough to dampen profits. As business spending dropped, so too would income growth and pricing power. The ability to service debt would diminish as a consequence. Minsky noted, 'A decline in the sum of investment, government deficit, balance of trade surplus, and consumption out of wages and profits decreases the validating cash flows. Investment spending, the balance of trade surplus, and consumption ratios of households are all sensitive to financial market developments' (Minsky, 1986, p. 166).

Profit shortfalls would dampen asset prices further. Increasing financial distress would lead to more restrictive financing conditions. Eventually, outright asset sales would be required to service debt commitments, forcing asset prices lower again. In Minsky's opinion, spender and lender of last resort responses by the government would be required to reverse this vicious spiral. There could be no illusions about the self-corrective nature of the market. As Minsky wrote, 'Instead of a disappointment of expectations setting up forces that correct the disappointment, the financial consequences of a shortfall of profits make the achievement in the future of results that validate the cost structure more difficult' (Minsky, 1986, pp. 165–6).

Keynes was conflicted on this subject, as his central concept of a marginal propensity to consume of less than one implied households would tend towards deficit spending as a recession deepened (Keynes, 1979, ch. 10, pp. 394–5). But this exit from the vicious spiral of debt deflation makes less sense if households enter a recession when they are already in a deficit spending position. In this instance, some other sector must be willing to deficit spend. Given the damage done to profits during recessions, the business sector may not be relied upon to spontaneously begin investing in plant and equipment. Instead, what Keynes referred to as loan expenditures, or deficit spending financed by new credit creation, is required of the public sector (Keynes, 1979, 'Means to prosperity', p. 354).

Therefore, one of the keys to defusing the debt deflation threat in any recession is to replace private sector deficit spending with deficit spending by the public or foreign sectors. If a fiscal deficit or a trade surplus can be achieved in a timely fashion, the domestic private sector can reduce its expenditures without undermining its income or distress selling its assets. Moreover, if government and foreign deficit spending persists, net nominal saving can be generated in the private sector, allowing room for private balance sheet repair. With a swing towards fiscal stimulus and a trade surplus sufficient to overcome the collapse in private investment spending and the rebound in household savings rate, profits can revive, further bolstering asset prices.

Applied to the recent situation, the break in equity prices has decisively driven investment expenditures into the ground. From the end of 2000 to the fourth quarter in 2002, the level of nominal non-residential fixed investment expenditures has dropped by $160 billion, with another $251 billion in nominal private inventory de-stocking.

Conventional expenditure multiplier relationships hold that lower investment spending should imply lower investment equipment production, lower capital goods employment and, so, lower household income. With lower household income should come lower household spending. Curiously, though, household expenditure as a share of GDP remains at post-war highs (Figure 3.9). Although some of this can be explained by fortuitous tax cuts and equity cash out mortgage refinancing activity (in part as rapid Fed easing encouraged lower mortgage rates), there may also be a larger issue of broken checks and balances in the consumer finance system at work here. Nevertheless, were households to try to close their financing gap as of this writing, and to return to the 2.5 per cent of GDP surplus they have averaged over the past half decade, another $296 billion direct hit to the economy would arise.

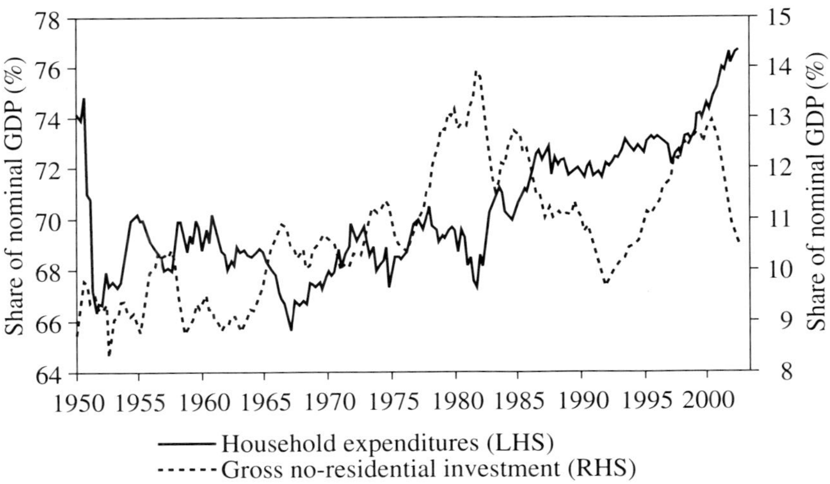

Figure 3.9 US household spending share remains aloft

Were consumers to get caught by credit rationing, forced sales of liquid assets to meet financial obligations might be required. Since the average share of equities in households is still above the historical norm and will tend to overshoot this average to the downside, it is conceivable that equity positions may be liquidated in order to meet debt commitments.[12] Mutual fund liquidation became persistent late in 2002, even though consumer debt was still mounting. Barring a shift in favor of equity allocations by another sector

– say corporate share repurchases or portfolio rebalancing by large institutional investors targeting fixed stock/bond weights – a recursive loop of forced equity sales, lower equity prices, lower household net worth and more equity sales could provoke debt deflation dynamics.

This is not to belittle the fact that the private financing gap closed to $133 billion by the third quarter of 2002, from a high of $547 billion in the third quarter of 2000. Although the combined government balance has swung favorably from a $128 billion surplus in the third quarter of 2000 to a $364 billion deficit in the third quarter of 2002 on further tax cuts and military expenditures following the 9/11 attack, this swing in the fiscal balance has been partially offset by a deteriorating current account balance. Without a reversal of the trade deficit, the private sector is unlikely to return to balance in the immediate future, and the risk of Fisher debt deflation dynamics will not disappear. Indeed, as of the second quarter in 2002, the non-financial corporate price deflator had slipped into outright deflation, and corporate profit margins, still near their post-war lows, were falling again.

CONCLUSION

While the generation of financial wealth in the US economy during the second half of the 1990s captured the attention of the world, this prosperity was clearly built on a house of cards. The complicity of macroeconomic policy-makers in allowing the US economy to enter into a state of unprecedented financial fragility cannot be overlooked. Ironically, while orthodoxy emphasized the need to get public finances in order, private financial balances were ignored and dangerously undermined.

Although the many private sector behaviors that fed the equity bubble and the attendant financial imbalances are now reversing, these unfolding adjustments make the return to sustainable growth more challenging. Since the policy response to date has been more rapid and more aggressive than usual, the US economy may as yet be able to avoid a full-blown debt deflation path. Early indications are that the swing in fiscal policy is proving sufficient to reduce private sector deficit spending. However, barring a wave of new equity issuance, outstanding private debt can only be paid off by persistent net private saving. To complete the repair process, not only must a deep fiscal deficit be maintained, but also the current account deficit must be reversed.

Even then, we may find business and household balance sheet repair is not a sufficient condition for returning the USA to a robust expansion path. The rupture of the euphoric return expectations on financial and real capital is likely to have a lingering effect. Given the alarming underperformance of stocks relative to bonds since the bubble burst – of a magnitude not experienced since the Great Depression – portfolio preferences could change for an entire investing generation. At a minimum, investor and lender risk perceptions of various asset classes are liable to shift for some time to come. With less euphoric portfolio preferences must come lower financial asset prices, and less gullible creditors. If, as argued above, asset prices can influence the desired rate of capital spending and the household propensity to save, these portfolio preferences shifts are likely to weigh on the rate of income growth achievable in the post-bubble economy.

More to the point, the enormous overhang of capital stock financed during the bubble years will need to depreciate away before the profit expectations of entrepreneurs revive. High-tech equipment put in place may depreciate quickly, and new waves of technological innovations cannot be ruled out. But by way of the macro profit equation, it is evident that a falling or stagnant investment share of GDP leaves any rebuilding of US profit shares at the mercy of (1) a stabilization in the household savings rate, (2) further tax cuts or public investment initiatives that raise the fiscal deficit, and (3) a reorientation of foreign economies away from export led strategies in order to help reverse the US trade deficit.

These are not impossible tasks, but they are not likely to emerge spontaneously either. Fortunately, such challenges open up room for creative initiatives that can speed the repair of the economy, as well as prevent severe disequilibria from developing in the future. In the wake of the disillusionment brought on by the bursting of asset bubbles comes the opportunity to refoot financial relations on a sounder basis. Such opportunities are indeed rare, but are rarely worth ignoring.

NOTES

1. Much of the framework for this analysis draws heavily from research begun in late 1998 with Frank Veneroso. In addition, suggested edits by L. Randall Wray proved especially helpful. However, any errors, omissions, or opinions expressed herein remain my own.
2. Furthermore, the pattern of the gross household saving rate is somewhat ambiguous over the course of post-war business cycles, contrary to the procyclical pattern suggested by Keynes.
3. This may help explain the difficulty of finding reliable evidence of any strong positive interest rate elasticities of saving.
4. Keynes once wrote 'any man who has thoroughly grasped this truism ... will never be, in his outlook on the practical world, quite the same man again'. See Keynes (1979, pp. 40–41). Fanning and O'Mahoney (1998) offer an interesting attempt to reconstruct the General Theory with a profit orientation.
5. Recall in the Keynes/Kalecki profit equation, investment is more than just non-residential investment, and the fiscal balance is on a current basis, and so is not to be confused with the government financial balance discussed in the next section. To calculate the combined drag, the fiscal share is subtracted from the net export share of nominal GDP.
6. This is not to be confused with the loanable funds fallacy. Deficit spending by one sector

does not require prior net saving by a second sector in economies operating with endogenous credit money. Rather, the deficit spending by one sector will create the income flows out of which new savings will be generated, as described in Meade's version of Kahn's expenditure multiplier.

7. Unlike Wynne Godley's (1999) approach, this is the financial balance for the business sector as a whole, not just the non-financial corporate segment, and all of the income/expenditure statistical discrepancy is attributed to this sector, rather than split with the household sector, on the belief that profits are most likely to be incorrectly counted.
8. Non-financial business debt is used here, despite the calculation of a financial balance for the business sector as a whole, because complex financial layering makes the interpretation of financial sector debt loads somewhat problematic.
9. The irony of this application deserves to be appreciated, as one of the early explorers of debt trap equations, Evsey Domar, concluded, because interest income is taxable, public debt trap dynamics are fairly limited.
10. Only two prior stretches in the post-war period show five-year declines in excess of this assumption: the periods ending in 1986–87, and the periods ending 1993–94.
11. One possible explanation of the high implied interest rate for this sector could be the rising share of debt held off balance sheet.
12. As of the third quarter in 2002, the share of equities (inclusive of mutual fund holdings) in total financial assets held by households and personal trusts was 29 per cent, slightly above the 50-year average of 25.6 per cent, and well over twice the 1982 low of roughly 12 per cent.

REFERENCES

Cadette, Walter M., David A. Levy, and Srinivas Thiruvadanthai (2001), *Two Decades of Overstated Corporate Earnings: The Surprisingly Large Exaggeration of Aggregate Profits*, New York: Levy Institute Forecasting Center.

Fanning, Connell, and David O'Mahoney (1998), *The General Theory of Profit Equilibrium: Keynes and the Entrepreneur Economy*, New York: St. Martin's Press.

Fisher, Irving (1933), 'The debt deflation theory of the Great Depressions', *Econometrica*, **1**, 337–57.

Galbraith, John Kenneth (1990), *A Short History of Financial Euphoria: Financial Genius Before the Fall*, Knoxville, TN: Whittle Communication L.P.

Godley, Wynne (1999), *Seven Unsustainable Processes*, New York: Levy Economics Institute.

Henry, David, and Christopher H. Schmitt (2001), 'The numbers game', *Business Week*, 14 May.

Kalecki, Michal (1971), *Selected Essays on the Dynamics of the Capitalist Economy*, London: Cambridge University Press.

Keynes, John Maynard (1953), *A Treatise on Money*, London: Macmillan.

Keynes, John Maynard (1964), *The General Theory of Employment, Interest, and Money*, New York: Harcourt-Brace-Jovanovich.

Keynes, John Maynard (1979), *The Collected Writings of John Maynard Keynes, Volume XXIX: The General Theory and After*, London: Macmillan.

Minsky, Hyman P. (1986), *Stabilizing an Unstable Economy*, New Haven, CT: Yale University Press.

Morck, R., A. Shleifer, and R. Vishny (1990), 'The stock market and investment: is the market a sideshow?', *Brookings Papers on Economic Activity*, **2**, 157–215.

PART II

Post Keynesian Approaches to Monetary Theory and Policy

4. Money in the time of the Internet: electronic money and its effects

Claudio Sardoni*

1 INTRODUCTION

In the last few years, much attention has been paid to the effects that the so-called information technology (IT) revolution can have on the monetary and financial system of advanced economies. This chapter considers the impact that these technological changes can have on central banks and their ability to implement an effective monetary policy, a topic recently discussed by many monetary economists. In this context, particular attention is paid to the role and effects of electronic money (e-money).

Some believe that recent technological developments can reduce significantly the importance of central banks and their ability to implement monetary policy. Others have responded by holding that IT advances do not imply radical changes of the existing monetary organization in advanced economies. In this debate, e-money is often regarded as an exemplification of what the IT revolution can bring about. After having defined precisely what is meant by e-money and having considered some basic characteristics of this new means of payment (section 2), I turn to consider the current debate on IT and the future of central banking (section 3). In the concluding section 4, I argue that, although in principle IT advances could imply a significant weakening of the central banks' power, this requires that e-money evolves into a means of payment different from the current one. In particular, I argue that in order to arrive at a world in which central banks have, mostly or entirely, lost their power, it is necessary that the economy adopts a means of payment not based on the existence of conventional money, as is the case for e-money currently in use.

2 MONEY AND E-MONEY

One problem with the discussion of the effects of e-money on the monetary system is that the term is not always clear. It is sometimes used in a very loose sense to indicate any means of payment implying the use of electronic devices at some stage of an economic transaction. Here, I adopt the definition of e-money given by the European Central Bank (ECB): 'electronic money is broadly defined as an electronic store of monetary value on a technical device that may be widely used for making payments to undertakings other than the issuer without necessarily involving bank accounts in the transaction, but acting as a prepaid bearer instrument' (ECB, 1998, p. 7). This definition is a good representation of the two main types of e-money currently available: e-money based on cards (multifunction pre-paid cards bought by buyers); e-money based on some type of software that allows buyers and sellers to transfer funds through an electronic network. Both types of e-money require the existence of conventional money. In fact, users buy cards or software from issuers by paying in advance with conventional money a certain amount that then they can spend electronically. Both types of e-money can be issued by banks as well as by firms outside the banking sector. Normally, e-money is denominated in the same unit of account of conventional money, but it does not necessarily have to be so.

E-money issued by commercial banks can be regarded as a form of demand deposit and, therefore, a component of money narrowly defined (M_1, base money plus demand deposits). When the public buys e-money, it undertakes an operation that is essentially the same as opening a current account with a bank. Banks, on the other hand, treat the liabilities created in this way as demand deposits, to which they apply a certain reserve ratio.[1] When e-money is created outside the banking sector, it cannot be regarded as similar to demand deposits. The diffusion of e-money issued by firms outside the banking sector can be considered as analogous to cases in which the demand for liquidity shifts from assets defined as belonging to the aggregate M_1 to assets classified under broader monetary aggregates (M_2, and so on). Therefore, given a constant total demand for liquidity, a positive demand for this type of e-money implies a reduced demand for M_1. A major implication of a positive demand for e-money issued by non-banking firms is that these firms would not have deposits (reserves) at the central bank, so that an increase in the demand for their liabilities may imply a reduction in the demand for base money. It is this type of e-money that could represent a threat for central banks.

Before turning to the debate on the impact of a large diffusion of e-money, it is useful briefly to consider some of the factors that can favor or hinder its adoption in the economy. The analysis of how the total demand for money is distributed among different instruments can be carried out in terms of a maximization problem. The use of each instrument implies some costs and benefits; agents choose that combination of currency, deposits and e-money that maximizes (minimizes) such benefits (costs).[2] If all the variables that affect the agents' decisions are collapsed into a single variable, called 'efficiency' (π), the efficiency of each means of payment can be regarded as a direct function of its degree of diffusion of in the economy. Money is an asset with a positive *network effect*: it becomes more useful (efficient) as its diffusion in the economy increases. Total efficiency then is

$$\pi\ (c, d, m) = \pi_c\ (c) + \pi_d\ (d) + \pi_m\ (m) \tag{4.1}$$

where c is the proportion of total money demanded in the form of currency, d is the proportion demanded in the form of deposits and m is the proportion demanded in the form of e-money. The agents' problem is to choose the vector (c^*, d^*, m^*) that maximizes $\pi(c, d, m)$.[3]

Apart from the trivial case in which there is no demand for e-money ($m^* = 0$), the maximizing solution could be such that the agents' demand for currency and deposits is very little, that is, both c^* and d^* are small and m^* is large. This solution could be justified by the typical characteristics of e-money. As is well known, currency is usually preferred to deposits because its cost of usage is virtually nil whereas deposits have a positive cost (trips to the bank, fees charged on them, and so on). On the other hand, deposits are safer than currency and make the payment of large amounts easier. E-money has both the advantages of currency and deposits: its cost of usage is very low and, at the same time, is safer than currency. For these reasons, e-money can be a good substitute for both currency and deposits, and the public could maximize the efficiency of exchanges by demanding very little conventional money.

However, because of network effects, e-money is more efficient than the other media only if its degree of diffusion in the system is larger than a certain critical value of m. The process through which conventional money is largely displaced by e-money can be described in the following terms: e-money owns some characteristics that make it a more efficient means of payment than conventional money, but this is true if e-money becomes sufficiently widespread in the economy. Once the degree of diffusion of e-money has reached this 'critical' value, positive network effects are able to induce a large reduction in the demand for the other means of payment.

However, there can be, several factors at work that prevent e-money from becoming the dominant means of payment in the economy. Goodhart (2000), for example, has mentioned some of these factors: the public's desire of privacy, the existence of illegal transactions and so on. Dowd and Greenaway (1993)[4] have shown that, despite the existence of positive network effects, there can be obstacles to the diffusion of a new more efficient means of payment. There can be some sort of 'inertia' due to a high 'switching cost' (the cost implied by moving from a means of payment to another) and to a problem of co-ordination: the new means of payment is actually more efficient than the old only if it is adopted by a large number of agents in the economy, but no single agent knows when and if the others are going to switch to the new means, so that nobody (or very few) will adopt the new instrument. The presence of inertia in the system means that, in many cases, the degree of competition among different means of payment is not very strong. The introduction of potentially more efficient means is not necessarily conducive to the displacement (or 'quasi-displacement') of 'inferior' instruments.[5]

3 THE IT REVOLUTION AND CENTRAL BANKING

The current discussion on the implications of the IT revolution for central banking is part of a more general debate on the implications of financial innovations for the working of monetary economies. In the early 1980s, the debate on these issues was started by the exponents of the New Monetary Economics. The basic idea behind this approach was that the significant reduction in transaction costs, brought about by innovations in the payment system, makes it possible to have a world without any medium of exchange and a unit of account different from conventional money. Transactions would be made through an accounting system, which works through book-keeping entries, debits and credits, while the role of unit of account (numeraire) can be played by any good (asset) or bundle of goods (assets) (see, for example, Fama, 1980; Greenfield and Yeager, 1983). In spite of some differences among them, the representatives of the New Monetary Economics shared the common conviction that a world without money[6] would be more efficient and more stable than the currently existing economies. In particular, this new world – with central banks much less, if at all, powerful than today – would be free of inflation and instability.[7]

The debate on the future of money has acquired new vigour more recently, especially in the second half of the 1990s. This more recent debate, inevitably, echoes many discussions of the 1980s, but with some distinctive characteristics. While new monetary economists shared a common hostility towards central banks and their deleterious effects on the economy, most participants in the current debate are not so interested in questioning the usefulness or necessity of monetary policy, but they rather concentrate on the question whether the IT changes imply significant effects on the central banks' ability to implement monetary policy.

Although opinions on such effects diverge, the participants in the debate agree on some basic issues. First, all are concerned with the central banks' ability to set the short-term interest rate; in other words, all accept the idea that monetary policy is essentially about the determination of the interest rate, rather than the quantity of money.[8] Second, in the discussion of the effects of IT on the demand for base money, all concentrate their attention on the demand for bank reserves at the central bank rather than on the public's demand for currency. All also agree that there is a secular tendency for bank reserves to decrease and that such trend can be reinforced by the IT revolution. It is on the extent and implications of such reduction that opinions diverge.

Benjamin Friedman (1999; 2000) is among those who are convinced that a significant reduction in the demand for banks' reserves implies a decrease in central banks' power. Although, already now, the central banks' open market operations are a very small proportion of total financial transactions, they can still affect interest rates – and, hence, the economy – because their transactions are fundamentally different from all the others: the central bank's purchases (sales) of securities always imply an increase (decrease) in the reserve account of the seller's (buyer's) bank. No other participant in the market has the same power to increase or reduce the total volume of reserves. The central bank is 'a monopoly supplier (and withdrawer) of reserves'. The central bank's ability to control the rate of interest, and hence implement monetary policy, crucially depends on the fact that there is a positive demand for reserves. For Friedman, should this demand significantly shrink, the central bank would see its power inevitably wane: 'being a monopolist is of little value if no one needs, or even wants, to have whatever the monopoly is of' (Friedman, 1999, p. 327).

The development of new technologies has created several possible alternatives to conventional money. One of those is e-money, the diffusion of which implies a reduction in the demand both for cash and bank deposits.[9] If the demand for deposits decreases, the banks' demand for reserves at the central bank also decreases. Banks, moreover, can reduce their deposits at the central bank also for other motives. They might reduce their demand for reserves at the central bank as new clearing systems develop. Banks demand reserves at the central bank essentially for clearing purposes, but competition can threaten this aspect of the central bank monopoly power. Competition can come from the creation and development of private clearing mechanisms (Friedman, 1999, p. 333), which can be favoured by the IT revolution.[10]

Friedman points out that e-money does not completely displace conventional money but, he argues, its adoption and diffusion in the economy could expand to a point in which conventional money would be required only at the initial stage of the value chain associated with transactions, that is, to buy e-money. Moreover, if e-money were issued by firms outside the banking sector, and third parties were willing to accept balances on the non-bank firm's books in payment for the firm that issues the card, there would be no need for bank balances to back up in full its corresponding liability. Transactions, in other words, would take place without using conventional money (cash and bank money) at all and, hence, independently of the need for banks' reserves at the central bank. In this way, e-money would develop to the point where it is not merely a means of payment, but also a means of settlement (Friedman, 1999, pp. 328–9). In such a world, conventional money still exists but the central bank's power would be seriously impaired.

In Friedman's terminology, the real threat to central banks' power derives from the possibility of a 'decoupling at the margin' of their operations from markets (Friedman, 2000). In other words, conventional money still exists, but with irrelevant effects on the working of the economy as a whole. Decoupling at the margin can take place at the quantity level and at the price level. From the quantitative point of view, there is decoupling if, at the margin, changes in the balance sheet of the central bank become less, or not at all, related to changes in the volume of assets and liabilities (money and credit) actually needed by the public. From the prices point of view, there is decoupling if the rate of interest set by the central bank becomes less, or not at all, related to the rates and prices that are relevant for the economy as a whole (Friedman, 2000, p. 263). The central bank can still fix the yield of its own liabilities, but this variable is no longer connected to other interest rates and asset prices. The central bank would simply maintain its monopoly power over something that is no longer demanded by a significant section of the economy, so that its decisions become largely irrelevant.[11]

Also Costa and De Grauwe (2001) have recently expressed the opinion that in a world in which currency issued by the central bank is replaced by privately issued liabilities, like commercial bank deposits and e-money, and there are no reserve requirements, the central bank would lose its ability to control the interest rate (Costa and De Grauwe, 2001, p. 4). The central bank would be a bank like any other banks and unable to force the others to hold deposits (reserves) with it. Banks' deposits with the central bank would be just regular bank deposits and it is unlikely that commercial banks wish to hold the full amount of such deposits in their asset portfolio. A large part of these deposits will be presented for conversion at the central bank, which must liquidate an equivalent amount of treasury securities. Therefore, the initial increase in the assets and liabilities of the central bank is eliminated and the amount of liquidity in the system can be expanded only to the extent that banks are willing to hold the liabilities of the central bank (Costa and De Grauwe, 2001, pp. 11–12). If central banks lose the ability to vary the amount of reserves, they also lose the ability to affect interest rates.

Palley (2001–02) has equally held that a wide diffusion of e-money would largely reduce the demand for commercial banks' reserves. He has also introduced the further concern for an increased degree of systemic instability, due to the diffusion of e-money. Central banks' could try to maintain their power by 'inducing' a significant positive demand for their liabilities; for example, by imposing that taxes are paid with conventional money and whoever chooses to exit the e-money circuit must be paid in conventional money. These measures, however, could imply a reduction in the degree of the system's stability, as they can increase the risk of something like bank runs. In a situation in which the public retains the option of demanding conventional money in settlements, 'there will always be the risk that agents will switch and demand payment in such form. If this happens, it will create a massive destabilizing liquidity shortage' (Palley, 2001–02, p. 219).

The positions of those who do not believe that the IT revolution will imply a significant reduction of the central banks' power follow two different, though complementary, lines of argumentation. On the one hand, it is held that, for several reasons, the demand for conventional money will not decrease significantly; on the other hand, it is argued that even a very significant reduction in the demand for conventional money, reserves in particular, will not impair the central banks' ability to set the interest rate and affect the working of the economy. Goodhart (2000), although firmly convinced that e-money is not going to displace conventional money, has argued that even the disappearance of conventional money would not reduce the power of central banks. His basic idea is that the central bank can retain its power to determine interest rate because it is the government's bank and, as such, it does not obey the logic of profitability (Goodhart, 2000, p. 190). The central bank can set the interest rate because it is always able 'to dictate the finest terms on either the bid, or ask, side of the money market'. Banks know that the central bank is backed by the government and this makes it unlikely that it has to undertake large-scale open-market operations to achieve its targets (Goodhart, 2000, p. 205).[12]

Also, Freedman (2000) has held that it is unlikely for e-money to displace currency or the current settlement services, but that even in the case of displacement the central bank would be able to set or influence the short-term interest rate. The fundamental reason why central banks have the power to implement effective monetary policies is that commercial banks want to hold reserves with them, even though there is no institutional reserve requirement. There are some important reasons why the central bank is the privileged locus of settlements for banks' payment imbalances; in particular, the central bank is risk-free and can be lender of last resort (Freedman, 2000, p. 222). Thanks to IT and e-money,[13] a private bank could act as settlement agent for all the others, but there are drawbacks to this type of arrangement: a private bank is not risk-free and the other banks would be uncomfortable about its competitive advantages. Another possibility could be that banks settle payments by transferring risk-free instruments like treasury bills (Freedman,

2000, p. 223). In this case, however, there would be no lender of last resort in case of shortfalls, so that banks should hold large amounts of bills to guarantee that they can meet their obligations.[14] Thus, Freedman's conclusion is that banks will continue to use the current system of settlement.

Freedman also considers the more general issue of whether the system may evolve in such a way that final payers and payees are connected directly through computers and no intermediation is necessary. For example, a software company could offer payments transfer services by using claims on itself as the medium of settlement or by using securities as the means of transferring value. Freedman, however, observes that this does not substantially change things. In the first case, the software company would act as a bank, with all the risks connected to a private bank acting as a settlement agency. In the second case, the use of securities to transfer values would have the same drawbacks as in the case in which banks use bills to settle payments (Freedman, 2000, p. 224). Thus, for Freedman, it is not clear why such futuristic systems should be more advantageous than the current one. However, even in such an unlikely environment, the central bank could influence the rate of interest. It could insist that settlement of its own transactions must be on its own balance sheet and refuse to settle on alternative mechanisms, an arrangement that would be more effective if the central bank continued to be the government's banker (Freedman, 2000, p. 225). Alternatively, the central bank could fix a 'corridor' for the overnight interest rate by providing standby facilities in which it was prepared to accept overnight deposits at a certain rate of interest and to extend overnight loans at a higher rate of interest. If, for example, the market interest rates tend to fall below the central bank's deposit rate, market participants would choose to hold overnight deposits with it (Freedman, 2000, p. 225).

Woodford, in order to show that the IT revolution does not represent a real threat for central banking and monetary policy, has developed a more technical and detailed analysis of monetary policy under different regimes (Woodford, 2000; 2001; 2002). In particular, he considers cases in which there are reserve requirements imposed by the central bank as well as cases in which there are no such requirements and the limit case in which commercial banks reduce their demand for reserves virtually to zero. Although deregulation (for example, the abolition of reserve requirements) and/or advances in IT can determine a reduction in the banks' demand for central-bank balances, this does not mean that the central bank is unable to influence short-term interest rates (Woodford, 2001, p. 319). It can do so by paying an interest on reserves. This method is followed by central banks that use a 'channel' system of interest rate control. With this system, 'there is little reason to expect monetary control to be any more difficult following the development of new electronic media for making payments' (Woodford, 2000, p. 244). With this sort of arrangement, there is no reserve requirement and banks still hold reserves at the central bank as settlement balances. The central bank chooses a target overnight interest rate, supplies a certain amount of settlement cash through open-market operations, and offers a lending facility by which it is ready to supply any amount of additional overnight settlement cash at a fixed interest rate, just above the target overnight interest rate (Woodford, 2000, p. 245).[15]

Woodford also considers the implications of possible, though for him unlikely, developments of payment systems that do not require clearing through the central bank's settlement balances. This would amount to a set limit to the banks' costs of clearing payments through the central bank. If these costs went beyond such a limit, banks would choose to abandon the clearing system through the central bank (Woodford, 2000, p. 254). If, for example, banks considered their balances with the central bank as useful as any other equally riskless overnight investment, their demand for them would be nil at any interest rate higher than the settlement cash rate and horizontal at any rate equal to or lower than the settlement cash rate. In such a case, banks would hold balances at the central bank only if the overnight rate is not higher than the central bank's rate paid on settlement balances. But the central bank could still control the equilibrium overnight rate by fixing a positive settlement cash target, so that the only possible equilibrium would be at an interest rate equal to the settlement cash rate (Woodford, 2000, pp. 255–6; 2001, p. 343). In this context, a perfect control of overnight rates should still be possible through adjustments of the rate paid on central-bank balances and changes in the target overnight rate would not have to involve any change in the settlement cash target, just as is true under current channel systems (Woodford, 2000, pp. 255–6). Thus, the central bank can set the equilibrium overnight rate without any change in the quantity of the balances held with it. Moreover, such constant supply of central bank's liabilities can be quite small, though positive, with respect to the aggregate volume of financial transactions in the economy.

This, for Woodford, is possible because there does not exist an inherent equilibrium value for a fiat unit of account like the 'dollar' (that is, the central bank's liability), unless a particular value is determined through the monetary policy commitments of the central bank itself (Woodford, 2000, pp. 256–7). In a completely deregulated context in which commercial banks do not settle through the central bank, it might seem that it is impossible for the central bank to select among alternative equilibria through the monetary policy. But this is not true because the unit of account in a purely fiat system is defined in terms of the central bank's liabilities. A contract promising to deliver a certain amount of dollars at a certain date implies a payment in terms of settlement balances at the central bank, or in terms of some kind of payment that the payee is willing to accept as a suitable equivalent. In any case, 'settlement balances at the central bank still define the thing to which these other claims are accepted as equivalent' (Woodford, 2000, p. 257). It is this factor that explains why the nominal interest yield on settlement balances at the central bank can determine market overnight rates. The central bank can define the nominal yield on overnight deposits in its settlement accounts as it wishes; it can also let banks exchange such deposits among themselves at whatever terms they wish. However, the value of a dollar deposit with the central bank cannot be anything other than a dollar. This is something that cannot be done by private financial institutions.[16] The special characteristic of central banks, therefore, is that they are institutions whose liabilities are used to define the unit of account in a wide range of contracts. But, even though it is true that the central bank can always fix the interest rate on its deposits, would this rate be relevant for other market interest rates? Woodford's answer is in the positive. The private sector could issue short-term claims that are as riskless as, for example, Treasury bills, but it could not offer an interest rate different from the rate on deposits at the central bank, otherwise there would be excess supply or demand for the private sector instruments (Woodford, 2001, p. 347).

Friedman (2000) has reacted to the idea that the central bank could determine the relevant interest rates in the economy even though the demand for its liabilities shrinks to a very large extent. In particular, he has objected to the positions put forward by Goodhart, Freedman and Woodford. For Friedman, in so far as the central bank is ready to lend to and borrow from banks in potentially infinite volume, it can affect the entire structure of interest rates and influence the working of the economy.[17] If, in the actual world, central banks can implement effective monetary policies without engaging in large transactions, this happens because

> market participants know that, under current circumstances, the central bank *can* make the interest rate whatever it wants – if necessary, by engaging in very large transactions – and as a result those large transactions are *not* necessary. The market watches the central bank's signals, and then establishes – mostly on its own – the interest rate level that the central bank seeks.
>
> (Friedman, 2000, p. 271)

In other words, the central bank can exert its power because the other players in the economy believe that it has the strength to make the market work as it wishes. It is basically for this reason that effective monetary policies can be currently implemented by central banks, but the present situation can drastically change if players change their conviction. In such a case, for Friedman, 'with nothing to back up the central bank's expressions of intent ... in time, the market would cease to do the central bank's work for it. This prospect is ultimately what the threat posed to monetary policy by the electronic revolution is all about' (Friedman, 2000, p. 271).

4 CONCLUSION

In the debate on the implications of IT, and e-money in particular, on central banking and monetary policy, two contrasting positions have emerged. Starting from the common acknowledgement that the IT revolution implies a reduction in the demand for base money, of reserves in particular, opinions diverge on the effects that such reduction can have on the central banks' ability to set the short-term nominal interest rate and, through it, affect the working of the economy as a whole. The idea that a significant reduction of the demand for reserves at the central bank implies a significant reduction in its ability to implement an effective monetary policy appears more convincing. The possibility of the central bank always being able to set the interest rate on its liabilities is of little relevance if such liabilities are no longer crucial for the working of the economy. It is true that, already, central banks are effective without engaging in large transactions, but this is true because markets know that central banks, if they wish, could always engage in much larger transactions and, hence, bring the interest rate to whatever level. This would cease to be true if there were no longer a significant market for the central banks' liabilities, that is to say, if the economy can work without using a relevant amount of conventional money.

Thus, in my opinion, it is possible that technological and institutional transformations lead to a world in which central banks have largely lost their power and their ability to implement effective monetary policies. But another issue arises: is it likely that e-money of the sorts that currently exist can actually determine such a significant reduction in the demand for conventional money? In my opinion, if conventional money is required to buy e-money, it is problematic to conclude that banks' reserves are no longer necessary or that their volume becomes irrelevant.

A world consistent with that envisaged by Friedman could be one in which all transactions are made via e-money, which is bought initially by income recipients. But income recipients must be remunerated in conventional money and, therefore, not only would conventional money exist but it would also be a relevant proportion of the total amount of money. Firms would have deposits with banks to pay the factors of production, which, on the other hand, would most probably have deposits with banks that are periodically transformed into e-money. Decoupling is more likely if the type of e-money used in the economy does not presuppose in any way the use of conventional money. For example, one could envisage a world in which factors of production are directly remunerated in e-money (issued by one or more firms) that is universally accepted as a means of payment in the economy.

More than 30 years ago, although in a different context, Kaldor had depicted a sort of world without conventional money and virtually without any role to play for central banks.[18] Kaldor's idea was that, if the central bank and commercial banks are not ready to increase their supply of (conventional) money, any excess demand for money would be filled by the creation of new means of payment also in the form of non-bank money. There would emerge some money substitutes, issued by firms or financial institutions. These substitutes would circulate in the same way as bank notes.

The system's response to cash scarcity would be, on the one hand, an extension of credit through a larger diffusion of credit cards and, on the other hand, the creation of substitutes for cash. Those who cannot use credit cards

> would get paid in chits which would be issued in lieu of cash by, say, the top five hundred businesses in the country (who would also, for a consideration, provide such chits to other employers). And these five hundred firms would soon find it convenient to set up a clearing system of their own, by investing in some giant computer which would at regular intervals net out all mutual claims and liabilities. It would also be necessary for the member firms of this clearing system to accord mutual 'swops' or credit facilities to each other, to take care of net credit or debit balances after each clearing. When this is also agreed on, a complete surrogate money-system and payments-system would be established, which would exist side by side with 'official money ...'
>
> (Kaldor, 1970, pp. 9–10)

Kaldor's 'chits' are an actual alternative form of money, because the issuers also create a clearing system that no longer requires conventional money. By creating a clearing system, the issuers do not even need a banking system. In Kaldor's example, this new money coexists with 'official money' but only because it is not used for all transactions and not because it needs at some point in time 'official money'.[19]

The evolution of the monetary system in the direction of a world where there is decoupling in Friedman's sense requires that e-money evolves into a means of payment that is substantially different from e-money as it currently exists. Markets could actually evolve in this direction, but central banks do not 'sit back' and watch passively the spontaneous evolution of markets. On the contrary, in order to reduce the risk that financial innovations in general, and those brought about by the IT revolution in particular, give rise to a system in which their power is largely reduced, central banks have been keeping financial markets under close scrutiny and have taken several measures to control their evolution.[20] Central banks can try to introduce new regulations, or adjust those already in existence, to face the new situation. Moreover, they can make the use of conventional money compulsory for certain classes of transactions (for example, the payment of taxes) and also impose that only ordinary banks can issue e-money. E-money issued by banks implies a lesser threat for the central bank's power because it is not substantially different from conventional money and it implies a positive demand for reserves; therefore its effects on the working of the monetary system are less disruptive than those produced by e-money issued by firms outside the banking sector.[21]

Thus, endogenous factors like inertia and co-ordination failure, jointly with the measures taken by central banks themselves, seem to lead to the conclusion that the power of central banks and their ability to implement effective monetary policies are not subject to immediate serious threats. In the near future, for good or bad, central banks will maintain their monopoly power and will affect the working of the economy as a whole.

NOTES

* I would like to thank J. Bibow, M. Sarcinelli and the editor of this volume for their helpful comments on an earlier draft of this chapter. The usual disclaimers apply.

1. The ratio of base money (H) to M_1 decreases whenever the public substitutes e-money for currency (provided that the e-money reserve ratio is less than 1); on the other hand, if the public substitutes e-money for conventional deposits, this produces a decrease in the ratio H/M_1 only if banks apply a lower reserve ratio to e-money than to conventional deposits. For a more detailed analysis of these aspects, see Sardoni and Verde (2002).
2. For simplicity, I consider here only currency, demand deposits and e-money. For a detailed analysis of this kind of problem, which considers several types of media of exchange, see Santomero and Seater (1996).
3. Subject to the constraints $c + d + m = 1$ and $c \geq 0$, $d \geq 0$, $m \geq 0$.
4. Dowd and Greenaway are mostly concerned with switching from one currency to another, but their analysis can be easily extended to the choice of competing means of payment.
5. Krueger (1999) has further elaborated on Dowd's and Greenaway's contribution. He draws a more precise distinction between switching from a medium of exchange to another and switching from a unit of account to another.
6. That is to say a barter economy even though a sophisticated barter economy (Greenfield and Yeager, 1983, p. 307).
7. 'No longer would there be any such thing as money whose purchasing power depended on limitation of its quantity. No longer, then, could there be too much of it, causing price inflation, or too little, causing depression, or a sequence of imbalances, causing stagflation. A wrong quantity of money could no longer cause problems because money would not exist' (Greenfield and Yeager, 1983, p. 305). For a more detailed exposition of the salient characteristics of the New Monetary Economics, see Krueger (1999). For a critique of some aspects of this theory see, for example, Cesarano (1995).
8. For a brief summary of the recent debate on the choice of central banks' monetary instruments, see Blinder (1999), who observes that 'interest rate targeting won by default', for the difficulty of targeting the money supply (ibid., pp. 25–51).
9. 'For most items, neither cash in one's pocket nor an adequate balance in one's chequing account is necessary at the time of purchase. More recent improvements like electronic cash and "smart cards" ... have accentuated this trend' (Friedman, 1999, p. 327).
10. See also Palley (2001–02, pp. 219–25), for the analysis of banks' demand for reserves.
11. Although not considering e-money explicitly, King (19 99) has taken a position that is

similar to Friedman's: 'there is no reason, in principle, why final settlements could not be carried out by the private sector without the need for clearing through the central bank' (King, 1999, p. 26). Once the central bank is no longer the institution that manages final settlements, it has virtually lost all its power and could not implement monetary policy (ibid., pp. 26–7).

12. However, the control of the interest rate by the central bank can determine a growing fiscal cost for the government, because the central bank must be ready to bear losses in order to set the interest rate. Such a cost poses a general question of what benefits are produced by a central bank that implements monetary policy discretionally, rather than on the basis of some automatic, or semi-automatic, mechanism (Goodhart, 2000, p. 207).
13. Especially e-money based on software to make transactions through a network (Freedman, 2000, p. 218).
14. Moreover, keeping treasury bills would be costly and they could become excessively scarce if the government's debt shrinks.
15. See also (Woodford, 2001, pp. 325–41) for a detailed illustration of the working of the channel system.
16. They can offer liabilities that promise to pay a certain amount of dollars in the future, but they also must accept the market's present evaluation of such liabilities. Even if these liabilities were not perfect substitutes for other financial instruments, private financial institutions could not determine both the quantity issued and the nominal yield, whereas the central bank can determine both the quantity of settlement balances in existence and the nominal yield on those balances.
17. Nobody should doubt that a large borrower or lender, willing to enter into transactions in infinite volume, can set market rates' (Friedman, 2000, p. 269).
18. Kaldor's interest in the possibility that there may exist alternative forms of money derived from his criticism of the monetarist hypothesis of exogenous money and, hence, of the possibility to control prices through the supply of money by the central bank.
19. Such chits could also be denominated in a different unit of account.
20. A large number of studies and researches on e-money and its implications have been promoted or carried out by central banks.
21. The ECB's *Report on Electronic Money* (1998) *is* a good illustration of the typical ways in which a central bank tries to limit the potential threats of e-money.

REFERENCES

Blinder, Alan S. (1999), *Central Banking in Theory and Practice*, Cambridge, MA and London: MIT Press.

Cesarano, Francesco (1995), 'The new monetary economics and the theory of money', *Journal of Economic Behavior & Organization*, **26**, 445–55.

Costa, Claudia, and Paul De Grauwe (2001), 'Monetary policy in a cashless society', CEPR discussion paper no. 2696.

Dowd, Kevin, and David Greenaway (1993), 'Currency competition, network externalities and switching costs: towards an alternative view of optimal currency areas', *Economic Journal*, **103**, 1180–89.

European Central Bank (ECB) (1998), *Report on Electronic Money*, Frankfurt: ECB.

Fama, Eugene F. (1980), 'Banking in the theory of finance', *Journal of Monetary Economics*, **6**, 39–57.

Freedman, C. (2000), 'Monetary policy implementation: past, present and future – will electronic money lead to the eventual demise of central banking?', *International Finance*, **3**, 211–27.

Friedman, Benjamin M. (1999), 'The future of monetary policy: the central bank as an army with only a signal corps?', *International Finance*, **2**, 321–38.

Friedman, Benjamin M. (2000), 'Decoupling at the margin: the threat to monetary policy from the electronic revolution in banking', *International Finance*, **3**, 261–72.
Goodhart, Charles A.E. (2000), 'Can central banking survive the IT revolution?', *International Finance*, **3**, 189–209.
Greenfield, Robert L., and Leland B. Yeager (1983), 'A laissez-faire approach to monetary stability', *Journal of Money, Credit and Banking*, **15**, 302–15.
Kaldor, Nicholas (1970), 'The new monetarism', *Lloyds Bank Review*, reprinted in Nicholas Kaldor (1978), *Further Essays on Applied Economics*, New York: Holmes and Meier, pp. 3–21.
King, Mervyn (1999), 'Challenges for monetary policy: new and old', *Bank of England Quarterly Bulletin*, **39**, 397–415.
Krueger, Malte (1999), 'Towards a moneyless world?', Department of Economics and Finance, University of Durham, working paper no. 9916, Durham.
Palley, T.I. (2001–2), 'The e-money revolution: challenges and implications for monetary policy', *Journal of Post Keynesian Economics*, **24** (2), 217–33.
Santomero, Anthony M., and John J. Seater (1996), 'Alternative monies and the demand for media of exchange', *Journal of Money, Credit, and Banking*, **28**, 942–60.
Sardoni, Claudio, and Alessandro Verde (2002), 'The IT revolution and the monetary system: electronic money and its effects', Dipartimento di Scienze Economiche, University of Rome 'La Sapienza' discussion paper no. 42, Rome.
Woodford, Michael (2000), 'Monetary policy in a world without money', *International Finance*, **2**, 229–60.
Woodford, Michael (2001), 'Monetary policy in the information economy', *Economic Policy for the Information Economy*, Kansas City: Federal Reserve Bank of Kansas City, pp. 297–370.
Woodford, Michael (2002), 'Financial market efficiency and the effectiveness of monetary policy', *Economic Policy Review*, Federal Reserve Bank of New York, **8**, 85–94.

5. Understanding the implications of money being a social convention

Thomas A. Swanke

INTRODUCTION

It is well known that many different objects have functioned as money. Money also fulfills many roles in the economy, and society. Yet, the attempts to define money seem to flounder on these observations, rather than reveling in explaining the reasons that these observations seem to be true. In fact, money is many different things to different people. Some see money as a means of transactions; others see it as an object of study. Money has many levels, they can be practical, emotional, theoretical or the subject of inner or overt desires. One way to explain all these different aspects of money, and what it means, is considering money as a socially created social convention.

The view that money is a socially constructed social convention explains many of the characteristics of money listed above. There are four reasons to believe that money is a socially created social convention. Along the way we will briefly examine the ways that customs, norms, social contracts, social conventions and the social creation of reality impact on the functioning of money. Lastly, we turn to the reasons that the neo-Chartalist view of money, by itself, does not explain why money works.

MONEY AS A SOCIAL CONVENTION

Money is a social convention for several reasons. There are many similar definitions of social conventions. Lewis (1969, p. 78) argues that:

> a regularity in behavior of members of a population when they are agents in a recurrent situation is a convention if and only if it is true that, and it is common knowledge in the population that, in almost any of these recurrent situations among the members of the population:
> a.) almost everyone conforms to the regularity
> b.) almost everyone expects everyone else to conform to the regularity

c.) almost everyone has approximately the same preferences regarding all possible combination of actions
d.) almost everyone prefers that any one more will conform to the regularity on condition that almost everyone conforms to the regularity
e.) almost everyone would prefer that any one more will conform to some other regularity, on condition that almost everyone conform to it.

Gilbert (1989, pp. 339–40) asserts:

> Conventions are regularities in behavior which are correlated with certain preferences and expectations, such that given these expectations the people in question prefer to perform the action in question. They are conceived of as law-like regularities, but the basis for the law-likeness is not made explicit and is not explicitly a matter of the consideration of precedent in the generation of expectations.

Social conventions, then, are actions undertaken because the actor believes that the action is appropriate in the circumstances and that other people will, or are, acting in the same fashion in similar circumstances. An example of this type of behavior is driving on the right-hand side of the road in the USA. People who drive on the right-hand side of the road believe that it is the correct action. Perhaps more importantly, people who drive on the right-hand side of the road do so because they expect that everyone else drives on the right-hand side of the road and that everyone else also expects the same behavior. Social convention determines the side of the road that everyone drives on because of the mutual expectation which enforces that behavior. There is also a law which forbids driving on the wrong side of the road. This law, however, is not the motivater which keeps people on the correct side of the road. People drive on the right side of the road because of the mutual expectations of where everyone will drive, rather than fear of a ticket. In summary, a convention is an action that people do because they have the mutual expectation that it is the correct action in that situation and because they believe that other people will act in the same way in similar situations.

The first reason that money is a social convention is that it operates because people expect it to be money. Recall that a social convention is the mutual expectation that something will act in a certain way. Economists commonly associate the functions of money to be a medium of exchange, a standard of value, a unit of account and a store of nominal value (Colander, 2001, p. 299; Keynes, 1930 [1976], pp. 3–4). Although there are some concerns about doctrinal markers associated with these different functions (Ingham, 1996, pp. 511–12, 517–20; Tcherneva, 2001, pp. 43, 45), we will approach these functions in the order listed, without any implication of the importance of each function. So, starting with the medium of exchange function, money functions because people believe that the money object will be accepted in exchange (Swanke, 1993, pp. 140–41). Social convention created money allows people to handle the radical uncertainty of the world (Swanke, 1993, pp. 145, 149–50). Thus, many different physical objects function as money and the two which are most commonly used for the medium of exchange are checks and currency (Colander, 2001, p. 301). People accept checks because they expect that they will be able to deposit them at their own bank and write their own checks. Similarly, people accept currency in transactions because they are confident that it will be accepted in exchange for what they desire. This confidence is due to the social convention, socially constructed, that it is a manifestation of money, called the money object, which works in exchange.

People's acceptance of checks and currency as money occurs because they 'know' that these things are money. There is no doubt that people will accept them and everyone 'knows' that. This confidence exists because people perceive the world as ordered and full of pre-defined objects (Berger and Luckmann, 1966, pp. 21–2). People use objects to understand the subjective intentions of other people (this is called objectifying) and that allows symbols to function (Berger and Luckman, 1966, pp. 35–7). Language depends the functioning of symbols and language is vital for creating the stock of knowledge that everyone 'knows' (Berger and Luckman, 1966, pp. 41–3). Language also allows the diffusion of the knowledge throughout society. Further, all human activities, either private or social, are subject to habitualization (Berger and Luckmann, 1966, p. 53). Habitualization means that a person repeats an action so frequently that it becomes a pattern of action that can be repeated with a minimum of effort, almost automatically (Berger and Luckmann, 1966, p. 53). For institutions to exist, the people involved must have different habitualized behavior (Berger and Luckmann, 1966, p. 53).

Institutionalization happens when there is a reciprocal typification of habitualized actions by types of actors (this reciprocation of habitualized actions is the institution) which can be available to anyone and is shared between the people acting (Berger and Luckmann, 1966, p. 54). For example, a workplace is an economic institution because those people identified as 'line-workers' come to work and assume a habitualized behavior (for example, punching their time cards, going to their station and starting to work, waiting for permission, or the habitualized break time to get a drink and so on, and generally following the orders of the 'supervisors'). Similarly, other people ('supervisors') come to the workplace, do not punch in (if they are paid a salary, as opposed to a wage), watch people, evaluate their work, monitor the supply chain or do their particular habitualized behavior. This interaction of habitualized actions is why a workplace is an economic institution.

Checks and currency function as socially created social conventions because people 'know' that they are money, because these media represent an institution. This means that people, as they grow, accept checks and currency as money because they view them as objective realities which exist in the same sense that a physical object does.

There are many other types of institutions, but according to Berger and Luckmann all institutions imply a history and some measure of control (1966, pp. 54–6). The history occurs because the repeated actions (in other words, the habitualized actions) are built up in the course of the shared history between the people involved (Berger and Luckmann, 1966, pp. 54–6). So currency and checks have evolved out of individuals' learning that checks and currency function to facilitate exchange (checks and currency's history) for those using them now. Further, people learn that there were objects of exchange before the emergence of checks and currency (wampum and gold coins, for example). The control happens because, by their existence, institutions select one action from many possible actions (Berger and Luckmann, 1966, pp. 54–6). So, Disney dollars are not acceptable in general exchange; people are exerting their control over what is socially sanctioned to fulfill that role.

According to Berger and Luckmann, institutions originate when at least two people habitualize some repeated action (but usually there are many more people involved). The people who started this habitualized behavior pattern almost certainly they did not plan to create an institution. The institution is created when new people begin to interact with those who act in the habitualized way and the newcomers adopt the habitualized behavior. The newcomers take the habituated actions as objects and that creates institution (meaning we have the institution of checks and currency functioning as media of exchange because that is the way it is) (this whole paragraph from Berger and Luckmann, 1966, pp. 56–8).

Because of the way an institution is created, people experience the institutional world as objective reality (Berger and Luckmann, 1966, pp. 58–61). Further, the relationship between man (the producer) and his world (the product) is a dialectic (Berger and Luckmann, 1966, pp. 58–61). The thesis of this dialectic is externalization, which is the creation of habituated realities in a social way (Berger and Luckmann, 1966, p. 61). In the case of checks, people accept that checks are media of exchange, generally habitually. The checks, or currency, are the external, physical, representations of the power to exchange. The antithesis is objectification, which is the treatment of socially created externalities as objects (Berger and Luckmann, 1966, p. 61). Thus checks themselves are equated with money in exchange because they are accepted in exchange. The synthesis is internalization, the process by which the objectivated social world is retrojected into people's consciousness during the course of their socialization (Berger and Luckmann, 1966, p. 61). This is when people 'know' that checks are accepted in exchange; they have internalized this social knowledge. These three parts correspond to some essential characteristics of the social world:

1. Society is a human product.
2. Society is an objective reality.
3. Humans are a social product (Berger and Luckmann, 1966, p. 61).

So, checks and currency are created by humans, but people treat them as separate entities (on par with a tree or rock; part of the world) and so people are shaped by this socially created reality.

We can detect institutions by the presence of roles, linguistic objectification and physical objects. Roles are a habituated behavior that people adopt to conform to the institutional expectations placed before them (Berger and Luckmann, 1966, p. 72). Roles represent institutional order on two levels (Berger and Luckmann, 1966, p. 74). First, the performance of the role represents itself and second, the role represents an entire list of institutional conduct (Berger and Luckmann, 1966, pp. 74–5). For the first meaning of roles, when someone spends currency they generally pay attention to the transaction, making sure that their interests are served – they count their change, they may bargain for a lower price. So currency is a marker of an institution because of the role that it plays in the institution of money. For the second meaning of roles, all that currency represents is inherent in its role; currency is power, access, ease, and so on. Roles imply a social distribution of knowledge, as often people get to inhabit certain roles because of knowing some specific sector of common knowledge very well, for example, part of the adult's role is knowing currency and check use, part of the role for financial planners is knowing annuities and bonds, and so on (Berger and Luckmann, 1966, p. 76). Other ways that institutions may also be represented are by linguistic objectification (when certain words mean an institution) and physical objects, which are brought to life by human conduct, that allow roles to function (Berger and Luckmann, 1966, p. 75). An example of a linguistic objectification is the expression, 'Let's see if he's worth his salt', which recalls when salt functioned as a medium of exchange. A physical object example is a dollar bill.

Given the way institutions gradually appear and change throughout history, people sometimes see them as non-human creations (this is called reification of social reality) (Berger and Luckmann, 1966, p. 88). Reification happens when the institutional order, or some parts of it, have ontological status separate from human activity and signification bestowed upon it (Berger and Luckmann, 1966, p. 90). For money functioning as a medium of exchange people are reifying when they assert that currency functions because the government decrees it, or because it represents some morally superior society.

Going back to the functions of money, money functions as a standard of value because money is a social convention. It is probably true, as the Chartalists and neo-Chartalists claim, that the government of Babylon fixed a shekel at 1.2 hectoliters of barley, and then 8.3 grams of silver (Ingham, 2000, p. 26). Yet, how does a government enforce its laws? It does not have the ability to check whether everyone is using the accurate amount of silver in the coins. Anderson argues that most citizens, who do not regularly interact with the government, imagine that they are part of a nation (1991, p. 6). Even if this is not true, and even if the rulers of Babylon could force the correct weight of their coinage, shekels soon became institutionalized in their society. In the manner explained above, this institution became part of the general knowledge of that society. This general knowledge would have spawned other institutions that were derived from the Babylonian one. So, the other societies of that time, and societies that developed after the Babylonians, would have had money as a standard of value as part of their general knowledge. Thus, it would be people's belief in money, and no other source, that would make money function as a standard of value. It is this mutuality of belief, this social convention, that makes money function as a standard of value. Ingham all but admits this when he points out that the medieval money of account depended on the glory of Charlemagne (2000, p. 28) and that money depends on a form of impersonal trust (ibid., pp. 29–30).

Following the social creation of reality ideas, people externalize the money object's value, in the Babylonian case as 8.3 grams of silver, so they do not check it. Further, people objectify the money object as it serves as a standard of value. For example, in the book of Genesis Abram's wealth was demonstrated by his many flocks (Gen. 12:16 in *New American Bible*, 1971). Finally, people internalize this idea that money measures value. Anyone can see this by noticing the transition that children undergo when they are somewhere between two and three years old. At age two, a child values four pennies over a nickel, yet when he or she is three, he or she desires the nickel instead of the four pennies.

Keynes identified the third function of money, the unit of account (1930 [1976], pp. 3–4). Money derives its power, to transact, preserve nominal value and be a standard of value from its unit of account (Keynes, 1930 [1976], p. 3). Further, according to Keynes the state determines the object which functions as the unit of account (1930 [1976], p. 4). Yet, the state does not make this decision in a vacuum, the socially created social convention is still at work in this process. A good example of this is the dollar being established as the unit of account of the USA. As a unit of money the dollar started out as a unit of account of the Holy Roman Empire and spread all over Europe, inspiring dollar units in Spain, Italy, Denmark, Sweden, Hawaii,

Ethiopia, Austro-Hungary and the USA (Weatherford, 1997, pp. 113–15). Thus, the dollar was already functioning as a unit of account before the founding of the British colonies in North America. Given its widespread use, the dollar had clearly been externalized and objectified as a unit of account. Further, the widespread use of the dollar as a unit of account shows that using it that way had also been widely internalized. Weatherford reports that Thomas Jefferson was a strong supporter of the dollar as the US unit of account, but it was not the only idea for the USA's unit of account (1997, p. 118). Of course, there were many non-dollar colonial units of account, but the most dominant one was the English system of shillings and pounds (Wilson, 1992, pp. 58–65). Ultimately, the USA under all its three forms of government, Continental Congress, Articles of Confederation and the Constitution, chose the dollar as the unit of account, mainly because it was already accepted and employed as the unit of account by the majority of the population (Weatherford, 1997, p. 118 [Weatherford only cites this point under the Constitution]; Wilson, 1992, pp. 65–6, 70–73). Both Weatherford and Wilson report that the justification of this choice of unit of account is that people were already employing the dollar, in this case, as a unit of account (Weatherford, 1997, p. 118; Wilson, 1992, pp. 67–72). Weatherford even reports that the value of the US dollar was based on the average weight of the Spanish dollars in circulation (1997, pp. 118–19). So, technically, the state did decide the unit of account, but they decided it respecting what people wanted. In effect, the state was adopting an already functioning system of exchange, a socially created social convention system of exchange.

The referee for this piece asserted that it is true that the objects which function as money are determined by social convention, but not the unit account. He or she asserted that the dollar as the US unit of account has not changed since the beginning. Yet, Keynes's assertion that the state determines what answers the definition of the unit of account allows that definition to change over time (1930 [1976], p. 4). Clearly, the dollar's definition is no longer the 371 and one-fourth a grain of silver that was defined 1785 (Weatherford, 1997, p. 119). In light of the changes that have occurred since then, we can consider the struggles ranging from the debates over The First Bank of the United States, to the floating of the dollar in 1971 as struggles over the unit of account. Looking at the more frequent changes in unit of account in other countries (particularly Latin American countries recently), it is clear that the USA has had a very long continuance of the same name of the unit of account, but it is different now than it was when it started. Why did the changes that created today's dollar happen? Why do other countries continually redefine their unit of account? The state proposes a unit of account and the people determine if it fits into their socially created social convention determined unit of account. If it does, the standard will last; if not, it will not.

Lastly, the store of value function of money also exists because money is a socially created social convention. First, money's ability to function as a medium of exchange is what allows it to be a store of value (Swanke, 1993, p. 151; Ingham, 2000, p. 29). This works because we know that people will accept that money object in exchange, so we keep these objects until such time as we need to exchange them, as a store of value. People know which objects store value due to the now familiar method of externalizing, objectifying and internalizing them, in the standard social creation of reality method. So, overall, the money object's ability to perform the four functions is a result of the working of the social convention, created socially.

The second reason why money is a social convention is people are continually modifying money, particularly the object which functions as money, to suit their needs and desires. Even if they did not empower the money object, by modifying it people are creating a new use, or view, of that thing. This is not surprising since people have always objectified their surroundings (Berger and Luckmann, 1966, pp. 34–5; Zelizer, 1994, pp. 211–13). Even during the USA's drive to standardize the money, from the 1860s to the 1930s, people were constantly personalizing, and earmarking, their money (Zelizer, 1994, pp. 17–18). Earmarking is 'creating distinctions between the uses and meanings of currency' (Zelizer, 1994, p. 18). People differentiated their money into housekeeping allowances, pin money, spending money, gift money, tips, Penny Provident savings, mother's pensions and into various distinct categories such as food money, rent money, school money, charity money, burial money, wedding money and many others (Zelizer, 1994, pp. 202–04).

Further, even in modern times, people actively reject 'official' money, or create their own money. In the USA, people rejected the use of the Susan B. Anthony dollar, with the exception of one area of which the author knows. Almost certainly it was not acceptable to the public because it was too easily mistaken for a quarter coin, yet it shows that people need to accept and verify an object, by using it, for it to function as money. The exception in the rejection of the Susan B. Anthony dollar coin is the Seattle public rapid transit system's use of it as change. So the public accepts it there, making it money. Another example of rejected money is the two-dollar bill. Although it is sometime seen in use, most people do not like to use two-dollar bills. Again, that prevents it from functioning as money. As before, there is also one area where two-dollar bills are widely accepted, making them function as money. This is the area of Charlottesville, Virginia, near Monticello, Thomas Jefferson's estate. Being near Monticello is the source of its acceptance, since Thomas Jefferson is on the two-dollar bill. Thus, Monticello transacts with its visitors using as many two-dollar bills (and nickels) as possible. This expected use there has caused general acceptance of the two-dollar bill in the Charlottesville area. These are important examples because these official, government sanctioned, currencies cease functioning since people do not expect them to be acceptable in exchange.

The opposite of the rejection of certain money objects, there are also instances where people have accepted non-money objects as money. Maybe the most famous example where a non-money object has been pressed into service as money is the case of the Allied prisoners of war in World War II adopting cigarettes as money in their camps (Radford, 1945). Another example is the acceptance of California's warrants as money during their 1992 budget impasse (Swanke, 1993, pp. 337–40). This event happened after the political parties in the California legislature were unable to agree upon a budget, so the State of California entered the new fiscal year without a budget. Like the other states, California cannot operate with a deficit, yet it did that for about five months in the fall of 1992, in effect issuing their own money in the form of warrants, or checks (Swanke, 1993, pp. 334–7). People in California, and the other places that California sent its warrants, accepted these as money and the whole economic system functioned as if there was nothing unusual about the situation (Swanke, 1993, p. 335). There was no economic crisis and the society, and economy, was not collapsing. The last example of how people create their own money outside the 'official' money system is the widespread existence of currency substitution (a few citations are Uribe, 1999; Schenk, 2000; Bahmani-Oskooee and Techaratanachai, 2001; Dean, 2001; Alami, 2001). Currency substitution is when people of one country use another country's currency instead of their own (Schenk, 2000, p. 741). In other words, they create a social convention that the other currency shall also act as their own currency. Although some examples of currency substitution do indicate political and economic collapse (for example, in the Asian contagion, Russia and Argentina are examples), there are examples of currency substitution in more normal, and long-lasting, conditions (for example, Hong Kong and China in the late 1940s [see Schenk, 20001, Israel and Latin America in the 1970s and 1980s, as well as the question of whether Mexico and Canada should dollarize now [see Dean, 2001] and current practices in some Central American countries).

The third reason why money is a social convention is the mutual expectation element of the working of money, for all of its functions; no other social construction relies on the functioning of mutual expectations (Swanke, 1993, p. 61).

At this point it may be helpful to summarize four views on social organization and distinguish between them. Customs are non-habitual actions which people perform because they have been done in that way for a long time (Ladd, 1967, p. 278). Norms are actions which people do because it is in the best interest of the group. There are strong positive and negative sanctions for respectively observing, or not observing, norms (Cancian, 1975, pp. 1–2).

Social contracts are agreements into which a group of people enter to make all the participants better off (Hobbes, 1651 [1985], pp. 190–92, 227, 229–39, 272; Locke, 1690 [1988], pp. 330–33). Finally, social conventions are actions that people undertake because they believe that these actions are the correct options in the given situation and that other people would act in the same way if confronted with the same, or similar, situations (Gilbert, 1989, pp. 339–40; Lewis, 1969, p. 78).

The basing of customs on ancient practices makes them different from the other forms. Norms are different from the other forms because they have normative content, so that not observing them properly evokes strong emotions. Social contracts are different from the other forms because they require agreement by the participants before the function. Social conventions are different from the other forms because they function by mutual expectations and they do not have a normative content.

Customs cannot be the reason that money functions because that would not allow the earmarking, and other evolution, of the objects which serve as money. Norms are not the foundation of money because money's object has no particular moral meaning; it is either paper, or computer memory or metal, none of which preserve some important social value (Swanke, 1993, pp. 60–61). Social contracts are not the reason that money functions, because every time a social contract creates a money, the social contract must be modified or it will collapse (Swanke, 1993, pp. 324–8).

The final reason that money is a social convention, socially created, is that it allows us to tell a tale of money's evolution. This allows for the many different kinds of objects which serve as money and the ability of people to modify money in ways that we have seen. As I explained above, money may have started when the Babylonians specified some weight of silver as a shekel. Money may also have started as a religious symbol in sacrificial food communion rituals (Desmonde, 1962, p. vii). Ingham also supports this second view when he asserts that money's endurance is based on socially constructed arrangements which seem natural, or supernatural (2000, p. 30). (This also supports the socially constructed, social convention view since the naturalness of the social arrangement is the result of reification.) Either way it started, money became an institution when people who were not involved in its origins were introduced to it (maybe as children) and accepted it as a concrete reality. This helped objectify the money object and people probably quickly began the reification of money. These processes occurred simultaneously with the concept of money, and how it worked, entering the general social knowledge of that society. Other societies probably began to copy Babylon's use of money, since institutions are sometimes created by imitating institutions which exist in other places (Berger and Luckmann, 1966, pp. 63–6; Sugden, 1989, pp. 93–4). So, the concept of money entered into these other societies' general knowledge too. One could say that the general, socially created, view of what society should be included the concept of money.

Continuing the story, in the beginning of the revival of money in the Middle Ages, in Europe, they relied on the general knowledge, or conception, of Charlemagne's monetary system to socially create a money of account (Ingham, 2000, p. 28). Then privately issued merchant bank money came to exist (Ingham, 2000, p. 28) again in the same social creation of reality fashion; someone came up with the practice and others began to act in the same way, creating the institution of private issued bank money, or giro money. Undoubtedly this became a separate socially created object and was probably subject to reification as well. Ingham reports that when states joined the giro systems, money proper evolved (2000, p. 28). Again, this had to have happened in the way that Berger and Luckmann report any institution is created and how that knowledge becomes common to the people in that society.

A similar story can relate the way the USA determines its money. A story as to why the USA chose dollars is that they wanted to be independent of Great Britain completely, so they chose a different money standard. Yet, dollars, from Spain's New World holdings, were common in colonial America, so another view of the choice is the government joined another, existing, giro system (this and the previous sentence's assertion was argued above). The early part of the USA's history of banking and money show that people, and firms, were firmly in control of the issuing of private currencies and making the system work (through the now-often-repeated way of creating an institution, injecting that knowledge into society all the way through the reification of the object). After 1865, as the US Federal government began to try to regulate currency and the banking system more obviously, people still socially created their own money object and unit of account (as explained in Zelizer, 1994 [briefly explained above], and the above discussion of the socially created social convention unit of account). Then in 1935 the Federal government imposed a social contract of equating the dollar to a certain amount of gold, and it was expanded internationally during the Bretton Woods conference of 1944. Yet, the people of the USA were not allowed to exchange dollars for the amount of gold they were 'worth', and the Bretton Woods agreement collapsed in 1971. So, through it all, money continued to function in the way explained above, a socially created social convention. The various objects which serve as money are an example of evidence of an institution because these objects' significance are socially created.

The previous story explains several things about money. First, it explains how so many objects can be pressed into service as the money object. Further, it provides a template for how the new money objects, and money instruments, can come to exist. People, by their actions, create and affirm that the money object is money, even when they are treating money as some non-social creation (reifying it). Thus, money objects change and multiply as people earmark their money, as well as when people and firms interact to create new instruments to move money in ways that had not previously been done. Second, the socially created social convention view of money explains the anomalies of currency substitution and how even legal money must be negotiated if it is to be accepted in non-standard uses. Lastly, this view of money explains how such strong emotions can be tied to the money object. Because people truly believe that the money object is existentially real, and not created socially (which is the view after reification happens), there are intellectual, emotional and physical reactions to money and the object which money inhabits, whether that object is gold, shells, paper representations or computer memory. This explains a variant of musings about money which other theories of why money works do not (for the musings of money's emotional impact, see, Needleman, 1991, and for a psychologically based money theory see Dostaler and Maris, 2000). This insight is the origin of the title of this chapter; money's socially constructed social convention means that how people use money objects (while forgetting that they are socially created objects, or never knowing that they were so created) determines it as money for them. There are levels of meaning for money and the money object. So, for some people currency is money, for others money is a loan, or a derivative, and for others money is a function that some object, or government declared entity, performs. Scholars are not immune to this emotional commitment to a certain view of money, as a recent lamentation of intolerance indicates (Rochon, 1999, p. vii).

GOVERNMENTS AND MONEY

A popular view of money builds on Keynes's assertion that the state creates the unit of account (Keynes, 1930 [1976], pp. 3–4). Some people call this view neo-Chartalism. In essence, neo-Chartalism asserts:

> it surely is now true and obvious that the state writes the 'description' of money when it denominates the tax liability in a money of account, and defines the 'thing' that 'answers to the description' when it decides what will be accepted at public pay-offices. The thing which answers to the description is widely accepted *not* because of sovereignty alone, *not* because of legal tender laws and *not* because it might have (or have had) gold backing, but because the state has the power to impose and enforce tax liabilities and because it has the right to choose 'that which is necessary to pay taxes.
>
> (Wray, 2000, p. 58)

Although Wray traces the origins of the creation of the standard of value to the system of weregeld in blood feuds in ancient times, he argues that the important insights are due to the modern powers of the state in creation of the unit of account (as explained in the above quote). Yet, states do not necessarily limit money supply to that which defines the unit of account, they do accept bank money, or other privately created money (Wray, 2000, pp. 49, 52–3). This means that the money supply is endogenous as it is created by the process of the economic activity. Still, the government's acceptance of private bank created money does not make banks the creators of the unit of account, because banks still must redeem their money from the government for the reserves that it holds (Wray, 2000, p. 58). Because the government determines the unit of account, determining the acceptable unit for paying taxes, most private objects of exchange are also defined in that unit. Neo-Chartalists assert that this power to declare the unit of account determines what is money in that state.

There are a couple of reasons to disagree with the neo-Chartalism explanation for the workings of money. First, the neo-Chartalist explanation of money gives a sparse explanation of how the state's 'ability to write, and rewrite, the dictionary' causes people to accept the state-preferred unit of account. Given the socially created social convention view developed above, it is clear that the government's choice of the unit of account is very influential for the rest of society. Yet, it requires the active participation by society to create it as the basis of money. As outlined above, people must externalize, objectify and internalize a social creation, especially that which serves as money, from medium of exchange to unit of account.

Second, the question of the pre-existence of private payment systems makes one wonder if the government did not just join a pre-existing giro system, rather than created one by declaring the unit of account. If the government just joined the giro system (which Ingham asserts, [2000, p. 28]), it is buying into the pre-existing money system and its unit of account, not creating its own. As we argued above, when the state, say the USA, creates a unit of account by declaring its standard is the dollar, it is also just co-opting an existing socially created social convention. The Uap explanation of the German imposed standard of value also relies on the Uapian system of exchange already existing. Furness reports that the natives had already established a unit of account, a *fei*, which was a stone that must have a certain fineness, color and evidence of labor expended on it (1910, p. 94). Additionally, the natives had a compete system of exchange worked out, based on the *fei* (ranging from pearl shells and cowry shells to specially woven mats, both used and unused) which allowed them to get 'change' (Furness, 1910, pp. 102–06). Furness also reports that this exchange system had functioned for at least two or three generations (with a story about the mental accounting of a *fei* which sank in the island's lagoon) (1910, p. 97). Using 20 years to a generation, this puts a functioning exchange system on Uap between either 1870 and 1850 (Furness published the book in 1910). Furness reports that Germany purchased Uap from Spain in 1898 (1910, pp. 17, 99). So, when the Germans declared that they owned some *fei* (by painting the German cross on them to get the natives to work on the road system), they were buying into a pre-existing exchange system (Furness, 1910, pp. 98–100). In light of these examples, a neo-Chartalist explanation must include how declaring a unit of account does not require a pre-existing exchange system if it is to deflect these points.

CONCLUSION

Money is a social convention since money functions because of people's mutual expectations. Money is a medium of exchange because people expect that the money object will be accepted in any situation. Money is a standard of value because people act to accept the money as a standard in non-coercive ways. Money is a unit of account because the government-declared units of account keep changing until one acceptable to the social convention is selected. Money is a store of value because of people's expectation that the money object will continue as a medium of exchange.

Secondly, money is a social convention because people are constantly modifying and earmarking money. People reject officially approved money objects and create their own money out of non-officially approved money objects. Thirdly, of the possible social mechanisms, social convention is the one that best fits the ways that money functions. Lastly, money being a socially created social convention allows us to understand why so many objects can function as money. Further, it shows how using money objects, officially approved or not, requires a negotiated process. Finally, money being a socially created social convention allows us to understand how people can be so emotionally committed to a money object.

REFERENCES

Alami, Tarik H. (2001), 'Currency substitution versus dollarization: a portfolio balance model', *Journal of Policy Modeling: A Social Science Forum of World Issues*, **23** (4), 473–9.

Anderson, Benedict (1991), *Imagined Communities: Reflections on the Origin and Spread of Nationalism*, revised edn, London and New York: Verso.

Bahmani-Oskooee, and Ampa Techaratanachai (2001), 'Currency substitution in Thailand', *Journal of Policy Modeling: A Social Science Forum of World Issues*, **23** (2), 141–6.

Berger, Peter L., and Thomas Luckmann (1966), *The Social Construction of Reality: A Treatise in the Sociology of Knowledge*, New York and London: Anchor Books Doubleday.

Cancian, Francesa M. (1975), *What Are Norms? A Study of Beliefs and Actions in a Maya Community*, Cambridge: Cambridge University Press, pp. vii–x, 1–10, 105–13, 135–59.

Colander, David C. (2001), *Macroeconomics*, 4th edn, Boston, MA: McGraw-Hill Irwin.

Dean, James W. (2001), 'Should Latin America's common law marriages to the US dollar be legalized? Should Canada's?', *Journal of Policy Modeling: A Social Science Forum of World Issues*, **23** (3), 291–300.

Desmonde, William H. (1962), *Magic, Myth, and Money: The Origin of Money in Religious Ritual*, New York: Free Press of Glencoe.

Dostaler, Gilles and Bernard Maris (2000), 'Dr Freud and Mr Keynes on money and capitalism', in John Smithin (ed.), *What is Money?*, New York and London: Routledge, pp. 235–56.

Furness, William Henry (1910), *The Island of Stone Money: Uap of the Carolines*, Philadelphia and London: J.B. Lippincott, pp. 11–106.

Gilbert, Margaret (1989), *On Social Facts*, New York and London: Routledge, pp. 1–21, 315–407.

Hobbes, Thomas (1651), *Leviathan*, reprinted 1985, Harmondsworth: Penguin Books, pp. 1–138.

Ingham, Geoffrey (1996), 'Money is a social relation', *Review of Social Economy*, **54** (4), 507–29.

Ingham, Geoffrey (2000), '"Babylonian madness": on the historical and sociological origins of money', in *What is Money?*, John Smithin (ed.), New York and London: Routledge, pp. 16–41.

Keynes, John Maynard (1930), *A Treatise On Money: Volume 1 The Pure Theory of Money*, reprinted 1976, New York: Harcourt, Brace and Co., pp. 3–6.

Ladd, John (1967), 'Custom', in *The Encyclopedia of Philosophy*, vol. 7, Paul Edwards (editor in chief), New York: Macmillian and Free Press, pp. 278–80.

Lewis, David (1969), *Convention: A Philosophical Study*. Cambridge, MA: Harvard University Press.

Locke, John (1690), 'The second treatise on civil government', *Two Treatises on Civil Government*, reprinted 1988, ed. Peter Laslett, Cambridge: Cambridge University Press, pp. 265–428.

Needlman, Jacob (1991), *Money and the Meaning of Life*, New York and London: Doubleday.

New American Bible (1971), New York, Nashville and Camden: Thomas Nelson.

Radford, R.A. (1945), 'The economic organization of a P.O.W. Camp', *Economica*, **XII**, 189–201.

Rochon, Louis-Philippe (1999), *Credit, Money and Production: An Alternative Post-Keynesian Approach*, Cheltenham, UK and Northampton, MA, USA: Edward Elgar.

Schenk, Catherine R. (2000), 'Another Asian financial crisis: monetary links between Hong Kong and China', *Modern Asian Studies*, **34** (3), 739–64.

Sugden, Robert (1989), 'Spontaneous order', *Journal of Economic Perspectives*, **3** (4), 85–97.

Swanke, Thomas A. (1993), 'Why is it money? Viewing money as a social convention', thesis submitted to the Graduate School of the University of Colorado.

Tcherneva, Pavlina R. (2001), 'Money: a comparison of the post Keynesian and orthodox approaches', *Oeconomicus*, Winter, 43–9.
Uribe, Martin (1999), 'Comparing the welfare costs and initial dynamics of alternative inflation stabilization policies', *Journal of Development Economics*, **59**, 295–318.
Weatherford, Jack (1997), *The History of Money: From Sandstone to Cyberspace*, New York: Crown, pp. 111–22.
Wilson, Thomas (1992), *The Power 'To Coin' Money: The Exercise of Monetary Powers by Congress*, Armonk, NY: M.E. Sharpe, pp. 57–90.
Wray, L. Randall (2000), 'Modern money', in John Smithin (ed.), *What is Money?*, New York and London: Routledge, pp. 42–66.
Zelizer, Viviana A. (1994), *The Social Meaning of Money: Pin Money, Paychecks, Poor Relief, and Other Currencies*, New York: Basic Books.

6. Demand management and the monetary system: do currency boards and currency unions spell the end for Keynesian policy?

Stephanie A. Bell

In 1943, Abba Lerner defended the virtues of discretionary fiscal policy in an article entitled 'Functional finance and the federal debt'. His defense went well beyond the standard pump-priming arguments favored by soft-core Keynesians like Alvin Hansen. That is, rather than arguing for *temporary* spending programs, designed to grease the wheels of commerce, Lerner argued that public policy should *always* be conducted in accordance with two fundamental 'laws' or principles. The first of his principles makes it incumbent on the government to maintain spending at the level necessary to generate full employment, while the second specifies the manner in which the first principle is to be carried out. Specifically, the second principle calls for the government to avoid raising taxes or borrowing in order to offset the spending it undertakes in accordance with the first principle. Lerner termed his approach 'Functional Finance' because it requires the government's financial activities to be evaluated on the basis of the way they work or function, instead of following established rules regarding fiscal piety.[1]

The problem with Lerner's 1943 article is that it made Functional Finance sound like a viable option for *all* nations, regardless of the monetary system in place. He said:

> Functional Finance is not especially related to democracy or to private enterprise. It is applicable to a communist society just as well as to a fascist society or a democratic society. It is applicable to any society in which money is used as an important element in the economic mechanism.
>
> (Lerner, 1943, p. 50)

Thus, Lerner seemed to suggest that any nation could reconsider its current approach to policy and then move swiftly to an adoption of his two principles of Functional Finance. That Lerner did not detail the prerequisites of his approach in his 1943 article is unfortunate, because it gave readers the impression that his approach could be adopted by any nation, as long as it wasn't committed to the principles of 'sound' finance.

But, as Lerner himself went on to recognize in his 1947 article, 'Money as a creature of the state', a nation's ability to implement public policy in accordance with the principles of Functional Finance requires more than simply the 'existence of money as an important element in society' (ibid., p. 00); it requires the government of that society to bear a particular relationship to the money of that society. Since the early 1990s, many nations have abandoned their sovereign currencies, choosing 'stateless' money systems such as currency board arrangements or currency unification. This chapter seeks to explore the potential for Keynesian-style demand management, *à la* Abba Lerner, under these kinds of monetary regimes.

THE HIERARCHY OF MONEY

In Lerner's view, a nation's power in the policy sphere derives from its power in the monetary sphere. Since the state's power in the monetary sphere is the basis for its power to conduct policy according to the principles of functional finance, it is important that this argument be laid out carefully. One way to accomplish this is by applying the state theory of money to the concept of a debt-pyramid or hierarchy of money.[2] Doing so allows one to infer something – based on the positioning of the various monies within the hierarchy – about the (relative) power of the parties issuing various monies.[3]

In the *Treatise*, Keynes distinguishes between the 'money of account' and 'money' by stating that 'the money of account is the *description* or *title* and the money is the *thing* which answers to the description' (1930, p. 3). He goes on to argue that 'if the same thing always answered to the same description, the distinction would have no practical interest. But if the thing can change, whilst the description remains the same, then the distinction can be highly significant' (ibid., p. 3). It is because different 'things' *do* answer to the 'description' of the money of account that there exists what has been referred to as a hierarchy of monies. The Chartalist theory can be used to describe the hierarchy in more detail.

The Unit of Account

The 'description' or 'title' referred to by Keynes is the *unit* in which all money in the hierarchy is denominated. In the USA, the unit of account is the dollar. Thus, all money in the hierarchy is dollar denominated. But why is it the dollar, and not some other unit, which serves as the 'title' or 'description' to which all money in the hierarchy must answer? The Chartalist theory of money as a creature of the state gives the answer.

Because the government's currency is the only legal means of discharging tax liabilities, and because tax liabilities *recur period by period*, the private sector will continuously need dollars. Thus, the ubiquitousness of dollar-denominated tax liabilities makes the dollar the standard unit of account for all money in the hierarchy. Because the private sector will always be indebted to the government in dollars, they will prefer to write all money contracts (that is, make all promises) in terms of dollars. In short, the unit in which state money is denominated and in which taxes are due determines the unit of account for all money in the hierarchy (Keynes, 1930; Lerner, 1947; Wray, 1998).

Money in the Hierarchy

All money represents a promise or an IOU. As Minsky (1986) emphasized, these promises or IOUs can be issued by anyone. But money, which *always exists as both an asset and a liability*, can only be created when one party agrees to *accept* the IOU or promise of another. Since not all promises will be considered equally desirable, the hierarchy of money can be thought of as a multi-tiered pyramid, where the tiers represent promises with *differing degrees of acceptability* (Foley, 1987). At the apex is the most acceptable form of IOU. But if all promises are denominated in the same unit of account, why are some considered more acceptable than others? Whose promises will be the most acceptable? And why would anyone agree to hold the *relatively* less acceptable promises? Let us investigate the different types of money included in the hierarchy.

In Knapp's treatment, all money represents a Chartal means of payment. That is, all money is a 'ticket' or 'pay-token', which gains acceptance by virtue of a proclamation that it will be accepted as a means of payment. These 'tickets' or 'tokens' exist as chartal money as soon as another party agrees to hold them. When, for example, the postal service proclaims that a $0.37 stamp will be accepted as payment for delivery of a small envelope, an individual/institution must accept the stamp as the debt of the postal service in order for it to become Chartal money. This is consistent with the requirement that money exist simultaneously as an asset and a liability; the stamp, an asset to its holder, is a liability to the postal service until it is used as a means of payment (affixed to a letter and relinquished for delivery). If this logic were applied to *all* forms of Chartal money, a list of every conceivable type of money could, theoretically, be constructed. Going back to Keynes, then, a great number of 'things' would answer to the 'description' or 'title' of money. That is, a complete hierarchy would include every plane ticket, prepaid phone card, movie ticket, subway token and so on. It will, therefore, be useful to narrow our focus and to proceed with a simplified discussion of the hierarchy.

The 'simplified' hierarchy can be envisioned as a four-tiered debt pyramid, with the debts of households, non-bank firms, banks and the state each occupying a single tier. The hierarchy will vary constantly in size and structure; its *volume* will increase when the total amount of new debt created rises faster than the total amount destroyed, while its *composition* will change with the circulation of these debts. All of the money in the hierarchy represents an existing relationship between a creditor and a debtor, but the more generally acceptable debts will be situated relatively higher.

The debts of non-bank firms and households occupy the third and fourth tiers, respectively. This is because there is at least some chance that they will not trade at par with government money (which is needed to pay taxes). For example, a firm may sell bonds to finance the purchase of a new plant. Although the firm promises to pay a certain *nominal* amount to the holders of these bonds, their value may vary over time (for example, with default risk and/or as interest rates change). Thus, as assets to their holders, these bonds will be relatively illiquid because they cannot necessarily be 'quickly converted into the medium of exchange *with little loss of value*' (Wray, 1990, p. 16; my emphasis). Still, the promises of non-bank firms are more liquid than households' promises because better secondary markets exist for their resale. To get business and household debts accepted, they might be made convertible into the debt of someone *higher* in the pyramid, and they might require interest payments to compensate for the risk associated with holding less liquid assets.

Unlike households and firms, state promises and certain bank promises would be accepted even if they were not convertible into anything else. That is, even though, banks currently make their promises (demand deposits) convertible, on demand, into the state's promises (government money), this is not the reason they are accepted. It is because bank money is accepted at state pay-offices that it, along with state-issued currency, is considered by Knapp to be the 'decisive' money of the system (1924, p. 95). Thus, even if convertibility to state money were suspended indefinitely (except at clearing houses), bank promises, as long as they were accepted in payment of taxes, would continue to be accepted. Likewise, the state's promises do not depend on convertibility into anything else.[4] As Foley noted, 'the State does not have to pay its liabilities by transferring something else' (1987, p. 520). Thus, neither the state nor the banks rely on convertibility for acceptance of their promises; what makes them both acceptable is their acceptance at state pay-offices.

Recall that the various monies are positioned within the hierarchy according to their *degree* of acceptability. As the 'decisive' money of the system, both the state's promises and banks' promises rank high among the monies of the hierarchy. Although bank money is part of the 'decisive' money of the system, its acceptance at state pay-offices really requires its conversion to state money (that is, bank reserves). In other words, bank money is converted to bank reserves so that (ultimately) the state actually accepts only its own liabilities in payment to itself. The debt of the state, which is required in payment of taxes and is backed by its power to make and enforce laws, is the most acceptable money in the pyramid and, therefore, occupies the first tier.[5]

As the most acceptable money in the hierarchy, the state's debts serve as both a means of payment and a medium of exchange in *private* transactions. But, as Lerner recognized, no law requiring that the state's debt be accepted in private transactions is necessary in this regard. Indeed, he stressed the irrelevance of legal tender laws for the establishment of (generally acceptable) money, stating that 'its general acceptability, which is its all-important attribute, stands or falls by its acceptability by the state' (1947, p. 313). Tobin agrees, suggesting that:

> In advanced societies the central government is in a strong position to make certain assets generally acceptable media. By its willingness to accept a designated asset in settlement of taxes and other obligations, the government makes that asset acceptable to any who have such obligations, and in turn to others who have obligations to them, and so on.
>
> (Tobin and Golub, 1998, p. 27)

Thus, the legal obligation to pay taxes and the state's proclamation that it will accept its own currency at state pay-offices elevate the state's liabilities to the *top* of the pyramid, rendering them the promises with the highest degree of acceptability.

Although the state's liabilities reign supreme among promises, certain bank promises, as a consequence of their acceptance at state pay-offices, also come to serve as means of payment and media of exchange. In particular, '[d]emand deposits have attained a special status in our economy because of the special role commercial banks have come to play' (Wray, 1990, p. 291). Because the central bank guarantees that demand deposits will trade at par with government currency and because they are accepted in payment of taxes, bank promises (demand deposits) are nearly as liquid as state money and, therefore, occupy the second tier in the pyramid.

In short, not all money is created equal. Although the government, banks, firms and households can create money denominated in the social unit of account, these monies are not considered equally acceptable (Hicks, 1989). Only the state, through its power to make and enforce tax laws, can issue promises that its constituents must accept if they are to avoid penalties. The general acceptability of both state and bank money derives from their usefulness in settling tax and other liabilities to the state. This makes them the 'decisive' money of the hierarchy and enables them to circulate widely as means of payment and media of exchange. The debts of households and non-bank firms are accepted because of their convertibility (at least potentially) into *relatively* more acceptable promises. These debts are not accepted at state pay-offices and, thus, are unlikely to become widely accepted means of payment.

Based on this argument, an examination of the hierarchy as it exists in the USA today would reveal something like the pyramid shown in Figure 6.1. When the state controls the money that sits atop its pyramid, it implies an intimate relationship between 'the fiscal, tax-raising, authority on the one hand and money creation on the other' (Goodhart, 1997, p. 1).[6] This relationship, when maintained, enables (or at least does not preclude) the use of counter-cyclical fiscal policy and may be the key to maintaining full employment, as Lerner (1947), Wray (1998), and Kregel (1999) have argued. When the intimacy of this relationship is challenged, however, a nation's potential for flexibility in the policy sphere is severely reduced.

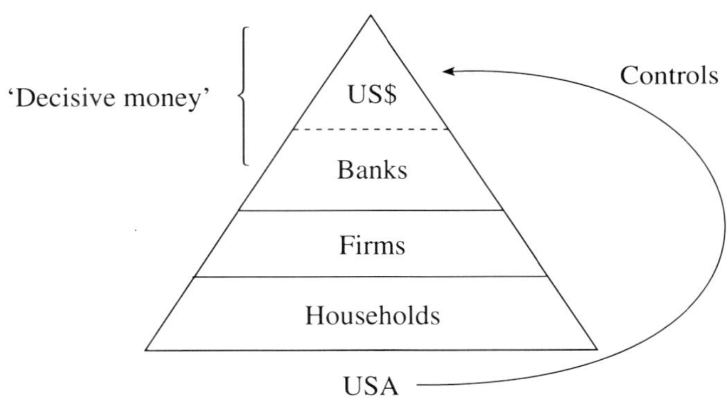

Figure 6.1 The US hierarchy

THE HIERARCHIES OF THE EUR-12

A nation's power in the policy arena is enhanced when it maintains the power to control the creation and destruction of the money that sits atop the hierarchy. If, however, the state has given up its sovereign currency or has otherwise compromised its power to create and destroy that currency at will, then it will have seriously limited its capacity to implement policy in accordance with Functional Finance.

Some Background on the New European Arrangements

As is well known, each of the members of the EUR-12 must accept the single monetary policy that is handed down by the European System of Central Banks (ESCB). Under current arrangements, the Governing Council formulates monetary policy for the entire Eurozone, while the Executive Board is charged with the implementation of the Community's monetary policy (Article 109a). National Central Banks (NCBs), such as the Banque de France and the Bundesbank still exist, but they are merely operating arms of the European Central Bank (ECB); they have no autonomous policy-making authority.[7]

While the Treaty clearly describes the manner in which monetary policy is to be implemented, it does not include such a precise blueprint for the implementation of fiscal policy. Indeed, rather than sketching out a program for the implementation of counter-cyclical fiscal policy, the Treaty imposes a set of rules and guidelines that are designed to *constrain* the use of discretionary fiscal policy. Specifically, by agreeing to the terms set out in the Maastricht Treaty, member states have subjected themselves to three distinct fiscal constraints.

First, member states have agreed to exercise a certain degree of *self-restraint* when it comes to matters of fiscal policy. The Treaty encourages 'close coordination of Member States' economic policies' (Article 3a), asking member states to 'regard their economic policies as a matter of common concern and … [to] coordinate them within the Council, in accordance with the provisions of Article 102a' (Article 103).

The second constraint on fiscal policy derives from the Stability and Growth Pact. Proposed by former German Finance Minister Waigel, the Pact makes more explicit the budgetary limits and financial penalties for non-compliance with Maastricht rules regarding fiscal discipline. The Pact, which was ratified at the June 1997 Amsterdam Summit, strengthens the surveillance of member states by forbidding countries from running deficits in excess of 3 per cent of gross domestic product (GDP) and requires that debt-to-GDP ratios be maintained below 60 per cent.[8]

There is strong disagreement regarding the severity of the deficit-to-GDP and debt-to-GDP constraints. For example, Pasinetti argues that 'the "pact" may entail severe costs on two counts: because it prevents expansionary policies in periods of recession and mass unemployment … and because, on top of that, it even imposes heavy fines' (1997, p. 9). Arestis and Sawyer concur, suggesting that the objective deficit-to-GDP 'constraint on the budget deficit clearly limits the use of national fiscal policy for demand management purposes' (1998, p. 2). DeGrawe (1996) and Eichengreen and von Hagen (1995) also oppose the objective constraint, arguing that member states should be free to pursue independent fiscal policy without arbitrary limits or penalties. In contrast, Mosler (1999) suggests that the objective constraints are relatively unimportant, since member states are unlikely to be able to secure financing for deficits in excess of 3 per cent of GDP except, perhaps, over very relatively short periods of time.

The final constraint on fiscal flexibility, mandated under Article 104 of the Maastricht Treaty, is the requirement that central governments abandon the use of 'overdraft facilities or any other type of credit facility with the ECB or with the central banks of the Member States' (Article 104). Article 104 forbids both the ECB and the NCBs from lending *directly* to member states or buying securities *directly* from them. Moreover, it states that the ECB should be mindful of this rule when carrying out monetary policy so that it does engage in operations that would amount to the *indirect* monetization of debt. Since NCBs are now forbidden to issue Treasury bonds on behalf of the government and the ECB is forbidden to directly or indirectly monetize government debt, governments wishing to deficit spend must now float bonds on the capital market, where they must compete with the financing needs of private borrowers.[9]

The Hierarchy of Money

Within the EUR-12, monetary contracts are now written in terms of the new European currency, the euro. Moreover, since taxes must ultimately be paid in euros, the euro should also be the most acceptable form of debt within the pyramid and should, therefore, sit at the top of the hierarchy. However, member states are incapable of creating and destroying euros at will. This is not only because they have handed over the power to conduct independent monetary policies (that is, the right to buy and sell bonds at will) but also because Article 104 of the Maastricht Treaty prevents them from 'printing' money by selling bonds directly to the ECB or their respective NCBs. Thus, as Figure 6.2 indicates, members of the EUR-12, lack the power to control the money that sits at the top of their hierarchies.

The fact that member states no longer control the money that sits at the top of their hierarchies implies something about the potential for policy flexibility in these regions.[10] Godley, recognized this, arguing that the abdication of monetary authority has brought about 'an end to the sovereignty of its component nations and their power to take independent action on major issues' (1992, p. 39). Sawyer, who also appreciates the importance of retaining a sovereign currency, has stated that by severing this relationship, 'national governments will no longer have the ability to "print money" to pay interest on bonds, and their ability to pay depends on their ability to levy the necessary taxation' (Sawyer, 1999, p. 11).

Thus, the traditional (institutional) link between a nation's treasury and its central bank has been severed under the new monetary arrangements. Having

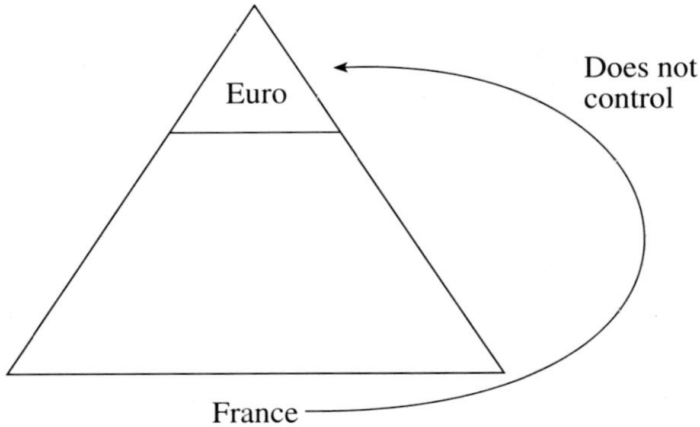

Figure 6.2 The hierarchy of a representative member state

broken this link, member states must rely on the willingness of commercial banks or other financial institutions when floating new issues. This means, of course, that they are (by definition) incapable of conducting policy according to the principles of Functional Finance.

THE HIERARCHY OF MONEY UNDER A CURRENCY BOARD ARRANGEMENT

In the previous section, we examined the limitations of policy flexibility under the European form of monetary union. As argued above, it is currently impossible for member governments to implement policy in accordance with the principles of Functional Finance. This is because unlike the USA, Canada, Australia and the UK, governments of the EUR-12 adopted monetary union *without* political union. By accepting an institutional framework that severs the traditional link between the treasury and the central bank, these governments cannot maintain full employment in accordance with the principles of Functional Finance.

The purpose of this section is to examine exchange rate pegging as an alternative method of fixing a nation's exchange rate. Even though most of the 181 IMF member countries do not currently peg their exchange rates, 66 of them – just over 36 per cent – *were* implementing some form of exchange rate peg in 1997. Figure 6.3 describes, from the least restrictive to the most restrictive, the various methods by which nations can allow exchange rates (Ers) to be determined.[11]

The most restrictive form of exchange rate regime, monetary union, has already been investigated. Thus, the primary concern in this section is with

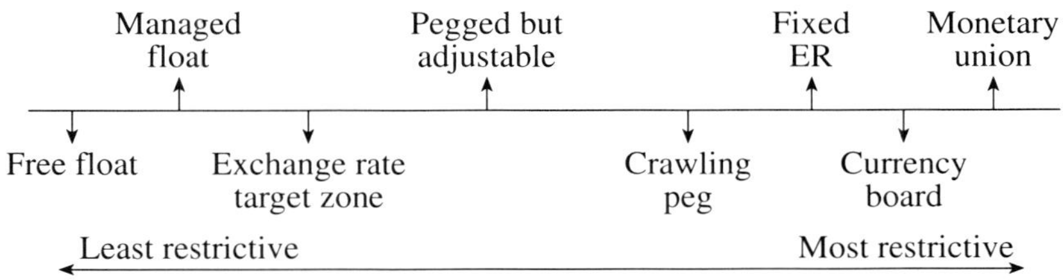

Figure 6.3 Exchange rate flexibility under different regimes

the limitations that a currency board arrangement imposes on a government's ability to implement policy according to the principles of Functional Finance.

What is a Currency Board?

A currency board is the hardest form of a pegged exchange rate regime, short of a currency union. Although they were popular in colonial times, currency boards fell into disuse when colonial regimes were dismantled.[12] In 1960, 38 countries or territories were operating under a currency board. By 1970 the number had fallen to 20, and by the late 1980s only nine remained. Recently, however, there has been a renewed interest in currency boards as a means of stabilizing currencies and restoring political confidence.

This renewed interest has led to an increase in the number of countries currently operating under a currency board – there are now 14. Hong Kong was the first to reintroduce a currency board in 1983, and Argentina followed with a similar arrangement in 1991. Then, following the disbanding of the Soviet Union in the fall of 1991, currency boards sparked further debate as officials began to search for a way to bring stability to the Baltic countries, Russia, and the other countries of the former Soviet Union. Estonia implemented a currency board in 1992, and Lithuania followed in 1994. More recently – 1997 – Bulgaria introduced a currency board after it experienced a severe financial crisis that lasted from 1996 until early 1997. There has also been serious discussion regarding the potential benefits of a currency board in Indonesia and Russia.

When a nation adopts a currency board, it pledges to back (usually by 100 per cent or more) the domestic currency with another currency (or a basket of currencies). Under less rigid exchange rate pegs, the monetary authority intervenes – buying or selling the domestic currency – in order to defend a target exchange rate, but it is not required to hold a specific quantity of foreign exchange. Thus, there is no guarantee that a depreciation of the domestic currency can be staved off by selling foreign exchange. This guarantee is supposed to be made credible under a currency board, since the monetary authority is required to hold enough of the reserve currency to convert the entire domestic money supply (notes and coins) into the reserve currency (and vice versa) at the fixed rate of exchange.[13]

Thus, the currency board simply pledges to convert the domestic currency and the reserve currency into one another at a fixed rate. By fully backing the domestic currency, investors are supposed to realize that the outstanding supply of domestic currency can easily be converted to the reserve currency, thereby discouraging speculative attacks against the domestic currency. Indeed, enhancing the credibility is one of the oft-cited benefits of a currency board system.

Deeper insight into the theoretical rationale for this form of arrangement derives from an affinity for commodity-money-like systems and a money supply that is determined entirely by market forces. Indeed, the currency board system is not substantively different from a gold standard.[14] Like a commodity money system, a currency board is supposed to foster 'free market principles', by 'curbing [the government's] functions and embedding them within a strict framework of rules' (Leontjeva, 1997). Thus, a desire for strict discipline in matters of government finance has also been a rationale for adopting this form of monetary arrangement.

Functional Finance under a Currency Board System

As Williamson explained, '[a] currency board is at bottom an arrangement that legislates a particular monetary rule: a rule that changes in the monetary base will be equal to the country's overall balance of payments surplus or deficit' (1995, p. 1).[15] Carbaugh has characterized the currency board system this way:

> A country that adopts a currency board thus puts its monetary policy on autopilot. It is as if the chairman of the Board of Governors of the Federal Reserve System were replaced by a personal computer. When the anchor currency flows in, the board issues more domestic currency and interest rates fall; when the anchor currency flows out, interest rates rise. The government sits back and watches, even if interest rates skyrocket and a recession ensues.
>
> (Carbaugh, 2000, p. 489)

The notion of a government that passively 'sits back and watches' as a recession ensues is wholly inconsistent with the policy approach advocated by Lerner. According to the principles of functional finance, the government should always strive to maintain full employment and minimize economic insecurity. However, as I have already demonstrated, not all nations are, given their current monetary systems, in a position to adopt policy according to Lerner's two fundamental principles. Below, I will demonstrate that not only must nations put monetary policy on 'autopilot' but that fiscal policy is similarly constrained when a currency board is adopted.

Recall that Lerner's second principle of functional finance decrees that the government should close the spending gap by 'printing money', by which he meant selling bonds to the central bank or to commercial banks, in exchange for a credit to its account. However, a currency board is not allowed to lend to the domestic government in this way. In fact, the only way that additional units of the domestic currency can be issued is through an expansion of the Board's holding of foreign exchange reserves.[16] Thus, under a currency board arrangement, the government can finance its spending only by taxing or borrowing; it cannot 'print money' in accordance with Lerner's second law.

What this means, of course, is that governments operating under a currency board, in order to deficit spend, must compete with other borrowers in order to secure funding. Worse, the terms of finance will be dictated by capital markets, which can refuse to facilitate expansionary efforts or even to roll over maturing obligations. Thus, as Hanke and Schuler note, even though governments can, in theory, continually borrow in order to finance growing deficits, 'in practice, lenders are unwilling to allow government budget deficits to persist forever' (2000, p. 5). Unless private lenders are willing to provide the *external* finance necessary to sustain a growing deficit, governments will be forced to run balanced budgets.[17] Given this, it should not be surprising to learn that in countries where a currency board is in operation, government budgets 'have historically been balanced or slightly in surplus' (Hanke and Schuler, 2000, p. 5).

The restrictive nature of a currency board arrangement is evidenced in Figure 6.4, which shows Bulgaria's budgetary stance before and after implementing its currency board in 1997. Importantly, the budget surplus coincides precisely with the implementation of the currency board system, further emphasizing the restrictive nature of such an arrangement.

The Hierarchy under a Currency Board Arrangement

When a nation chooses to peg its currency via a currency board arrangement, contracts can be written in terms of the domestic currency or in terms of the reserve currency. Thus, in Bulgaria, money contracts can be written in Bulgarian levs or in euros. However, as Hanke and Schuler have recognized, '[t]he ultimate reserves in a currency board system are the monetary base of the reserve currency' (2000, p. 26). Thus, as Figure 6.5 shows, the euro must sit atop Bulgaria's hierarchy.

However, Bulgaria cannot control the creation and destruction of euros. Instead, the currency board responds passively, converting the reserve cur-

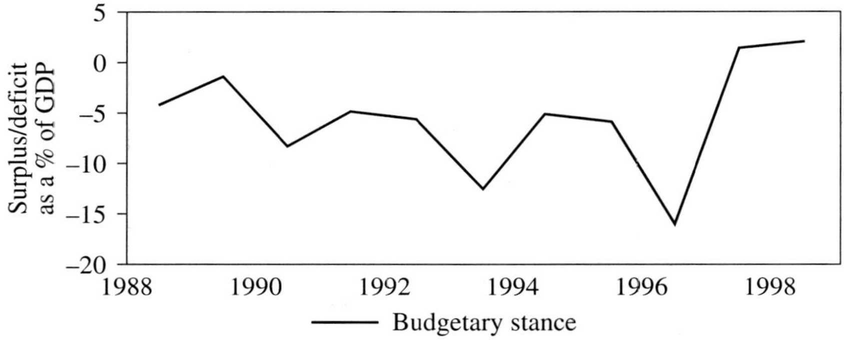

Source: Bulgarian National Bank: http://www.bnb.bg

Figure 6.4 Pre- and post-currency board budgetary stance in Bulgaria (as % of GDP)

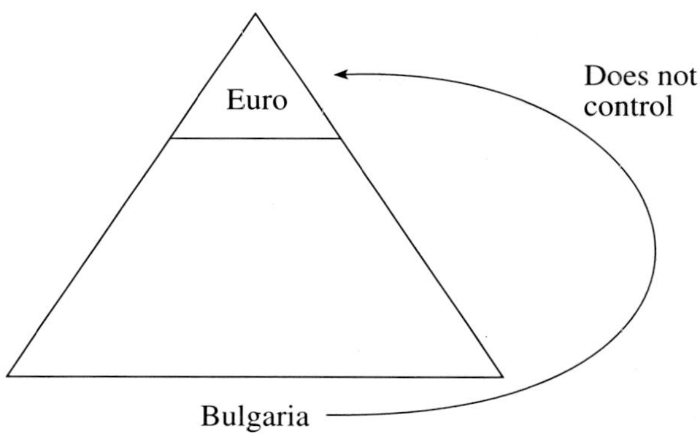

Figure 6.5 The Bulgarian hierarchy

rency and the domestic currency into one another at the fixed rate of exchange. Government spending, though done in terms of the domestic currency, is constrained by the availability of the reserve currency. Unless the state acquires additional units of the reserve currency, the deficit and, hence, the domestic base, cannot increase. Here, again, it is lack of power in the monetary sphere, which limits flexibility in the sphere of public policy.

CONCLUDING REMARKS

The fundamental relationship between sovereignty over money and sovereignty over policy was recognized by Lerner (1947) and has been developed more fully by Goodhart (1998), Wray (1998) and Bell (2001). However, the economics profession has generally failed to pay sufficient attention to the theory or to the policy implications that follow from it. Indeed, one would be hard pressed to find any mention of functional finance or the state theory of money in modern economics texts. Instead, the profession has tended to focus on the existence of federal budget constraints and on money as a 'thing', which is (or should be) in scare supply.

The belief that money should be kept scarce derives from the profession's continued support for the quantity theory of money, which Keynes (1936) so forcefully attacked in *The General Theory*. Although it is true that not all economists view changes in the money supply as the single most important determinant of short-run changes in GDP, the idea that an independent central bank, following a set of predetermined (and rigidly adhered to) rules, has won significant acceptance within the profession. Palley has characterized the profession's current state aptly:

> [D]evelopments in the economics profession increasingly cast a deflationary shadow across the world's economies. This is because most economists support policies of zero inflation achieved by high real interest rates, fiscal austerity, balanced budgets, limited social and infrastructure spending, free trade, and the globalization of financial markets. Since economists act as policy advisers around the world, the economics profession has become a de facto means for coordinating and implementing deflationary policy on a global scale.
>
> (1996, p. 58)

As Minksy (1982; 1986) emphasized, it takes an entity capable of injecting large quantities of liquidity (that is, a 'big bank' lender of last resort) and an entity capable of spending enough to sustain business profits (that is, a 'big' government) in order to avert a debt deflation. But the monetary system adopted by the member states of the EUR-12 as well as the monetary systems adopted by nations operating currency boards violate both of Minsky's conditions. Instead, countries operating under these new regimes have chosen to constrain government spending and to eliminate lender-of-last-resort facilities. Thus, it is possible that a strain on domestic banks will be met with an attempt to liquidate bank assets, which could very well lead to a Fisherian (1933) or Minskian (1982) debt deflation. The inability to cope with such a state of affairs is the logical implication of abandoning a nation's chartal money.[18]

The above, while wholly inconsistent with the central tenets of Functional Finance, is precisely consistent with the recent wave of monetary reforms that have taken place in the 1990s. In particular, the introduction of various forms of 'stateless' money (for example, the euro and the monies that have been rigidly pegged via a currency board arrangement) has promoted the neoliberal agenda, which seeks to paralyse policy-makers in order to promote market forces. This is to be accomplished through the creation of 'independent' central banks and currency boards that cannot be used as fiscal arms of their respective governments. These reforms, which are predicated on the assumption that capitalist economies will (more-or-less) automatically revert back to a stable equilibrium, following any deviation from such a position, leave their adopters with little (if any) capacity to stimulate aggregate demand in the event that things fail to work as expected.

NOTES

1. This is of course very different from the practice of so-called 'sound' finance, which appears to have been embraced by virtually all nations today.
2. Several economists (e.g. Minsky, 1986; Foley, 1987; Wray 1990) have used the concept of the debt-pyramid or hierarchy of money. The primary advantage of this approach is that it demonstrates clearly why the state's power is unique in this regard.
3. For more on the Chartalist (or state) theory see Knapp (1924), Lerner (1947), Wray (1998) or Bell (2001).
4. Here, I am referring specifically to state-issued fiat money. State promises could, of course, also take the form of government bonds, but, while these promises also have a place in the hierarchy, unless they are accepted in payment of taxes, they will be situated below state and bank money.
5. One might object that the position of the state's money at the top of the pyramid follows not from the imposition and enforcement of taxes but from the market's identification of these debts as possessing the highest degree of 'moneyness'. This objection might follow, for example, from Menger's theory, as reformulated by Mises (1881 [1935]). For Mises, any commodity has the potential of emerging spontaneously as money, but the one with the highest degree of marketability (the one most likely to be accepted in exchange) would be expected to rise to the top of the pyramid. Thus, the Austrians might contend that the state's debts sit atop the pyramid because of an *ex post* sanctioning of the 'money' selected spontaneously by the market, rather than the state's power to tax. Knapp's state theory of money, then, could be viewed simply as a 'special case', which is not necessarily inconsistent with the neoclassical story. But this objection is simply not compelling, for as Wray argues, the Chartalist theory is a *general* theory, which can be applied 'to the entire era of Chartal, or state, money' (1998, p. 43). To properly defend the argument, a detailed analysis of the history and evolution of money would be necessary. Interested readers should refer to Wray (1998) for more on this.
6. The relationship between the tax-raising authority of the state and the relative value of the state's debt follows directly from the state theory of money.
7. The NCBs will continue to perform many of their original duties, but they 'now engage in monetary policy operations only when and as instructed by the ECB' (Stevens, 1999, p. 1).
8. In the event that a country does not fulfill the two fiscal criteria – for the budget deficit and public indebtedness – the excessive deficit procedure pursuant to Article 104(c) will apply. Under the Excessive Deficit Procedure, deficits exceeding 3 per cent of GDP are subject to a fine as declared by the European Council upon a report by the European Commission and a judgement by the Monetary Committee.

9. As Parguez recognizes, this means that markets will make lending decisions on the basis of their perception of member states' creditworthiness, which is based on a state's ability to 'pledge to balance its budget, to get a zero *ex post* deficit, so as to protect the banks against the risk of accumulating public debt' (1999, p. 72). Since markets will perceive some members of the EUR-11 as more creditworthy than others, financial markets will not view bonds issued by different nations as perfect substitutes. Therefore, high-debt countries may be unable to secure funding on the same terms as their low-debt competitors. This was recognized by Lemmen and Goodhart, who suggest that 'governments with above-average deficits and debt will find that they have less financial flexibility within EMU than [was previously] the case' (1999, p. 77).
10. Again, this is because member states must now compete for euros by selling bonds to private investors (including private banks) who will not view the various obligations as perfect substitutes. Thus, governments must float bonds on the capital market, where they must compete with debt instruments offered by other (government and non-government) entities. The result, as Taylor recognizes, is that 'debt issuance by Euroland's governments [will] take place in a new environment of market discipline' (1999, p. 16).
11. Each member of the IMF, as specified in the Second Amendment to the Articles of Agreement of the International Monetary Fund, is free to choose the method by which its own exchange rate will be determined. These include: (1) the maintenance by a member of a value for its currency in terms of the special drawing right or other denominator, other than gold, selected by the member, or (2) co-operative arrangements by which members maintain the value of their currencies in relation to the value of the currency or currencies of other members, or (3) other exchange rate arrangements of a member's choice (quoted in Kenen, 1989, pp. 3–4).
12. They were initially enacted as a way to connect distant colonies to the monetary system of their parent countries.
13. As with the implementation of other forms of exchange rate pegs, the choice of the peg depends, among other things, on the strength of the currency as well as the trading ties. Both Hong Kong and Argentina, with strong ties to the USA, elected to peg to the US dollar. However, Estonia, which conducts substantial trade with Finland and Sweden, opted for the strength of the Deutschmark when it introduced its currency board in 1992.
14. The analogy will be drawn out more carefully in the following section.
15. Millier (1999, p. 44) explains that in Bulgaria, the currency board is set up in such a way that 'changes in foreign currency reserves do not necessarily lead to equivalent changes in M0', but this condition tends to hold elsewhere.
16. In addition to current account surpluses, the reserve currency can be gotten through direct investment, portfolio investment, or the sale of Eurobonds.
17. Balances cannot be created *internally* as in the USA, Canada, the UK or Australia.
18. As Grabel (2000) notes, adherents to the new-classical branch of macroeconomics have added the criterion of 'policy credibility' to the profession's list of appropriate policies.

REFERENCES

Arestis, Philip, and Malcolm Sawyer (1998), 'Prospects for the single European currency and some proposals for a new Maastricht', draft manuscript.

Bell, Stephanie (2001), 'The role of the state and the hierarchy of money', *Cambridge Journal of Economics*, **25** (2), 149–63.

Carbaugh, Robert J. (2000), *International Economics*, 7th edn, Cincinnati, OH: South-Western College Publishing.

DeGrawe, Paul (1995), *The Economics of Monetary Integration*, Oxford: Oxford University Press.

Eichengreen, Barry, and Jurgen von Hagen (1995), 'Fiscal policy and monetary union: federalism, fiscal restrictions, and the no-bailout rule', *Monetary Policy in an Integrated World Economy*, ed. Horst Siebert, Schriftleitung: Harmen Lehment.

Fisher, Irving (1933), 'The debt deflation theory of business cycles', *Econometrica*, October, pp. 337–57.

Foley, Duncan (1987), 'Money in economic activity', *The New Palgrave: Money*, eds John Eatwell, Murray Milgate and Peter Newman, New York and London: W.W. Norton, pp. 519–25.

Godley, Wynne (1992), 'Maastricht and all that: letter from Europe', *London Review of Books*, **14** (19), October.

Goodhart, Charles (1997), 'One government, one money', *Prospect*, March.

Goodhart, Charles (1998), 'The two concepts of money: implications for the analysis of optimal currency areas', *European Journal of Political Economy*, **14**, 407–32.

Grabel, Ilene (2000), 'The political economy of "Policy Credibility": the new-classical macroeconomics and the remaking of emerging economies', *Cambridge Journal of Economics*, **24** (1), 1–19.

Hanke, Steve, and Kurt Schuler (2000), *Currency Boards for Developing Countries: A Handbook*, accessed at http://users.erols.com/kurrency/icegrev.htm.

Hicks, John (1989), *A Market Theory of Money*, Oxford: Clarendon Press.

Kenen, Peter (1989), *Exchange Rates and Policy Coordination*, Ann Arbor, MI: University of Michigan Press.

Keynes, J.M. (1930), *A Treatise on Money*, New York: Harcourt Brace.

Keynes, J.M. (1936), *The General Theory of Employment, Interest and Money*, New York: Harcourt, Brace & World.

Knapp, G.F. (1924), *The State Theory of Money*, abridged and trans. by H.E. Batson, London: Routledge and Kegan Paul.

Kregel, J.A. (1999), 'Currency stabilization through full employment: can EMU combine price stability and income growth?, *Eastern Economic Journal*, **25** (1), 35–47.

Lemmen, Jan J.G., and Charles A.E. Goodhart (1999), 'Credit risks and European government bond markets: a panel data econometric analysis', *Eastern Economic Journal*, **25** (1), 77–107.

Leontjeva, Elena (1997), 'An epitaph to the currency board', *The Free Market*, accessed at www.freeman.org/NewsLetter/monetary.policy/1997.5epitaph.pthml.

Lerner, Abba P. (1943), 'Functional finance and the federal debt', *Social Research*, **10**, 38–51.

Lerner, Abba P. (1947), 'Money as a creature of the state,' *American Economic Review*, **37** (2), 312–17.

Millier, Jeffrey B. (1999), 'The currency board in Bulgaria: the first two years' in Zeljko Sevic (ed.), *Banking Reform in South East European Transitional Economies*, Bulgaria and London: University of Greenwich Business School.

Minsky, Hyman P. (1982), *Can 'It' Happen Again? Essays on Instability and Finance*, Armonk, NY: M.E. Sharpe.

Minsky, Hyman P. (1986), *Stabilizing and Unstable Economy*, London: Yale University Press.

Mises, L. von. (1881), *The Theory of Money and Credit*, reprinted 1935, New York: Harcourt Brace.

Mosler, Warren (1999), *The Launching of the Euro: A Conference on the European and Monetary Union*, Annandale-on-Hudson, NY: The Bard Center.

Palley, Thomas I. (1996), 'The forces making for an economic collapse', *Atlantic Monthly*, July, 43–58.

Parguez, Alain (1999), 'The expected failure of the European economic and monetary union: a false money against the real economy', *Eastern Economic Journal*, **25**, 63–76.

Pasinetti, Luigi L. (1997), 'The myth (or folly) of the 3% deficit/GNP Maastricht "Parameter"', unpublished paper.

Sawyer, Malcolm (1999), 'Minsky's analysis, the European single currency, and the global financial system', The Jerome Levy Economics Institute working paper no. 266, pp. 1–18.

Stevens, Ed (1999), 'The euro', *Federal Reserve Bank of Cleveland, Economic Trends*, 1 January, accessed at www.clevelandfed.org/research/com99/0101.pdf.

Taylor, Christopher (1999), 'Payments imbalances, secession risk and potential financial traumas in Europe's monetary union', draft 24 May.

Tobin, James, and Stephen S. Golub (1998), *Money, Credit, and Capital*, New York: Irwin/McGraw-Hill.

Williamson, John (1995), *What Role Currency Boards?*, Washington, DC: Institute for International Economics.

Wray, L. Randall (1990), *Money and Credit in Capitalist Economies: The Endogenous Money Approach*, Aldershot, UK and Brookfield, USA: Edward Elgar.

Wray, L. Randall (1998), *Understanding Modern Money: The Key to Full Employment and Price Stability*, Cheltenham, UK and Northampton, MA, USA: Edward Elgar.

PART III

Post Keynesian Contributions on Development, Growth and Inflation

7. Stability conditions for a small open economy

Etelberto Ortiz

THE ISSUES

Is there any good reason to believe that the standard policy recipes conceived out of common views and problems of the 1980s, should work in an entirely different environment nowadays? This question is addressed to the current orthodox view in response to whichever disequilibrium appears: *sound macroeconomic conditions rest on a null fiscal deficit and negligible inflation.* Nevertheless in the 1998 address to the World Bank Conference on Trade and Development, Joseph Stiglitz expressed his doubts about the form in which the 1995 Mexican and the 1997 South-East Asian crises exploded. In both cases we were in the presence of 'successful models', at least according to the view of the World Bank and the IMF. Both engaged in long successful efforts to reduce the public deficit to zero and the rate of inflation to a single digit. Both were the 'stars' of structural change policies on the basis of trade and financial liberalization. Nevertheless, both collapsed into severe payments and financial crisis. Undoubtedly there are many common features with the recent collapse of the Argentinean economy.

This chapter takes the view that current economic policies look as if they were drawn only from inflationary experiences of the 1970s and 1980s, when monetization of chronic public deficits were the original sources of inflationary pressures. But today's crises may not necessarily be the result of excess drawing of the government on the Central Bank. In fact the core of our argument is that current anti-inflationary policies, aimed to stabilize macroeconomic conditions, may well be at the root of those new crises.

It is striking that the orthodox menu of disequilibria phenomena reduces to inflation and public deficit, while today the real world reflects other extremely important phenomena: *deflation, recession, bankruptcies* and *unemployment.* Within the orthodox view, these are but occasional disarrays from a fundamental equilibrium, caused either by a market or government failure, but in no way fundamental disruptions produced by the way a market economy expresses its capabilities of adjustment. Within that view, market failures do not express an essential limitation of a market economy, but external interference on its normal process of adjustment.[1]

The usual standard characterization of macroeconomic stability and policies of the 1970s and 1980s may well be represented as in the following list:[2]

1. Public deficits were attributed to 'fat' public sectors.
2. Backed by 'monetization' of public deficits.
3. That turned into high inflation rates.
4. Poor export performance associated with rigid import requirements.
5. Growing foreign debt associated with public sector and current account deficits and capital flights.
6. Public deficits turned into savings deficits.
7. Public deficits turned into external deficits.
8. Presumption of investment higher than savings, and 'crowding-out'.

Nevertheless, it resulted in high rates of growth (over 6.5 percent in Mexico)

Standard policy prescriptions of the time adopted the following approach:

1. Structural reform.
2. Liberalization of trade and finance.
3. Reduction of public deficits to zero.
4. Privatization of public enterprises.
5. More emphasis to rules than to discretionary intervention.
6. Independence of the central bank at least on control of the monetary base.
7. Emphasis on anti-inflationary policies.
8. 'Pegging' the rate of exchange to control inflationary expectations.
9. High interest rates to promote higher savings ratios and more investment.

Nevertheless, there is a growing consensus that the relevant political agenda of today differs, essentially as a result of orthodox stabilization policies, but particularly is to be attributed to the impact of policies for structural change.

How can the 'new model' be characterized? Our contention is that the new behaviors cannot be reduced to some change of parameters within the same old model, but that there is a new, essentially different, behavioral pattern.

There is a growing literature that characterizes the new agenda with a strong emphasis on a new 'structural behavior', particularly on the monetary and fiscal determinants, that could be described as follows. The relevant stylized facts for a small open economy nowadays are:

1. The urge for financial resources to serve the external debt, imposes the prominence of anti-inflationary policies.

2. Actual anti-inflationary policies work through 'pegging' the exchange rate, therefore pressing for higher rates of interest (Edwards, 1999).
3. Monetary policy actually works from the rate of interest and the exchange rate (Blinder, 1998).
4. Total savings turn higher than total investment (Ortiz, 1997b; Edwards, 1999).
5. External savings expand at the expense of domestic savings without expanding total savings (Ortiz, 1998; Edwards, 1999).
6. Stagnant and smaller investment rate (Ortiz, 2002; Edwards, 1999).
7. A deflationary and recessive drive pervades economic performance, with lower and more erratic growth rates (Ortiz and Motamen, 1998).
8. There is a tendency for overvaluation, under any exchange rate regime.
9. Private deficits are the main source of public deficits (Ortiz, 1998).
10. External deficits are turned into public deficits.
11. Export leaders receive indirect subsidies, through exchange rate overvaluation (Ortiz and Motamen, 1998).
12. Competitiveness of domestic market producers rests on low wages.
13. Export led growth does not produce a reasonable growth rate, even with very fast export growth (Ortiz and Motamen, 1998; Edwards, 1999).
14. Growing weight of public debt service in total public expenditure leads to the reduction of real public consumption (Ortiz, 1998).
15. Growing marginality of precarious labor (Ortiz, 1997b).
16. Recessive environment with a very slow growth of GDP (Ortiz, 2002; Ros, 2000).

There is a new behavioral pattern attributable to essential characteristics of the relationship between external disequilibria and the accompanying domestic disequilibria. Our rejection of the standard open IS-LM model, as in a conventional Mundell-Fleming formulation[3] arises from its poor representation of the relationship of domestic and external disequilibria. But it is interesting that even current descriptions of critical episodes, as in Mundell (1997), might not fit with the standard orthodox approach. We call attention particularly as they relate to the imbalances between investment and savings, and the corresponding fiscal and trade balances. This analysis is particularly relevant for recent experiences of small open economies subject to structural reforms, where the impact of monetary and financial disequilibria on public finance has been much more significant than generally has been admitted.

This framework is particularly important for countries like Mexico and Argentina, which have initiated significant structural reforms during the last 15 years. Our contention is that this behavior cannot be properly represented on the theoretical lines of the standard orthodox approach, (Krugman, 1997), particularly because the issues have changed as a consequence of policies for structural change during the last 20 years. More precisely, the new dominant phenomena cannot be reconstructed theoretically without considering the strong link between real and monetary phenomena. A fundamental role arises from the impact of monetary policy on fiscal balance, that generally the orthodox model overlooks.

This chapter initially discusses the monetary policy model, and the way in which the macroeconomic model can be put together. But the whole model is based on the Mexican experience of the last 15 years, and emphasizes the relationship between external and domestic disequilibria in a small open economy.

The final section discusses the impact of monetary policy given its strong incidence on the productive structure and prices, in the context of a small open economy. A model of monetary policy that relies on fixing the exchange parity, compensated with increases in the interest rate, is found to be contradictory to the standard aims for structural change and monetary policy. It is shown that such monetary policy would necessarily result in fiscal and balance of payment deficits. Furthermore, given its recessive impact, it may well induce a strong recurrence of instability and crises.

THE MONETARY POLICY MODEL

In an open economy, monetary policy has an impact on three different but closely interrelated aspects:

- the formation of prices, (in a forthcoming paper)
- the balance of public income and expenditure
- the external balance.

Evidently none of this may occur but there may be an impact on the level of investment and income. The overall view is based on the *non*-neutrality of money, which is discussed here.[4] We observe that monetary policy is defined by a pair [E, i], rates of exchange and interest, and not by a monetary quantum M, Blinder (1998). The amount of means of payment and money, M, becomes completely endogenous; according to that pair $[E, i]$ determined by the monetary authority and the banking system.[5]

This approximation allows us to work out the impact of monetary policy without resorting to the quantitative theory of money, since it would be redundant within this approximation.

Anti-inflationary policy presumably works through an expectations model such that $E(\dot{P}) = E(\dot{E})$. Therefore it is expected that the reduction of the devaluation expectation should reduce the inflationary expectations. Somehow this model recognizes the importance of the 'inertial components' of inflation. One important consequence of this view, is that the actual realm of monetary policy might reach to the determination of the wage rate, w.

If monetary policy has a real incidence through real and monetary prices and the effective demand, the initial consequence of this argument is that neither the IS nor the LM schedules can be identified, because there would appear circularity in its argument (Hicks, 1980–81). The reason is that something in the money sphere would have an incidence on the level of public expenditure and investment, and therefore on the level of demand.

Savings and Investment

The investment decision in this model plays a critical role in two areas:

- microeconomic – in the formation of prices.
- macroeconomic – in the determination of effective demand and macroeconomic equilibrium.

Total investment will be the sum of each sector's investment decisions. These are nourished by the prospective evaluation of profitability perspectives in different activities in regards to a target profit rate, denominated r' that can be assimilated to the concept of marginal efficiency of investment (MEI) as in Keynes (see Davidson, 1994; Ortiz, 1997); so that $I_i = \Psi\ (r' - r_i)$. However, it is important to establish that profitability conditions are a variable that is affected by the level of activity. To the extent that through an expansion we can expect a positive relationship of income growth to income-yield capacity of investment and, reciprocally during a recession, we will find a negative impact on profits. Therefore the investment function can be expressed, as in Kaldor, as a positive function of the rate of growth of the productivity of labor: $I_i \leq \Sigma_t\ [\lambda - w]$, where λ represents the productivity of labor and w the wage rate.

Worker's consumption will be equal to their wages, so that $C_w = W$. At the same time, capitalist's consumption will be given by a standard consumption function $C_k = c(\Pi)$. Domestic savings are established as a passive function, determined by current income level. Thus, capitalist's savings will be given by: $S_d = s\ (\Pi)$. On the other hand, external savings will be determined by the difference of interest rates, that is, $i' = i'_d - i'_x$. Therefore, $S_x = \varphi\ \{\ (i'_d - i'), E'\}$. In this case E' establishes the prospective exchange rate, or shows the devaluation expectation. This function is characterized by: $\varphi'_{id} > 0$ and $\varphi'_{r'} > 0$. But $\varphi'_{E'} < 0$. Accordingly, total savings will be, generally: $S_t = S_d + S_x + S_g$. The suggested behavior of domestic savings is based on the idea that reductions in the real exchange rate are associated with increases in the domestic interest rate. Both movements linked with increases in the external savings rate provoke the effect of a peculiar 'crowding-out' on domestic savings. This condition implies that increases in the interest rate will be associated with reductions in the domestic savings rate. Overall, investment determines savings.

However, the aggregated savings function, while it is a function of the profit rate, it is also a pro-cyclical function of the level of income. Beyond a point like *a* in Figure 7.1, successive increases in the interest rate lead to reductions in the investment rate, thus in income and, accordingly, in total domestic savings.

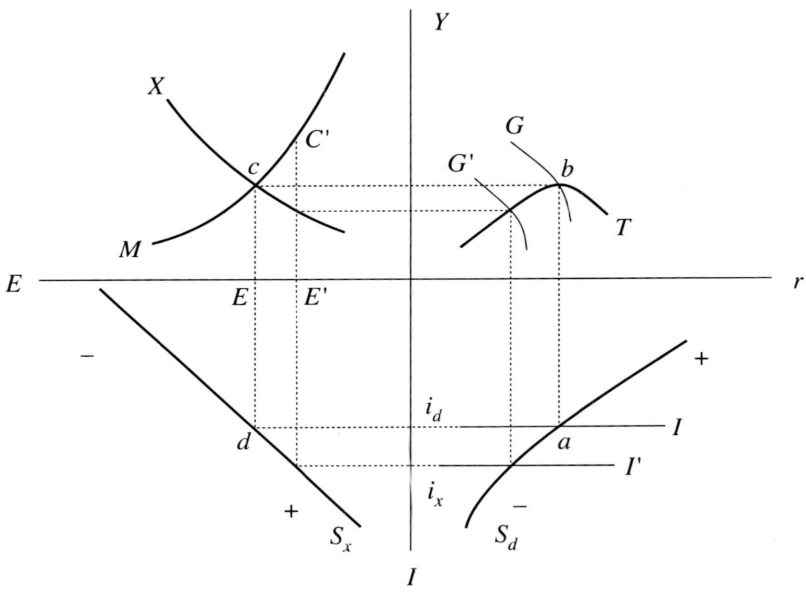

Figure 7.1 Trade disequilibria with fiscal and savings equilibrium

On the other hand, the external savings flux is defined by the differential between domestic and external interest rates in real terms. Accordingly, monetary policy has a very clear effect on the flux of external savings through the rate of interest.

Foreign Trade

The external sector is represented by a relationship of the flows of trade and capital considered before. The difference between the flow of exports and imports will equal the flow of external savings. Trade behavior usually considers that exports represent a positive function on the real exchange rate and the income level of the rest of the world Y^*. Nevertheless according to the stylized facts already highlighted, it is important to observe that there is a tendency for overvaluation of the rate of exchange with a parallel phenomenon of loss in terms of trade. This problem cannot be reduced to find an exchange rate that brings the balance of trade to equilibrium. The difficulty concerns the problem for a small open economy to retain its advances in productivity, following Prebish (1962). Let λ be the rate of growth of labor productivity in the home country and λ^* in the rest of the world, and P and P^* the corresponding growth rates in prices. The terms of trade could then be represented as a relationship of labor productivity and prices:

$$\frac{\lambda_i}{\lambda_i^*} \geq = \leq \frac{P_i}{P_i^*} \tag{7.1}$$

And the problem is if there exists an E' that can bring them to equality. Such an E' could be interpreted as the rate that equates returns to both countries, although not necessarily the balance of trade. But the importance for a small open economy relies on that it express the incidence of the rate of exchange to preserve productivity gains.

Consequently we shall present a model with the income term, given that it works as an exogenous variable of pro-cyclical nature, but considering the terms of trade as follows: $X = \chi(Y^*, \lambda, P)$, where λ is for the productivity of labor, and λ to P represents the terms of trade. The price of exports in domestic currency is $P_3 = P_3^\$ E$. Imports are modeled as a positive function of income and a negative function of the terms of trade, given the productivity and prices in the rest of the world. $M = \mu(Y, \lambda^*, EP^*)$. Accordingly, $(X - M) = [\chi(Y^*, \lambda, EP) - \mu(Y, \lambda^*, EP^*)]$.

Fiscal Constraints and Budgetary Disequilibrium

Public income is essentially defined by tax income: $T = \tau(Y, r)$. The idea is that an increase in profits allows for an increase in tax collection. Though the inverse function of τ on r, the rate of profit, shows the resistance of capitalists to tax increases. Public spending is also perceived as a positive function of income and a progressive function of interest rates for domestic and external public debt: $G = \gamma(Y) + i_d D_d^g + i_x D_x^g$. Generally, we adopted the following expressions for tax receipts and public spending: $T = \tau(Y, r)$, and $G = \gamma(Y, r\{i\})$. Characterized as follows: $\tau'(Y) > 0$ and $\tau''(Y) < 0$ and with a limit at $\tau'(r) > 0$ as at point b in Figure 7.1. From there on, it will be negative with: $\tau'(r) < 0$, and $\tau''(r) < 0$. Public expenditure behaves as follows: $\gamma'(Y) > 0$, and

$\gamma''(Y) < 0$ with a limit at point b of Figure 7.1. And $\gamma'(r) > 0$ with a limit at point b. From there on, it will be negative with: $\gamma'(r) > 0$, and $\gamma''(r) < 0$. And finally $\gamma'(i) < 0$ and $\gamma''(i) < 0$.

The overview of the problem is that, an increase in income given a determined tax rate, τ, produces an increase in tax revenue. However, the relationship is not linear. Up to a point, further increases in income tax will be resisted by social agents, and could be perceived as having a negative effect on actual tax collection.

The impact of the interest rate on public spending operates in two ways: directly through the public debt cost, and indirectly through the impact that increases in i could have on r. However, the most important effect will be observed in the displacement effect on the component of current spending $\gamma(Y)$, due to increases in service on the public debt, which appear as $\gamma'(i) < 0$. The form of the functions can be represented in the space $\{Y, r, T\}$: Consequently the budget restriction is:

$$T = \gamma(Y) + i_d D_d^g + i_x D_x^g. \tag{7.2}$$

The behavior of autonomous spending, may be a function of the level of income. Variations in the rate of interest will impact service on the domestic and external public debt, such that will affect G as shifts of its curve toward the r axis. This represents lower public spending with a lower level of income. In the $\{T, r\}$ space, two curves are represented, one with a positive slope that represents increases in tax collection associated to increases in income and profits, that might be called a Kaleckian drive. Nevertheless, in Figure 7.1, starting at point b, the curve bends down, representing the behavior of enterprises to resist greater increases in tax collection, since they would perceive it as a reduction in profits. The resulting decrease in public spending would lead to a reduction in income, and thus, in the level of effective demand and income.

The Relationship of Domestic and External Disequilibrium

The solution for the model requires that we initially represent the conditions of domestic and external equilibrium separately.

The macroeconomic model proposed in the previous pages is put together including the conditions for each subsector and its impact on effective demand. Substituting in $(S - I) = (T - G) + (X - M)$; we have:

$$\begin{aligned}[s(\pi) - I(\lambda - w)] = {} & [\tau(Y, r) - \{\gamma(Y) - i_d D_d^g - i_x D_x^g\}] \\ & + [\chi(Y^*, E\lambda EP) - \mu(Y, \lambda^*, EP^*)]\end{aligned} \tag{7.3}$$

Regrouping terms, it can be expressed as:

$$[s(\Lambda - W) - I(\lambda - w)] = [\tau(Y,r) - \gamma(Y) - i_d D_d^g - i_x D_x^g] + [\chi(Y^*, \lambda, EP) - \mu(Y, \lambda^*, EP^*)] \quad (7.4)$$

There are two ways to deal with this equation: the first, working out the overall magnitudes of effective demand; the second, analysing the dynamic paths suggested by the functional relationships.

The first track, putting together the model, we can observe that the equation allows us to establish aggregate demand through the budget restriction established by net savings, or after serving the public debt and imports. The model operates on four variables: [*Y*, *i*, *E*, *r*]. But they can be broken down into two subsystems, one internal and the other external, in such a way that an analytical solution can be expressed for the whole model:

- The internal as:

$$[s(\pi) + i_d D_d^g] - Ir = \tau(Y,r) - \gamma(Y) \text{ which is in the space } \{Y, r, i.\} \quad (7.5)$$

- And the external as:

$$[S_x[id - i^*), E] + i_x D_x^g] = [\chi(Y^*, e) - \mu(Y, E)] \text{ in the space } \{Y, i, E.\} \quad (7.6)$$

The dynamic operation of the model has to be understood considering that the monetary and financial side of the model appears in the quadrant in [*E*, *i*]. It represents the impact of monetary policy across the economy, but reflected in the savings deficit, therefore in the external savings flow that is necessary to close the external balance.[6]

The need of external savings necessary to close the savings and trade deficit affects the availability of domestic savings, through the impact of the interest rate on public spending, net external savings and the rate of investment.

In Figure 7.1, the terms of the model have been split so that those having an effect on external equilibrium are on the left-hand side (*Y*, *E*, *i*) and those that correspond to domestic equilibrium are on the right-hand side (*Y*, *r*, *i*).

The construction initially represents a situation of equilibrium in the entire system, since the interest and exchange rates find a solution in which there are no trade, fiscal or savings deficits. Generally, the existence of a solution is postulated, since from the point of view of effective demand we have nine equations and nine unknowns: $\{Y, S_d, S_x, S_g, I, M, X, T, G\}$. The specification of the model considers the following parameters as givens: $\{w, Y^*, i^*, r', P^m, \mu, \chi, D_d^g, D^g\}$ besides monetary policy parameters [*E*, *i*].

We can observe that the public spending and tax curves are graphed in such a way that public spending is determined up to an income level, since its pro-cyclical nature is recognized in profits and income growth. However, starting at point *b*, an increase in public spending and taxes can lead to a reduction in profits, even if it is still associated with a higher income level. Domestic savings is a curve of available net savings for investment, since service on the domestic public debt must be discounted. The volume of net domestic savings cuts the investment curve from below and is relatively inelastic to the interest rate. The idea is that the interest rate is not a determinant of investment. At point *a*, savings is equal to investment, but this equality is restricted to a certain level of income and price.

We postulated the existence of a solution of equilibrium.[7] However, our interest is on the way in which macroeconomic relationships in disequilibrium are articulated. Any point to the right of the savings and investment intersection, as point *a*, show us the savings deficit. Any increase in *I* above this point would only be possible with a lower rate of interest which would break the external and domestic equilibrium.

We will first analyse a situation of external disequilibrium, but from a situation of fiscal and savings-investment equilibrium. In Figure 7.1, we depart from equilibrium. However, whether it be because of needs in servicing the external debt or because of a disequilibrium generated by autonomous capital inflows, now with the pair $[E', i']$ we find a trade deficit as long as $i'_d > i^*$. Evidently the situation is introduced by anti-inflationary policies. We can observe that any point to the left of *d* represents a situation of 'easier money', and points to the right represent greater astringency of means of payment. Thus, in the initial disequilibrium, we have a situation of excess demand in the commodities market, but curiously, we also have a situation of excess total savings. This means that if the monetary authority has implemented a restrictive monetary policy, given the availability of savings resources, the perception will be that there is no reason to reduce monetary astringency, but rather to accentuate it, either through an increase in the interest rate or a reduction of credit.

If there is price discrimination in the capital market, and in emerging markets in countries going through strong structural change there are likely to be, we have agents with the possibility of obtaining credit at a rate of i^* lower than the domestic rate, for example, export leader sectors.

Availability of resources obtained by these enterprises cannot affect the domestic interest rate, since pressure on the trade deficit and external savings remains. Accordingly, we now know that some agents will have the possibility of operating with an interest rate of i^* while others will have to accept price discrimination at a higher rate i_d. Paradoxically, the increase in the domestic interest rate leads to an excess in savings, which, under normal conditions, the banking system can turn into an incentive for overindebtedness in the economy as a whole.

Also, an increase in the domestic rate of interest causes an increase in public and private debt service, both domestic and external, and for this reason two possibilities arise. At the existing savings rate, the higher public debt service implies that total public spending increases to serve the debt, or that the autonomous component, $\gamma(Y)$, contracts. In the second case, the situation implies moving from G to G', so that, the restrictive adjustment is transformed into a lower income level or to a growing public deficit. If the source of disequilibrium remains, new flows of external capital will be necessary, so that monetary policy will now move to a new pair $[E'', i'']$. The result is that the external disequilibrium has become accentuated with two consequences: point c″ means that now a fiscal deficit has been caused, whose management, in order to reduce pressure on the interest rate, requires that domestic investment contracts. This contraction will come through a reduction in credit and income, and accordingly, a decrease in profits and investment opportunities. The combined result will be essentially recessive.

However, the general argument can be demonstrated by showing the impossibility of a solution through free market play. Accordingly, we can assume that the pair $[E', i']$ is established by the free flow of the capital market, and the Central Bank only passively follows its signal as in a floating rule. The main problem is not why capital flows are encouraged above the needs to refinance the external debt, or the primary deficit, as demonstrated in Cornford and Kregel (1996). The problem is whether the Central Bank has the capacity to stop the flow of capital or neutralize its impacts within the economy. As long as the capital flow continues, not only is there *no* reason for the disequilibrium to close, but it could even be encouraged and grow. Since the gap in the interest rate encourages a situation in which, despite an excess in total savings, the external savings gap continues to open, thus imposing greater flows of external financing.

Why does the Central Bank allow this? Or is it the case that it just cannot help it? Probably, to some extent the main determinant of its behavior is to obtain international liquidity at any cost, whether to cover the debt service or to finance the deficit in current account. The main problem is that the Central Bank, once engaged in a strategy for setting the exchange rate, in the event of a capital reversal flow, cannot step back without causing significant inflationary impacts.

The comparative statistic's of the situation that has been described shows that a recessive adjustment predominates, as is evidenced by the shift in investment and real public spending. The obvious question is whether the dynamic market adjustment process will correct the disequilibrium. The orthodox view stresses that the adjustment relies exclusively on the assumption that a zero fiscal balance and a very low inflation rate are necessary and sufficient conditions to create expectations for stability and growth. In McKinnon and Huw's argument (1995), the revaluation of real assets as related to financial assets, caused by an anti-inflationary policy, should be transformed into improved conditions for the valuation of real assets, leading to an increase in the investment rate. Financial liberalization, based on anti-inflationary policies, within that view, should thus lead to an increase in investment associated with an increase in savings. The difficulty is, as is recognized even by McKinnon, that such an adjustment demands the pre-existence of stability, particularly in the capital market. But stabilization policies, in fact, are accumulating pressure in the capital market. The difficulty then is that it shows circularity in his argument. But considering the view here developed, the essential difficulty is that such a stabilization program in fact turns disequilibria into a growing trade and fiscal deficit.

The second approach, introduces the dynamic path and might be very appealing, given that it can be represented in the realm of the monetary policy variables. The idea is to reflect the behavioral pattern of macroeconomic variables within the space of the variables that the Central Bank decides: [*w*, *E*, *i*], and a 'real variable' which is the result of the level and pace of economic activity, namely, the productivity of labor.

Our last expression is:

$$[s(\Lambda - W) - I(\lambda - w)] = [\tau(Y,r) - \gamma(Y) - i_d D_d^g - i_x D_x^g] + [\chi(Y^*, \lambda EP) - \mu(Y,, \lambda^*, EP^*)] \quad (7.7)$$

Reordering the system we have:

$$S_x(E,i) = [s(\pi) - I(\lambda - w)] = [\tau(Y,(\lambda - w)) - \lambda(Y) - i_d D_d^g - i_x D_x^g] + [\chi(Y^*, \lambda, EP) - \mu(Y,, \lambda^*, EP^*)] \quad (7.8)$$

or

$$= [\tau(Y,(\lambda - w)) - \gamma(Y) - i_d D_d^g - i_x D_x^g] + [\chi(Y^*) - \mu(Y)] + [\chi\lambda - \mu\lambda^*] + [\chi(EP) - \mu(EP^*)] \quad (7.9)$$

Therefore, for each deficit we can represent:

- The investment and savings function can be projected in the $\{\lambda - w\}$ space.
- The $I(\lambda - w)$ is a positive function in both parts of the argument, perhaps more flexible to increases in labor productivity. But both can also be expressed as closely related to income.

- The saving function $s(\Lambda - W) = s(\pi)$, relates to total income, therefore it can safely be related as a function of income: $S = s(Y)$.
- Tax revenue and government expenditure is reflected considering the debt service burden in the $\{w, i\}$ space.
- Tax revenue $\tau(Y, (\lambda - w))$ is a positive function in both elements in its argument, although as we have already established with a limit on the second.
- Expenditure considers two components, the first on income, $\gamma(Y)$ which is positive in its argument. The second part, which although is expressed as deduction, nevertheless its growth, for example due to rising rates of interest, $(i_d D_d^g + i_x D_x^g)$, exerts an overwhelming effect of reducing public consumption in order to keep fiscal balance.
- Exports and imports are reflected from the point of view of the movement of terms of trade and rate of exchange, for given levels of income, in the $\{E\ \lambda\}$ space, considering three different components:
- An income elasticity effect: $[\mu(Y)/\chi(Y^*)]$, which is a decreasing function to the rate of exchange and positive on the rate of productivity of labor, as in *Ye*.
- A productivity component that reflects real terms of trade, $[\chi,(\lambda)/\mu(\lambda^*)]$, which is a positive function on both parts of its argument; as in λ.

In a world where rates of exchange express actual productivity, these last two functions should be equal. Our view is that for small open economies they are not, and the real productivity is up to the nominal rate, representing then a loss in terms of trade.

Finally, the savings deficit, namely the demand for external savings appear in the $\{E, i\}$ space.

The initial position is conceived as a sort of 'equilibrium', where the whole system may well have a solution. This is possible because now the system works on 11 equations and has 11 unknowns. But it is clear that this is an oversimplifying representation, because our initial argument amounts to the fact that at least the investment function, the public expenditure functions, the debt burden function and the terms of trade function might not be linear at all.

Now let us assume the introduction of an anti-inflationary policy by the Central Bank, consisting of 'pegging' the rate of exchange and compensating with increases in the interest rate in order to bring the gap in the balance of trade and also serve the external debt (Figure 7.2).

The impact is straightforward. The increase in debt service brings a reduction of public consumption from γY_1 to γY_2 , and a reduction of the investment rate from $s(\pi_1)$ to $s(\pi_2)$. All this can occur with an excess of total savings, but

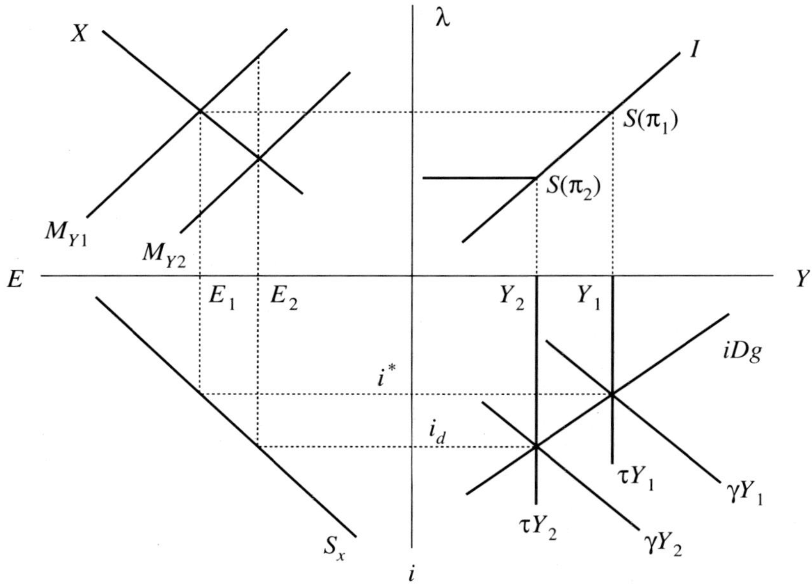

Figure 7.2 The dynamics of monetary policy and real effects

evidently with a lower income level. This excess of savings is produced by the flows of external savings at higher rates of interest, but with a smaller income effect on domestic savings. The adjustment then is necessarily on the level of income and employment, hindering on the possibilities to stimulate the growth of labor productivity.

But the external balance suffers for another far-reaching reason. At a lower rate of exchange the distance between the real (labor) terms of trade are far away from the nominal terms of trade at a particular income effect. The loss in terms of trade now is worse than at the first position. This has a perverse impact on the income level that widens the gap between real and nominal terms of trade.

If there is an affect on the price level it is through the recessive impact, and evidently at a lower income level. Except for one possibility. If the owners of capital observe the interest rate as something that reflects inflationary expectations, the adjustment described before might produce an opposite effect, inducing the expectation of a higher inflation rate, that nevertheless remains 'repressed' in so far as the flow of external capital allows it.

TENTATIVE CONCLUSIONS: MONETARY RULE VS. GROWTH, OR THE 'CATCH 22' SYNDROME

Orthodox literature insists that recent financial crises are rooted in the phenomena of overindebtedness generated by the simultaneous implementation of processes of structural change and financial liberalization. A priori, any difficulty is to be attributed to lack of fiscal and monetary discipline. Nothing is more illustrative of this than the recent Argentine debacle.

The model here advanced allows the refutation of both ideas, since both overlook the basic nature of the relationship between domestic and external disequilibrium and the characteristics that structural change in progress has created. The core of structural change rests on the particular characteristics of monetary policy, which turns out to be decisive for the operation of the whole model.

Ironically, the search for stability through monetary restraint and fiscal discipline may well lead to induce external and fiscal disequilibria through the excess of saving. Although this fact is somehow recognized, it is not identified theoretically, because the standard model cannot treat it properly.

We have stressed the passive nature of fiscal policy, tied to maintain a balanced budget, and the decisive role that monetary policy plays. The result is that, through free market play, economies with these characteristics systematically enter into processes of recurrent and accumulative destabilization. The recessive drive pervades the economy and makes it extremely vulnerable. We find the origin of this instability in the ambiguous impact generated by the present monetary policy model on the various economic actors.

It is important to observe that our argument is not a call for irresponsible fiscal deficits or monetary chaos. All we have shown is that the search for stability through the orthodox recipe seems to be contradictory in its own terms. To the early examples of the 1990s now has to be added the Argentinean collapse, obsessively looking for fiscal balance. As in the paradox of 'Catch 22', every time fiscal balance was achieved, the conditions for its destruction would come about through the reduction of output and employment, and consequently on tax collection. Fiscal crisis was another consequence of the full operation of the model. Over 20 per cent of open unemployment was the limit that Argentineans accepted, but the social cost of the real and financial collapse will be considerably higher.

The most important consequence is that the operation of standard stabilization models, even when rigorously observing the condition of fiscal equilibrium as a base for macroeconomic stability, necessarily leads to a collapse of the fiscal equilibrium and cannot generate conditions for its endogenous stabilization. Furthermore, we see that the fiscal and external disequilibria continue to worsen as income contracts.

Based on the factors considered, with no consideration of dynamic growth impacts, the essential nature of the monetary policy model is not reduced to its recessive drive. Its negative impacts on the investment rate and, accordingly, on loan recovery conditions for banks is reinforced by an increase in the total availability of savings in the economy. These savings, however, have limited possibilities for use in productive investment. The paradox is that the availability of total savings will be higher than the need for savings for investment and for financing the public deficit, because it is obtained through a very high interest rate. The result is the impossibility of loan recovery, which bankrupts the financial system.

Another important result is that now the relationship between the price level and the exchange rate is clearer. If the nominal interest rate incorporates inflationary expectations, it is not possible to reduce inflation by pegging the exchange rate E.

If pegging E is achieved at the cost of a loss in terms of exchange, it will not be able to have a full impact on lowering the price level, except by strangling productive sectors that otherwise may well be competitive.

In the most general sense, we can see that the problem is not reduced to exchange rate policy. The difficulty is not flexible exchange rates against fixed exchange rates. The issue is the conception of monetary policy as a whole, in terms of trade, savings, industrial and fiscal policy, and evidently the way in which institutions can manage the growth and structural change process coherently.

Under the current monetary policy model, it is impossible to avoid a reduction in domestic savings, a reduction in the real investment rate and the generation of a fiscal deficit. A growing service on internal and external debt closes the grip, making long-term growth and development policies inconceivable. All of this can occur with a condition of total savings in excess of investment.

A fundamental criticism is that macroeconomic stability cannot be postulated as null fiscal deficit and zero inflation. The trouble is that it is just meaningless. Nominal stability cannot be pondered at the cost of the level of income and a loss in terms of trade and employment. The lower part of Figure 7.2 is concerned with the usual 'macroeconomic fundamentals'. But its fulfilment cannot make 'essential productive and investment' fundamentals in the upper half of the figure.

An alternative policy framework would have to consider the following ideas:

1. A complete reconsideration of the role of central banks. These institutions must come to terms with the idea that monetary policy cannot be neutral in any single form. A full consideration of non-neutrality must

give way to policies where central banks are fully responsible for the real effects of monetary policy, particularly on growth and employment.
2. Instead of giving away central banks, as with the models of 'dollarization' or the creation of 'monetary councils', there needs to be a neat intervention by central banks to consider and manage the common impacts on structural change on growth. Small open economies require stronger institutions, not giving them away because they are not 'efficient'.
3. To stop the growth of public debts on account of private deficits, which has turned fiscal policy meaningless. Growth and structural change demand the possibility of active fiscal policies in accordance with monetary and financial policies for growth.
4. Monetary policy should not lead to loss of control on capital flows over their real needs. Growth based on external savings and excess expending create conditions for financial fragility and lower growth.
5. The current emphasis on anti-inflationary policies should be avoided, in so far as in a recessive environment, this creates conditions to prompt payments and a fiscal crisis which are far more disruptive.

NOTES

1. Hahn and Solow (1998) argue that for current orthodox macroeconomics has come to a point where two essential economic problems appear as 'illegitimate facts', namely, inflation and unemployment.
2. Current literature has an abundant description on most of these issues as in Edwards (1997; 1999), Feldstein (1999) and Krugman (1997).
3. See Pentecost (1993).
4. This is an important issue on which we take the discussion as in Davidson (1994) or Snowdon, Vane and Wynarczyk (1996), but we will not take the discussion here.
5. See Blinder (1998), Wray (1998) and Davidson (1994).
6. See Cornford and Kregel (1996).
7. It would also be pointless to go into the discussion of the scope of 'General Equilibrium' models.

REFERENCES

Blinder, Alan (1998), *Central Banking in Theory and Practice*, Cambridge, MA: MIT Press.

Cornford, A., and Kregel J. (1996), 'Globalization, capital flows and international regulation', Jerome Levy Economics Institute working paper no. 6, Washington, DC.

Davidson, Paul (1994), *Post Keynesian Macroeconomic Theory*, Aldershot, UK and Brookfield, US: Edward Elgar.

Edwards, S. (1997), 'Exchange rates, inflation, disinflation: Latin American experiences' in S. Edwards (ed.), *Capital Controls, Exchange Rates and Monetary Policy in the World Economy*, Cambridge, MA: Cambridge University Press.

Edwards, S. (1999), 'Capital flows to Latin America', in M. Feldstein (ed.), *International Capital Flows*, Chicago, IL: University of Chicago Press, NBER.

Feldstein, M. (1999), *International Capital Flows*, Chicago, IL: University of Chicago Press, NBER.

Hahn, F., and Solow, R. (1998), *A Critical Essay on Modern Macroeconomic Theory*, Oxford: Blackwell.

Hicks, J. (1980–81), 'ISLM: an explanation', *Journal of Post Keynesian Economics*, **3** (2), 139–54.

Krugman, Paul (1997), *Currencies and Crises*, Cambridge, MA: MIT Press.

McKinnon, R., and Pill Huw (1995), 'Credible liberalizations and international capital flows', mimeo, Stanford University, Department of Economics.

Mundell, R. (1997), 'Stabilization and liberalization policies in semi-open economies', in S. Edwards (ed.), *Capital Controls, Exchange Rates and Monetary Policy in the World Economy*, Cambridge, MA: Cambridge University Press.

Ortiz, Etelberto (1997), 'Disequilibrium pricing, critical equilibrium and the real cycle', in P. Davidson and J. Kregel (eds), *Improving the Global Economy*, Cheltenham, UK and Lyme, USA: Edward Elgar.

Ortiz, E. (1997a), 'El cambio estructural en México y las empresas pequeñas y medianas', *Comercio Exterior*, **47** (1), 16–26.

Ortiz, E. (1997b), 'Políticas de Cambio Estructural, política cambiaria y distorsiones entre costos sociales y privados', *Economía Teoría y Práctica, Nueva Época. Num 7*, México: UAM.

Ortiz, E., and Sima Motamen (1998), 'Successful integration and economic distress: the case of Mexico in NAFTA', in Christos Paraskevopoulos (ed.), *Global Trading Arrangements in Transition*, Cheltenham, UK and Lyme, USA: Edward Elgar.

Ortiz E. (1998), 'Déficit Privado, Financiamiento del Desarrollo e Inestabilidad en México', *Comercio Exterior*, **48** (6), 461–72.

Ortiz, E. (2002), 'Formación de precios, inflación y política monetaria en una economía pequeña y abierta', in Guadalupe Mántey y Noemi Lévy (ed.), *Globalización financiera e integración monetaria. una perspectiva desde los países en desarrollo*, México: Edit Porrua-UNAM.

Pentecost, Eric (1993), *Exchange Rate Dynamics*, Aldershot, UK and Brookfield, US: Edward Elgar.

Prebish, Raúl (1962), 'The economic development of Latin America and its principal problems', *Economic Bulletin for Latin America*, **7** (February), 1–22, New York, ECLA, United Nations.

Ros, J. (2000), 'Employment, structural adjustment and sustainable growth in Mexico', *Journal of Development Studies*, **36** (4), 100–19.

Snowdon, B., H. Vane, and P. Wynarczyk (1996), *A modern Guide to Macroeconomics*, Aldershot, UK and Brookfield, US: Edward Elgar.

Wray, Randal (1998), *Understanding Modern Money: The Key to Full Employment and Price Stability*, Cheltenham, UK and Lyme, USA: Edward Elgar.

8. Mexico: strong currency and weak economy

Arturo Huerta

THE IMPORTANCE OF NOMINAL EXCHANGE RATE STABILITY IN THE CONTEXT OF FINANCIAL LIBERALIZATION

Financial liberalization, free capital mobility and the resulting internationalization of capital markets have increased the importance of managing the exchange rate. With currency devaluation in emerging market economies, financial investments lose in dollar terms; but with nominal exchange rate stability and appreciation they gain through increased profits in dollar terms. Exchange rate determination, therefore, becomes subordinated to the demands of international financial capital. Governments and central banks in emerging market economies are forced to work towards low inflation and to equalize their inflation with that of developed countries. The emphasis on inflation is forced upon them in order to avoid shocks in nominal exchange rate parity and to safeguard profitability conditions for international financial capital, thereby ensuring a positive capital flow to these countries. Exchange rate stability also becomes necessary in order to avoid speculative practices that are likely to cause instability in financial markets.

POLICIES TO ACHIEVE EXCHANGE RATE STABILITY

The Latin American economies do not have the macroeconomic, productive and domestic financial conditions to lower inflation *and* achieve nominal exchange rate stability via traditional means. Countries with low productivity and strong pressure on their macroeconomic fundamentals have been able to lower inflation through promoting capital inflow. They are then able to cover their current account deficit and increase international reserves in order to face attacks from fluctuations in international financial markets and to ensure nominal exchange rate stability and free convertibility. As a result, this policy broadens foreign capital's sphere of influence at the national level. Foreign capital demands policies related to accelerating liberalization, deregulating the economy, privatizing, increasing foreign influence on national assets and establishing conditions of profitability and confidence. A United Nations Conference on Trade and Development (UNCTAD) report says, 'it may be very difficult for any single country to resist the strong trend towards liberalization of capital movement if it has close links with international markets through FDI and trade flows' (UNCTAD, 2001, p. 110).

In order to achieve the macroeconomic performance that ensures exchange rate stability, Latin American governments give priority to restrictionist fiscal and monetary policies, convinced that they will prevent demand pressures on prices, the external sector and public finances. Sustained by a decrease in public expenditure and the privatization of public assets, fiscal discipline expands investment boundaries to private national and foreign capital, thus promoting capital inflow. Accompanying this process, the central bank gives exclusive priority to restrictionist policies through high interest rates that are aimed to increase financial profitability to draw capital. Carsten Hefeker's stance defends these positions by saying that 'in order to achieve credibility, monetary policy rules are required to prevent inconsistent policies. Fixed exchange rates are seen as an obligatory compromise' (Hefeker, 2000, p. 162).

EXCHANGE RATE APPRECIATION POLICY AND EXTERNAL FINANCING

Anchoring the exchange rate, high interest rates, fiscal discipline and the increasing takeover of national assets by foreign capital are all policies that are essential to promoting capital inflow. They create the financing pattern that allows globalization, brings about exchange rate stability and lowers inflation. In relation to this, María Concepción Tavares states that 'overvaluing the exchange rate is a typical sign of a model to finance a monetary pattern through external indebtedness' (Tavares, 1999, p. 66).

The conjunction of external factors and so-called market-oriented structural reforms (that have increased profitability and scope of influence for international capital) has facilitated financing to lower inflation in the Latin American economies. The US economic dynamic in the nineties played an important role in the flow of foreign exchange to Mexico through both the growth of exports to the USA and greater capital inflow due to created growth expectations. This acted in favor of nominal exchange rate stability.

When an economy presents a fixed or stable exchange rate together with growth expectations, it draws capital, thus generating stock market booms that stimulate greater capital inflow into these markets. This increases the supply of foreign exchange, which appreciates national currencies and lowers inflation. Since external factors play an essential role in nominal exchange rate stability, it becomes highly vulnerable to the behavior of these factors.

THE EXCHANGE RATE DISSOCIATED FROM THE PURCHASING POWER PARITY PRINCIPLE AND FROM ADJUSTMENT OF THE FOREIGN TRADE BALANCE

Economic policy is circumscribed to reaching the goal of lowering inflation through nominal exchange rate stability (or appreciation). Thus, a country abandons its active exchange rate policy (which is flexible with regard to the internal versus external price differential) in order to adjust its trade balance. The free capital mobility, capital market internationalization and increasing capital inflow required by the Latin American economies hinder the active use of the exchange rate. This dissociates it from the purchasing power parity principle since the exchange rate does not align with price differentials, which is required in order to guarantee the law of a single price needed for tradable goods to maintain the same price in both countries. This alignment also counteracts productivity differentials both to protect and develop the national productive plant vis-à-vis imports, improves the accumulation dynamic of national firms and decreases the trade deficit and dependence on capital inflow.

In spite of pressure on the trade balance, the Mexican government has defended nominal exchange rate stability. Table 8.1 shows exchange rate

Table 8.1 Nominal and real exchange rate (December 1996 = 100)

	1996	1997	1998	1999	2000	2001
Nominal exchange rate (ER)	7.876	8.136	9.912	9.415	9.444	9.146**
Real ER	7.876	8.962	10.461	11.443	12.05	12.029
ER appreciation %	0	10.15	5.54	21.53	27.70	31.51

Notes:
* December each year.
** May 2001.
Real exchange rate = Nominal ER * (Mexican prices/US prices).

Source: Banco de México, Indicadores Económicos; US Department of Labor, Bureau of Labor Statistics.

appreciation of around 31 percent (accumulated percentage) since 1996 to mid-2001. The trade balance, however, went from a surplus of 6831 million dollars in 1996 to a deficit of 8049 million dollars in the year 2000. The surplus of the balance of payments capital account went from 4069 million dollars to 17 920 million dollars in the same period.

By facing the current account deficit through a surplus of the balance of payments capital account, nominal exchange rate stability and the high interest rate policy become essential to develop the financial market and enable capital inflow. In fact, exchange rate depreciation will not adjust the foreign trade balance sufficiently in order to reach the necessary trade surplus to finance the payment of the foreign debt service. (In Mexico, by the end of 1994 and at the beginning of 1995, the exchange rate was devalued in order to adjust the foreign deficit, and the trade surplus that was reached, approximately $7 billion, did not suffice to finance the debt service payment that reached close to $14 billion) (Huerta, 1997).

THE FLEXIBLE EXCHANGE RATE AND ITS APPRECIATION

After the fixed exchange rate led Mexico and other countries to exchange rate crises, a flexible exchange rate was chosen with the idea that it was the best alternative to adjust the foreign sector, face fluctuations in international financial markets and avoid financial and exchange rate crises. Those who defend this exchange rate regime claim that it allows economic policy-makers a greater margin of flexibility both to reduce interest rates and increase money supply and public expenditure for growth. In the context of financial liberalization, however, the floating exchange rate does not take place around the internal versus external price differential that is necessary (at least in principle) to avoid distortions in the external sector. Although the government claims that it is working with a flexible exchange rate, actual free floating does not take place.

Exchange rate flexibility depends on the behavior of supply and demand for foreign exchange. The government therefore formulates economic policies aimed at increasing foreign exchange supply and reducing foreign exchange demand, thereby assuring a high enough surplus of the balance of payments capital account to maintain nominal exchange rate stability and its appreciation. This approach explains why financial liberalization is accompanied by fiscal discipline policies (sustained by cutbacks in expenditure and the sale of public firms), conservative management of the money supply, high interest rates, permanent privatization processes and increasing foreign influence in the economy. These policies ease the pressure of demand on prices and the external sector as well as on the demand for foreign exchange. In turn, these policies stimulate capital inflow, and increase foreign exchange supply.

Even though a government decides in favor of a flexible exchange rate, the same economic policies prevailing under the fixed exchange rate regime continue operating. Economic policy management, therefore, does have the margin of freedom that flexible exchange rate proponents offer. The IMF, the World Bank and the US Federal Reserve are constantly propping up the national currencies of Mexico and other large Latin American countries by paying their foreign debt through the transference of financial resources. By ensuring capital flow, the monetary and fiscal authorities no longer adjust the exchange rate around the internal versus external price differential in order to adjust the trade deficit. Instead, they create an appreciated exchange rate that maintains latent pressures on this deficit.

Exchange rate appreciation places national production at a competitive disadvantage vis-à-vis imports, which acts against the companies' accumulation dynamic. It decapitalizes them, increases unemployment, increases the levels of internal and external indebtedness, and increases insolvency and banking instability. It also increases the trade deficit, which eventually depreciates the national currency. Cardim de Carvalho et al. say that 'instead of producing convergence, fixed exchange rates ... produce divergence among the situations of the economies in the region' (Cardim et al., 2001, p. 451). These policies accentuate the differences in competitiveness in detriment to the countries that establish them, affecting their accumulation dynamic and therefore investment growth. This result shows the high cost of adjusting the external sector through capital inflow.

PRICE STABILITY AND INTEREST RATE

The monetary authorities introduced the goal of lower inflation under the precept that it would reduce the interest rate, thus promoting both the investment dynamic and the economy. The prevailing exchange rate regime, however, has not allowed a discretionary management of the internal interest rate favoring growth due to the fact that the achieved exchange rate flexibility was, in actuality, obtained from the behavior of the supply and demand for foreign exchange where the interest rate plays an active role. The prevalence of high interest rates is due to the financial and short-term nature of the prevailing capital that flows into the country. Although in the second half of the year 2001, the interest rate in Mexico came down significantly in relation to the previous year (from 18 per cent at the end of the year 2000 to 7 per cent at the beginning of November 2001), it continues to maintain an attractive real margin in relation to the interest rate in the USA (that in real terms was below 1 per cent in November 2001).

The prevailing exchange rate policy maintains latent pressure on the external deficit, which forces the government to establish high real interest rates in order to avoid capital flight and continue drawing capital to finance the deficit. These forces lead to a vicious circle that takes the country to higher levels of external indebtedness and an increased presence of international financial capital in all national markets. The problem is that the increase in the interest rates forced by nominal exchange rate stability impacts public and private finances, as well as the productive sector, the banking system and the external sector. This situation continues demanding high interest rates in order to draw capital to finance these imbalances. High interest rates restrict and raise the cost of productive investment and productivity growth, which places national production at a greater disadvantage vis-à-vis imports; not to mention that exchange rate appreciation and high internal interest rates lead companies to search for external financing since it is less costly. The private sector has thus significantly increased its external debt.

The interest and exchange rates cannot respond to domestic financial and growth needs, but instead are established in response to capital inflow needs. Basil Moore states that 'the higher and lower limits – of the internal exchange rate – will depend on the level of the world interest rate, the level of the internal exchange rate and the size and openness of the domestic economy, where interest rate differentials induce international capital flows in the exchange markets' (Moore, 1988, p. 380). Along the same lines, María Concepción Tavares says, 'we are prisoners of the interest and exchange rates and depend more on the fluctuations of financial markets' (Tavares, 1999, p. 22). Since the interest rate does not accompany the lowering of inflation, capital inflow continues and nominal exchange rate adjusts even less to the internal versus external price differential. The problems of low accumulation dynamic and insolvency continue, as well as pressures on the foreign trade balance and the increasing requirements of capital inflow, thus maintaining exchange rate risk.

MEXICO ATTEMPTS TO LEVEL ITS INFLATION WITH INFLATION IN DEVELOPED COUNTRIES

Mexico aims to equalize its inflation with that of the USA in order to avoid losing competitiveness. The drawback is that it intends to do this through stabilizing the exchange rate in nominal terms. With this exchange rate parity, Mexico imports low inflation from the USA, its main trade partner, mainly through tradable goods. However, the domestic prices of non-tradable goods, the goods that explain the internal versus external price differential, continue increasing. This way of reducing inflation turns out to be costly and counterproductive for Mexico. However much this exchange policy lowers inflation, Mexico's competitiveness in relation to the USA will never improve. This results in a higher trade deficit, a lower capital accumulation dynamic and greater external vulnerability.

INTERNATIONAL RESERVES AND EXCHANGE RATE STABILITY

Mexico is forced to ensure large amounts of international reserves in order to meet the demand for foreign exchange and to consolidate nominal exchange rate stability. Mexico gives priority to contractionary monetary, credit and fiscal policies in order to keep the foreign deficit from increasing and pressuring the reserves. High interest rates are important to ensure permanent capital flow with which to finance the current account deficit. International reserves increase at the cost of high interest rates, contracting economic activity, maintaining latent liquidity and insolvency problems, and increasing foreign influence over the country's economy. The high cost of exchange rate stability is once again noted. The UNCTAD report notes that 'maintaining a high level of reserves for this purpose would be a very expensive way of securing insurance against financial panic' (UNCTAD, 2001, p. 111).

In the context of globalization, monetary policy links the money supply to the amount of the international reserves in order to ensure convertibility and confidence in exchange rate stability. This policy subscribes to the theory that associates the balance of payments with the money supply and attributes the problems of the balance of payments to expansionist behavior. Attempts are thus made to ease pressure on the external sector and international reserves through contractionary fiscal and monetary policies. The increase in international reserves, via an increase in the interest rate, is also accompanied by an increase in the domestic public debt, which ends up by pressuring public finances.

However much the Latin American governments attempt to maintain higher international reserves, protection from external shocks and nominal exchange rate stability is not completely ensured; since it depends not only on the amount of the reserves, but to a large extent on its composition. It makes a difference whether the reserves are constituted by resources derived from a surplus in the balance of payments current account or from a surplus in the capital account. Capital inflow constituted by long-term resources is also different from capital inflow constituted by highly speculative short-term capital. Besides, it is not the amount of the international reserves that determines exchange rate stability, but, as Tavares notes, 'the viability of resisting an attack against currency depends on the capacity to ensure an uninterrupted and sufficiently large foreign exchange flow congruent with our cash needs' (Tavares, 1999, p. 67). The problem with Mexico and the rest of Latin America is that permanent capital inflow has not been ensured due to their internal problems (that is, high deficit of the external sector and high levels of indebtedness) that end up by dissimulating capital flow, adding to the instability of both the economy and international markets. When international reserves are insufficient to calm speculative demand for foreign exchange, nominal exchange rate stability comes to an end and gives way to an increase in the real exchange rate as well as to a drop in the capital market (stock market crash), creating a context of insolvency, depreciated assets, banking instability and financial crisis.

NOMINAL EXCHANGE RATE STABILITY AND CONTRACTIONARY POLICIES

When the economy is left to the free movement of goods and capital, and exchange rate appreciation prevails, pressure on the external sector deficit increases. In order to prevent an aggravation of the external sector deficit that would upset the exchange rate and encourage speculative action, the monetary authorities give priority to permanent monetary, credit, fiscal and wage adjustments to ease the pressure of the domestic demand, making the economy depend on the external demand. The fiscal policy has been subordinated to play an important role in nominal exchange rate stability and in promoting capital inflow. Fiscal cutbacks and the privatization of public firms are carried out in order to reduce the amount of the public debt and achieve fiscal discipline with the goal of creating confidence in price and exchange rate stability so as to draw capital to finance the existing deficits.

The Latin American governments, particularly the Mexican government, prefer to give priority to these policies in spite of their recessive effects, rather than devalue and reformulate the prevailing economic policy. They consider that reducing the real interest rate differential and expanding the monetary and exchange rate policy would cause greater harm to the economy, because capital markets would destabilize and invested capital would devalue. This would encourage heavy capital outflow that would decapitalize the economy, leading to monetary problems and to a greater vulnerability within the international financial system.

In the context of globalization, monetary and fiscal policies cannot be dissociated from the goal of reaching nominal exchange rate stability. By increasingly depending on capital inflow in order to ensure nominal exchange rate stability,

Mexico no longer has an economic policy to face national productive issues and increase the domestic market, productivity, import substitution and the national content of exports. Prevailing policies, however, do not achieve the desired monetary stability. What they do achieve is nominal exchange rate stability, which is far from being monetarily stable. If monetary stability were attained, monetary, credit and fiscal restrictions would not prevail, nor would placing government bonds at high interest rates to draw capital in order to increase the reserves to finance nominal exchange rate stability.

If monetary stability is not attained, it is not due to the lack of discipline in the implemented policies, but a consequence of the contradictions of these policies, which act against the productive, financial and macroeconomic conditions that are necessary for monetary stability. Tavares states that

> anti-inflation policy is intended to defeat inflation, but not to ensure macroeconomic stability. Abrupt opening of the economy, overvaluing the exchange rate, and a high interest rate are aimed to ensure prices at any cost, but they destabilize the other macroeconomic variables (activity level, consumption, investment and balance of payments) and dismantle part of industry and agriculture without making them more competitive.
>
> (Tavares, 1997, p. 15)

Sooner or later, this situation comes to an end, compromising the conditions of confidence and the exchange rate stability financial liberalization demands. It thus tends to generate negative expectations that curb capital inflow and encourage capital outflow, leading to a crisis.

THE EXCHANGE RATE IS A MACRO PRICE AND ITS DISTORTION THEREFORE HAS STRONG IMPLICATIONS

The exchange rate reflects the relation between internal and external prices. In the context of an open economy, it therefore represents the economy's main price; since the protection of production, national employment vis-à-vis external employment, the accumulation dynamic and capitalization levels in the productive sphere to a certain extent depend on it. Eatwell and Taylor state that 'a change in the exchange rate will affect the internal prices of all tradable goods. In this sense, the exchange rate is a macro price' (Eatwell and Taylor, 2000, p. 70). This variable is crucial to the adjustment of the external sector, to the value of both productive and financial assets and liabilities, as well as to the stability of the banking sector. Its determination and management therefore cannot be left in hands of free-market forces commanded by international financial capital. It must instead respond to the macroeconomic needs for sustained growth.

Nominal exchange rate stability and its resulting appreciation have been used to lower inflation. The fact that national currency parity in relation to the dollar moves below inflation and the differential between internal and external inflation (inflation in the USA, our main trade partner) determines a relative price distortion imported goods are favored in detriment to national products, which have a higher cost structure than imported goods given lower productivity levels in relation to imported goods. The accumulation dynamic, together with the growth of national production and employment, are therefore constrained to the productive sphere. Productive chains are destroyed and the levels of indebtedness as well as the trade deficit increase, which leads us to a greater dependence on capital inflow.

Exchange rate appreciation, high interest rates and fiscal discipline distort profits, thus altering the economic structure. They affect the productive sphere in favor of capital markets and money. This makes most capital inflows gravitate toward the non-productive sector and re-create financial and speculative actions in detriment to sustained growth.

EXCHANGE RATE APPRECIATION AND MANUFACTURED GOODS EXPORTS

The exchange rate that is appreciated in order to favor capital inflow affects the growth of national exports (particularly of firms that are not integrated into the US economy) and reduces the national component in exports. It favors exports by transnational corporations located in Mexico since it allows them to reduce the costs of the inputs they import (mainly from Asia), thus improving their competitiveness to export to the USA with a low national added value. Exchange rate appreciation in Mexico also favors US exports to Mexico since it increases the competitiveness of US products in relation to Mexican products.

NOMINAL EXCHANGE RATE STABILITY AND LOWERING INFLATION DO NOT PROMOTE INVESTMENT AND GROWTH

Inflation is commonly accused of causing a loss of competitiveness as well as the resulting external trade deficits and financial instability. These problems, however, currently emerge in the context of low inflation that has been based on contractionary policies and exchange rate appreciation, which affect productive plant competitiveness and capitalization, increase the trade deficit, create insolvency problems, increase the instability of the banking sector and put undue pressure on public finances. This contradicts the position held by conventional theory which notes that exchange rate stability and the lowering of inflation are a better option to promote investment and growth. In contrast, managing the exchange rate through devaluation creates a context of exchange rate uncertainty in which the future exchange rate is also uncertain. This leads agents to postpone their investment decisions and re-create speculative practices. Nevertheless, policies related to fiscal and monetary restriction and nominal exchange rate stability, in spite of being aimed to ensure the certainty of stability and profitability for financial capital, do not represent a better option to stimulate the investment decisions agents make in the productive sphere. Instead, they contract the domestic market, decrease the accumulation dynamic, cause higher levels of internal and external overindebtedness, as well as insolvency, credit restriction and deficits in the external sector, which thus reverts to the detriment of the desired monetary stability and economic growth.

EXCHANGE RATE AND EXPECTATIONS

The expected exchange rate is determined by capital flows that finance the external gap and increase the amount of the international reserves. Its behavior is related to the economic growth expectations and the behavior of economic fundamentals, from the perspective of whether they guarantee exchange rate stability and the reimbursement of the yields this capital expects. Other important elements in the behavior of capital flow are the privatization process and the behavior of the capital market.

The stock market boom encourages greater capital inflow, thus appreciating the currency even more. This contributes to a lowering of inflation and a greater availability of credit (so long as capital inflow is enough to generate growth expectations). However, in underdeveloped countries, these elements precede any financial, exchange rate and banking crisis. Exchange rate appreciation, on the one hand, increases the external sector deficit and, on the other, affects the accumulation dynamic, which increases the levels of overindebtedness in firms and generates insolvency problems that destabilize the banking sector. Credit is then restricted, giving rise to pressure on public finances. This ends by changing the agents' expectations. Capital outflow causes a stock market crash, which is accompanied by a devaluation of the exchange rate. Both crises accentuate the instability of the banking sector, due to capital depreciation, the high interest rates that are established in order to curb capital outflow, and the contraction of economic activity and income that results. All this generates insolvency problems.

Even though the implemented economic policy may not succeed in ensuring macroeconomic balance, capital may nevertheless continue flowing to the economies provided that they establish high interest rates, carry out budget cutbacks and tax increases aimed at reducing the fiscal and trade deficits, and accelerate the privatization process and foreign takeover of attractive assets. This situation makes the economy capable of working with an appreciated exchange rate in spite of the external imbalance. This is possible thanks to capital inflow that finances the appreciated exchange rate and increases international reserves. Expectations of exchange rate stability are created, which may change when stability and reimbursement conditions are no longer perceived. J. Pinto de Andrade and M.L. Façao Silva state that 'ex-post devaluation of the domestic currency by the government depends on the expectations of private agents and the latter depends on the credibility associated with government policies' (Andrade and Silva, 1999, p. 317).

When the economy no longer offers stable macroeconomic conditions (in public finances and the external sector) by being unable to pay yields corresponding to the invested capital, having difficulties in deepening the privatization process as well as the foreign takeover of strategic assets or in offering or granting them as a guarantee to international capital, the latter changes its expectations about the country. Mario Presser claims that 'even when the need to mitigate exchange rate volatility is acknowledged, in an atmosphere of high capital mobility the instruments used to attend to the objectives that are causing conflict are discovered to be insufficient' (Presser, 2000, p. 38).

COST OF EXCHANGE RATE STABILITY

Financial liberalization, nominal exchange rate stability and currency convertibility are turning out to have a high cost for Mexico since it does not have a monetary, credit and fiscal policy for sustained and generalized growth. Industry has been reduced, the agricultural sector has been reduced and the banking system does not grant credit. We have fewer national assets, a higher internal and external debt, and we are vulnerable in relation to international events. Giving priority to capital inflow as the financing pattern condemns Mexico to contractionary policies and appreciated exchange rate parities results in the loss of the national production competitiveness as well as the permanent sacrifice of the national patrimony owing to the expansion of profitability and the sphere of influence of foreign capital. The greater the pressure on the economic fundamentals, the more it costs the government to maintain nominal exchange rate stability since it is forced to grant or transfer greater concessions and assets to international capital.

Mexican firms have had to search for international partners in order to achieve levels of liquidity and capitalization to remain in the market. Large firms that offer higher expectation of profitability are mainly involved in this process. The exchange rate policy thus generates a patrimonial adjustment favoring international capital. The process through which both firms and assets fall under foreign influence represents a high cost; since it implies an economic liberalization policy and nominal exchange rate stability, which instead of generating endogenous conditions for growth, creates backwardness and vulnerability.

CURRENCY APPRECIATION AND BUSINESS AND FAMILY INCOMES

Eatwell and Taylor note that 'weak currency tends to reduce real income flow and real wealth in families and businesses' (Eatwell and Taylor, 2000, p. 74). It should be explained that this is applicable if businesses and families have financial assets since these assets lose value with currency devaluation and non-inflation-adjusted wages. However, if the currency is appreciated ('strong'), it affects the incomes and wealth of businesses and families located in the productive sphere due to the loss of competitiveness and to the negative consequences derived from contractionary policies and the high interest rate accompanying exchange rate appreciation. Anti-inflation policies reduce business profits and individual incomes. It is therefore no use to increase the purchasing power of the Mexican peso in relation to the dollar, if business and family incomes with which goods are purchased are reduced, thus overall affecting Mexican goods.

In the face of the impossibility of using the exchange rate policy to improve national production competitiveness and to adjust the foreign trade balance, the Mexican authorities have told business people that if they want to improve competitiveness, they have to adjust wages. The purpose of decreasing real wages is to counter the profit problems exchange rate appreciation generates and to lower domestic inflation even more to avoid greater exchange rate appreciation and greater loss of competitiveness. The drop of real wages has nevertheless allowed Mexico to continue with exchange rate appreciation without counteracting the negative effects exchange rate parity causes. Exchange rate adjustment is simply postponed at the cost of a greater impoverishment of the population.

Productivity differentials between the USA and Mexico largely favor the USA. In spite of low wages in Mexico, this does not improve its competitiveness nor the situation of the external sector. The decrease in real wages does not therefore encourage a greater economic dynamic, but to the contrary, leads the Mexican economy into a vicious circle by contracting the growth of the domestic market even more and making it become more dependent on exports and the US dynamic. Over 85 per cent of total Mexican exports go to the USA, which makes Mexico highly vulnerable to the behavior of the US economy.

CAPITAL INFLOW DOES NOT COUNTERACT THE NEGATIVE EFFECTS GENERATED BY THE POLICY THAT PROMOTES IT

Capital inflow does not counteract the problems derived from the policy aimed to promote it, such as the contraction of the domestic market, decapitalization of the productive sphere and insolvency, all of which restrict credit availability. Capital inflow generally flows to the financial sphere or is associated with exports or buying national enterprises. Capital inflow has not improved the productive sphere or insolvency in the banking sector. Neither has it improved public finances or the public sector. On the contrary, the policy formulated to favor capital inflow has acted in detriment to these sectors, which places us in a situation of higher external vulnerability and hinders sustained growth.

ECONOMIC LIBERALIZATION DOES NOT ENSURE THE MACROECONOMIC CONDITIONS TO MAINTAIN THE EXCHANGE RATE STABILITY IT REQUIRES

Working with nominal exchange rate stability demands a foreign trade surplus and/or large capital inflows and international reserves, in order for the economy to face the external shocks emerging in international markets. The context of economic liberalization in which Mexico and the other Latin American economies operate, does not create a foreign trade surplus that can reimburse external financial obligations; nor does it ensure conditions of confidence for permanent capital flow that allows the external imbalance and nominal exchange rate stability to be financed.

Currency appreciation, together with the contraction of the domestic market, reduces tax collection. Firms increase their levels of overindebtedness and re-create insolvency problems and instability in the banking sector. The government must transfer resources to that sector, thus increasing public debt and pressure on public finances, which are also affected due to the increase in public debt derived from sterilizing capital inflow. The high interest rates established to ensure capital inflow for exchange rate stability, upsets public finances and re-creates the problems the national banking sector faces, which in turn contracts investment growth.

The external sector faces pressure as a consequence of the exchange rate policy, the opening of trade, and restrictionist anti-inflation policies (related to monetary, credit and fiscal issues). As opposed to what conventional theory claims, the current account deficit is not derived from monetary and fiscal expansion. On the contrary, prevailing contractionary monetary and fiscal policies, together with high interest rates act in favor of capital inflow, thus appreciating the exchange rate. This reduces competitiveness and affects the productive sphere, thus increasing pressure on the trade balance.

Pressure on public finances, the external sector and the banking system combined with the vulnerable nature of international financial markets eventually weakens nominal exchange rate stability and the lowering of inflation, discourages capital inflow and compromises exchange rate stability and growth.

EXCHANGE RATE APPRECIATION AT THE COST OF A WEAK ECONOMY THAT ENDS UP QUESTIONING IT

Exchange rate appreciation does not at all imply the Mexican currency is strong, and far less does it imply that the economy is strong. The Mexican economy has been weakened as a result of the damage caused by exchange rate appreciation itself and the policies that caused it. The lowering of inflation is no longer sustainable since it relies on capital inflow to finance the current account deficit and maintain nominal exchange rate stability. Capital inflow only postpones the emergence of a greater crisis since capital inflow and the economic policy accompanying it maintain exchange rate appreciation and therefore maintain the pressure on the trade deficit. Besides, the financial obligations derived from greater capital inflow also increase. This places the economy in a context of insolvency that leads to restraining capital inflow and outflow, as well as to currency devaluation and a financial crisis. R. Blecker says that 'The debt positions created by these inflows are unsustainable over time, causing abrupt outflows of speculative capital, which in fact accelerate the balance of payments crisis and Draconian adjustment policies that reduce growth and create massive unemployment' (Blecker, 1998, p. 29). History has shown the transitory nature of exchange rate anchors, whether they are sustained by capital inflow, price control or severe monetary and fiscal control policies. The market eventually corrects prolonged exchange rate distortions at a high devaluatory, inflationary and recessive cost that implies greater subordination to the interests of international creditors.

EXCHANGE RATE APPRECIATION AND THE CURRENT RECESSION

The contraction in the US economy since the second half of the year 2000 has affected the growth of exports from Mexico to the USA, which previously had been the engine of growth for Mexico. The trade deficit has increased as well as the requirements for capital inflow to bridge this gap and ensure nominal exchange rate stability. The change in the international context, the aggravation of domestic problems and the payment difficulties tend to curb capital flows and compromise nominal exchange rate stability.

There are no endogenous perspectives to face external adversities, decrease the foreign trade deficit and maintain nominal exchange rate stability. In the face of this situation, Mexico maintains relatively high real interest rates (higher than in the USA), credit and fiscal restrictions, and exchange rate appreciation in order to prevent capital from leaving the country and to continue promoting capital inflow. This places Mexico at a greater competitive and productive disadvantage in facing its export contraction. Besides, these policies act in a pro-cyclic manner. Instead of increasing public expenditure and credit availability, reducing the real rate of interest in order to improve domestic liquidity and flexibilizing the exchange rate to counteract the drop in exports and reactivate the economy, exchange rate stability continues to be favored in order to prevent capital outflow and a financial crisis.

Nominal exchange rate stability, however, cannot be maintained in the context of a low accumulation dynamic, increasing pressure on the trade deficit, high levels of indebtedness and credit restrictions, since this places us in a context of high external vulnerability that will end by triggering the financial crisis Mexico wants to avoid. The international context accentuates the pressure on the national external sector and the insolvency problems of the private sector (highly indebted in dollars), which takes us further away from international financial markets and hinders financing for growth and exchange rate stability.

TO WHAT EXTENT CAN MANAGING THE MONETARY AND EXCHANGE POLICY BE RESUMED IN THE CONTEXT OF FINANCIAL LIBERALIZATION?

Monetary authorities in Latin American countries cannot flexibilize their monetary policy and reduce the real interest rate to the same level as developed countries in order to give way to greater exchange rate flexibility, since both variables are key pieces to ensure the capital inflow that is needed to finance the current account deficit and avoid speculative practices that would lead to financial crises.

The exchange rate in emerging market economies cannot flexibilize to promote exports and adjust the trade deficit, since the devaluation of the exchange rate is dysfunctional to financial liberalization, because it devalues the financial capital operating in those economies. Devaluation would lead to severe problems in the capital market, encourage capital outflow and curb capital inflow. This would compromise the financing of the external deficit and the payment of the foreign debt. It would aggravate the financial problems of both public and private sectors, which are highly indebted in dollars, thus preventing an increase in investment that could take advantage of the new exchange rate parity. The interest rates would increase in order to curb capital outflow, which would aggravate insolvency problems and banking instability.

A mere adjustment of relative prices would not ensure the protection of the productive plant. It would not improve competitiveness in order to better the accumulation dynamic and the foreign trade balance. Economic liberalization has increased import coefficients. Imports, thus, show a strong price inelasticity that would prevent devaluation from reducing them significantly in order to adjust the trade deficit. Besides, manufactured goods exports would not grow significantly due to their high import coefficients as the low dynamism of the world economy and the large investments that are needed to increase the productive capacity. This requires a credit availability that does not exist due to the problems the banking system is facing, which would only worsen in the face of devaluation.

Devaluation would have repercussions on inflation due to an increase in productive and financial costs, which would nullify the initial effect of the relative price correction to improve competitiveness and move forward in import substitution and increase exports. Investments would not thus flow in that direction, the external sector would not be able to be adjusted and economic growth would not be promoted.

HOW CAN THE MANAGEMENT OF THE ECONOMIC POLICY BE RESUMED?

In order to avoid permanent pressure on the exchange and interest rates, and to resume the sovereign management of the economic policy favoring the productive sphere and sustained growth in the Latin American economies, it is necessary to control capital mobility in order to detach from nominal exchange policies and contractionary monetary and fiscal policies. The payment of the foreign debt service must be reformulated and restructured in order to ease pressure on the external sector and on the requirements for capital inflow and to stop formulating policies that favor foreign capital.

Economic relations with developed countries must be reformulated in order to improve long-term and investment credit flows as well as trade and technological treatment, to overcome productive lags, increase productivity and reconstruct domestic productive chains that allow improvements in work, income and solvency conditions. This is the only way we will be able to ease pressure on the external sector, achieve banking stability and resume monetary, credit and fiscal policies for growth.

Only by regulating capital mobility and reducing the requirements for capital inflow can Mexico recover the sovereign management of its economic policy in order to meet its national demands.

REFERENCES

Andrade, J., and F.M.L. Silva (1999), 'Divergencias e Convergencias sobre as crisis cambiais', in Organizadores, Tadeu Lima, Joao Sicsu and L.F. de Paula, Campus Editora. *Macroeconomia Moderna, Keynes e a Economia Contemporanea*, Rio de Janeiro, Brasil.

Blecker, R. (1998), 'Interational capital mobility, macroeconomic imbalances, and the risk of global contraction', Center for Economic Policy Analysis New School University working papers.

Cardim de Carvalho, F., F.E. Pieres de Souza, J. Sicsu, L.F. Rodríguez de Paula, and R. Studart (2001), *Economia Moderna e Financiera, Teoria e Practica*, Brasil: Campus Editora.

Eatwell, J., and L. Taylor (2000), *Global Finance at Risk: The Case for International Regulation*, New York: New Press.

Hefeker, Carsten (2000), 'Sense and nonsense of fixed exchange rates: on theories and crisis', *Cato Journal*, **20** (2), 159–79.

Huerta, A. (1997), *Carteras Vencidas, Inestabilidad Financera, Propuestas de Solucion*, México, DF: Editorial Diana.

Moore, Basil (1988), 'The endogenous money supply', *Journal of Post Keynesian Economics*, **10** (3), 372–85.

Presser, F.M. (2000), 'Polticas macroeconomicas e regimes cambiais: uma resenha critica da contribucao do main strem na decada de 80', *Economia e Sociedade*, no. 14, Instituto de Economia, UNICAMP, Brasil, June.

Tavares, M.C. (1997a), 'Globalizacao e o Estado Nacional', *Journal Folha de S. Paulo*, 12 October.

Tavares, M.C. (1997b), 'Canido na real', *Correio Brazilense*, 9 November.

Tavares, M.C. (1997c), 'A economia politica do real', draft, Brasilia: Brasil.

Tavares, M.C. (1998), 'A crise mundial e o Brasil', *Journal Folha de S. Paulo*.

United Nations Conference on Trade and Development (UNCTAD) (2001), *Trade and Development Report*, New York: United Nations.

9. Economic policy of sustainable development in the countries of transition towards a market economy

Rumen V. Gechev

During the 1980s, Council for Mutual Economic Assistance (COMECON) economies entered the stage of irreversible economic degradation. All extensive factors of production were exhausted. The level of productivity remained far below the productivity of the developed countries. The standard of living was deteriorating. Even the massive foreign credits did not help and just prolonged the agony of the so-called command economy on the expense of mounting foreign debt, deepening financial and economic disproportions, and increased dependence on import of consumer goods.

Abolition of the old system and establishment of modern market economy was a great challenge for the people in Eastern Europe. They had to go through a unique process of transformation at a time of worsening internal and external economic conditions, difficult and contradictive political democratization, and ideological prejudices. The most complicated problem was the development of such a model of transition which could minimize its economic and social price. Despite the many similarities, every country from the region had to apply nationally adapted or modified reform mechanisms. Three main factors have determined the outcome of the reforms: complexity, consistency and dynamics. Today, most of the main objectives are fulfilled but at a different cost.

There is a common understanding that a universal model of transition towards market economy does not exist. Some common principles are observed, including privatization, trade liberalization, general economic restructuring, monetary reforms, political pluralism and others, but the concrete mechanisms of implementation have to be different. These different models and mechanisms are based on the varieties in the level of economic and technological development, established trade patterns, foreign debt volume, dependence on the international financial institutions, degree of political pluralism, traditions, cultural peculiars, geographical proxy to European Union (EU), and so on.

Some economists view the models of reforms as two possible alternatives: 'shock therapy' or 'gradual reforms'. They assume that the first model leads to great instability and high social price in the short run but eases the fast establishment of market institutions. This model was tested in a few countries, including Poland, Hungary and Bulgaria. We may assume that the supporters of that model believed that the short-term disproportions and 'social pain' are an acceptable sacrifice for the expected mid- and long-term prosperity. It is a matter of discussion, but this mechanism brought relatively good results in Hungary and Poland. In some other countries, for example Bulgaria and Romania, the results are much more doubtful and need further clarification.

The Czech Republic is the best example for the advantages of the consistent, gradual implementation with a relatively dynamic and systematic approach. This country has the lowest dependence on the international financial institutions, relatively high and stable economic growth, impressive by Eastern European standards gross domestic product (GDP) per capita (above $7500, measured through the PPP Index), lower unemployment and acceptable inflation, large foreign direct investment (FDI) inflow, a competitive national economy, and so on. Actually, an ideal model does not exist. My personal experiences as an economic policy-maker proved that we should use the more precise definitions as 'rational' and 'irrational' models instead of using political definitions like 'leftist' or 'rightist' (liberal) model of transition. The rationality is based on three interrelated indicators: (1) clear and well balanced objectives; (2) consistent and adequate mechanism of reforms which is particular to the environment; (3) appropriate harmonization of the economic, social and political changes. Finally, when compared with the other EU candidate countries, the model applied in the Czech Republic is the closest one to the criteria of sustainable development.

ECONOMIC SYSTEM AND ENVIRONMENT

Heavy industry used to be the main engine of economic growth in Eastern Europe but it was also an environmentally destructive factor because of its low efficiency and overconsumption of energy and raw materials. The economic policy evaluation was based exclusively on quantitative indicators. When analysing energy and raw materials consumption we have to keep in mind that the price system was absolutely distorted. The extracting industries were heavily subsidized, keeping the prices below the cost of production. It was also true for the oil and the natural gas supplied at discounted prices by the former Soviet Union. That is why the price system chain was sending wrong signals to the whole economy. The command economy was extensively using those resources at the expense of future generations instead of improving the technologies and decreasing the consumption of non-renewable resources per unit of production.

Sustainable development has its clear indicators and evaluation criteria. However, these indicators have to be analysed systematically. Because if one takes into account some isolated indicators, the command economy can be presented as one close to sustainable development. The former socialist countries have demonstrated large-scale industrialization and high economic growth, full employment, free education and free health care, housing for everyone, an acceptable standard of living and a relatively low crime rate. But most of these 'positive' trends were at the expense of deepening foreign credits dependence, overuse of the extensive factors of production and speedy environmental degradation. It is not accidental that in most of the Eastern European countries the democratic movement has started as a pro-environment one. In conclusion, the centrally planned economy failed to achieve the basic objectives of sustainable development. All Eastern European countries went through sharp financial, economic and political crisis which in fact paved the road towards modern market economy and democracy.

We should clarify the method of analysis when evaluating the macroeconomic and overall socio-economic development in the former socialist block countries. Special attention has to be paid to the distinction between the short-term and the long-term results. It would be a misleading approach if we build the comparative analysis on sustainable development on short-term outcomes only. All the former socialist countries lost about 35–55 per cent of their GDP within the first four to five years. We have witnessed serious economic crisis, galloping inflation, unusually high unemployment, large-scale bankruptcies, volatile exchange markets, eroded purchasing power and shrinking export potential. The end of the highly protected COMECON 'market' in 1990 left the state-owned companies with broken foreign trade channels. It made technological and product innovations very difficult.

I would agree that the unsustainable development at that time was caused mainly, but not only, from the reshaping of the whole economic and political system. Such necessary steps as privatization, closing of ailing banks and loss-making companies, and redirection of foreign trade turnover have caused additional burdens on the economy and everyday life of millions of people.

ECONOMIC RESTRUCTURING: A PRECONDITION FOR SUSTAINABILITY

Economic restructuring plays a vital role for the old system conversion into a new, functional market economy. In my view, it includes the following components: (1) privatization; (2) isolation or liquidation of the loss-making companies; (3) technological and product innovation; (4) redirection of foreign trade mainly toward EU and other developed countries; (5) establishment of a well integrated financial system (capital markets including), and (6) creation of a highly competitive environment. It is impossible to cover all the components in this chapter but we shall focus on those which reflect core economic indicators and have intensive interrelations with the ecosystem.

I would underline the necessity for GDP 'dematerialization'. As we mentioned before, the potential for further utilization of the extensive factors is exhausted and too expensive. As Professor Friedrich Schmidt-Bleek (1998, s. 93–4), pointed out, only the new technologies allowing less production will make possible the improvement on the standard of living. Lower material quantity per unit of production saves money, decreases the consumption of non-renewable and renewable resources, limits pollution and creates conditions for environmentally friendly economic growth. Also, high material consumption combined with obsolete production technologies produces far more damage to the ecosystems.

More dynamic development of the service sector is another way to ease the GDP reduction. This sector produces more than 55–60 per cent of GDP in the most developed countries. It enables, other things being equal, the slowdown or minimization of environmental degradation, decreased energy and material consumption, and the creation of better working conditions.

Nevertheless, it does not mean that the industrial production is the most damaging one by definition. Actually, the environmental side effect depends on the kind of technology and the type of product. Process and production methods (PPMs) are among the most important economic policy issues. These methods may have a positive or negative effect on the environment. The product itself may pollute or degrade the environment when it is used or consumed. The negative effect can be generated earlier, also at the stage of production or consumed at the end of its life. These are the so called 'non-product related PPMs'. The distinction is not clearly defined by the World Trade Organization (WTO) rules yet and is a matter of intensive discussions among the trading partners. This problem deserves additional clarification. We may witness a scenario when the developed countries 'filter' the import and allowing the import for 'green' products only while the damage from the 'gray' technologies of production are left for the less developed countries. It is especially true for the Eastern European countries which will not be accepted as full members of the EU in the coming five to ten years. But such geographical reallocation of the negative effect on the environment will rather worsen the situation than solving the problem. Such an undesirable scenario has to be avoided by the Eastern European countries as they apply to well selected and balanced economic and administrative instruments, including the introduction or extension of eco-labeling, lowering or removing any tariff and non-tariff barriers for import of environmentally sound technologies, preferential stimulus for export of green products, trade bans or quotas for environmentally hazardous products, implementation of tax incentive measures (tax vacations vs tax increase, flexible custom duty policy), gradual elimination of budget subsidies in the heavy industry, and so on.

The implementation of more efficient technologies and product innovation comply with the Kyoto protocol (1997) which was signed recently by all the EU candidate-countries. Its main goal is consistent decrease of the carbon dioxide emissions. The actual harm caused to the environment is measured as quantity of carbon dioxide per capita or quantity of carbon dioxide per unit of GDP. If measured with the first indicator, Poland, Hungary and the Czech Republic are in a better position than developed countries such as the USA, Canada and Belgium. The emissions per capita in Hungary are even below the level in Japan, respectively 4 tons and 6 tons of carbon dioxide per capita.

Unfortunately, this optimistic differentiation is because of the shrinking of the GDP in Eastern Europe. Simply, the volume of underproduction and consequently the volume of pollution are larger than the harmful effect from using less developed technologies. If measured by the second indicator, which is more precise and more long-term oriented, the result is quite different: whereas the carbon dioxide emissions are within 0.2–0.4 t/GDP in Switzerland, France, Sweden, Norway, Austria and Japan, in Poland, the Czech Republic and Hungary these emissions are 1.5, 1.2, 0.7 t/GDP respectively (OECD Environment Centre).

If it is to be fulfilled, Kyoto protocol requires intensive economic restructuring and technological innovation. In the concrete conditions the FDI are to play a leading role in that process. The governments should also try to mobilize more resources. Some disadvantages might be converted into advantages. Unused production capacity could be used for active participation in the trade with pollution permits which will generate additional financial resources for the governmental programs toward sustainable development.

More attention has to be paid on the ratio between the GDP share of the industrial, agricultural and service sectors. Other things being equal, the larger the service sector, the better for the environment. When doing comparative analyses we should count the differences in the composition between EU and the candidate countries in the composition of value added: the service sector exhibits up to about 15 per cent higher share within EU, while the heavy industry products, agricultural and the natural resource branches constitute significantly larger shares. Therefore, higher share of services moves the economy closer to the criterion of sustainable development. But it may lead to wrong conclusions in some cases when the reason for such a high share is simply the industrial sector collapse. It is highly recommendable for both relative and absolute values to be used when analysing the GDP's structural aspects. Frankly speaking, the GDP qualitative parameters are as important as the quantitative ones.

There are some substantial differences between economic growth, economic development and sustainable development. The last one fully integrates economic, social and environmental criteria. However, it does not mean that a thorough GDP analysis should be neglected. Most of the scientists share the understanding that the main objective is to develop a model of development which allows de-coupling environmental degradation from economic growth. The process of de-coupling is expressed as a percentage of energy and non-renewable resources use per unit of GDP. Recent research concludes that 'The use of energy and other resources, like agricultural raw materials, water and metals, now appears to be increasing at a slower rate than GDP in many OECD (Organization for Economic Co-operation and development) of the countries, and the pollution intensity of output is growing even more slowly' and that 'OECD countries are expected to reduce the energy intensity of their economies by 20% to 2020, while increasing total energy use by 35%. Even with the use of new, more efficient, energy and transport technologies, it is unlikely that total emissions from these sources will decrease much over the next two decades' (OECD, 2002, pp. 20–21).

The expected trends are rather negative. Although more environmentally sound technologies will be applied, total energy and material consumption will continue to rise at unacceptable high rates. There is an additional question which has to be investigated: to what extent will the process of de-coupling environmental degradation from economic growth in OECD be based on real technology and product improvements, and what will be the role of transferring 'undesirable' technologies and products towards the less developed countries, including those in Eastern Europe? It could lead to an absolutely wrong decision because it will only reallocate the problem instead of solving it. Hopefully, the further EU enlargement will eliminate the possibility of such a scenario.

Undoubtedly, the restructuring of the energy sector is crucial for the restructuring of the whole Eastern European economy which has to meet two interrelated preliminary requirements: environmentally friendly energy production at relatively low price. The subsidization cannot continue to be a hidden competitive tool. Most of the countries from the region follow fast-track reduction of energy subsidization. It is also one of the prerequisites of the International Monetary Fund (IMF) when approving balance-of-payments support.

Energy sector restructuring towards sustainability requires further clarification of the nuclear energy future. Nuclear energy plants have been producing up to 40–60 per cent of electricity in a few Eastern European countries, including Bulgaria, Romania, the Czech Republic and Poland. It used to be a common belief that nuclear energy was the cheapest one because of the artificially low price of nuclear fuel and the miscalculation of the economic and environmental cost of the nuclear waste collection, transportation and storage. There are enough convincing arguments that the full cost of this kind of energy is unacceptable and much higher than some other alternative energy sources. It is widely accepted that 'nuclear power is no longer an economically viable energy source … When the costs of decommissioning nuclear plants, which may rival those of construction, and the costs of disposing of nuclear waste are incorporated into cost calculations, it seems clear that nuclear power has no economic future' (Brown, 2001, p. 272).

Nuclear reactor shutdowns would create different kinds of problems to be faced by the policy-makers. Eastern Europe is no exception. There are a number of reasons why the countries from the region postpone or modify the EU request. First, the replacement cost is often higher then the losses caused by the nuclear energy sector. This is true when the comparative analysis is based on a short-term period. The positive outcome of the replacement might be expected in the long term only. The question is whether or not the Eastern European economies are able to bear the short-term burden and, if so, at what price?

Bulgaria is fast emerging as a key regional electricity producer, able to serve neighbors with rapidly growing demand. In 2001, electricity exports reached 7 billion kilowatt hours – its main clients Turkey, Federal Republic of Yugoslavia, Macedonia, Albania and Greece. Bulgaria covers about 40–50 per cent of the electricity deficit in the Balkans. An earlier than projected closing of the nuclear reactors will complicate the energy supply at a regional level.

In some countries, like Bulgaria for example, the problem is even more complicated. The country has invested more than US$1 billion for the construction of the second nuclear energy plant in the town of Belene. The money (about 10 per cent of the current GDP!) has been frozen for more than 12 years. It is difficult to prove that the construction of an alternative electric power plant will compensate the accumulated losses. If the Bulgarian government decides to proceed with the project, it has to overcome serious resistance of the EU authorities, neighboring countries and different local and international non-governmental organizations (NGOs) (Lovins, 2002).

The governments of the Czech Republic, Romania and Poland have similar problems. We should take into account the specifics of each country when applying the common criteria for sustainable development of the energy sector in conjunction with the environmental, economic and safety standards. The tragedy in Chernobyl has activated the anti-nuclear energy movement which is based on safety precautions rather than on economic reasoning.

Safety has to be the first priority for all parties involved in the decision-making, but it does not mean that a very detailed, complex and interdisciplinary analysis should not take place. The Eastern European countries are able to take long-term oriented decisions only if there is appropriate support to overcome the expected disadvantages in the short-term period.

Energy use per unit of GDP in Eastern Europe is two to three times higher than in the developed countries. This is because of the technology gap and the inefficient economy structure. As Lovins describes 'it is much cheaper to save energy than to buy it' (Ginsburg, 2001, p. 198). So, the restructuring of the energy sector has to be organized in conjunction with the restructuring of the whole economy, and vice versa. Attention has to be paid to the technology transfer opportunities in such fields as state of the art electrical production based on wind, sun and hydrogen energy. These restructurings may lead to the desired environmentally friendly production combined with efficient energy use. 'Among the strongest economic advantages of focusing on energy productivity instead of energy production is that building, for example, super window and efficient-lamp factories instead of power stations and transmission lines requires about a thousand fold less capital per unit of extra comfort or light … ' (Hawken, Lovins and Hunter Lovins, 1999, p. 25).

The trends towards decreased use of fossil oil and coal are positive phenomena. Additional pressure for further limitation of nuclear energy production is expected at the same time. It makes the installation of environmentally friendly and efficient alternative energy sources a must. Any model of macroeconomic and investment policy in particular has to be in keeping with the new realities at the beginning of the twenty-first century. The World Bank, European Bank for Reconstruction and Development (EBRD) and the European Investment Bank (EIB) are playing an active role in this process. Some of the leading corporations from the energy power sector are ready for different forms of co-operation, including joint ventures, turnkey operations, concessions and so on. There are concrete projects for further modernization and extension of the infrastructure for natural gas transportation from Russia to South East Europe. It is an important, transition step from the old to new energy sources which are more economically efficient and meet the criteria for sustainable development.

The experts in this field argue that the same set of pipelines can be used for transportation of hydrogen fuel in the future. Actually, by helping the modernization of the Eastern European energy sector, the developed countries directly or through the international financial and banking institutions will ease the road towards sustainability at a regional and global level. It is beneficial both for the countries in transition and the rest of the world.

FDI AND PRIVATIZATION AS A POWERFUL DRIVE TOWARDS SUSTAINABLE DEVELOPMENT

Improving the energy sector efficiency is only one of the steps towards sustainable development. Two additional structural changes have to be made: first, decreasing the energy and material consumption per unit of GDP and, second, improving the structure of the GDP itself. The most suitable mechanisms and stimuli have to be found which may ease the transfer of recently developed patents, licenses, know how as well as new products. One of the most realistic solutions is further encouragement of foreign direct investment. Eastern European countries do not have enough resources for research and development under existing fiscal restrictions. Many laboratories, scientific institutions and programs were closed or their activities limited. It will take a long time before the regional research and development (R&D) activities catch up with similar programs in developed countries. Hungary, the Czech Republic and Poland managed to attract massive foreign direct investment through the process of cash privatization, joint ventures and greenfield operations. These countries introduced foreign trade liberalization, tax holidays, free land, unlimited profit repatriation, free exchange market, aggressive promotion activities, and so on at the very beginning of the reforms. Others like Romania and Bulgaria were late with privatization and it led to a significantly lower level of FDI per capita. The Hungarian absolute amount of FDI in the mid-90s was nearly equal to the overall FDI in the rest of Eastern Europe. This explains why the Hungarian economy is among the most competitive and meets the Maastricht and Copenhagen criteria for EU full membership.

An important FDI advantage is gaining an additional world market share. It increases investment returns, lowers investment risk and has an additional positive effect on balance of payments. These imported technologies are usually more sophisticated, environmentally friendly, energy saving and use fewer materials per unit of production.

The economic restructuring, and privatization in particular, play a vital role for the creation, dynamics and further development of the social economy which integrates different forms of economic activities (based on private and public property, corporations, co-operatives and small and mid-size enterprises (SMEs) and social activities and objectives. All these forms of economic activities have to be reshaped following the social economy enterprise model. Such an approach may develop the necessary conditions and factors for further strengthening of sustainable development. The Seventh European Conference on Social Economy which took place in 2001 concluded that: 'the social economy in a modern society can be described according to five main themes: social responsibility, citizen participation, social capital, empowerment and third sector' (Presidency Summary, 2001, p. 1). EU candidate countries must meet all the economic, political, social and environmental criteria, and the achievement of social economy is one of the milestones when evaluating the process of transition.

Privatization is the most crucial component of economic restructuring. It paves the way towards the establishment of a market economy and its mechanisms and institutions. In Bulgaria, about 1100 state-owned companies were privatized by vouchers in 1996. Nearly 3.3 million eligible citizens (at least 18 years old) took part directly or indirectly (through privatization funds) in the process of property transformation, and became shareholders. The cash privatization in some reform-leading countries such as the Czech Republic, Hungary and Poland is nearly completed already. More than 60–70 per cent of the GDP in Eastern Europe is produced in the private sector. The new business environment generates opportunities for the emergence of thousands of new SMEs. We witness an increasing role of trade unions, NGOs, associations of producers, consumers, civil society groups, and so on. All these recent developments are necessary steps towards a more transparent and functional social market economy.

The process of privatization deserves much broader analyses but I will concentrate mainly on its 'cross point' with environmental issues. Our countries have inherited from the past on-site and off-site heavily contaminated state-owned companies. As a result, the environmental problems became one of the most complicated issues in the privatization deals. A number of serious problems had to be overcome, among them damage estimation in market value, evaluation of the recovery cost, time frame determination for partial and full recovery, allocation of the clean-up responsibilities between the buyer and the seller, and calculation of the possible price discount when appropriate.

All state-owned companies in the metallurgical, chemical production, extraction industries and pharmacies, for example, had and still have such problems. Preliminary estimations in the Czech Republic made at the beginning of the 1990s showed that the clean-up costs for about 2500 state-owned enterprises exceeded US$ 1 billion (Lawson, 1994). For the whole region the accumulated damages are tens of billions of dollars. In most of the cases a compromise solution has been made: the buyers were responsible mainly or only for the 'new pollution'. Poland was a leading country in that respect, using appropriate economic and legal techniques. Nevertheless, the economic and legal burden from the past contaminations appears to be one of the most complicated obstacles in the privatization procedures for both domestic and foreign buyers. Now:

> An enduring puzzle for CEE (Central and Eastern European) governments is how to appeal to foreign investors who are reluctant to purchase old, primarily state-owned

> industrial properties in CEE. These governments are capable of instituting more flexible requirements governing future uses and cleanup of contaminated properties. Authorities can also adapt various economic incentives to lure foreign investors. (Aver, Reuveny and Adler, 2001)

Theoretically, the clean-up cost can be higher than the company's assets value. By economic perspective it means that the seller has to pay the buyer who actually bears the environmental responsibility. There are few privatization deals when the seller (government) has arranged (at its expense) a credit from the World Bank or other financial institutions. Such credits, serviced by the taxpayers, were used for clean-up operations. For example, it was a preliminary condition of Belgian investors who signed the privatization contract for the Bulgarian metallurgy giant MDK. The government arranged such indirect discount for the buyer and US$20 million were allocated for the company's environment recovery.

The mechanism of a so-called escrow account is another tool for minimization of the conflict of interests between the sellers and the buyers of contaminated companies. A certain percentage of the selling price is kept on that account and can be used only for clean-up procedures in case the actual expenditures are higher than the preliminary estimate. This technique was widely applied first in Poland and later in all countries in transition. The experiences in that respect allow shortening of the overall privatization procedures and assuring higher environmental standards at the newly privatized companies. It brings benefits to all, including companies, employees, local citizens and the whole society. The positive outcome reflects the whole region and has a trans-border effect.

EXPECTED OUTCOME OF EU ENLARGEMENT AND FOREIGN TRADE LIBERALIZATION

The process of EU enlargement is speeding up the implementation of the environmental protection law in Eastern Europe. Most of the candidate countries have not yet complied with the EU environment acquisition but the progress in that direction is promising. Countries like Slovenia, the Czech Republic and Hungary are well ahead but others like Romania and Slovakia must work more intensively for the implementation of the acquisition. It is understandable that at the time of the EU accession the environmental legislation of the new member states has to be in harmony with the EU's legislation. There will be exclusion in respect of that rule only for a few, preliminary specified programs, which require massive public investments. Such investments are not available at the current stage because of overall economic problems and budget restrictions. The Habitat Directive, for example, has to be implemented before 2004/05 but other 'expensive' programs will be given priority after the accession. There is no reason to believe so far that the introduction of more strict and transparent environmental standards in Eastern Europe would discourage FDI. The better developed the environmental legislation, the more intensive FDI inflow will be. Countries like Poland, Hungary and the Czech Republic have proved this to be the case.

Most of the Eastern European countries are applying or preparing to apply the 'Flower Program' which started in the EU 10 years ago. This eco-labeling initiative promotes sustainable consumption and production. It was set up to encourage business to produce and market greener products and to enable consumers to make informed environmental choices. Today, the EU 'Flower Program' covers 99 licenses, 19 product groups, several hundred products and over 15 million eco-labeled articles. In the past year alone, the number of licenses has increased by 75 per cent (European Commission, 2002).

Textile and indoor paints and varnish products are among the most often eco-labeled products and the process spreads throughout the whole economy. In correspondence with the EU three year eco-label development plan, the number of eco-labeled products will increase by 25 per cent annually. From that perspective, the eco-parameters of Eastern European exports are not only a matter of competitiveness but a matter of eligibility as well. We shall assume that the eco-labeling process and the production of environmentally sound products are imperative for the process of accession. It could pave the way to further adaptation to the EU economic and legal environment.

The new EU Environmental Program covers the issues of upcoming enlargement. It recognizes both the existing problems and the new opportunities when the candidate countries join the EU from 2003 onward. It will strengthen the environmental standards in Europe. Substantial natural resources and rich biodiversity will be added to the European heritage. Preliminary estimates are that the candidate countries have to transpose about 270 legal Acts. In order to reach the higher standards these countries need huge investments, mainly in the development of new infrastructure or updating the existing one. Special programs are needed for the recovery of heavily polluted industrial sites. As the EU Environment Commissioner Margot Wallstrom pointed out, 'We are well aware of the challenges they are facing and we realize that they will need transitional periods to cope. But, of course, we would like to keep these periods as few and as short as possible' (Wallstrom, 2001, p. 4).

European Union integration is intensifying the process of economic internationalization and globalization. The outcome of this process is a matter of interesting discussions and quite opposite conclusions. The evaluation of this outcome depends on the point of view, time frame perspective, reliability of selected indicators, and so on. There are not only positive or only negative effects. The question is how to gain from the new opportunities and how the undesirable side effects can be minimized or eliminated. However, judgment has to be based on the improvement of natural resource use. Most probably, processing of natural resources will be shifted more closely to the place of their extraction. This will create new jobs in the resource-affluent countries with all the associated desirable social and economic effects, but will create new environmental problems at the same time.

The existing order of international economic relations, and WTO rules in particular, do not yet guarantee that such development can be prevented. Even for the most developed countries the environmental cost for certain productions are too high. It is unrealistic to expect that less developed countries will be able to solve the problems alone without closer and more efficient financial and technological co-operation with developed countries. Both sides have their own responsibilities which are related to the economic restructuring and new law enforcement. Nevertheless, there is no other solution than combining the mutual responsibilities with joint actions, where every partner participates in harmony with its economic and intellectual potential.

It is widely accepted that competitiveness is a major criteria for a functional market economy. The difference between the domestic and the world markets are diminishing. Our economies have reached a high degree of interrelation and interdependence. The accession to the EU will deepen these trends. I share the understanding that foreign trade characteristics (export and import volume, structure by articles and group of commodities, geographical position, way of financing, and so on) are the most reliable criteria for market reforms assessment and for assessment of the level of sustainability as well.

About 70–85 per cent of the foreign trade turnover of the former socialist countries used to be within former COMECON. The situation is quite different now. The EU is the main trade partner and more than 50 per cent of the export/import operations are with EU companies. We may expect that this percentage will be even higher in the near future. No doubt such 'geographical' restructuring of our trade flows is desirable. The trade flow is not only an exchange of commodities but an additional opportunity for industrial co-operation, transfer of technologies, ideas, managerial know-how, development of joint-venture production or sale operations, and so on.

Compensation of the technological gap and the establishment of the market mechanisms cannot be done overnight. I am rather skeptical that the foreign trade flows between the developed countries and countries in transition can be restructured substantially in the short run. However, it is not an excuse for the unused opportunities of better designed foreign trade policy, for delayed economic restructuring and missed foreign investment opportunities.

During the last five years Hungary, Poland and the Czech Republic enjoy positive economic growth in the range of 1.5 to 5 per cent. Romania has maintained positive growth since 2000, 1.6 to 3.8 per cent. Bulgaria emerged

Table 9.1 Current account percentage of GDP

	1999	2000	2001	2002*
Bulgaria	–5.2	–5.8	–6.3	–5.9
Romania	–3.8	–3.8	–6.1	–6.3
Slovakia	–3.6	–5.1	–5.2	–3.9
Czech Republic	–4.5	–4.2	–4.9	–4.3
Hungary	–3.3	–2.3	–3.2	–2.7
Poland	–6.3	–6.3	–4.2	–4.4

Source: *Emerging Europe Monitor* (2002), **9** (2), p. 1.

from economic recession in 1998 and since then has increased its real GDP by 3.5 to 5 per cent annually. As we see from Table 9.1, growth is import oriented. All the countries have relatively high current account deficit: about 6 per cent in Romania and Bulgaria and approximately 3 to 4 per cent in Poland, the Czech Republic and Hungary. Last year, the highest trade deficit per capita ($357) was in Poland, while the lowest ($128) was in Romania. In the Czech Republic this indicator is nearly three times as high as in Romania ($305) but the trade deficit is twice as low as the percentage of export for the same indicator in Romania (calculations based on data from *Emerging Europe Monitor*, 2002).

In addition to this, all countries except Romania and the Czech Republic face complications with the foreign debt service. The debt burden is 45–80 per cent of their GDP, but payment of the debt is much more difficult for Bulgaria and Romania than for the better developed candidate countries. In the short run we shall see two opposite influences on economic development: first, 'transferring' impulses towards sustainability (import of technologies, know-how, patents and licenses; easier access to the EU and world markets) and, second, causing bankruptcies or establishing entry barriers for the newly emerging businesses. Substantial foreign borrowing will be necessary to cover the trade deficits and the capital outflow.

To be sustainable, the world economy needs much improved foreign trade rules. The pure economic interests used to have a priority for WTO and its predecessor General Agreement on Tariffs and Trade (GATT). The environmental issues of trade were often neglected. Finally, with the beginning of the Millennium Round in Seattle (1999), criteria are in process of changing towards greater sustainability and less profitability. The liberalization and globalization of the world market make sense only if environmentally friendly foreign trade is promoted. I doubt that there is an automatic positive effect towards sustainable development. If not directed by appropriate market and administrative instruments, globalization can easily speed up environmental and social degradation (Tainter, 1988, pp. 1–5).

The transition towards market economy appears to be a longer and more complicated process than expected at the beginning of the 1990s. Despite the unprecedented problems during the transformation, the candidate countries are closer to the criteria of sustainability than 10–12 years ago. Ten countries most probably will become full EU members within two to three years; others will meet the criteria during the second half of this decade. We agree that sustainable development is a difficult task which require more close co-operation and interaction between government institutions, economic agents, NGOs and society as a whole. Eastern Europe must respond appropriately to the challenge of United Nations (UN) Agenda 21 and the new realities. Further efforts are necessary for the design and implementation of suitable economic, social, legal and political incentives which can better motivate sustainable development at local, national, regional and global levels.

REFERENCES

Auer, Matthew R., Rafael Reuveny and Lisa Adler (2001), 'Environmental liability and foreign direct investment in Central and Eastern Europe', *Journal of Environment & Development*, **10** (1), 5–34.

Brown, Lester R. (2001), *Eco-economy*, New York: W.W. Norton.

Emerging Europe Monitor (2002), **9** (1) and (2).

European Commission (2002), *Environment for Europeans*, **10**, April, p. 12.

Ginsburg, Janet (2001), 'Amory Lovins: "Efficiency goes straight to the bottom line"', *Business Week*, 7 April, p. 198.

Hawken, Paul, Amory Lovins and L. Hunter Lovins (1999), *Natural Capitalism*, New York: Little Brown.

Lawson, M.L. (1994), 'New owners bear brunt of their property's old ecological problems', *Prague Post*, 20 April, p. 1.

OECD (2002) *Environmental Outlook*, Paris: OECD.

OECD Environment Centre (2001), 'Environmental indicators', www.oecd.org.

Presidency Summary (2001), 'Presidency Summary of the Troika meeting on the occasion of the 7th European Conference on Social Economy', Ministry of Industry, Employment and Communications, Stockholm, www.industry.ministry.se.

Schmidt-Bleek, Friedrich (1998), *Das MIPS-Konzept. Weiger Naturverbrauch-mehr Lebensqualitat durch Faktor 10*, Munchen: Droemer.

Tainter, Joseph (1988), *The Collapse of Complex Civilizations*, Cambridge: Cambridge University Press.

Wallstrom, M. (2001), *Environment for Europeans*, **6**, March, 4.

10. Allied, German and Latin perspectives on inflation

Alcino Câmara and Matias Vernengo[1]

INTRODUCTION

Post Keynesian authors have emphasized in the last decades that the balance of payments constitutes the main constraint to growth (Davidson, 1990). In this respect, post Keynesians have refuted neoclassical views that assume a supply constrained economy, and have extended Keynes's principle of effective demand into the long run (growth theory). Hence, growth is seen as being demand led. While these ideas are certainly important, post Keynesians have neglected, for the most part, the importance of the balance of payments constraint in explanations of the inflationary phenomena.

High inflation and hyperinflation are not very common phenomena. In the twentieth century episodes of high inflation and hyperinflation occurred after the two World Wars, after the Latin American debt crises and after the collapse of the socialist block. In all these historical events balance of payments crises, severe depreciation and fiscal crises were present. Neoclassical economics always emphasized the fiscal component and neglected everything else. On the other hand, post Keynesians generally looked at normal times, inflation in developed countries, and emphasized the role of distributive conflict. However, German authors during the 1923 hyperinflation, and Latin American authors during the 1980s, have emphasized the importance of balance of payments crises.

This chapter brings those ideas to the fore by discussing the contributions of the German Balance of Payments School and the Latin American neo-structuralists. Three important points are raised. First, the origins of high inflation and hyperinflation processes are to be found in balance of payments crises. Second, fiscal deficits are the result, and not the cause of the inflationary processes. Third, interest rate (monetary) policy, within a post Keynesian framework, cannot simply be reduced to 'cheap money' once balance of payments considerations are introduced.

ALLIES, GERMANS AND LATINS[2]

According to the post Keynesian approach inflation is the result of a conflict over the distribution of income. Rowthorn (1977) provides a possible formalization of post Keynesian views. In his model inflation increases profits by reducing the real purchasing power of workers, since the latter are not able to protect them against it. The model assumes that conflict is a direct function of effective demand, which in turn depends on the exogenous money supply. Demand-pull inflation and exogenous money are both characteristics of monetarist models of inflation. Hence, the main difference between Rowthorn's model and the conventional monetarist story is that excess demand affects balance of power between workers and capitalists and only indirectly the price level. In the monetarist approach effective demand affects prices directly.

Several post Keynesian authors have constructed conflict models of inflation in which excess demand is not a relevant component of the explanation. Further, in these models the money supply is endogenous. In other words, inflation reflects only the inconsistency of the desired mark-up of firms and the target real wage that workers consider fair.

These post Keynesian models contrast with the conventional neoclassical interpretation of inflation. But, as much as neoclassical models, most post Keynesian models have neglected balance of payments considerations. Although, the neoclassical view of inflation, based ultimately on the Quantity Theory of Money (QTM), has a long and established tradition, the discussion of high inflation goes back to Bresciani-Turroni (1931) and Cagan (1956).

The view according to which deficit spending was the main cause of German inflation was named the English or allied view by Constantino Bresciani-Turroni (1931, p. 46) in his classic *The Economics of Inflation*. In this view, the burden imposed by the internal war debt, the payment of pensions to war veterans, widows and orphans, the reconstruction of the few devastated regions, and the process of war demobilization were too heavy for the young Weimar Republic and the leftist Social Democrat government to carry. In addition, the incapacity to raise fiscal revenues implied that the increasing fiscal spending had to be financed by the Reichsbank.

In this view, the rise in money supply precedes the rise in the price level. Also, given the dominance of purchasing power parity as the explanation of exchange rate determination, the rise in the domestic price level precedes and causes the depreciation of the Deutschmark. There is a chain of causality that runs from the exogenous money supply to the price level and then to the exchange rate. For Bresciani-Turroni, the solution to the inflationary problem was simply to cut the fiscal deficit. Once the principles of sound finance were re-established, the price level would be stabilized. The German government is to blame then.

One should note that Keynes's own views on inflation in the early 1920s – as expressed in his *Tract on Monetary Reform* (Keynes, 1923) – would put him firmly in the allied or English camp. There are a couple of qualifications that should be made, however, regarding Keynes's views on inflation at this time. First, one should note, that the *Tract* represents the departing point of his long road towards the *General Theory*. Second, and more importantly, his policy prescriptions are far more heterodox than one might expect from somebody that still accepts the Quantity Theory. He was clearly against burdening Germany with excessive debts, that it could not repay, as his famous book *The Economic Consequences of the Peace* makes clear.[3]

The German officials that had to deal with the day-to-day problems of running an economy under hyperinflationary conditions saw the problem, not surprisingly, from a different perspective than the allied and Keynes view. The most notorious defender of the so-called balance of payments theory was Karl Helfferich. His views were named the German view by Bresciani-Turroni (1931, p. 47).

Helfferich had a high position in the Deutsche Bank, and was a defender of the permanence of Germany on the Gold Standard. During the war he joined the German Treasury Office, and was a member of the Reichstag from 1920 until his death. For Helfferich the main cause of hyperinflation was to be found in the reparations of the Versailles Treaty.

In the first place, the disruption of the war led the German government to regulate the foreign exchange 'by way of a direct control of all foreign payments and credits' (Helfferich, 1927, p. 259). However, 'as the collapse of the German nation shows, the force of circumstances proved more powerful than any policy of exchange control' (ibid., p. 262). That is, trade deficits led to depreciation despite the control of the German authorities. As correctly noted by Howard Ellis (1934, p. 224), 'the balance theory takes as its point of departure the decline of German exports'. Helfferich argued that the permanent unfavorable trade balance, caused by the war and the impositions of the Versailles Treaty, led to depreciation. This was the root of German problems. In other words, causality runs from the exchange rate to the price level. That means that the rise in the price level cannot be related to the increase in the money supply. The opposite must be true.

Graham (1930) defended Helfferich's position in what was to become, up to the publication of Bresciani's book in English, the most influential view of the German hyperinflation. Graham (1930, p. 172) argues that 'the proximate ... chain of causation, up to August 1920 at least, and perhaps at other times, ran from exchange rates to prices to volume of circulating medium rather than in the reverse direction'.

According to the balance of payments view it is not possible to stabilize the economy without stabilizing the exchange rate. This was only possible if foreign reserves were available. The renegotiation of reparations in 1922 and the loans obtained through the Dawes Plan in 1924 allowed the stable foreign value of the rentemark to be maintained. It is clear that the pressures on the balance of payments imposed by reparations are to be seen by the Germans as the main cause of inflation.

The Latin American debate on hyperinflation in the 1980s recovered some of the ideas of the debate between allies and Germans in the 1920s. Latin American structuralists emphasize the role of distributive conflict within a cost-push approach. Also, given the recurring balance of payments problems of the region, structuralist authors have paid more attention to open economy issues. Juan Noyola (1956) and Osvaldo Sunkel (1958) are generally regarded as the seminal contributions to the structuralist theory of inflation. According to the structuralist view, inflation has its origins in the supply side. In that sense, excess demand caused by fiscal deficits is irrelevant. In particular, the inelasticity of food supply that results from the concentrated structure of land ownership is seen as the major cause of inflation.

Also, the structural dependency of capital imports, and the lack of foreign reserves means that Latin American countries have recurrent balance of payments problems. Currency depreciation is endemic, with or without foreign exchange control or other types of capital control. Hence, depreciation is also seen as an essential part of the inflationary problem.

In that sense, the structure of land ownership and the dependence on foreign exchange are seen as the main problems. Shocks to the terms of trade provide the spark that ignites the inflationary process. Structuralists emphasize both the shocks that initiate inflation and the propagation mechanism that maintains it. It must be noted that some structuralists, in particular Noyola (1956) and Furtado (1958), argue that the propagation of inflation is the result of incompatible income claims. If after an inflationary shock a group is dissatisfied with its income share it will try to pass its losses to another group.

Further, for structuralists inflation is not a monetary phenomenon, and results from real disequilibria. Hence, monetary policy is a passive element in the inflationary process. The notion that monetary policy is passive is close to the post Keynesian view on the endogeneity of the money supply as developed by Kaldor (1982).[4]

Brazilian neo-structuralists provided an important contribution to the understanding of inflation.[5] The Brazilian experience with indexation, and the failure of austerity measures to bring down inflation during the 1970s led many authors to argue that inflation in Brazil was mainly inertial.[6] These authors called for a 'heterodox shock' (Arida and Lara-Resende, 1985). Given their distrust in orthodox policies, the inertialist authors became known as neo-structuralists. However, the connection between inertialist and the old structuralists is almost uniquely related to their common rejection of tight money policies. It is interesting to note that for them, although inflation is essentially inertial, stability can only be achieved if fiscal balance is also present. Clearly, there is a demand-pull element in their theory.

The failure of heterodox stabilization plans in Latin America led many neo-structuralist authors to rediscover orthodoxy. Amadeo (1994) suggests that in a wage-led economy, as many Latin American economies are assumed to be, a heterodox shock package involving wage, price and foreign exchange rate freeze, and contract deindexation will increase effective demand. Rising effective demand is the result of the elimination of the inflation tax, and the fact that the redistribution of income towards workers leads to a consumption surge. As the economy is assumed to be near full employment, excess demand pulls up prices. Thus, according to this view a combination of austerity with a social compromise to reduce wage-price spirals is needed for a successful stabilization.[7]

Germans and Latins provide an alternative to the conventional (allied) views of inflation, which are based on the quantity theory. However, no alternative model in which a balance of payments crisis is the main cause of inflation has been developed. The next section tries to fill this gap.

A MODEL OF BALANCE OF PAYMENTS CONSTRAINT AND INFLATION[8]

The following model is an extension of German and Latin ideas of the previous section, and tries to show that stabilization does not depend on fiscal austerity, but only on favorable balance of payments conditions, since the main cause of inflation is a balance of payments crisis. External shocks affect the cost structure and may change the income distribution equilibrium of the economy. Wage indexation is the main propagation mechanism, however, inflation is not essentially inertial. That is not to say that formal contracts do not have a role in the inflationary process, but that for simplicity's sake they can be eliminated without significantly changing the picture.

First, we must look at the effects of the exchange rate dynamics. Many countries in Latin America from the 1960s onwards adopted depreciation rules to stimulate exports. Crawling pegs can have several objectives, such as keeping the trade account balanced, or keep the real exchange rate constant and eliminate the difference between domestic and foreign inflation. We assume that the depreciation formula is given by

$$\frac{\dot{e}}{e} = \alpha\frac{\dot{p}}{p} + \beta(\overline{\varepsilon} - \varepsilon) \qquad (10.1)$$

where the dot over the variables represents the time derivative, e stands for the nominal exchange rate, defined as the domestic price of foreign currency, p is the domestic price level, ε-bar is the target real exchange rate and ε is the real exchange rate. The target real exchange rate is fixed by the central bank, which tries to guarantee that the real exchange rate is such that an export surplus to pay for the service of the foreign debt will always exist.[9] Hence, when the costs of servicing the foreign debt increase the target real exchange rate will increase.

The rate of change of the real exchange rate is then given by

$$\frac{\dot{\varepsilon}}{\varepsilon} = (\alpha - 1)\frac{\dot{p}}{p} + \beta(\bar{\varepsilon} - \varepsilon) \tag{10.2}$$

where $0 < \alpha, \beta < 1$. In other words, the rate of change of the real exchange rate is inversely related to the rate of inflation.

The next step is to look at the domestic price level dynamics. Real wage changes are also inversely related to the rate of inflation, since the change in the real wage can be defined as the difference between the change in the nominal wage and inflation. Also, we assume that the government imposes nominal wage increases that are proportional to the impact of domestic inflation on the nominal exchange rate. Thus, we have

$$\frac{\dot{\omega}}{\omega} = \frac{\dot{W}}{W} - \frac{\dot{p}}{p} = \alpha\frac{\dot{p}}{p} - \frac{\dot{p}}{p} = (\alpha - 1)\frac{\dot{p}}{p} \tag{10.3}$$

where ω is the real wage and W is the nominal wage.

Further, firms determine their prices as a mark up on variable costs in the traditional Kaleckian way. This is represented by

$$p = \frac{(Wb - ep^{*}m)}{(1 - \pi)} \tag{10.4}$$

where b is the inverse of labor productivity, p^* is the price of imported goods, m is the import coefficient and π is the share of profits in total income. We assume that the law of one price is not effective, and as a result domestic prices may differ from foreign prices. If the law of one price were effective, then we would have $p = p^*$ and either π or W would have to be endogenous. We take p^* equal to one, and assume it is constant.

Finally, the economy is divided between workers and capitalists, who try to increase their share on total income at the expense of each other. The profit share is positively related to the degree of monopoly as represented by the mark-up. Hence, whenever the actual share of profits falls below the target share firms will increase domestic prices. This is represented as follows

$$\frac{\dot{p}}{p} = \bar{\pi} - \pi \tag{10.5}$$

where π-bar represents the target profit share desired by capitalists. Also, for simplification we assume that whereas firms have the ability to impose a higher degree of monopoly, workers are relatively passive and are unable to fight reductions in their relative income share.[10]

Equation (10.4) can be rewritten as

$$\pi = 1 - \omega b - \varepsilon m \tag{10.6}$$

where all the variables have the usual meaning. From equations (10.1) to (10.6) we can derive the dynamic behavior of the system, which sets the real exchange rate and the real wage in the economy. We have

$$\frac{\dot{\varepsilon}}{\varepsilon} = (\alpha - 1)(\bar{\pi} - 1 + \omega b + \varepsilon m) + \beta(\bar{\varepsilon} - \varepsilon) \tag{10.7}$$

$$\frac{\dot{\omega}}{\omega} = (\alpha - 1)(\bar{\pi} - 1 + \omega b + \varepsilon m) \tag{10.8}$$

Solution of the system formed by (10.7) and (10.8) is presented in Figure 10.1. Initially assume that the real exchange rate and the real wage both rest in the ε-dot schedule. If ω increases, then π falls and for given π-bar prices will rise, pushing down the real exchange rate. In addition, assume that real exchange rate and the real wage lie in the ω-dot schedule. If ε increases, then π falls and for given π-bar prices will rise, pushing down the real wage rate. Stability requires that the ε-dot schedule is flatter than ω-dot schedule.[11]

Let us assume that an external shock affects the ability to service foreign debt, and as a result has an effect on the target real exchange rate.[12] If the interest rate on foreign debt rises, then the target real exchange rate will have to be higher to generate a larger export surplus.[13] Accordingly, the ε-dot schedule moves to the right and the real exchange rate depreciates. Depreciation, in turn, implies rising variable costs and a lower profit share, which leads to price inflation for given π-bar. Nominal wages are readjusted, but less than fully, since $0 < \alpha < 1$. Therefore, in the new equilibrium the real wage is smaller than before the external shock, as shown in Figure 10.2. Furthermore, if the economy is wage led, then a reduction in real wages has a

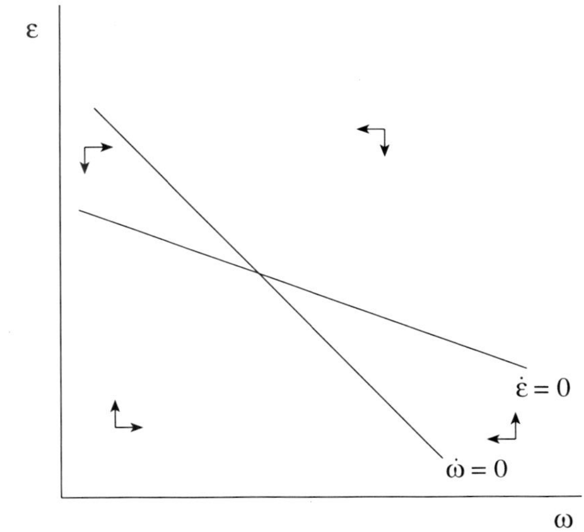

Figure 10.1 *Exchange rate and wage dynamics*

negative effect on capacity utilization and the economy stagnates. In sum, the external shock leads to stagflation.[14]

Inflation in the model in Figure 10.2 is represented by the transition between two steady-states (E_0 and E_1). Exchange rates are depreciated to bring enough export surpluses to service the debt, and real wages are brought down. These results are in accordance with the stylized facts of high inflation and hyperinflation situations.

Stabilization in this case requires a solution for the balance of payments crises. Short-run solutions may require a contraction of domestic demand. In the long run a reversion of capital flows may reduce the external pressure, and allow for a more appreciated exchange rate target. The ε-dot curve moves inwards, and deflationary pressures are then felt. Other things equal, stabilization might have a positive effect on income distribution by allowing for a higher real wage.

It is important to note that fiscal deficits, and all other excess demand pressures are absent, so that high levels of inflation are compatible with an economy that is below full employment, and stabilization is independent of fiscal adjustments. However, this does not imply that the model has no fiscal implications. The target real exchange rate is manipulated through the interest rate. The fiscal implications of these policies are discussed in the following section.

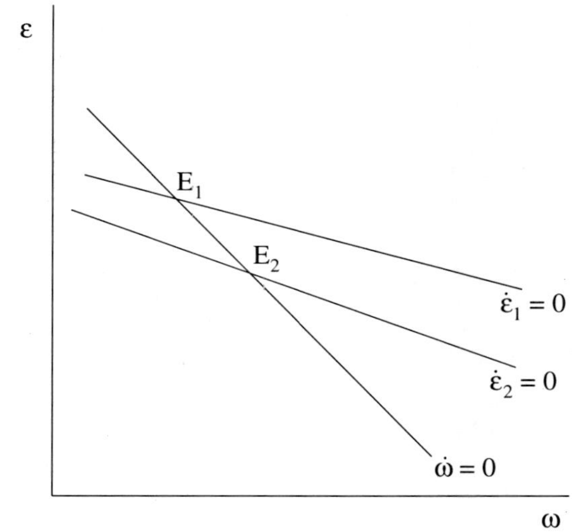

Figure 10.2 External shock dynamics

FISCAL DEFICITS AND MONETARY POLICY

As we saw in the previous section, fiscal policy has no direct role in the model presented. In that case, it follows that fiscal austerity is not part of the stabilization process. The stabilization process then depends on the reversion of the external shock. For example, a recession in the creditor countries that forces a reduction in foreign interest rates allows a reduction of the target real exchange rate, since lower interest rates reduce the costs of debt servicing.[15]

This leads to an inward change of the ε-dot schedule and the real exchange rate appreciates. Appreciation, in turn, implies falling variable costs and a higher profit share, which leads to price deflation for given π-bar. Nominal wages are readjusted, but less than fully; hence the real wage is higher than before the positive external shock. Thus, initially at least the stabilization process goes hand in hand with an improvement of income distribution.

Two points must be then emphasized. First, progressive income distribution may very well lead to higher levels of capacity utilization and growth. However, there is no reason for higher effective demand to affect prices in the model presented. Higher effective demand will only have an impact on prices if it affects the income distribution equilibrium. Also, other macroeconomic factors may reverse the initial positive effects on income distribution and growth.

Second, and more importantly, the appreciated currency may imply that interest rates are kept high in order to attract foreign reserves, to defend the currency, on the one hand, and to close the balance of payments, on the other, since the appreciated currency leads to current account deficits. High interest rates, on the other hand, have a negative impact on debt servicing.

Increased debt servicing means, as the experience of some Latin American countries shows, that even if primary balances (excluding interest payments) are in surplus, operational balances (including real interest payments) will be deeply in the red. Hence, fiscal crises are the result and not the cause of inflationary crises, and may not disappear with stabilization.

In fact, without the depreciation of the value of accumulated debt (non-indexed bonds) caused by inflation, one would expect that fiscal crises get worse during the stabilization process. Also, since stabilization requires a relatively appreciated currency, which leads to current account deficits, then foreign debt also piles up. The effect is the accumulation of twin debts (foreign and domestic).

This set-up imposes severe trade-offs for policy-makers. In particular, the central bank has to decide whether to keep a high rate of interest in order to maintain the appreciated currency and stability, on the one hand, or to reduce interest rates to avoid the increase of the fiscal deficit, on the other. Recent experience in Latin America shows that most central bankers will take the first route to its ultimate consequences, that is, to the point where no interest rate is high enough to attract capital, and the exchange rate must be floated (usually concomitantly with default).

CONCLUDING REMARKS

The conventional view of inflation in the developed world has been based on the quantity theory of money. Post Keynesians have challenged this view, and put forward a view of inflation based on distributive conflict. German and Latin contributions during hyperinflationary periods provide another alternative that emphasizes the role of balance of payments crises. This chapter provides a model that contains the main arguments of the German Balance of Payments School, and of some neo-structuralists authors. Not only inflation results from balance of payments crises, but fiscal crises also are the result of the initial balance of payments crises within this framework. Finally, this approach emphasizes the harsh trade-offs imposed on central bankers.

NOTES

1. We would like to thank Luis Carlos Bresser Pereira, Korkut Erturk, Julio Lopes, Antônio Carlos Macedo e Silva, Noemi Levy Orlik, Randy Wray and an anonymous referee for their comments. The responsibility for any remaining errors is ours entirely.
2. This section relies heavily on Câmara (1990) and Câmara and Vernengo (2001).
3. Keynes also defended a non-orthodox policy regarding British return to the Gold Standard. While the Cunliffe Committee – based on Arthur C. Pigou's intellectual authority – proposed a return to Gold at the pre-war parity, Keynes preferred a devalued parity. By 1925, when Churchill returned to Gold at the pre-war parity, Keynes had moved to attack the Gold Standard *tout court*. See Vernengo (2001).
4. In many respects the structuralist discussion on passive money precedes the post Keynesian discussion on endogenous money. See Olivera (1970) for a typical structuralist view, and Wray (1998) for a recent exposition of the post Keynesian views.
5. The origins of the inertialist view of inflation are to be found in work done by Bresser Pereira in the late 1970s. See Bresser Pereira and Nakano (1987).
6. Some post Keynesians authors emphasized also the role of expectations in producing price inertia, rather than the role of contracts (Carvalho, 1993).
7. See also Taylor (1991, pp. 99–105).
8. This section is based on Vernengo (2002).
9. The main instrument used by the central bank is the rate of interest. This reflects, for example, the policies pursued by the Brazilian central bank between March 1995 and January 1999, when a crawling peg maintained the real exchange rate relatively constant.
10. Also, it is implicitly assumed that firms have a constant market share. This model, one should note, does not emphasize disputes between firms, which might be an important part of inflationary phenomena.
11. We have

$$\frac{\partial \varepsilon}{\partial \omega}\Big|_{\dot{\varepsilon}=0} = \frac{(\alpha-1)b}{(1-\alpha)m+\beta}$$

and

$$\frac{\partial \varepsilon}{\partial \omega}\Big|_{\dot{\omega}=0} = -\frac{b}{m}$$

Simple inspection shows that both are negative and that the stability condition is satisfied, since $0 < \alpha, \beta < 1$.
12. Several external shocks would befit the analysis. For example, a fall in export revenues following the collapse of the international price of commodities, or the reversal of capital flows caused by contagion effects, would be representative of the types of shocks we have in mind.
13. Clearly, we assume that the so-called Marshall-Lerner condition is satisfied.
14. The introduction of staggered price and wages adjustments would lead to inflationary inertia. Inertia and a stable adjustment process as the one presented fit the stylized facts in Latin America, where some countries suffered high but relatively stable inflation. We assume continuous adjustment for simplicity.
15. The US recession of the early 1990s and the lower interest rates that followed – together with the Brady Plan – are usually part of the explanation of the increase of capital flows to Latin America.

REFERENCES

Amadeo, E. (1994), *Institutions, Inflation and Unemployment*, Aldershot: Edward Elgar.

Arida, P., and A. Lara-Resende (1985), 'Inertial inflation and monetary reform in Brazil', in J. Williamson (ed.), *Inflation and Indexation*, Washington, DC: Institute for International Economics.

Bresciani-Turroni, C. (1931), *The Economics of Inflation: A Study of Currency Depreciation in Post-War Germany*, reprinted 1937, London: Allen & Unwin.

Bresser Pereira, L.C., and Y. Nakano (1987), *The Theory of Inertial Inflation: The Foundation of Economic Reform in Brazil & Argentina*, Boulder, CO: Lynne Rienner.

Cagan, P. (1956), 'The monetary dynamics of hyperinflation', in M. Friedman (ed.), *Studies in the Quantity Theory of Money*, Chicago, IL: Chicago University Press.

Câmara, A. (1990), 'Plano Collor: Raízes e Frutos', in M.C. Tavares, A. Teixeira and M.V. Junho Penna (eds), *Aquarella do Brasil*, Rio de Janeiro: Rio Fundo Editora.

Câmara, A., and M. Vernengo (2001), 'The German Balance of Payments School and the Latin American neo-structuralists', in L.-P. Rochon and M. Vernengo (eds), *Credit, Interest Rates and the Open Economy*, Cheltenham, UK and Northampton, MA, USA: Edward Elgar.

Carvalho, F. (1993), 'Strato-inflation and high inflation: the Brazilian experience', *Cambridge Journal of Economics*, **17** (1), 63–78.

Davidson, P. (1990), 'A post Keynesian positive contribution to "theory",' *Journal of Post Keynesian Economics*, **13** (2), 298–304.

Ellis, H. (1934), *German Monetary Theory: 1905–1933*, Cambridge, MA: Harvard University Press.

Furtado, C. (1958), *The Economic Growth of Brazil*, reprinted 1963, Berkeley, CA: University of California Press.

Graham, F. (1930), *Exchange, Prices, and Production in Hyperinflation: Germany, 1920–1923*, Princeton, NJ: Princeton University Press.

Helfferich, K. (1927), *Money*, New York: The Adelphi Company.

Kaldor, N. (1982), *The Scourge of Monetarism*, Oxford: Oxford University Press.

Keynes, John M. (1920), *The Economic Consequences of the Peace*, New York: Harcourt, Brace and Howe.

Keynes, J.M. (1923), 'A tract on monetary reform', in D. Moggridge (ed.), *The Collected Writings of John Maynard Keynes*, vol. 4, repr. 1971, London and Cambridge: Macmillan and Cambridge University Press.

Keynes, John M. (1936), *The General Theory of Employment Interest, and Money*, New York: Harcourt, Brace & World.

Noyola, J. (1956), 'El Desarrollo Económico y la Inflación en México y otros Países Latinoamericanos', *Investigación Económica*, **14**, 4.

Olivera, J. (1970), 'On passive money', *Journal of Political Economy*, **78**, 805–14.

Rowthorn, R. (1977), 'Conflict, inflation and money', *Cambridge Journal of Economics*, **1**, 215–39.

Sunkel, O. (1958) 'Inflation in Chile: an unorthodox approach', *International Economic Papers*, **10**, (first published in English in 1960).

Taylor, L. (1991), *Income Distribution, Inflation and Growth: Lectures on Structuralist Macroeconomic Theory*, Cambridge, MA: MIT Press.

Vernengo, M. (2001), 'Sraffa, Keynes and "The Years of High Theory"', *Review of Political Economy*, **13** (3), 343–54.

Vernengo, M. (2002), 'Conflicto de Distribución en una Economia Abierta', *Cuestiones Económicas*, **18** (3), 209–20.
Wray, R. (1998), *Understanding Modern Money*, Cheltenham, UK and Lyme, USA: Edward Elgar.

PART IV

Kaleckian Perspectives on Growth, Inflation and Distribution

11. Commodity prices and the dynamics of inflation in Australia*

Harry Bloch and David Sapsford

INTRODUCTION

Explanations of inflation tend to emphasize domestic market conditions, particularly labor market institutions and the strength of demand for domestic output relative to productive capacity. In the present chapter we examine an additional influence on the inflationary process, namely the prices of primary commodities. Our approach is to incorporate primary product prices into a structural model of pricing that is developed from the pricing analysis of Michal Kalecki.

Kalecki (1971, ch. 5) treats the cost of finished goods as determined by both the prices of primary commodities used as raw materials and the wage rates of industrial labor. He then argues that primary commodity prices have a stronger positive relationship to the business cycle than do wage rates, so the ratio of primary commodity prices to wage rates is pro-cyclical. Further, prime costs are marked up to determine finished goods prices, implying cyclical variation in the real wage rate and distribution of income.

We employ Kalecki's pricing analysis to consider the implications for the dynamics of inflation arising from the cyclical behavior of primary product prices. Our particular concern is that the pro-cyclical movement in primary commodities relative to wage rates can set off a wage-price spiral for finished goods through the resulting pressure on the nominal wages of industrial workers. Of course, this scenario can also work in reverse, as Beckerman and Jenkinson (1986) suggest in explaining the fall of the rate of inflation in the UK in the early 1980s. The general issue is whether, and to what extent, shocks to nominal commodity prices impact on the aggregate price level as well as on the relative price of primary commodities and manufactured goods. We examine this possibility by estimating an econometric model of the inflationary process in the Australian economy over the period since the float of the Australian dollar in 1984.

Kalecki develops his pricing analysis for the case of a closed economy, so we extend his framework two ways to apply it to the open Australian economy.

First, we allow the price of competing foreign products to affect prices of domestic finished goods, following Bloch (1996) in treating the degree of monopoly for domestic products as influenced by the relative price of domestic and competing foreign products. Second, we introduce an exchange rate equation to provide a link between foreign and domestic prices. Bloch (1991) shows that this is particularly important in the case of Australia, as primary commodities have been so dominant in Australian exports that the Australian dollar is generally considered to be a 'commodity currency'. We therefore need to establish whether the Australian dollar price of raw materials follows the worldwide pattern or deviates due to offsetting fluctuations in the exchange rate.

Our estimating model is described in the following section, which also contains a discussion of the predicted impacts for key variables. The data, estimation method and empirical results are discussed in the following section. The final section presents conclusions and discusses the implications for economic policy in Australia.

MODELING COMMODITY PRICES AND AUSTRALIAN INFLATION

Markets for primary commodities are notoriously volatile, arising from the interaction of inelastic demand (for both price and income) and supply. They are also prone to periods of boom and bust of significant magnitude (see Sapsford and Morgan, 1994, for an overview). Maizels (1992) demonstrates how volatile prices have been in the 1980s. Sugar, for example, has seen world market prices vary between 2.5 and 41 US cents per pound, while coffee has ranged between 60 and 303 cents per pound. 'Hard' commodities have not been insulated from this volatility either, with aluminum prices varying between 42 and 162 cents and copper between 58 and 159 cents. While only a limited sample, it is illustrative of the more general experience of price uncertainty and variability in primary commodity markets.

Kalecki (1971) treats primary commodity prices as determined by supply and demand forces in world markets. He also notes that primary commodities are used as raw materials for the manufacturing process, so that demand increases with industrial production. Figure 11.1 shows the rates of change in OECD industrial production and in the IMF index of primary commodity prices over the period from 1984, quarter 2, through 1998, quarter 4. The peaks and troughs occur at similar times, but there is substantially greater volatility in primary commodity prices.

In Bloch and Sapsford (1991–92), we expand this treatment to include other influences on the demand and supply of primary commodities and to treat primary commodity prices as determined in world markets. World de-

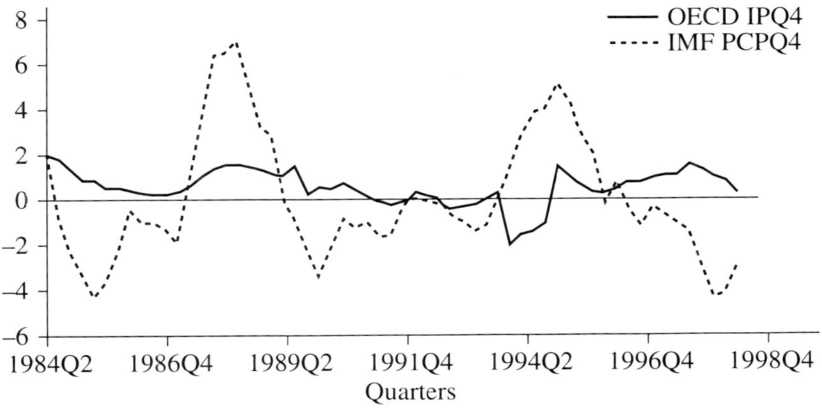

Figure 11.1 OECD industrial production and IMF primary commodity prices ($US) – quarterly percentage change (four quarter moving average)

mand increases with industrial production and with the prices received for manufactured products. Kalecki treats manufacturing as generally operating with excess capacity, but primary commodity production is generally subject to capacity constraints in the short to medium run, which shift with changes in productive capacity due to investment or technical progress.

A short-run world pricing equation for primary commodities in general form is:

$$pc = f[X, px, \varepsilon, TC] \quad (11.1)$$

In equation 11.1, *pc* is the world price of the primary commodity expressed in US dollar terms. *X* and *px* are measures of total world industrial production (given by the sum of X_j over all countries) and the average price at which this product is sold in the various countries, respectively, ε is a disturbance term for the influence of supply shocks (such as droughts, floods and earthquakes). Finally, *TC* is an index of productive capacity across primary producers.

Pro-cyclical movement in primary commodity prices is expected in equation 11.1, as the primary commodity demand moves in the same direction as industrial production and primary production is supply constrained. By similar argument, prices of industrial products are expected to have a positive influence on primary product prices. Finally, a negative impact is expected for increases in capacity due to investment and technical progress, which increase short-run commodity supply.

Australia's foreign exchange rate is linked to primary product prices through their influence on her terms of trade. Bloch (1991) finds that Australia, as a substantial net exporter of primary commodities, has terms of trade that move directly with the price of primary commodities on world markets. The path of the IMF primary commodity price index and the value of Australian currency expressed in terms of US dollars per Australian dollar are shown in Figure 11.2. Parallel movement in the indexes is particularly noticeable from the beginning of the period through 1989 and again from 1996 onwards.

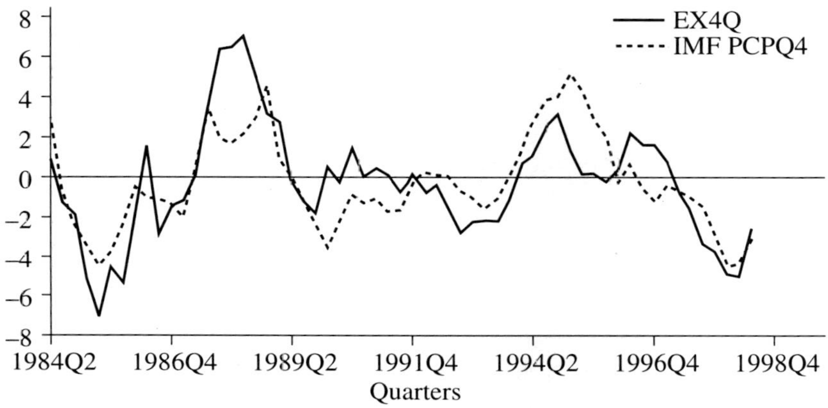

Figure 11.2 *US\$/A\$ exchange rate and IMF commodity prices – quarterly percentage change (four quarter moving average)*

Gruen and Wilkinson (1994) find some evidence that the Australian dollar moves directly with Australia's terms of trade (after controlling for the influence of interest rate differentials). Further, Blundell-Wignall and Gregory (1990) argue that increases in Australia's terms of trade require appreciation of the real exchange rate to achieve product market equilibrium. Thus, the nominal exchange rate expressed as foreign currency per Australian dollar is expected to move directly with commodity prices, after controlling for domestic and foreign price levels. Our equation for estimating the determinants of Australia's foreign exchange rate includes primary commodity prices, along with the domestic price level, foreign price level and other macroeconomic variables used in monetary and portfolio balance theories of the determinants of exchange rates. Our estimating equation is of the general form:

$$E_{A,j} = f[pc, px_A, px_j, Z_{A,j}] \tag{11.2}$$

In equation 11.2, $E_{A,j}$ is the foreign exchange rate expressed as currency of the *j*th country per Australian dollar, px_A is the Australian domestic price level, px_j is the domestic price level in country *j* and $Z_{A,j}$ is a vector of other variables, such as interest rates, affecting the exchange rate between Australia and country *j*. Due to the importance of the US dollar in international transactions, especially transactions in primary commodities, we limit our focus to the exchange rate between the Australian and US currencies.

Our direct interest is in the determinants of the aggregate price level in Australia. Primary commodity prices have a potential influence through the use of these commodities as raw materials in manufacturing, as well as entering directly as final products in the food sector. Kalecki (1971) treats the prices of finished goods as determined by marking up unit prime cost, where unit prime cost consists of unit labor cost and unit materials cost. Bloch and Olive (1999) find that prices in Australian manufacturing industries are very closely related to domestic production costs. However, they also find that in industries with high concentration, output prices increase with prices of competitive foreign products when the market share of competitive imports is high and that output prices increase with the level of aggregate output (real GDP) when the market share of competitive imports is low. This implies that, for high concentration industries, the degree of monopoly increases with either the price of competing foreign products or real GDP. Thus, we allow for the aggregate price level in Australia to be affected by prices of competitive foreign products and real GDP, as well as by input prices that affect production costs.

We estimate a pricing equation for finished goods, combining the factors that affect the degree of monopoly with those that affect unit prime cost. The variables affecting the degree of monopoly are real GDP and the price of competitive foreign product, while unit prime cost depends on the wage rate, the price of primary commodities and time as a proxy for technology. The estimating equation is of the general form:

$$px_A = f[X_A, px_{A,j}, pc_A, w_A, T] \tag{11.3}$$

In equation 11.3, X_A is a measure of aggregate production in Australia (measured by real GDP), while $px_{A,j}$ is a measure of the average price of competitive foreign products as expressed in Australian dollars. w_A and pc_A are measures of the nominal wage rate in Australia and of the price of primary commodities expressed in Australian currency, respectively. *T* is time, which we use as a proxy for technology available for manufacturing in Australia.[1]

Wage rates are generally given more prominence in discussions of the determinants of inflation than are primary commodity prices. We explicitly include wages in our model of inflation through a Phillips-curve relationship of the variety commonly used in Australia (see Gruen, Pagan and Thompson, 1999), so that the wage rate equation is explicitly in log difference form, except for the unemployment variable, as follows:

$$\Delta\log(w_A) = f[\Delta\log(px_A), U_A, \Delta\log(pc_A), \Delta\log(TW_A)] \qquad (11.4)$$

In equation 11.4, U_A is the Australian unemployment rate and TW_A is an index of the productivity of labour in Australia (either proxied by time or measured by labor productivity).

Blanchard and Katz (1999) discuss the difference between the type of Phillips curve relation in equation 11.4, excluding primary commodity prices and labor productivity, and a 'wage curve' in which the level of the wage rate is a function of the level of unemployment and the level of the reservation wage. They show that the two are consistent provided that (1) neither the expected real wage nor the reservation wage in the 'wage curve' is a function of labor productivity and (2) the reservation wage in real terms moves exactly with lagged real wages. We test below to determine whether labor productivity and primary price terms add to the explanatory power of our wage rate equation. If not, the estimated Phillips curve may be taken as also representing an underlying 'wage curve'.

SOME EMPIRICAL EVIDENCE

The previous section specifies a four-equation model consisting of equations describing the determination of world primary commodity prices, equation 11.1, Australia's exchange rate, equation 11.2, Australia's domestic aggregate price level, equation 11.3, and Australia's wage rate, equation 11.4. This section reports the results that are obtained when this model is estimated against quarterly data spanning the time period from the first quarter of 1984 through to the final quarter of 1998. We restrict our attention to the period after the Australian dollar was floated in December 1983, to focus on the interrelationship between movements in prices in international commodity markets and the value of the Australian dollar in international currency markets, as a central element of our model. Blundell-Wignall and Gregory (1990) show clearly that the inflationary impact of terms of trade movements changed dramatically after 1983 when the Australian dollar moved from an adjustable peg to a managed float.

For purposes of estimation we take the world price of the primary commodity (pc), the Australian exchange rate vis-à-vis the US dollar ($E_{A,j}$, where j denotes the USA) as well as Australia's prices and wage rates (px_A and w_A, respectively) as endogenously determined. The remaining variables of the model are each treated as exogenous. These remaining variables are the world finished goods production (X), productive capacity in primary production (TC) [proxied by time], domestic price level in the outside world (px_j) [proxied by the US GDP deflator], the vector of 'other' macroeconomic variables affecting the Australian–US dollar exchange rate ($Z_{A,j}$), Australian real GDP (X_A), technological capacity in the production of finished goods within Australia (T) [proxied by time], the Australian unemployment rate (U_A) and labor productivity in Australia (TW_A).[2]

The world primary commodity price series analysed in this section is obtained from the International Monetary Fund, International Financial Statistics (IFS) database. This series provides an index of the prices of 33 internationally traded primary commodities expressed in US dollars. Our proxy for world production of finished products is the OECD index of industrial production and is obtained from its Main Economic Indicators database. The remaining series employed are obtained mainly from the DX database, supplemented in the case of some of the domestic variables by data collected from the Australian Bureau of Statistics and Reserve Bank of Australia sources, or the IFS. Full details relating to both the sources and definitions of the series used may be found in the Data Appendix.

Testing the variables of a model for stationarity *prior* to regression analysis is now well established as an essential component of econometric practice. The results that are obtained when the Dickey-Fuller and Augmented Dickey-Fuller (both with and without trend) tests are applied to the variables of our model lead us to reject, for each variable expressed in growth rate form as the first difference of natural logarithms, the null-hypothesis of a unit-root.[3] In essence, these results indicate that the *levels* of the logarithms of the various variable discussed above are each I(1) variables.

Since each of the variables entering the right-hand side of the world primary commodity price equation 11.1 is exogenous, unbiased estimates of the parameters of this equation can, in principle, be obtained by a suitable single equation method of estimation. As indicated above, our proxy measure for world production of finished products (X) is the OECD's index of industrial production. In light of the unit-root test results described above, our model is estimated with all variables specified in logarithmic first-difference form, with the consequence that each estimated parameter may be straightforwardly interpreted as an estimate of the relevant elasticity. As regards equation 11.1, this particular specification for the estimating equation has the additional implication that when TC is proxied, as is frequently the case, by a time trend then its coefficient corresponds directly to the intercept that is estimated from the equation expressed in logarithmic first-difference form. Since we are working with quarterly seasonally unadjusted data a set of three seasonal dummies is introduced into the analysis, corresponding to the first through third quarters of the year (denoted hereafter by SD1, SD2 and SD3, respectively).

The results that are obtained for equation 11.1 are set out as equation number 1.1 in Table 11.1. We allow for possible lagged effects in the determination of world primary commodity prices using the 'general-to-specific' methodology. The results of this exercise lead us to choose only the current value of the world industrial production variable. This exercise also reveals no evidence that the world aggregate price level, px (whether proxied by the US GDP deflator or the US producer price index), exerts any current or lagged effect on world primary commodity prices. Due to the presence of autocorrelation, this equation is corrected using the exact AR(1) Newton-Raphson iterative method, which converges after five iterations.[4]

In terms of both its overall degree of fit and the signs of its various estimated parameters, this estimated equation provides an encouraging degree of support for the simple model of price determination in the world market for primary commodities presented above. The estimated coefficient of world finished goods production, X, (measured by OECD industrial production) shows the expected pro-cyclical movement in primary commodity prices and is statistically significant at the 5 per cent level Our estimates imply an elasticity of world primary commodity prices with respect to OECD industrial production over the study period of 0.46. This estimated elasticity compares to the estimate of 1.46 reported by Bloch and Sapsford (2000, p. 474) for the longer period 1948 through to 1993. The difference between these two estimates supports the view expressed by some analysts (for example, Winters and Sapsford, 1990) that at the global level, primary commodity prices in the 1980s were less sensitive to fluctuations in the level of world industrial production than in earlier periods.[5] Our estimates also reveal the presence of a distinct seasonal pattern in world primary commodity prices, with a significant increase being evident in the first quarter of the year, accompanied by a fall of roughly equivalent magnitude in the third quarter.[6]

The results that are obtained when the Australian exchange rate equation 11.2 is estimated are summarized as equation number 1.2 in Table 11.1. In view of the endogeneity of both the primary commodity price (pc) and Australian domestic price level (px_A) variables, equation 11.2 is initially estimated using the generalized instrumental variable (GIVE) technique. In this equation, the Australian GDP deflator measures the domestic price level, while the US domestic price level (px_j, with j = US) is measured by the US GDP deflator.

Experiments utilizing the generalized instrumental variable estimation (GIVE) technique conducted over a range of alternative specifications, yield no evidence to suggest that movements in either the Australian or US price levels exert any significant impact on the exchange rate between their two

Table 11.1 Primary commodity prices and inflation in Australia, 1984Q2–1998Q4

Equation number	Dependent variable												
	pc	Constant	X	SD1	SD2	SD3	R^2	D-W					
1.1		–0.0028	0.4588	0.0225	–0.0003	–0.0201	0.3090	2.1371					
		(0.331)	(2.472)	(3.253)	(0.045)	(3.145)							
	$E_{A,US}$	Constant	pc(–2)	r_A	$r_A(-1)$	r_{US}	$i_A(-2)$	$i_{US}(-3)$	SD3	R^2	D-W		
1.2		–0.0043	0.4836	–0.4999	0.2309	0.5094	0.1578	–0.1679	–0.0188	0.4330	1.8299		
		(0.841)	(3.060)	(3.782)	(2.0617)	(3.467)	(2.510)	(2.186)	(1.567)				
	px_A	Constant	$X_A(-1)$	$X_A(-3)$	$w_A(-1)$	$w_A(-2)$	$w_A(-3)$	$w_A(-4)$	$pc_A(-3)$	$pc_A(-4)$	R^2	D-W	LM_1
1.3		–0.0042	0.3877	–0.2547	0.1696	0.2187	0.3553	0.2571	0.0844	0.0378	0.5527	1.4001	6.9453
		(1.932)	(3.468)	(2.327)	(2.187)	(2.965)	(4.650)	(3.565)	(3.942)	(1.828)			
1.3 (cont)		LM_2	LM_3	LM_4									
		1.5189	0.0998	0.3783									
	w_A	Constant	px_A	pc_A	SD1	SD2	SD3	R^2	D-W	LM_1	LM_2	LM_3	LM_4
1.4		0.0018	0.9773	0.0340	0.0039	–0.0060	–0.0019	0.4038	2.0287	4.2941	1.0639	0.1982	0.8251
		(0.647)	(3.548)	(1.153)	(1.564)	(2.631)	(0.807)						

Notes: Figures in parenthesis are absolute '*t*' ratios. LM_1 denotes the Lagrange multiplier test for serial correlation, LM_2 denotes Ramsey's RESET test of functional form, LM_3 denotes the Jarque-Bera test for residual normality, while LM_4 denotes the Lagrange multiplier test for heteroscedasticity. On the relevant null-hypothesis these test statistics are distributed as χ^2 with 4, 1, 2 and 1 degree of freedom respectively.

currencies. This finding is consistent with the evidence in Olekalns and Wilkins (1998), who find that purchasing power parity applies to the Australian exchange rate only over the long run. The results in equation number 1.2 in Table 11.1 are obtained with the two price level variables omitted on the grounds of their insignificance.

For the purpose of the current exercise we consider only short-term and long-term interest rates for both the US and Australia as possible components of the Z vector. Long-term rates are used as proxies for inflation expectations, while short-term rates are used as proxies for financial market intervention by the monetary authority in each country. In the particular specification reported in 1.2, the interest rate variables for each country are entered separately, so that the separate effects exerted by domestic and foreign (US) interest rates may be isolated. The long-term interest rate variables employed in 1.2 are the 10-year Australian bond rate and US long-term Treasury bond rate, denoted by r_A and r_{US}, respectively. The corresponding short-term rates are the 13-week Australian Commonwealth note rate and the three-month US Treasury note rate (for constant maturity), denoted by i_A and i_{US}, respectively.

To allow for possible lags in the influences on Australia's exchange rate a range of alternative lag lengths are applied in the context of the 'general-to-specific' technique. The results of this exercise indicate the existence of significance at two quarters for the *pc* term, two quarters on the US short-term interest rate, three quarters on the Australian short-term interest rate, and both the current value and the one-quarter lag on the Australian long-term interest rate.[7] Once the price level variables and the current value of commodity price level are omitted, there are no current endogenous variables on the right-hand side of our chosen specification and we estimate equation number 1.2 in Table 11.1 using a single-equation method. Finally, diagnostic tests on ordinary least squares regression results lead us to adopt a one-period moving average adjustment scheme.[8]

The parsimonious model reported in 1.2 reveals that primary commodity prices lagged two quarters exert the hypothesized positive effect on US dollar per Australian dollar exchange rate (implying appreciation of the Australian dollar following an increase in primary commodity prices). The elasticity of 0.4836 suggests that the Australian dollar in the period since the float exhibits the characteristics of a commodity currency, once the influences of foreign and domestic interest rates are included in the specification. However, the elasticity value indicates slightly less than half of the change in world commodity prices is offset by a change in the value of the Australian dollar, so that prices of primary commodities expressed in Australian dollars are still pro-cyclical with world industrial production.[9]

Both short-term and long-term interest rates in Australia and the US are shown to significantly influence the value of the Australian dollar in 1.2.

Evidence of overshooting is found for the adjustment of the exchange rate to changes in the long-term Australian interest rate, but there is no evidence of dynamics found for the US interest rate. The direction of the net influence for each long-term rate is as expected for measures of inflationary expectations, with a higher Australian rate associated with depreciation of the Australian dollar and the US long-term rate having the opposite effect. The opposite direction of impact is expected for short-term interest rate variables as measures reflecting the impact of monetary policy. This is what we find, namely, that the Australian dollar appreciates with an increase in Australian short-term interest rates but depreciates with an increase in US rates.[10]

Experiments conducted with estimation of equation 11.3, describing the determinants of Australia's aggregate price level, using the GIVE technique suggest that the rate of growth of Australia's domestic price level (proxied by the GDP deflator) over the post-float period is significantly and positively related to growth in real output, X_A (proxied by GDP at constant prices), growth in nominal wages, w_A and growth in primary commodity prices denominated in Australian dollars, pc_A. However, our initial results provide no evidence that the average price of competing foreign products expressed in Australian dollars (proxied by the US GDP deflator multiplied by the prevailing rate of exchange between the two dollars) exerts a significant effect, so this variable is excluded.

To allow for the possible existence of lags in the impact of the remaining variables on the domestic price level, a range of alternative lag lengths are applied in the context of the 'general-to-specific' technique. The results obtained when the model is re-estimated after exclusion of non-significant lag terms are reported in equation number 1.3 in Table 11.1. Since the particular specification reported in 1.3 contains no current endogenous variables on its right-hand side, it is legitimately estimated by OLS rather than GIVE.

The various diagnostic statistics for 1.3 provide no evidence of serial correlation, heteroscedasticity, non-normality or functional form misspecification problems. The results suggest that growth in Australia's domestic price level is positively and significantly related to growth in real GDP lagged one quarter, but negatively and significantly related to real GDP lagged three quarters. This is arguably consistent with the existence of an endogenous lagged supply response of the cobweb variety.

In addition, the results in 1.3 indicate that the effect of growth in nominal wages, w_A, is distributed over a four-quarter period commencing with a one-quarter lag, with all four of the lag coefficients correctly signed and significant at the 5 per cent level. The sum of the wage coefficients indicates a full impact elasticity of approximately 1.0 (1.0064 to be exact) within five quarters. This implies that a 1 per cent increase in nominal wages leads to a 1 per cent increase in the GDP deflator within five quarters, so that domestic producers are restoring fixed mark-ups on changes in unit labor costs due to wage changes over the five-quarter period.[11]

Simple dynamics on the primary commodity price term denominated in Australian dollars, pc_A, indicate that this variable exerts the expected positive on the price level at both three and four quarter lags at the 5 per cent significance level.[12] The full impact elasticity of primary commodity prices on inflation, as indicated by the sum of the lagged coefficients of the primary product price, is approximately .12 within five quarters.

Equation number 1.4 in Table 11.1 reports GIVE estimates of the parameters of the Australian wage equation 11.4. Once again the diagnostics show no evidence of serial correlation, functional form misspecification, non-normality of errors or heteroscedasticity. In contrast to Gruen, Pagan and Thompson (1999), who estimate a Phillips curve type formulation for quarterly Australian data covering the longer period 1965, quarter 2, through 1997, quarter 4, our results provide no evidence of a significant unemployment term over the post-float period, so this variable is omitted from the estimated specification reported as equation number 1.4 in Table 11.1.[13] Despite its parsimonious nature, 1.4 reveals that movements in Australia's domestic price level (as proxied by movements in the GDP deflator) exert a positively signed and significant effect on movements in average weekly earnings. The estimated coefficients of the seasonal dummies suggest the presence of a seasonal pattern according to which average weekly earnings rise (fall) significantly during the first (second) quarter of the year.

Although correctly signed, the primary commodity price variable (expressed in Australian dollars) fails to achieve significance. Likewise, despite experimentation with a range of alternative proxy measures for labor productivity, we could find no evidence to suggest that this variable exerted a significant effect on the rate of growth of Australian nominal wages over the post December 1983 period. We retain the intercept as a proxy for the time trend in labor productivity and the primary product price variable in 1.4 to test the conditions proposed by Blanchard and Katz (1999) under which a Phillips curve relationship can also be interpreted as a wage curve. These conditions are satisfied, as we are unable to reject the null hypothesis that each coefficient is equal to zero. However, as noted above we are unable to find any significant impact on wage rates for the unemployment variable, implying that both the Phillips curve and the wage curve are vertical.[14]

CONCLUSIONS

We examine the impact of primary commodity prices on inflation in Australia. We begin with the observation that commodity prices are highly volatile and are dependent on the world business cycle as suggested by Kalecki (1971, ch. 5). This has potentially complex implications for Australia, given her position as a commodity exporting country. Primary commodity prices have a positive impact on the aggregate price level through the use of commodities as raw materials in industrial production. However, the Australian dollar may behave as a 'commodity currency' and appreciate (depreciate) with increases (decreases) in commodity prices, thereby offsetting the direct effect of changes in commodity prices on the cost of production.

We estimate a system of four equations for determining in turn: a price index of primary commodities on world markets, the foreign exchange rate for the Australian dollar in terms of US dollars, the GDP deflator in Australia and the average weekly earnings in Australia. We find that primary commodity prices are strongly pro-cyclical with world industrial production as suggested by Kalecki, explaining part of their overall volatility. We also find that this volatility impacts on the value of the Australian dollar (relative to the US dollar) through the type of relationship to commodity prices expected for a 'commodity currency', although the long-run elasticity of the Australian dollar to commodity prices that is substantially less than one (about equal to one half). Thus, primary product prices expressed in Australian dollars are shown to move pro-cyclically with world industrial production.

Our results for determining the aggregate price level in Australia show a positive and significant impact of primary commodity prices (expressed in Australian dollars). We estimate an elasticity of the GDP deflator with respect to primary commodity prices equal to 0.12, so that a 10 per cent increase in primary products prices directly leads to an extra 1.2 per cent inflation in overall prices. In addition, we find a positive, although statistically insignificant coefficient, for primary commodity prices in the earnings equation of .03, so that there may be a small additional impact of commodity prices through wages. Both these effects are enhanced through a positive feedback mechanism between wages and prices. In particular, we estimate an elasticity of wages with respect to current aggregate prices equal to 0.98 and an elasticity of aggregate prices with respect to various lagged values of wages equal to approximately 1.0, implying an extremely strong wage-price spiral that can continue virtually indefinitely once shocked by a change in commodity prices.[15]

The strength of the wage-price spiral found in our results has very great consequences for Australia's inflationary experience. The high degree of volatility in primary commodity prices is only partially offset by changes in the exchange rate for the Australian dollar as a 'commodity currency'. This means that the Australian inflation rate is subjected to substantial shocks through the Australian dollar price of primary commodities that feed through, albeit with a lag and only partially, to the rate of inflation in the GDP deflator.

Given the strength of the price-wage spiral found in our results, there is no endogenous dampening force to dissipate the force of this shock over time. Without a reversal in commodity prices or a change in the rate of growth of domestic GDP, our results suggest that a rise (or fall) in inflation caused by such a commodity price shock will be sustained indefinitely. This means that the ultimate impact on the price level grows without bounds.

In closing it is worth speculating on the implications of our findings for other industrialized countries, particularly those that are importers rather than exporters of primary commodities. Changes in primary commodity prices can be expected to lead to changes in the currency value for such countries that are opposite to those experienced in Australia, for example a commodity price boom would lead to a depreciation of the currency. The domestic currency price of primary commodities would then magnify the change in world prices. The potential magnitude of an inflationary (or deflationary) shock is then especially great. Of course, there is no guarantee that the strength of the wage-price spiral would be as great as what we find for Australia. Examination of the impact of primary commodity prices in other countries is the subject of our continuing research.

NOTES

* Financial support from the Australian Research Council is gratefully acknowledged, as is research assistance from Michael Dockery. Previous versions of this chapter were presented to seminars at Curtin University of Technology, University of Adelaide, University of New South Wales, Australian National University, Industry Economics Conference at the University Melbourne and Seventh International Post Keynesian Workshop at the University of Missouri, Kansas City. We gratefully acknowledge helpful comments from participants at these sessions and from an anonymous referee for this volume. However, all remaining errors and omissions are the full responsibility of the authors.

1. See Bloch and Sapsford (1991–92) for a more detailed derivation, which does not, however, allow for variables influencing the degree of monopoly.
2. It should be noticed that the price of primary commodities expressed in Australian dollars (pc_A) is given, by construction, as the world price expressed in US dollars (pc) and divided by the exchange rate prevailing at the time in question between the US and Australian dollars ($E_{A,j}$, where j denotes the US). Since both of these individual 'components' of pc_A are treated as endogenously determined, pc_A is to be treated likewise. The price of competing foreign products expressed in Australian dollars ($px_{A,j}$), is similarly the product of two components px_j (with j = US) and $E_{A,j}$ (where j again denotes the US). This variable is also treated as endogenous as it comprises the product of an exogenous variable (px_j) and an endogenous variable ($E_{A,j}$).
3. The full set of test results is available from the authors upon request.
4. The estimated autoregressive error specification is as follows:

$$U(t) = \underset{(4.29)}{0.4878}\ U(t-1) + \varepsilon$$

where $U(t)$ denotes the error corresponding to time t, ε denotes a disturbance term and the figure in parenthesis is the 't' ratio based on the asymptotic standard error. The log-likelihood ratio test of the AR(1) specification versus the (unadjusted) OLS specification yields a Chi-square value, with one degree of freedom, equal to 16.289.

5. The greater volatility of primary commodity prices in the 1980s, as noted by Maizels (1992), plausibly was due to supply-side shocks or alteration in the protection of primary commodities, rather than the influence of demand-side shocks. Maizels notes a number of supply-side developments and, especially increases in protection by agricultural commodity importers, when explaining the volatility of primary commodity prices in the 1980s.
6. The wage cost variable (w) is dropped from the estimated equation, as we could find no evidence of significance for this term using the data series employed in our earlier study (Bloch and Sapsford, 2000). This may reflect the poor quality of data on wages in developing countries that account for the bulk of production of agricultural primary commodities. Alternatively, the capital-intensive nature of most mining and energy commodity production might give capital costs a greater impact than labour costs.
7. It should be noted that once these lags are imposed, only the third-quarter seasonal dummy variable approaches significance; hence the exclusion of the dummies for the first and second quarters from the specification estimated as equation 1.2.
8. The estimated moving average error specification is as follows:

$$U(t) = E(t) - \underset{(1.91)}{0.3559}\, E(t-1)$$

where $U(t)$ denotes the error at time t, E denotes the error term before applying the moving average and the figure in parenthesis is the 't' ratio based on the asymptotic standard error. The coefficient of the lagged error is significant at the 6 per cent level.

9. Bloch (1991) finds a powerful impact of the terms of trade between primary commodities and manufactured goods on the value of the Australian dollar using annual data over a period mostly preceding the float. The results reported in equation number 1.2 are more consistent with those in Gruen and Wilkinson (1994), who find that Australia's real exchange is most strongly influenced by the differential in long-run interest rates, rather than the terms of trade, during the post-1983 period of a floating exchange rate.
10. The lags that we find for the impact of short-term rates are consistent with exchange rates responding to monetary policy following their influence on the respective domestic economy rather than through a direct effect on foreign exchange markets.
11. This implies that the mark up on unit prime cost actually rises when nominal wages rise. This evidence of a rising mark-up following a nominal wage increase contrasts with a decreasing mark-up following real wage increases found by Bloch and Madsen (2001) in a study of mark-ups and employment across Australian industrial sectors. One possible reason for the difference in results is that mark ups at the industrial sector level are subject to the competitive influence of prices in other domestic industries. In contrast, we find no significant role for competing foreign prices in influencing the aggregate price level in the present study, suggesting that there is no influence on the corresponding aggregate mark-up.
12. Bloch and Sapsford (1997; 2000) find evidence to suggest that primary commodity prices lagged one year exert a significant positive effect on the prices of finished goods averaged over all OECD countries during the post-1948 period.
13. This finding is not altogether unusual in the Australian context. Gruen, Pagan and Thompson (1999) point out that the Australian evidence is perhaps to be expected to be less revealing of a Phillips curve type (inverse) unemployment effect given the fact that Australian wage data reflect, in addition to pressures generated by the forces of excess demand or supply in the labour market, various institutional factors associated with centralized wage bargaining. It is perhaps worth noting that estimation of specifications of equation 11.4 by ordinary least squares does, however, yield a correctly signed and, according to standard OLS hypothesis testing techniques, significant unemployment term. However, the analysis of this chapter suggests that such findings are invalid. The estimators in question are inconsistent, by failing to allow Australia's domestic prices and primary commodity prices to be endogenous within the wage equation.

14. Dungey and Pitchford (2000) note difficulties in identifying a unique relationship between the unemployment rate and inflation from data for Australia over recent decades. Our results cast further doubt on the existence of an Australian NAIRU (the non-accelerating inflation rate of unemployment). However, as in the results of Dungey and Pitchford, we find that output growth significantly impacts on the rate of price increase in the results reported in equation number 1.3. This means the inflation rate responds positively to economic activity, as measured by the rate of growth of output, rather than responding to labour market conditions, as measured by the unemployment rate.
15. It is worth noting that we find no evidence that unemployment can be used by policymakers to control inflation, as the unemployment rate has no significant impact on the rate of wage increase in the results in equation number 1.4 of Table 11.1. This is consistent with the finding in Bloch and Madsen (2001) that real wages in Australia have no significant impact on employment. Both findings are consistent with the post Keynesian view that unemployment and inflation are largely separable phenomena.

REFERENCES

Beckerman, W., and T. Jenkinson (1986), 'What stopped the inflation? Unemployment of commodity prices?', *Economic Journal*, **96**, 39–54.

Blanchard, O., and L. Katz (1999), 'Wage dynamics: reconciling theory and evidence', *American Economic Review, Papers and Proceedings*, **89**, 69–74.

Bloch, H. (1991), 'The impact of world manufacturing growth on Australia's trading position', *International Review of Applied Economics*, **5**, 100–15.

Bloch, H. (1996), 'International competition and the degree of monopoly in Australian manufacturing', *International Review of Applied Economics*, **10**, 373–87.

Bloch, H., and J. Madsen (2001), 'A model of employment and real wages under imperfect competition', *Journal of Post Keynesian Economics*, **24**, 165–78.

Bloch, H., and M. Olive (1999), 'Cyclical and competitive influences on pricing in Australian manufacturing', *Economic Record*, **75**, 268–79.

Bloch, H., and D. Sapsford (1991–92), 'Postwar movements in prices of primary products and manufactured goods', *Journal of Post Keynesian Economics*, **14**, 249–66.

Bloch, H., and D. Sapsford (1997), 'Some estimates of Prebisch and Singer effects on the terms of trade between primary producers and manufacturers', *World Development*, **25**, 1873–84.

Bloch, H., and D. Sapsford (2000), 'Whither the terms of trade? An elaboration of the Prebisch-Singer hypothesis', *Cambridge Journal of Economics*, **24**, 461–81.

Blundell-Wignall, A., and R.G. Gregory (1990), 'Exchange rate policy in advanced commodity exporting countries: Australia and New Zealand', in V. Argy and P. De Grauwe (eds), *Choosing Exchange Rate Regime: The Challenge for Smaller Industrial Countries*, Washington, DC: International Monetary Fund.

Dungey, M., and J. Pitchford (2000), 'The steady inflation rate of economic growth', *Economic Record*, **76**, 386–400.

Gruen, D., and J. Wilkinson (1994), 'Australia's real exchange rate – is it explained by the terms of trade or by real interest differentials?', *Economic Record*, **70**, 204–19.

Gruen, D., A. Pagan and C. Thompson (1999), 'The Phillips curve in Australia', Reserve Bank of Australia research discussion paper 1999–01.

Kalecki, Michal (1971), *Selected Essays on the Dynamics of the Capitalist Economy*, Cambridge: Cambridge University Press.

Maizels, A. (1992), *Commodities in Crisis*, Oxford: Clarendon Press.
Olekalns, N., and N. Wilkins (1998), 'Re-examining the evidence for long-run purchasing power parity', *Economic Record*, **74**, 54–61.
Sapsford, D., and W. Morgan (eds) (1994), *The Economics of Primary Commodities: Models, Analysis and Policy*, Aldershot, UK and Brookfield, US: Edward Elgar.
Winters, L.A., and D. Sapsford (eds) (1990), *Primary Commodity Prices: Economic Models and Policy*, London: Cambridge University Press.

DATA APPENDIX

World price of the primary commodity (*pc*)
Source: IMF Index of Primary Commodity Prices in US$, International Financial Statistics (various issues).

Australian primary commodity prices in AU$ (pc_A)
Source: Reserve Bank of Australia Index of Primary Commodity Prices, DX Database.

Australian exchange rate vis-à-vis the US dollar, expressed as US$ per A$ ($E_{A,US}$)
Source: DX Database.

Australian price level (px_A)
Source: Australian GDP Deflator, DX Database.

Australian wage rates (w_A)
Source: Average Weekly Earnings, DX Database.

World finished goods production (X)
Source: OECD Index of Industrial Production, OECD Main Economic Indicators.

World/US long-term interest rate (r_{US})
Source: US 10-year Treasury Bond Rate, IFS Database.

World/US short-term interest rate (i_{US})
Source: US 3-month Treasury Bill Rate (constant maturity), IFS Database.

Domestic price level in the outside world ($px_{A,US}$)
Source: US GDP Deflator and US Producer Price Index, US Department of Commerce Bureau of Economic Analysis Database.

Australian real GDP (X_A)
Source: GDP at constant prices, DX Database.

Australian long-term interest rate (r_A),
Source: Australian 10-year Bond Rate, DX Database.

Australian short-term interest rate (i_A),
Source: Australian 13-week Commonwealth Note Rate, DX Database.

Australian unemployment rate (U_A)
Source: Australian Bureau of Statistics Database.

Labor productivity in Australia (TW_A)
Source: DX and Australian Bureau of Statistics Databases.

12. Innovation and investment in capitalist economies, 1870–2000: Kaleckian dynamics and evolutionary life cycles

Jerry Courvisanos and Bart Verspagen

INTRODUCTION

Innovation is a concept that has recently been analysed with much empirical evidence to indicate its crucial role in the long-run dynamics of modern capitalism. Classical economics recognized that innovation embodied in the form of new machines through fixed capital investment is the essential process for realizing economic development. Going forward in time, the 1990s strong growth path of the US economy and its satellites (like Australia) show the potency of innovation in helping to deliver this growth. This chapter aims to use Kaleckian theory with evolutionary features to analyse historical data on innovation in order to place this concept centrally within a post Keynesian analysis of endogenous investment.

As Sawyer (1996, p. 107) notes 'Kalecki's analysis provides for an endogenous rate of growth, albeit one which rests on the stimulating effect of innovation on investment indicates'. This means Kalecki viewed innovation as inciting investment with consequent impact on cycles and growth. Courvisanos (2001) argues for a more inclusive role for innovation in the post Keynesian analysis through the untapped insights of Kalecki and linking them to evolutionary economics studies that has researched innovation very effectively in a long-run context over the last 15 years.[1] This chapter attempts to do this with historical data as it shows the relation between innovation and investment, and its impact on the instability of business cycles and thus affecting the trend growth of these cycles. This way any strong upswing in a cycle must be related to the following downswing and its implication for new investment and further growth.

The next section is an exposition of the Kaleckian framework of analysis with Schumpeterian evolutionary dynamics used in this study to link the two concepts of innovation and investment together. The particular historical quantitative approach to the analysis of time series data follows, along with a precis of the empirical data used. The pattern-matching explanation of the time series data is then developed, followed by a short section on the limitations of this study and then a conclusion.

FRAMEWORK OF ANALYSIS

Schumpeterian Dynamics of Technology

Innovation dynamics in Schumpeter's theory is based on the distinction between radical innovations and incremental innovations. Radical innovations are major breakthroughs that provide radical breaks with past technological systems. Examples are the steam engine, the internal combustion engine, the digital computer or gene technology. Incremental innovations are small improvements of these basic innovations, aimed at refining and exploiting the potential offered by the breakthroughs. These incremental innovations are quite similar to Kalecki's concept of 'endogenous' innovations. This latter innovation is most common in business enterprises and it involves new investment spending as a matter of course when business activity is ongoing. In relation to the Kaleckian investment cycle, such innovation is called endogenous because it is the cycle itself that induces the innovation and, with it, higher levels of investment orders.[2]

Schumpeter's theory states that basic innovations lead to waves of incremental (or endogenous) innovation, in the form of 'bandwagons' of imitation and improvements. Such imitation and small improvements take the form of incremental (or endogenous) innovation, and is introduced into the economy by means of new investment. Hence diffusion, incremental innovation and investment are closely interlinked. Such a bandwagon of diffusion gives rise to long periods of rapid economic growth. Ultimately, however, decreasing returns to investment in incremental innovation sets in, because technological opportunities of the basic innovation become exhausted. This is when technology-based growth ceases, and a downturn sets in.

While clearly taking the Schumpeterian idea of radical innovations on board, we will not strictly adhere to a long wave perspective, partly for the reason that the data we will consider does not seem to provide strong support for a strict long wave pattern. Our Schumpeterian perspective will rather be one in which radical innovations arrive (exogenously) in a somewhat irregular pattern, such as, for example, in the case of Poisson distributed random process (see, for example, Sahal, 1974; Silverberg and Lehnert, 1993). This implies a 'liberal' attitude with regard to the timing of basic innovations compared to the old Schumpeterian hypothesis that basic innovations cluster strongly during depression periods. On the other hand, such a view leaves enough space to consider the process of diffusion of basic innovations as an irregular and non-smooth process over time, in which there are indeed periods during which radical innovation is more important than incremental innovation, or vice versa. Historical circumstances as well as factors endogenous to the investment process may lead to such large historical differences in timing of the diffusion of basic innovations. Our position is thus one of long-run variations in diffusion rates and the associated historical differences in growth, rather than that of the pure long-wave theorist.

The first stage of the life cycle of a basic innovation is called the embryonic phase. This is when the new paradigm (or basic innovation) is 'in the air'. The scientific and technological knowledge necessary to develop a new technological system is available among front-runners in academia and business. However, there is no ultimately clear understanding of the commercial opportunities of the new paradigm, or of the exact ways in which the technology needs to develop in order for these opportunities to materialize. Thus, the embryonic stage is characterized by a large degree of strong uncertainty, and there is ample opportunity for 'psychological factors' to play a large role in technology-investment decisions.

The next stage we call the early phase of the life cycle. This corresponds to Schumpeter's bandwagons of incremental innovations. The technological and commercial opportunities of the basic innovation are now more or less clear. Investment opportunities are high, and decision-making concerning investment is more or less 'normal', that is, less dependent on the psychological factors that were highly important during the embryonic phase.

Finally, the maturity phase sets in. In the Schumpeterian setting, this relates to the period when technological opportunities of the basic innovation become exhausted. Profit rates based on the, by now, old paradigm are falling, and competition becomes more intense. In terms of calendar time, this will often overlap with increasing opportunities for new basic innovations, and hence with the embryonic stage of a next paradigm.

The brief description of the three stages of the life cycle of a basic innovation already underlines the large role for investment. There is strong two-way interaction between investment and the development of the life cycle of a basic innovation. This is why we stage our theoretical argument in the context of (shorter-run) investment dynamics in the next section.

Kaleckian Framework of Analysis Incorporating Schumpeterian Dynamics

Using the extended reproduction model in Kalecki (1954), three observable variables are central to Kaleckian investment decision-making firms. These are profits, increasing risk (extending to the gearing or leverage ratio) and excess capacity. Within an institutional framework of monopoly capitalism, a susceptibility cycle model is developed by Courvisanos (1996), which measures the tensions that are built up when investment decisions are being made, with the three variables above acting as the barometers of this tension. This is the human agency investment mechanism that generates the innovation and investment patterns described in this research. The decision-making is not symmetrical over the investment cycle or even over different innovation paradigms.

During an investment boom, susceptibility tensions grow to such an extent that investment is highly susceptible to a collapse. In a historical context, such high susceptibility can be identified with falling profit rates, increased finance costs and gearing ratios, and falling utilization rates. This build-up of tension is based on the implementation of a long-run firm investment strategy. When high susceptibility is reached, any minor factor (endogenous or exogenous to the susceptibility cycle) can add another small amount of tension that will be enough to suspend or cancel investment orders, sending the investment (activity) cycle down as a result.

At the upper turning point of the susceptibility cycle, all firms experience high susceptibility and thus fragility of the situation induces a reversal in investment orders. The investment downturn that follows is timed tightly around the pressures to contract investment which affect all firms to a varying degree, but at around the same time. The timing and amplitude of the lower turning point is much more problematic than the upper turning point. Pressures to contract investment orders come from too high susceptibility across all firms. Pressures to expand investment orders come when susceptibility is low, and it depends on the more problematical issue of when a firm (or industry) wants finally to take the plunge. Tightly owned companies with less risk aversion tend to lead investment orders out of the doldrums, while the state tends to assist firms during this period by reducing costs of production through direct (for example, subsidies) and indirect (for example, unemployment benefits) deficit spending. These two factors strongly determine the timing and nature of the upturn.

The classic proposition comes from Schumpeter (1939) and developed further by Goodwin (1991), where the investment function responds to waves of optimism and pessimism that create clusters of innovation and thus, bunching of investment ('clust-bun' effect). This leads to susceptibility for unstable investment cycles and the development of a trigger mechanism to initiate fundamentally new innovation systems with long-wave implications. Kalecki (1962) reinforces the cycle-trend effect that innovation has on the investment function.[3] The intensity of innovation affects both the amplitude of investment cycles and also shifts the trend path of investment growth, by flows of vicious and virtuous circles. Virtuous circle effect occurs as innovation intensity rises, increasing the amplitude of the upper turning point of the investment cycle and shifting the trend path upwards.[4] Vicious circle effect increases the amplitude of the lower turning point and shifts the trend downwards. Steindl (1979, p. 7) formalizes this by considering the pace of innovation as a shift parameter of the Kaleckian investment function.

The common Kaleckian feature of expanded reproduction appears in the innovation and investment story that has not been recognized by the protagonists in this clustering debate. The prerequisite for clustering is deep depressions or breakthroughs in technology, both reflect reactions by the private sector (in the former case) and the public sector (in the latter case) to deep problems in the downswing of the previous business cycle. Then, the bunching requires effective demand stimulus through widespread diffusion of a cyclical cluster effect that can only be done through the availability of a surplus for investment (private profits and public deficit spending). Roadblocks to this 'clust-bun' effect reside in the institutional frameworks of nations; particularly the ones with still dominant mature industries with older technologies (Freeman and Perez, 1988, pp. 58–65). Increased uncertainty arising from large investment in the new technology systems also adds a roadblock through increased macroeconomic volatility, which Toivanen, Stoneman and Diederen (1999) empirically identify as slowing down the diffusion process.

In order to analyse the interaction between 'Schumpeterian' and 'Kaleckian' dynamics, we will distinguish the situations of high and low susceptibility in the Kaleckian cycle, and the three stages of the Schumpeterian life cycle of a basic innovation that were introduced above. The guiding principle for bringing the two types of dynamics together will be the opportunities for incremental, or endogenous, innovation. Incremental innovations play a large role during the early and mature phases of the life cycle, but much less so during the embryonic stage. High (low) technological opportunities are found during the early (mature) stage of the life cycle. Our main theoretical conjectures are summarized in Scheme 1 (see Figure 12.1).

Owing to the nature of the 'creative destruction' phenomenon, the mature stage of the life cycle of an 'old' basic innovation will usually overlap with the embryonic stage of the life cycle of a 'new' basic innovation. Hence, the first and last lines in our scheme cannot really be distinguished in a useful way in practice. We nevertheless make the analytical distinction, keeping in mind that these situations must be analysed in conjunction.

First we look at how Schumpeterian dynamics of innovation impact on Kaleckian dynamics of investment cycles. Research and development (R&D) expenditure plays an important role in this process. Research and development enables the firm to develop a set of incremental innovations, which may be held ready to be applied when susceptibility is relatively low. The firm's

Life-cycle stage of basic innovation	Low susceptibility of investment	High susceptibility of investment
Embryonic	Cautious and fragile upturns induced by early diffusion of new technological system; best circumstances for 'take-off' of new paradigm	Possible roadblock to diffusion of new basic innovations
Early or growth	Long upswings, rapid and strong upturn, rapid diffusion of new technological system	Short downswings, weak downturn, slow diffusion of new technological system
Mature	Rapid build-up of susceptibility: short and weak upswings; pressure for the 'old' paradigm to breakdown	Strong and rapid downturn; possibly long downswings; best circumstances for 'sailing ship' effect

Figure 12.1 Scheme 1: Interaction between Schumpeterian and Kaleckian dynamics

R&D is a form of intangible investment to be incorporated in the long-term business investment plan. Research and development may be constant throughout the investment cycle, or may vary under the same susceptibility pressures as means of production (MOP) commitments. Which of the two it is depends on how important R&D is for the firm and industry. In an industry where innovation is a regular competitive strategy, R&D would be large and would vary under the same susceptibility pressures as capital expenditure. In an industry where innovation is only occasionally implemented, R&D would be small and constant over the investment cycle.

When a firm decides to increase investment at relatively low susceptibility under competitive pressures and higher costs of postponement, innovations resulting from R&D investment in the past are ready to be implemented.[5] In this way endogenous innovation can be 'generated and directed by a process of investment' (Steindl, 1952 [1976], p. 133). This means that the diffusion of the new technological system is speeded up by the favourable circumstances in the investment cycle. Alternatively, during the early life-cycle phase of a new paradigm, a large, 'exogenous' boost to industry investment is produced at low susceptibility points. This investment boom relates to paradigm changes in single (but large) important industry sectors that adopt new technology systems, or to innovations that affect the whole economy (for example, steam-engine innovations). Either way, the investment boom is strong and resilient over a series of future cycles in susceptibility. Thus, a high availability of incremental, endogenous innovations stimulates investment, that is, the investment cycle expansion phase may be expected to be stronger and longer in the early life-cycle stage of a basic innovation.

At high susceptibility, firms are under pressure to postpone investment orders and with it shelving of endogenous innovations (R&D generated patents) and possible reduction of R&D. This alleviates pressure of growing susceptibility, by concentrating on profit returns from old MOP that have a proven track record from their production, rather than the higher but more unpredictable returns from new MOP.[6] Only small increases in capacity investment to protect existing MOP emerge at high levels of susceptibility. Thus, endogenous innovation postponement is induced from high susceptibility and it then adds pressure for the slowdown and eventual contraction of investment orders.

At low susceptibility firms introduce endogenous innovations, both in the form of process and product innovation, under the pressure of competition. Given that the technostructure needs to implement the long-term investment strategy with innovation incorporated therein,[7] this need creates increasing competitive pressure during the contraction of the susceptibility cycle when investment orders are declining and little new investment is going on. The costs of postponing a long-term investment strategy increases over time with the knowledge that other large firms, in the industry or ready to come into the industry, have the technology also to increase their market share and growth. These pressures, along with pressures for state-based stimulus, lead to some increase in investment embodied with endogenous innovation.

The creation endogenously of innovations out of low susceptibility makes some MOP obsolete and thus not part of excess capacity calculation. Also, oligopoly firms (and industries) lobby for the assistance of governments in reducing social costs of production (through subsidies, tax concessions or protection) when these firms attempt to expand their market by innovations in order to utilise new, and decommission old, idle productive capacity (O'Connor, 1973, p. 27). Such innovation and underwriting of the related risks reduce the rate of increase in susceptibility and encourages an investment recovery. However, these actions by firms and governments are not guaranteed to occur at any particular time or with any particular force. The institutional framework of a country (and region) will have a lot to do with the strength and timing of the upturn in investment orders.

Expectations are that the impact of high susceptibility will be more pronounced during the mature stages of the life cycle of a basic innovation, when opportunities for incremental innovation are already low. Hence, we would expect the downturn of the investment cycle to be more abrupt during such periods, and also for the downswings to be longer and more pronounced.

Summarizing life-cycle innovation and the investment process: at the early stage of the life cycle of a basic innovation, technological opportunities are high, and hence one may expect a stronger link between investment and innovation. Situations of low susceptibility can thus expect to be sustained longer, and consequently the associated upswing in investment will be stronger and more prolonged. Similarly, during the mature stage of the life cycle of a basic innovation, one may expect high susceptibility to generate more rapid, stronger and longer downturns of the investment cycle.

We now turn to the impact of the Kaleckian investment cycle on Schumpeterian dynamics, in the introduction of new basic innovations. As noted above, Schumpeter's original theory suggests that the introduction of basic innovations takes place during the depression periods of the long wave. Our focus on investment, however, puts more emphasis on the early upswing, which is associated with investment and hence with periods of low susceptibility. Freeman, Clark and Soete (1982) also put much emphasis on this stage, which they discuss in the context of diffusion (through investment) of the new paradigm.

Hence, we would expect 'exogenous' innovation to occur in an industry generally at the low susceptibility point, where competitive pressure exists on entrepreneurs to introduce it. When investment activity is high and susceptibility is high, entrepreneurs are not receptive to major new developments, but rather continue squeezing profits from the old paradigm, given the already large commitments made to this old paradigm during the rise of investment from the trough. As susceptibility is falling with investment order downturn, the financial constraints of high gearing in the industry are eased as debts are paid off or receivers are appointed. At low susceptibility the industry is financially restructured and becomes conducive to new investment orders. However, at this point it is not clear if or when the lower turning point of investment orders will be based on the decreasing opportunities from the old paradigm (providing only a modest upturn) or on the uncertainty of the new paradigm. Uncertainty of future profits reduces investment orders and susceptibility further. At this point even replacement investment is postponed, sending the susceptibility cycle even lower. One would thus expect that, due to the major uncertainty associated with the embryonic stage of the new basic innovation (or paradigm), the investment upswing associated with low susceptibility would be cautious and fragile.

Changes in technological systems or paradigms arise only after all the minor improvements (endogenous innovation) are squeezed out of the old systems and paradigms by 'monopoly capital' entrepreneurs who want to protect existing MOP and delay the new paradigm taking over. There is also a 'log jam' in endogenous innovations based on the new paradigm which compounds the latter's slow initial adoption. This occurs when established powerful entrepreneurs, with much old MOP, cannot justify the entire shake-up of industries, since not enough interrelated clusters have been formed.

This has been termed by Rosenberg (1976) the sailing-ship effect, due to the large amount of incremental innovations in sailing ships that emerged after the introduction of the steamship.

The circumstances for the sailing ship effect to occur are best under periods of high susceptibility, when the 'security' of the old paradigm will have relatively high appeal to investing firms as compared to the uncertainty of a new paradigm. Any long postponements of new innovative capital investment would produce a mismatch of current investment to new available technology in the economy, creating a roadblock to the 'clust-bun' effect.

One remaining question concerns the degree of 'radicalness' of the basic innovation. In Schumpeter's original view, basic innovations are associated with 'gales of creative destruction'. However, the breakdown of an old technological paradigm may also be smoother due to the readapting of the old paradigm through the adoption of new inventions that require relative minor innovations. As the institutional framework slowly adapts to the new technological system, entrepreneurs' reactions against uncertainty of profits come from competitive pressures and growing inefficiencies of old MOP. This indeed induces (slow) adaptation (by industries) and imitation (within industries) to technological trajectories that are totally new, establishing at very low susceptibility, the new investment upturn. It is creating a new investment boom and at the same time 're-establishing the conditions for a new phase of steady development' (Vercelli, 1989, p. 135).

A paradigm shift occurs when the new adapted technological systems pervade the whole economy. Some from the evolutionary school identify such innovation-based shifts with the beginning of new long waves in the economy's development (see Kleinknecht, 1987), others see these shifts as variations driven by more short-term economic motives embodied within business cycles (Silverberg and Verspagen, 2003).

The Hypothesis

The Kaleckian and Schumpeterian cycles feed on each other, but to different extents during different time periods. When basic innovations are new and have been built up, creating a cluster of innovations, then the Schumpeterian cycle is strong. This can be compared to when this cycle is weak, with basic innovations becoming exhausted. Such differing cycle pressures feed directly into the investment decision processes. The two versions of the Schumpeterian cycle can be ameliorated or intensified as a result of what is happening in the Kaleckian susceptibility cycle. Low susceptibility encourages technological innovation by powerful strategic competitive pressures and removal of postponement of investment pressures. High susceptibility discourages technological innovation with large roadblocks to diffusion of innovations and increased pressures to postpone investment decisions.

The empirical analyses conducted in the next section aim to understand these dynamic processes for the period 1870 to 2000. The analyses will enable a plausible story to be told which is consistent with the hypothesis outlined.

THE HISTORICAL QUANTITATIVE APPROACH ON THE TIME SERIES DATA

Five major capitalist economies are examined in this study: the USA, Germany, Japan, the UK and France. Three sets of time series data for each economy are used in the empirical analysis that follows, based on the three variables in the framework of analysis outlined in the previous section:

1. Pat: newly registered patents at the USA Office on the basis of the country of origin of each patent. This data represents the innovation input into the cycles. The data are taken from the US Patent and Trademark Office.
2. Inv: fixed capital investment of each country. This data set represents the investment that is crucial in the operation of the vicious and virtuous circles. The data set are taken from Maddison (1995) and updated with new data from the Groningen Growth and Development Centre.
3. GDP: gross domestic product of each country. This data set represents the GDP variable that is the basis for determination of profits. The source of these data is the same as for the investment data.

The period for which there is data varies across the five economies. In general, the data is extended as far back as statistical data collection allows. The aim is to have data sets that allow for an analysis from the late nineteenth century (including the 1890s deep recession) to the present day (2000).

The data is examined in three forms:

- raw data – the actual data of all three variables in log-form
- deviation from trend – the log-form deviations from the given trend of all three raw data series
- MV5 – the moving variance in continuous five-year periods based on the detrended data for each variable.

The deviation data represents the nature of the cycles of investment, innovation and GDP (or business cycle); identifying the peaks and troughs in the cyclical processes at work and the extent of upswings and downswings in the cycles. The MV5 data represents the extent of instability in each of the cycles, smoothing out seasonal bumps by the five-year moving variance of the data. The MV5 data identifies instability by the extent the data moves above zero. The higher the MV5 data moves above zero, the greater is the extent of volatility in the respective cycle of the variable denoted. The three data sets in graphical form for each country (with accompanying trend equations), are published as Appendix A in Courvisanos and Verspagen (2002, pp. 73–80).

A historical quantitative approach is applied to data. This approach identifies summary five-OECD country patterns and US patterns in the cyclical processes that relate to the dynamic model sketched in section above. These patterns are matched and compared across the five different economies to provide a plausible dynamic exposition of innovation and investment, using the important linkages set out in the framework of analysis. Such dynamic linkages would be completely missed when examined through conventional static analysis.

In terms of evolutionary industry life-cycle form, the whole period 1870 to 2000 is separated into sub-periods to examine how the changes in technological paradigms through these sub-periods affect differently investment cycles and GDP growth trends. The sub-periods examined are:

- Period I – from the start of each data set to the beginning of World War I in 1914, reflecting the rise of the USA as the predominant economic power based on railways and electrification
- Period II – covering the rise of mass production during the interwar period and the two World Wars
- Period III – from 1946 to 2000, covering the late twentieth century developments, particularly the maturation of the mass production mode and the rise of the 'New' Information Economy.

The above data with the periods described are combined with two other sets of time series data compiled by other authors to provide a summary perspective of how the Kaleckian susceptibility cycle across the five countries in our sample interrelates with Schumpeterian dynamics.

ANALYSIS OF DATA

Kaleckian Dynamics

We consider two sets of summary data for interpreting susceptibility to investment from a Kaleckian perspective, based on Courvisanos (1996). The analysis ignores innovation effects until the Schumpeterian dynamics are incorporated in an integrated interpretation in the forthcoming sub-section.

Initially we set up the perspective of the whole period 1870 to 2000 by the graph that combines the GDP figures for all the five countries in our sample to show a regression equation and its trend line. This graph, in Figure 12.2 suggests a pattern of three 'stages' that correspond to the three sub-periods delineated above. The first period is up to 1914 in which the GDP consistently remains above the trend line. The second period we date from the peak in 1914, when the GDP begins a downswing that takes the combined five-country GDP to below the trend and keep it there through the next two business cycles (with peaks in 1929 – just before the Great Depression – and the war related 1943–44).

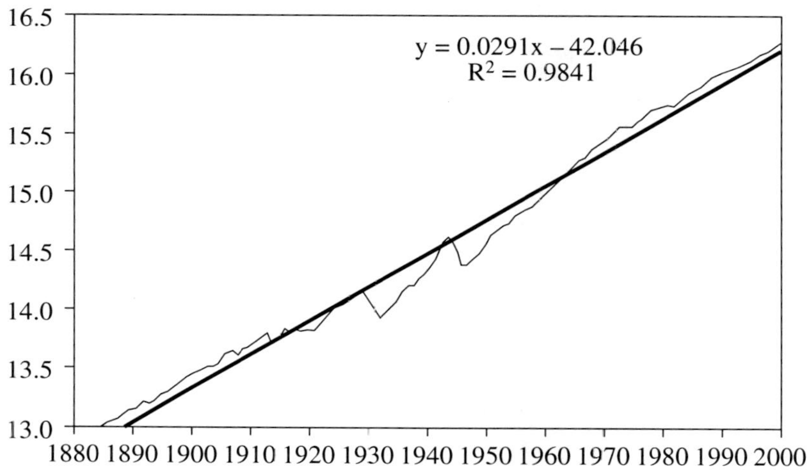

Key: Thin line is natural log of actual data, thick line is estimated trend with trend equation.

Figure 12.2 Combined GDP (in 1990 prices) of the five sample countries: Germany, France, Japan, UK, USA

The third period we date from 1946, when the data is in a trough and begins an upswing that takes the combined GDP to eventually cross over above the trend line in 1964 (the first time it does this since the 1914 peak – except momentarily in the peak of 1943–44). Then the GDP remains above trend for the next two business cycles (with peaks in 1974 and 1989; and troughs in 1981–82 and 1992–93).

The pattern of 'deviation from trend' investment data in the five individual countries is now considered within the context of these three stages of GDP.

We take the USA on its own first in the context of Figure 12.2, since it has such a prominence throughout the twentieth century as an economic power. The first period up to 1914 shows great investment cycle volatility, reflecting large swings in susceptibility in a period when the US state plays no significant intervention role. This volatility is clearly evident in the USA MV5 data with the investment variance index remaining very high through this early period. The large investment peaks in 1880 and 1890 keep the US GDP data significantly above the zero index. Then follows a relatively very strong investment upswing in the post-1890s depression (from trough in 1895 to highly volatile peak period around 1910), reaching very high susceptibility by the end of Period I.

Period II in the USA has strong investment downswings with weak upswings. The decreasing trend in US MV5 data (except for the 1930 spike) supports this subdued susceptibility-based investment cycle period. Second World War distortion is evident by the only large diversion between investment and GDP data, but investment keeps rising out of the 'Great Depression' investment collapse, with a notable upswing into Period III from the 1946 investment trough. The post-Second World War period is one with relatively low susceptibility until the mid-1960s, followed by an investment trend downswing till the 1992–93 recession. Lower investment volatility accompanies low susceptibility through this early post-Second World War period. Some volatility increase post-1964, especially during the recessions, indicates rising susceptibility. Only since the last recession (1992–93) have we seen in the USA a revival of a strong upswing in investment and with it significantly higher susceptibility.

Dumenil and Levy (1993) have US profit rates and capital utilization data to support the above pattern of investment susceptibility. Profit rates decline in five significant time periods, which signal peaking of investment susceptibility. These are 1880–90, 1906–14, 1923–32, 1952–58 and 1965–82. All five periods provide signs of high susceptibility and future severe declines in the investment cycle as noted above. The strong Second World War spike in profit rates shows the significant impetus a major war effort by the USA has on the profitability of capitalism, which is replicated in a more subdued way during the Korean War (1951–52) and the Vietnam War (mid-1960s). The virtual exclusion of the US military in the First World War is evident by some multiplier expansion in profit rates from 1914 onwards, but without the spike-effect as the military withdrew from the other US war efforts.

The US capacity utilization data in Dumenil and Levy (1993) show a similar pattern to the profit rates, but with a lag between one and two years. The lag is evident due to the stimulus in investment by rising profits, which then feeds into stronger economic activity (GDP) and higher capacity utilization of given capital stock. This exemplifies low susceptibility and sets up the basis for an upswing in investment activity. The Dumenil-Levy data identifies such circumstances when utilization rates are at their trough and business cycle contractions are continuing their downward slide. These periods of low susceptibility occur towards the end of recessions: notably around the late 1890s, early 1910s, mid-1930s, late 1940s, early 1960s, mid-1980s and mid-1990s.

Declining profits reflect, with a lag, falling utilization rates which first come about due to expanding capital stock and then reduced economic activity. These circumstances lead to growing susceptibility, reaching peak high susceptibility in mid-downswing of utilization rates: notably 1890, 1910, 1930, 1946, 1958, 1973 and 1980. These dates closely correspond with the end of the declining USA profits rate periods.

Taken together, the two sets of data for the USA show seven peaks of high susceptibility in investment that closely relate to the beginnings of business cycle contractions. Business cycle upturns are more problematic, depending on low susceptibility and the incentive to invest primarily coming through innovations. This integration of innovation and investment is examined in the next section. However, the data indicates seven periods when the US economy was receptive to some investment spurt as identified by the low susceptibility dates above.

We now look at the other four economies together. From the summary data in Table 12.1 below, the raw data shows Japan as having the strongest GDP and investment rates by far, with Germany having the next strongest investment rate, but this is not reflected in Germany's growth rate. The USA has a stronger GDP growth rate despite a much lower investment rate. The French have a very strong investment rate also, but like Germany, it is weakly reflected in the growth rate. Meanwhile the UK suffers in comparison, with overall the weakest in terms of both rates. There is a need to examine the innovation element before some clear explanation can be provided for the relatively poor investment rate 'efficiency' in relation to translating strong investment activity into much weaker GDP growth for the two European economies in this study.

What emerges from the discussion of the US data is that a combination of high MV5 and rising deviation above the investment trend creates a high and

Table 12.1 Summary Data Comparison of the Five Economies

	USA	UK	Japan	Germany	France
Growth rate (%)	3.18	1.83	4.13	2.74	2.20
Investment rate (%)	2.91	2.71	6.09	4.30	5.47
Patent rate (%)	0.77	1.36	9.15	2.49	2.59

rising susceptibility. While a low MV5 and falling deviation below the trend line creates a low and falling susceptibility. This pattern guide is used to analyse the deviation and volatility in investment of the four economies together.

Period I has the UK and Japan with similar deviation and MV5 patterns to the USA, that is, strong volatility overall with growing susceptibility of investment as the economy expands out of the 1890s depression. UK has one difference and that is the timing of investment is earlier in both its investment booms of about five-to-eight years. Germany and France have much lower volatility, but there is no investment data for this early period. The minimal GDP deviation from trend in these two economies suggests much lower investment and thus limited susceptibility to investment. Period II starts with strong dips in deviation for the European economies due to the First World War, that is not evident in Japan or the USA. Except for the UK, the rest experience expansion in the 1920s with growing susceptibility to investment.

A close basic pattern for all the five economies emerges from 1930 onwards. The 'common' MV5 pattern is starkly represented by the French data. The patterns of both GDP and investment resemble a reverse J-curve from the high variance after the Great Depression of the early 1930s, to strong reduction in variance through the 1950s and 1960s, only to see variance rise again in mid-1970s, with greater volatility of the variance data. From the extreme volatility (and high susceptibility) after the 1929 stock market crash, all the economies move through to the stabilising aggregate demand-induced influences that war and reconstruction-based investment activity provided with reduced volatility and subdued susceptibility. Only with the stagflation of the mid-1970s, and the accompanying difficult structural adjustment problems through the 1980s, that variance picked up again, but nowhere as high as in the 1930s.

The 1990s are very recent in historical overview terms, but the tails of the data show differences that seem to suggest some divergence from the 'common' pattern. The USA is clearly showing a rising deviation in investment that is being followed with a weaker rise in the UK. The two European economies and Japan are showing a tail that is deviating downwards and falling below the trend line in both investment and GDP. Susceptibility is thus much higher in the USA and UK relative to the other three economies as we enter the twenty-first century. Innovation should be able to shed light on this divergence as well as indicating the difference in investment opportunities in respect of these economies over the next few years.

Innovation Integration with Schumpeterian Dynamics

Schumpeterian dynamics are developed by comparing a time series on basic innovations compiled from data in Van Duijn (1983) and Haustein and

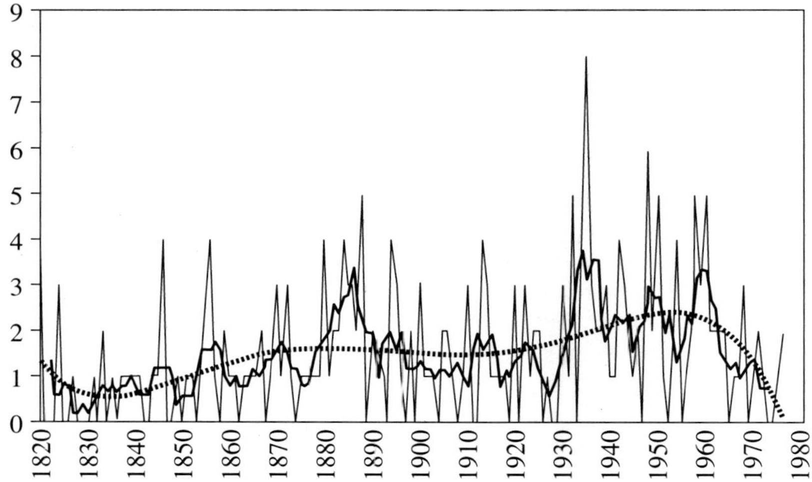

Key: Thin line indicates actual data, thick irregular line a five-year moving average of these, and thick smooth line a five-degree polynomial fitted trend.

Figure 12.3 Basic innovations 1820–1975

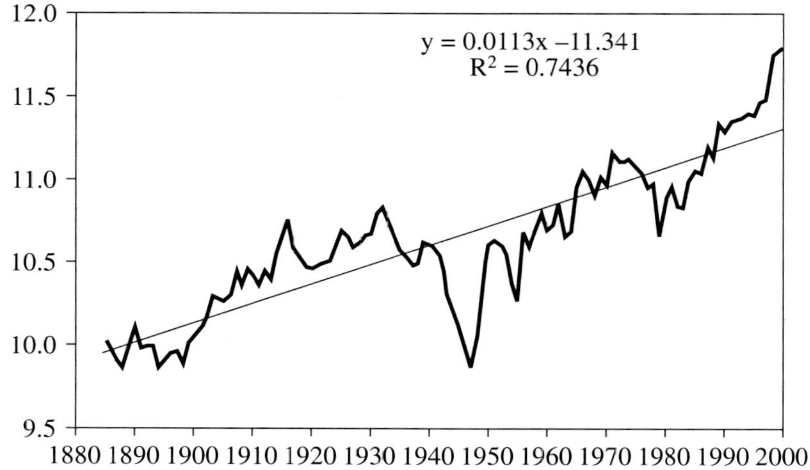

Figure 12.4 Total number of patents in the five countries together, including estimation of trend (estimated by OLS)

Neuwirth (1982) depicted in Figure 12.3,[8] with the time series aggregating patents awarded in the USA to inventors from the five sample countries in Figure 12.4. The latter is an indicator of incremental (endogenous) innovations that depend to a large extent on major breakthroughs in radical innovations indicated in the basic innovation series. The basic innovations graph is constructed as a five year moving average (dated at the 'centre' year), and a five-degree polynomial trend (estimated by Poisson regression). These two approximations of the trend in the basic innovation data suggest a pattern of three 'stages'.

The first stage is 1840–90, where the rate of basic innovations goes up with local peaks in 1846, 1856, 1870–72. The second stage, 1890–1930, settles at a rate that is about half of that during the peak years of 1880–90. The third stage, 1930–60, is again one of high activity, with local peaks 1935, 1948 and 1958–60. After 1960, the trend for the basic innovation data decreases sharply, however to a large extent, this must be considered as an artefact of the data collection method. What can be considered as a basic innovation becomes apparent only after a fairly long time period. Because most of the work on constructing the basic innovations time series underlying this data was done in the 1970s and early 1980s, it is therefore only logical that the time series stops somewhere in the 1960s. Combining these three stages with the three periods of Kaleckian investment activity identified in the previous sub-section and their accompanying incremental innovation pattern provides this integrated analysis.

From Figure 12.3, the very early (pre-1890) data supports the view that basic innovations are increasing, culminating in a period of relatively high activity in 1880–90. Integration with the Kaleckian perspective indicates that this embryonic innovative activity was on the basis of a low susceptibility of investment that allowed for a strong 'take-off' with very few roadblocks. The cluster of innovations led to a quick diffusion of these innovations through patents (see Figure 12.4 just prior to 1890) and the bunching of investment.

After the early 1890s recession, incremental innovation activity (patents in Figure 12.4) is on a steady increase through to the end of Period I. Radical innovation is about half of that of its peak 1880s activity. This reflects the early 1900s growth stage with higher susceptibility of investment, and where investment tends to lead the diffusion innovation process. For this reason, the volatility of investment becomes more intensified leading to a peak of susceptibility with concomitant investment collapse at the end of Period I.

Period II of mass production investment is supported by incremental patent activity staying above the trend level until the impact of the Great Depression. Then the subdued susceptibility-based investment cycle period also results in declining patent applications from around 1935. Patent activity continues to decline through into the Second World War due to crisis and secrecy, which 'bottles up' incremental innovation. The war allows a major thrust in basic innovation under cover of defence needs that help to establish the new embryonic technological systems for the electronic information age. The high susceptibility at the end of the Second World War kept embryonic basic innovation from being rapidly diffused until the short collapse of investment ended at the end of the 1940s.

Immediately after the Second World War basic war-inspired innovation reaches a local peak in 1948. Incremental patent innovation sees a sharp upward erratic trend from the mid-1950s to the early 1970s. This matches Kaleckian dynamics of relatively low susceptibility that increases through this whole period as investment drives this incremental innovation, with rising profit and utilization rates. All the signs of a mature stage in industry life cycle are evident by the late 1960s as energy-driven economies come under pressure of profit squeeze and capacity constraints. The end comes with the economic downturn of the mid-1970s and with it a collapse of innovation.

The strong rising patent activity after the early 1980s recession leads to strong information-based technology developments through the 1990s. Efforts to reform industries by deregulation and privatization are accompanied by state support for business and dismantling the welfare systems of the advanced economies. These efforts create the competitive climate for incremental innovation to spur on sustained investment activity under conditions of relatively low susceptibility of investment.

Finally, we examine the country differences in Table 12.1 patent rates in the context of the above stated integrated pattern. Japan is the standout in incremental-based patent rates on the table and reflects also the highest investment and growth rates. This tells a story of a strong Kaleckian susceptibility pattern in which the Japanese entrepreneurs react to the commercialization and diffusion of innovation in the way that relates closely to the variables of profits, capacity and debt levels that drive investment cycles. On the other hand, the USA reflects an economy with strong radical basic innovation and a low patent rate. Radical innovation and the national USA innovation pattern establish the basic investment cycle that drives countries like Japan (and smaller economies that are linked to the USA, like Australia and Canada).

The three European economies all suffer from poor investment rate efficiency in the context of growth rates. The patent rates in Germany and France show stronger incremental innovation than in the USA but well behind Japan. On examination, much of the investment in Germany and France is basic infrastructure from which GDP benefits. It implies a weaker entrepreneurial economy in the true Keynesian sense. The UK suggests a greater problem that combines weak entrepreneurial innovation activity with poor infrastructure investment. In the UK, the data shows continuing lower deviations from the trend after the 'high watermark' of the 1870s until the 1955–70 patent-based investment growth. Since then there has been a collapse of patent activity and with it endogenous investment activity.

LIMITATIONS

Collating and Analysing Data

The well-known problems of choosing weights for a deflator for both GDP and investment, as well as choosing an exchange rate to compare between countries, become more problematic the longer the time series get. The common approach is to use a benchmark study to obtain a purchasing power parity index (PPP, essentially an exchange rate) for a single year, to use this to calculate values for a common currency in that year, and to apply fixed price country-wise data to extrapolate this benchmark forward and backward in time. In order to perform this extrapolation, one may either choose a fixed weight deflator, or a chain-weighted deflator (where the weight changes on a yearly basis). The current data were based on a fixed weight approach. Hence, both the benchmark PPP and the weight used for the deflator refer to a single point in time (1990), and the further away the data points are from this point in time, the less reliable the method gets. Using a chain weighted price index and applying more than one benchmark can solve this problem, but this is problematic because the data needed to do this do not exist for the older period. In addition, national accounting standards were non-existent for the pre-Second World War period, and hence the data for these years are generally less reliable than the more current data.

With regard to technology, it must be noted that patents are not a perfect indicator of innovation. By definition, knowledge described in a patent must be new, imitations are to a certain extent ruled out. Thus imitation being an important component of incremental innovation does not appear in the patenting statistics. Also, for countries other than the USA, patents refer to foreign patents, and hence the sample may be biased towards firms with internationally oriented firms. Also, the US patent system has been subject to institutional changes and bureaucratic problems (see Griliches, 1990). Finally, with regard to the nature of the data on basis innovations, a number of problems have already been discussed in the analysis.

Applying the Results

In applying the results, the analysis relies on patent application data as a measure of the level of incremental innovation. This data is important for small and large firms, but the investment effects from patents are tenuous as many small firms fail and the innovation process itself becomes complex and convoluted before it registers through the investment process. Despite these limitations, the lagged patent data is the only innovation-based data that has a consistent set of numbers going back over a century.

The use of secondary source basic innovation data allows the extent of such innovation to be analysed in concert with incremental innovation patterns of patents. This two-innovation approach provides a reality check to the investment data and its links to innovation. Investment and GDP data are much less problematic in their link to economic activity in the standard Keynesian formulation.

The 'clust-bun' effect identified in the results comes from a pattern-matching exercise across five OECD countries. This method provides only a plausible explanation for patterns describing the susceptibility-based causal mechanism, rather than any tight econometric fit of the data to any output of mathematical modelling. The pattern-matching exercise allows for the maximum amount of dynamic human agency interpretations, but limited static testing of results

CONCLUSION

A clear Schumpeterian innovation pattern emerges with two distinct periods of high numbers in basic innovations, which lead investment. Generally, these periods are characterized by lower than average activity in incremental innovation. These periods are then followed by periods of low numbers of basic innovations, but relatively high periods of incremental innovation that accompany investment activity. These two patterns indicate how the 'clust-bun' effect works. In the 'basic' case, innovation drives investment and with it major structural change over the long waves of economic development. In the 'incremental' case, innovation is driven by investment over the business cycle. Kaleckian dynamics show that this latter pattern is embellished by bunching of investment activity, matching the clustering effects that give rise to strong economic activity that is represented by rising GDP data.

NOTES

1. For a review of the literature on innovation and investment from the post Keynesian economics and evolutionary economics perspectives, see Courvisanos and Verspagen (2002, pp. 34–9).
2. Steindl (1952, [1976], p. 133) describes this endogenous innovation very neatly: 'Techno-

logical innovations accompany the process of investment like a shadow, they do not act on it as a propelling force.'

3. Kalecki (1967, [1991], p. 455) endorses the Schumpeterian view when he states that 'capitalists investing "today" think to have an advantage over those having invested "yesterday" because of technical novelties that have reached them'. Note, Kalecki often uses the word 'invention' instead of 'innovation' in many of his discussions of technical progress. See Courvisanos (1996, p. 107) for resolution of this confusion.
4. Empirical evidence by Toivanen, Stoneman and Diederen (1999) support the notion of this virtuous circle effect.
5. The firm can also buy out smaller uncompetitive firms during the contractionary stage of the investment cycle, taking advantage of innovations developed by failed firms.
6. For empirical support, see Toivanen, Stoneman and Diederen (1999).
7. See Galbraith (1967, [1974]) on the role of technostructure in planning investment strategies and specific technologies for the ongoing survival and growth of the large corporation. For a recent reinterpretation of the technostructure from a post Keynesian perspective, see Dunn (2000).
8. More details on how these two basic innovation series are combined can be found in Silverberg and Verspagen (2002). This reference also gives details on the estimation of the five-degree polynomial fitted trend, using Poisson regression.

REFERENCES

Courvisanos, J. (1996), *Investment Cycles in Capitalist Economies: A Kaleckian Behavioural Contribution*, Cheltenham, UK, and Brookfield, US: Edward Elgar.

Courvisanos, J. (2001), 'Michał Kalecki as a behavioural economist: implications for modern evolutionary economic analysis', University of Tasmania School of Economics discussion paper 2001–08, Hobart.

Courvisanos, J., and B. Verspagen (2002), 'Innovation and investment in capitalist economies 1870–2000: Kaleckian dynamics and evolutionary life cycles', *Investigación Económica*, **62** (242), 33–80.

Dumenil, G., and D. Levy (1993), *The Economics of the Profit Rate: Competition, Crises and Historical Tendencies in Capitalism*, Aldershot, UK and Brookfield, US: Edward Elgar.

Dunn, S.P. (2000), 'Galbraith, uncertainty and the modern corporation', in M. Keaney (ed.), *Economist with a Public Purpose: Essays in Honour of John Kenneth Galbraith*, London: Routledge.

Freeman, C., and C. Perez (1988), 'Structural crises of adjustment, business cycles and investment behaviour', in G. Dosi, C. Freeman, R. Nelson, G. Silverberg and L. Soete (eds), *Technical Change and Economic Theory*, London: Pinter, pp. 38–66.

Freeman, C., J. Clark, and L. Soete (1982), *Unemployment and Technological Innovation: A Study of Long Waves and Economic Development*, London: Frances Pinter.

Galbraith, J.K. (1967), *The New Industrial State*, Boston, MA: Houghton Mifflin, reprinted 1974, 2nd revised edn, Harmondsworth: Penguin.

Goodwin, R. (1991), 'Economic evolution, chaotic dynamics and the Marx-Keynes-Schumpeter system', in G. Hodgson and E. Screpanti (eds), *Rethinking Economics*, Aldershot, UK and Brookfield, US: Edward Elgar.

Griliches, Z. (1990), 'Patent statistics as economic indicators: a survey', *Journal of Economic Literature*, **28**, 1661–707.

Haustein, H.-D., and E. Neuwirth (1982), 'Long waves in world industrial production, energy consumption, innovations, inventions, and patents and their identification by spectral analysis', *Technological Forecasting and Social Change*, **22**, 53–89.

Kalecki, M. (1954), *Theory of Economic Dynamics*, London: Allen & Unwin.

Kalecki, M. (1962), 'Observations on the theory of growth', *Economic Journal*, **72**, 134–53.

Kalecki, M. (1967), 'The problem of effective demand with Tugan-Baranovsky and Rosa Luxemburg', *Ekonomista*, **2**, 241–9, reprinted in J. Osiatyński (ed.) (1991), *Collected Works of Michał Kalecki, Volume II: Capitalism – Economic Dynamics*, Oxford: Clarendon Press, pp. 451–8.

Kleinknecht, A. (1987), *Innovation Patterns in Crisis and Prosperity: Schumpeter's Long Cycle Reconsidered*, London: Macmillan.

Maddison, A. (1995), *Monitoring the World Economy 1820–1992*, Paris: OECD Development Centre.

O'Connor, J. (1973), *The Fiscal Crisis of the State*, New York: St. Martin's Press.

Rosenberg, N. (1976), *Perspectives on Technology*, Cambridge: Cambridge University Press.

Sahal, D. (1974), 'Generalized Poisson and related models of technological innovation', *Technological Forecasting and Social Change*, **6**, 403–36.

Sawyer, M. (1996), 'Kalecki on trade cycle and economic growth', in J.E. King (ed.), *An Alternative Macroeconomic Theory: The Kaleckian Model and Post-Keynesian Economics*, Boston, MA: Kluwer Academic, pp. 93–114.

Schumpeter, J.A. (1939), *Business Cycles; A Theoretical, Historical and Statistical Analysis of the Capitalist Process*, 2 vols, New York: McGraw-Hill.

Silverberg, G., and D. Lehnert (1993), 'Long waves and evolutionary chaos in a simple Schumpeterian model of embodied technical change', *Structural Change and Economic Dynamics*, **4**, 9–37.

Silverberg, G., and B. Verspagen (2003), 'Breaking the waves: a Poisson regression approach to Schumpeterian clustering of basic innovations', *Cambridge Journal of Economics*, **27**, 671–93.

Steindl, J. (1952), *Maturity and Stagnation in American Capitalism*, Oxford: Blackwell, repr. 1976, 2nd edn, New York: Monthly Review Press.

Steindl, J. (1979), 'Stagnation theory and stagnation policy', *Cambridge Journal of Economics*, **3** (1), 1–14.

Toivanen, O., P. Stoneman and P. Diederen (1999), 'Uncertainty, macroeconomic volatility and investment in new technology', in C. Driver and P. Temple (eds), *Investment, Growth and Employment: Perspectives for Policy*, London and New York: Routledge.

Van Duijn, J.J. (1983), *The Long Wave in Economic Life*, London: Allen & Unwin.

Vercelli, A. (1989), 'Uncertainty, technological flexibility and long-term fluctuations', in M. Di Matteo, R.M. Goodwin and A. Vercelli (eds), *Technological and Social Factors in Long Term Fluctuations*, Berlin: Springer-Verlag, pp. 130–44.

13. Kalecki's theory of income distribution: the answer to a maiden's prayer?[1]

Anthony J. Laramie, Douglas Mair and Peter J. Reynolds

In short, Kalecki's formulation is not the answer to any maiden's prayer.
(Bronfenbrenner, 1971, p. 411)

INTRODUCTION

As our opening quotation suggests, Kalecki's theory of income distribution has not met with universal endorsement. The most persistent criticism that it is a tautology is a canard that Kalecki himself as well as more recent commentators denied (King and Regan, 1976). However, there are still weaknesses in Kalecki's theory that need to be addressed. A problem identified, for example, by Mitchell (1988) and Sawyer (1999), is Kalecki's failure to furnish in *Theory of Economic Dynamics* (1954) a satisfactory explanation of the process by which the price/cost mark-ups between competing firms are established and maintained. In Kalecki's theory, the price/cost mark-up is an important determinant of the degree of monopoly and, hence, of the distribution of income. Kalecki's failure to provide a convincing explanation of this process weakens his theory. Mair and Laramie (forthcoming) have proposed a solution that we discuss below.

A second criticism, which is the focus of this chapter, is Kalecki's failure to adduce empirical evidence in support of his theory (King and Regan, 1976). In light of what we consider to be fundamental weaknesses of the marginal productivity theory of income distribution – the Cambridge controversy and all that – it is all the more important to demonstrate that Kalecki's theory can be tested empirically. An early attempt was Reynolds (1983) and in this chapter we seek to improve on Reynold's previous work. In addition to refining what Kalecki himself thought were the determinants of the degree of monopoly and identifying additional possible determinants, we also examine the role of j, the ratio of material costs to wage costs, which Kalecki also thought would influence the distribution of income.

The chapter is structured as follows. First, we examine what Kalecki considered to be the political aspects of the determination of price/cost mark-ups and offer an explanation of how these may be established and sustained, something he failed to do in his own approach. Thereafter, we proceed to estimate the determinants of the degree of monopoly from two samples of data from the UK manufacturing sector in the 1980s and 1990s. Finally, we examine the contribution of *j*, the ratio of material to wage costs, as a determinant of the distribution of income.

POLITICAL ASPECTS OF PRICE/COST MARK-UPS

In order to appreciate fully what lies behind Kalecki's theory of income distribution, it is important to assess it in light of his earlier work, particularly 'Political aspects of full employment' (PAFE) (Kalecki, 1943). Mair and Laramie (forthcoming) argue that conventional interpretations of PAFE as a seminal essay in the theory of the political business cycle are misleading. Essentially, PAFE should be thought of as an early essay in rent seeking. The central issue in PAFE is Kalecki's implicit recognition of the Prisoners' Dilemma problem of the conflict of interest between the private interests of individual business people and their collective interest as a class. Individually, business people will welcome full employment with its concomitant higher profits. Collectively, they will see it as a threat to their hegemony over politicians and over their workforces. While it is not in the interests of any one business person to forego the higher profits of full employment, collectively it is in their interest to do so. Business people are, therefore, playing for big stakes. Indeed, the stakes could hardly be higher involving as they do the very survival of capitalism.

But how will capitalism's survival be assured under the institutions of the normal capitalist system? While Kalecki was undoubtedly aware of the Prisoners' Dilemma problem facing business people of how to reconcile their private and collective interests, he failed, in our opinion, to provide a convincing explanation in PAFE and, by extension, in *Theory of Economic Dynamics* as to how it might be achieved.

Mair and Laramie (forthcoming) argue that an answer to this Kaleckian Prisoners' Dilemma problem can be found by linking Kalecki with the ideas of Mancur Olson. A solution to the resolution of the conflict of interest between private and collective action was provided some 20 years after PAFE by Olson in *The Logic of Collective Action* (Olson, 1965) and its sequel, *The Rise and Decline of Nations* (Olson, 1982). According to Olson (1982, p. 21), the paradox is resolved if organizations are fortunate enough to find a selective incentive through which they are motivated to pursue a common goal.

For the business community, selective incentives, for example, may take the form of fiscal, legal or other trading advantages. However, selective incentives have little applicability to large groups except where the large groups can be federations of small groups capable of interaction (Olson, 1982, p. 24). But, the sector of society that has the largest number of lobbies working on its behalf is the business community.

Olson (1965, p. 143) concludes that, because the number of firms in an industry is often no more than would comprise a 'privileged' group, these industries will normally be small enough to organize themselves into active lobbies with the political power that 'naturally and necessarily' flows to those who control the business and property of the country. This contrasts with the position of workers who are normally members of large latent groups that can only organize and act effectively when their latent power is crystallized by some organization that provides political power as a by-product.

Olson's general thesis (1982, p. 34) is that groups that have access to selective incentives will be more likely to act collectively to obtain collective goods than those that do not and that smaller groups will have a greater likelihood of engaging in collective action than larger ones. All the essential elements of Olson's theory of collective behaviour are in Kalecki, particularly explanations for the persistence of involuntary unemployment in cyclically fluctuating capitalist economies. Of particular relevance is the emphasis in Kalecki of the *product* market rather than the *labour* market as the principal arena in which real wages and income shares are determined. The key to reconciling Kalecki and Olson is to be found in a passage from Olson where he expresses essentially the same problem that had bothered Kalecki in PAFE 40 years earlier:

> For the economist, it is natural to ask who in government *or elsewhere* might have an interest in blocking the mutually advantageous transactions with the involuntary unemployed ... political parties would not have any *direct interest* and *the business community as a whole would want the extra employment for the extra demand it would bring to business in general.*
>
> (Olson, 1982, p. 201, emphasis added)

But there may be exceptions to this general desire to reduce involuntary unemployment. There is the possibility that 'insiders' with the same or competitive skills would have an incentive to block the employment of similarly qualified 'outsiders'. But also:

> *The only other group that could have such an interest would be a monopsonistic (or buyers') cartel or lobby of employers; it would need to block mutually advantageous transactions between individual employers and workers to keep wages below competitive levels. No model of involuntary unemployment or theory of*

> *macroeconomics that ignores the motive that makes unemployment occur can be satisfactory.*
>
> (Olson, 1982, pp. 201–2; emphasis in original)

Olson's 'selective incentives' and Kalecki's 'degree of monopoly' can be thought of as complementary concepts. Olsen-type activities in which businesses will engage in pursuit of goals that are collectively advantageous will, in the main, be overt, politically legitimate (at least some of the time!) and, by their very nature, undertaken in collaboration with other firms in the same industry. Kalecki-type activities, on the other hand, will be pursued by the individual firm acting on its own, except under tacitly collusive or formal cartel conditions, and will be intended to advance or, at least, maintain the firm's market position vis-à-vis its competitors. Kalecki-type activities are in the pursuit of the private interest of the business class, while Olsen-type activities are in the pursuit of its collective interest. Businesses may engage in either or both at the same time. Kalecki-type activities are a necessary, but not a sufficient condition for the long-run survival of the business class.

Thus, there is more to the degree of monopoly than just industrial structure which is just one of a number of factors affecting the intensity of competition. For example, Olsen-type activities to influence matters of mutual concern such as the legal framework, thereby affecting firms' propensity to collude may be one. The height of trade barriers or the level of the exchange rate and their effects on the intensity of competition in domestic or overseas markets interacting with Kalecki-type activities may be another. It is the sum of these and other factors that, we argue, constitute the 'degree of monopoly' or 'selective incentives'. This wider behavioural interpretation of Kalecki's degree of monopoly accords with Olson's assessment of the purposes and achievements of business groups:

> The judgement that the 'special interests' – the individual industry groups – have disproportionate power, though the business community as a whole does not, is apparently consistent with the general trend of current affairs. For it seems that the particular interests do win tax loopholes, favourable tariffs, special tax rulings, generous regulatory policies and the like.
>
> (Olson, 1965, p. 148)

It may seem somewhat strange to post Keynesians for us to link Kalecki and Olson in this way. However Olson (1982) had great difficulty in finding a macroeconomic framework into which to integrate his ideas. He evaluated Keynesian, monetarist, 'disequilibrium' and rational-expectations 'equilibrium' models and found them all unsatisfactory for a common reason, namely, a lack of congruity with their microeconomic foundations. Olson's preference was for what he considered 'an important but inadequately appreciated insight of Robert Clower's' (Olson, 1982, pp. 207–10). The details of the Clower insight do not concern us here. What is important is that what Olson called the 'Clower-Olson' approach provides an explanation of frequent fluctuations in the level of real output or business cycles in societies with a significant degree of institutional sclerosis which is at no point inconsistent with any valid economic theory (Olson, 1982, p. 210). Had he chosen to consider it, we think that Olson would have found that Kalecki's model also met his criteria.

EMPIRICAL ESTIMATES OF THE DEGREE OF MONOPOLY

The second substantive criticism that can be made against the degree of monopoly theory is Kalecki's failure to provide empirical support. For example, King and Regan conclude:

> His [Kalecki's] analysis of the determinants of *k* [the mark-up] is piecemeal ... Kalecki offers no evidence ... although ... some at least could readily be obtained ... we must conclude that Kalecki's account of relative shares tells us very little. His own empirical work, moreover, simply *measures W/Y, j* and *k* and cannot be seen as providing empirical verification for *any* theory of relative income shares. Kalecki's assumptions (constant *AVC* and *SMC*, mark-up pricing) are entirely realistic, but without an analysis of the determinants of the degree of monopoly his model yields no unambiguous predictions.
>
> (King and Regan, 1976, pp. 55–6, emphasis in original)

In light of our discussion above, the issue of how to measure the degree of monopoly becomes more problematic. If we think of it in terms of Olson-type selective incentives, then it is not possible to generate empirical measures of the lobbying and other collective activities that firms find it profitable to employ. However, the factors that Kalecki identified in *Theory of Economic Dynamics* as determining the mark-up are, in principle, quantifiable as well as others that might also be properly considered. In this section we identify a number of possible factors. We present our justification for their inclusion and describe the ways we have sought to quantify them. Given the complementarity that we argue exists between the non-quantifiable Olsen-type activities and the quantifiable Kaleckian-type, we have no *a priori* expectation of the strength of the impact of the latter on the size of the mark-up.

In addition to the role of 'giant' firms that we have already discussed, Kalecki (1954, p. 17) identified three other factors that he thought would influence the degree of monopoly. These are the development of sales promotion through advertising, selling agents and so on, the influence of changes in the level of overheads in relation to prime costs, and the power of trade unions.

Concentration and S-C-P

It is possible to regard the extent of industrial concentration, the ratio of advertising to sales and other possible influences as structural characteristics of an individual industry within the static Structure-Conduct-Performance (S-C-P) paradigm, as is common in much of the industrial economics literature. We begin by examining the factors listed by Kalecki from an S-C-P perspective. He suggested that: 'the influence of the emergence of firms representing a substantial share of the output of an industry can be readily understood … the firm can fix its price at a level higher than would otherwise be the case' (Kalecki, 1954, p. 17).

This statement would appear to be consistent with the static S-C-P approach, implying a monotonic relationship with the level of concentration and the mark-up. However, there is a problem with this interpretation. Although the extent of concentration may be expected to affect the intensity of competition, a monotonic relationship with any specific measure of concentration is not assured. Whether the process of competition is more intense with, for example, two firms in an industry rather than three remains an open question. This will depend on how each firm responds (or is expected to respond) to a change (or expected change) in the behaviour of its rival(s), which in turn will be influenced by a host of historical, legal and other influences.[2]

Advertising: Sales Ratio

A high ratio of advertising to sales may suggest an industry approximating to the Chamberlinian large group case, where advertising is used to create perceived differences between products so that competition by advertising replaces competition by price. Thus, an increase in competitive pressure is manifested either in terms of reduced mark-ups or via increased expenditures on advertising. If, by the term 'high degree of monopoly', is meant a less intense competitive process, then a 'high degree of monopoly' may lead either to high mark-ups or to low expenditures on advertising. On this interpretation, a 'high degree of monopoly', implying a weak competitive process, may be associated with relatively low or relatively high spending on advertising. For a given degree of monopoly, this would lead us to expect a negative association between the mark-up and the ratio of advertising to sales.

Set against this, a high ratio of advertising to sales, by increasing perceived product differentiation, tempers the degree to which the firm is influenced by the pricing behaviour of its rivals, thereby increasing the degree of monopoly of the individual firm. The pressure to reduce mark-ups is thereby alleviated and they may even rise. Thus, the advertising to sales ratio may be thought of as one of the institutional or environmental factors both affected by the intensity of the competitive process and contributing to it.

Cyclical Variations in Mark-ups

Kalecki (1954) recognized that during a recession there may or may not be a rise in profit margins. This would depend on whether the squeeze on profits caused the competitive pressures to intensify or whether there would be tacit agreement to maintain or increase margins. On this point Kalecki wrote:

> If the level of overheads should rise considerably in relation to prime costs, there will necessarily follow a 'squeeze on profits' unless the ratio of prime costs to proceeds is permitted to rise. As *a result, there may arise a tacit agreement among the firms of an industry to 'protect' profits and consequently to increase prices in relation to unit prime costs. For instance, the increase in capital costs per unit of output as a result of the introduction of techniques which increase capital intensity may tend to increase the degree of monopoly. The factor of 'protection' of profits is especially apt to appear during periods of depression ... there is a tendency for the degree of monopoly to rise in the slump, a tendency which is reversed in the boom.*
>
> (Kalecki, 1954, p. 17–18), emphasis added)

In this passage, Kalecki is again focusing on the importance of the degree of monopoly as a selective incentive in a way that is entirely consistent with Olson's requirement that an acceptable macroeconomic theory must be consistent with booms as well as busts.

The Influence of Trade Unions

> The existence of powerful trade unions may tend to reduce profit margins for the following reasons. A high ratio of profits to wages strengthens the bargaining position of trade unions in their demands for wage increases, since higher wages are then compatible with 'reasonable profits' at existing price levels.
>
> (Kalecki, 1954, p. 18)

One of Kalecki's many significant contributions was to clarify that if trade unions are to influence labour's share of national income, then this will be achieved via a constraining effect on the mark-up. Kalecki (1971) referred to the power of trade unions as being manifested in 'the extent of wage rises demanded and achieved'.

ESTIMATING THE MARK-UP

We now report econometric results obtained from regression analysis of two data sets from samples of UK manufacturing industries that we have used to estimate the mark-up. The first data set relates to the period 1985–90 and the second to the period 1992–96. Because of differences in definitions, for example, the introduction in the UK of a revised Standard Industrial Classification in 1992 and in the availability of data between the two time periods, we report them separately. We describe the variables we include in our model and the data sources from which obtain them.

As we have seen, the various factors Kalecki thought would influence the mark-up include:

1. *Industry concentration*: a number of studies (Domowitz, Hubbard and Petersen, 1986; Conyon and Machin, 1991), have sought to find empirical confirmation of the link between industry concentration and industry price-cost margins. Much of the emphasis in these studies has been on the relationship between price-cost margins, concentration and unionization. There appears to be considerable agreement from both American and British studies that margins vary cyclically and that more highly concentrated industries have smaller increases in profit margins as unemployment rises.

   However, we believe that there are still conceptual and empirical problems to be resolved. For example, if the focus of interest is market concentration, then the market must be identified. If it is the domestic market that is of interest, then account must be taken both of the degree of penetration by foreign firms and of the proportion of domestic production which is exported.

   To keep faith with Kalecki, we follow the same procedure. We take the Annual Census of Production (ACOP) five-firm concentration ratios for the industries in our samples and multiply them by a weighting factor, $(1 - R1)$, where $R1$ is equal to imports divided by home demand and home demand is defined as manufacturers' sales plus imports minus exports. This measure, $CR5(1 - R1)$, comes closer to reflecting market concentration than the ACOP five-firm concentration ratios which relate to the industries in which goods are produced rather than the markets in which they are sold.

   However, we consider earlier studies still to be problematic because, as an indicator of market concentration, the $CR5(1 - R1)$ measure is deficient in industries where foreign firms are among the dominant suppliers. Also, it relates only to the domestic market. The degree of import penetration, measured by $R1$, is one of the institutional features that may influence a firm's behaviour. A high degree of import penetration in the manufacturing sector may be indicative of an industry dominated by trans-national firms where competitive pressures are reflected in aspects of marketing other than price. Thus, we include in our regressions as separate factors both *R*1, the ratio of imports to home demand and *R*4, the ratio of exports to the sum of manufacturers' sales plus imports. In this way, we address one of the criticisms of King and Regan (1976, p. 55) that Kalecki makes what they call the implicit and very questionable assumption of a closed economy.

2. *Advertising:sales ratio*: expenditures on advertising are included with other costs as part of a general category of overheads in the ACOP and are not separately identified. Consequently, we have used data from the *Advertising Statistics Yearbooks*. These data show advertising expenditure by product and it was necessary to allocate the product advertising expenditures to the Standard Industrial Classification three-digit industry classification.
3. *Influence of changes in overheads in relation to prime costs*: the ratio of overhead costs to prime costs can be obtained from ACOP data. However, as prime costs appear as the denominator both in this variable and in the mark-up (the dependent variable) inclusion of both in our model would result in bogus correlation. Furthermore, since advertising expenditure is included as an overhead cost in the ACOP, using ACOP overhead costs as an independent variable will lead to problems of multicollinearity. As a result, we adopt an alternative approach. If, as hypothesized, mark-ups do indeed increase during a recession due to the increased pressure of overhead costs, then the extent to which this occurs can be measured directly by including a cyclical variable as a regressor. This also serves to test the supplementary hypothesis, referred to above, whereby competitive pressure might increase during a recession, causing mark-ups to be reduced. We use the real rate of growth of output to examine for these effects. We have not found satisfactory data by which to measure changes in capital intensity, although to some extent we might expect this to be captured by *E(MCR)* (see below). Even so, the capital:output ratio used to determine *E(MCR)* is obtained from fairly aggregated data and is, therefore, a rather crude indicator of the degree of capital intensity of an individual industry.

Influence of trade unions: Implicit in Kalecki's approach is the assumption that the mark-up is fully determined by the firm in the sense that prices respond immediately to changes in prime costs. As discussed in Reynolds (1996), the aggregate, *ex post*, mark-up is also affected by the relative speeds with which prices adjust to money-wage price increases and money-wages respond to price increases. To capture this requires a dynamic specification, which we do not develop in this chapter. Within the model presented in this chapter, we have used the annual growth rate of earnings per head, $\hat{w}$, with various lag structures, to try to capture the influence of trade unions.

4. *Other institutional influences*: in the light of the Kalecki-Olson interpretation we develop earlier in this chapter, it is appropriate to consider other institutional factors or features of a firm's environment that might affect the mark-up. Hence, following Reynolds (1983) we investigate the effects of entry barriers. One possible reason for including entry barriers is to investigate the extent to which they lead to 'limit pricing' as an entry-deterring strategy. Four entry barriers are frequently discussed in the literature. These are:

   - the minimum capital requirement – *E(MCR)*
   - the percentage effect of economies of scale – *E(%)*
   - product diversification, proxied by the Specialization Index, *SI*, from the ACOP.

   For the reasons we discuss above with regard to modifying the five firm concentration ratio to take account of import penetration, we think it is important to make the same adjustment to *E*(%) to recognize that what is important is *MES* in relation to the size of the domestic market. Accordingly, we introduce $E(\%)[(1 - R1)]$ as a variable in the model.

   Following Reynolds (1983), we proxy *MES* by an estimate of the size of plant producing at the mid-point of the cumulative size distribution of the industry. The studies cited above have estimated *MES* by taking the net output of the size class containing the mid-point of the cumulative distribution of industry net output divided by the number of plants in the class. However, since this is often the largest size class, representing over 50 per cent of industry output, this represents only a crude estimate of *MES*. Furthermore, if the mid-point of the distribution lies close to a class boundary, a minor change in the composition of classes can lead to a very large change in the estimate of *MES*. To overcome both of these problems, we estimate *MES* by interpolating the mid-point from an approximation to the cumulative frequency polygon. In effect, we take a weighted average of the two class mid-points which lie on either side of the mid-point of the entire cumulative distribution.

Regression Results

The arguments in the previous section lead us to specify the following equation:

$$k = \alpha_0 + \alpha_1[CR5(1 - R1)] + \alpha_2(A:S) + \alpha_3[E\%(1 - R1)] + \alpha_4[E(MCR)] + \alpha_5 R1 + \alpha_6 R4 + \alpha_7 SI + \alpha_8 \hat{g} + \alpha_9 \hat{w} + \varepsilon \quad (13.1)$$

where:

k	= mark-up on prime costs (ratio of gross output: wage plus material costs) (*source*: *Business Monitor PA1002*, HMSO).
$CR5(1 - R1)$	= five-firm concentration ratio multiplied by one minus index of import penetration (*sources*: *Business Monitor PA1002*, HMSO; *Business Monitor MQ12*, HMSO): expected sign of α_1 is positive or negative.
$A{:}S$	= advertising:sales ratio (*source*: *Advertising Statistics Yearbook*, Advertising Association): expected sign of α_2 is positive or negative.
$E(\%)(1 - R1)$	= percentage effect of scale economies (minimum efficient scale divided by net output) multiplied by one minus index of import penetration. This measures minimum efficient scale as a percentage of the UK home market (*sources*: *Business Monitor PA1002*, HMSO; *Business Monitor MQ12*, HMSO): expected sign of α_3 is positive.
$E(MCR)$	= minimum capital requirement effect of scale economies (minimum efficient scale multiplied by capital:output ratio) (*sources*: *Business Monitor PA1002*, HMSO; *UK National Income Accounts*, HMSO): expected sign of α_4 is positive.
$R1$	= ratio of imports to UK manufacturers' sales plus imports minus exports. This measures the extent of import penetration in the UK home market (*source*: *Business Monitor MQ12*, HMSO): expected sign of α_5 is positive or negative.
$R4$	= ratio of exports to UK manufacturers' sales plus imports. This measures extent of UK export penetration (*source*: *Business Monitor MQ12*, HMSO): expected sign of α_6 is positive.
SI	= specialization index (*source*: *Business Monitor PA1002*): expected sign of α_7 is positive.
$\hat{g}$	= annual growth rate of industry output deflated by producer price index (*sources*: *Business Monitor PA1002*, HMSO; *Annual Abstract of Statistics*, HMSO): expected sign of α_8 is positive.
$\hat{w}$	= annual growth rate of earnings per head (*source*: *New Earnings Survey*, Part C, HMSO): expected sign of α_9 is negative.
ε	= error term.

If a firm is in 'equilibrium' in the sense that the mark-up has been adjusted to that which the firm intends, given the prevailing institutional and environmental influences, then equation13.1 may be expected to hold. Thus, equation 13.1 may be thought of as an 'equilibrium' relationship.

Industrial Sample 1985–90

We now estimate the determinants of the mark-up for two separate time periods. The first period is 1985–90 and the sample comprises 15 manufacturing industries (see Appendix). The choice of industries was determined (1) by the availability of data on advertising from the *Advertising Statistics Yearbook*; and (2) the requirement that an industry should have a *Specialization Index* of 90 or greater to ensure a high degree of product homogeneity. It was not possible to extend the time period back prior to 1985 because of a lack of data on advertising expenditures; and it was not possible to extend the sample period beyond 1990 because the Office of National Statistics discontinued publication in that year of *Business Monitor MQ12*.

The OLS results of the pooled regression for the 15 industries over the six-year period 1985–90 of the model specified in equation 13.1 are presented in Table 13.1. The coefficient of the annual growth rate of earnings per head, $\hat{g}$, was not statistically significantly different from zero and that variable has been omitted from the table. Because of the importance which earlier studies of the determinants of firms' mark-ups have attached to industry concentration and the importance we attach to modifying the definition of concentration to recognize the importance of the relevant market, we include $CR5(1 - R1)$ in the table despite the fact that its coefficient, too, is not significantly different from zero.

The coefficients of $R1$ (import penetration) and $R4$ (export penetration) are both positive and significant, although small in magnitude. This confirms that the degree of openness of the market is a relevant consideration. The positive coefficient on $R1$ can be interpreted as indicating that foreign firms may be attracted into the UK market by the existence of high mark-ups. Alternatively, foreign firms exporting to the UK may enjoy a high degree of monopoly in their own domestic markets which they are able to transfer to the UK market. The positive coefficient on $R4$ may indicate that UK firms use their position of domestic market strength as a platform for sales in overseas markets. Or there may be product characteristics of foreign manufactured goods which enable them to operate high mark-ups in the UK market, for example, wine, food, designer clothes and footwear. The results reported predate the creation of the Single Internal Market in 1991 which is likely to have strengthened still further the influence of external factors on mark-ups.

Table 13.1 Degree of monopoly for sample of manufacturing industries, 1985–90: Pooled regression, ordinary least squares estimation

Regressor	Coefficient	Standard error	T-ratio	[Prob]
Constant	.56858	.018870	3.131	[.003]
Specialization Index	.0028633	.9929E-3	2.8836	[.005]
Import penetration	.0034376	.0012327	2.7885	[.007]
Export penetration	.0038649	.794SE-3	4.8643	[.000]
Advertising:sales ratio	.96053	.27781	3.4574	[.001]
Minimum capital requirement effect of scale economies	.4148E-6	.8188E-7	5.0658	[.000]
Five-firm concentration ratio (1 – Index of import penetration)	.2032E-4	.1918E-4	1.0592	[.293]
% effect of scale economies (1 – Index of import penetration)	–.3359E-3	.8515E-4	–3.9444	[.000]
Real annual growth rate	.38321	.12150	3.1540	[.002]

Notes:

R-squared	.62345
R-bar-squared	.58626
Residual sum of squares	.86699
SD of dependent variable	.16084
F-statistic F (8, 81)	16.7639 [.000]
SE of regression	.10346
Mean of dependent variable	1.4329
Maximum of log-likelihood	81.2099

Dependent variable is mark-up
90 observations used for estimation from 1 to 90

The negative sign of $[E\%(1 - R1)]$ reflects, we think, the interaction between it and the other variables in the model designed to capture the influence of entry barriers. Again, we draw attention to the importance of modifying the definition of entry barriers to reflect the degree of openness of an industry. The significance of the annual rate of growth of gross output in real terms, confirms the importance of including a cyclical variable in the model.

We next estimated equation 13.1 including a set of time dummies in the model (not reported). The hypothesis that the time intercepts have the same value was not rejected by an F-test, for $\alpha = 0.02$. We then reran the regression to include a set of industry dummies. The hypothesis that the industry intercepts have the same value was rejected by an F-test for $\alpha = 0.02$. We examined the differences in the industry intercepts further. We estimated a constrained model by regressing the residuals of the equation on the industry dummies 1985–90 [RSS_0]. We then estimated two unconstrained models: (1)

the residuals were regressed on the industry dummies 1985–87 [RSS_1]; and (2) the residuals were regressed on the industry dummies 1988–90 [RSS_2]. The null hypothesis that the industry coefficients 1985–87 = the industry coefficients 1988–90 was tested by an F-test. The computed value of F^{15}_{60} = 6.477 compared to the critical value F^{15}_{60} = 2.50 (α = 0.02). Thus, the null hypothesis of no difference in the industry coefficients 1985–87 and the industry coefficients 1988–90 is rejected.

This suggests that there has been a process at work influencing the mark-ups of the industries in our sample over the period 1985–90. At the beginning of the period, the industry mark-ups were what they were as a result of the histories of these industries prior to 1985. By the end of the period, these mark ups had changed somewhat as a result of events during the period 1985–90. We have captured any purely cyclical influence by the inclusion of the real annual rate of growth in the model and, as we report above, the differences in the intercepts of the time dummies are not significantly different from zero. There were shocks to the UK economy in the period 1987–90, for example the UK's exit from the Exchange Rate Mechanism (ERM) and the subsequent devaluation of sterling. There was also the adjustment process towards the full operation of the Single Internal Market in 1991 which may account for the somewhat different pattern of behaviour in the latter part of the period. The point we wish to emphasize is the importance of recognizing that there is a process at work. We have demonstrated in Table 13.1 that it is possible to estimate the 'degree of monopoly' from industry data. We have further evidence that the institutional and environmental factors, which the degree of monopoly reflects, have changed over the period. It is important, therefore, to view the degree of monopoly as a dynamic phenomenon which may change materially over even as short a period as six years.

Industrial Sample 1994–97

We now report the results for the second period for which we have data. These are for the period 1994–97 and are based on the revised 1992 Standard Industrial Classification. We are able to identify 30 separate industries (see Appendix). The sample for the period 1994–97 is over twice the size of the sample for the period 1985–90 and, consequently, covers a wider range of industries.

There is, however, a major difference between the two samples. In the 1985–90 period, the ACOP reported separately data on 'operatives wages' and 'salaries of administrative, technical and other employees'. This enabled us to calculate the mark-up, k, in the required Kaleckian manner as gross output divided by the sum of wage and material costs. In the 1994–97 period, the ACOP reports only a combined figure for wages and salaries. Thus, we are unable to compute k directly in accordance with Kalecki's definition. We address the problem by computing two alternative measures of k. We calculate $k1$ as gross output divided by material costs and $k2$ as gross output divided by wages and salaries plus material costs. The regressions are basically similar with the principal difference that the coefficients of the import and export penetration variables are statistically significant with $k2$ as the dependent variable but not with $k1$. Neither is wholly satisfactory but we report below our regression with $k2$ as the dependent variable. The other difference between the two periods is that the ACOP for 1994–97 does not publish the Specialization Index and we are therefore obliged to omit it. Otherwise, the variables are as defined above.

We report in Table 13.2 our results with $k2$ as the dependent variable for the period 1994–97. Because of the differences in the definition of the de-

Table 13.2 Degree of monopoly (k2) *for sample of manufacturing industries, 1994–97: ordinary least squares estimation*

Regressor	Coefficient	Standard error	T-ratio	[prob]
Constant	1.4299	.041515	34.4442	[.000]
Advertising:sales ratio	.030564	.0058656	5.2108	[.000]
Minimum capital requirement effect of scale economies	–.2119E-6	.9252E-7	2.2902	[.024]
% effect of scale economies (1 – Index of import penetration	.95573	.42684	2.2391	[.027]
Import penetration	–1.7459	.49796	–3.5061	[.001]
Export penetration	2.4560	.81649	3.0080	[.003]
Five-firm concentration ratio (1 – Index of import penetration)	–.35543	.11095	–3.2036	[.002]
Real annual growth rate	.0085103	.7756E-3	10.9731	[.000]

Notes:

R-squared	.61342	
SE of regression	.17212	
Mean of dependent variable	1.4724	
Residual sum of squares	3.3179	
Akaike info. criterion	37.0173	
R-bar-squared	.58926	
F-stat. F(7, 112)	25.3887	[.000]
SD of dependent variable	.26856	
Equation log-likelihood	45.0173	
Schwarz Bayesian criteron	25.8673	

Dependent variable is $k2$

120 observations used for estimation from 1 to 120

pendent variable, differences in the composition of the sample and differences in the specification of the model, direct comparison of the results of Tables 13.1 and 13.2 is difficult. The advertising:sales ratio, export penetration and the annual growth rate of output are all statistically significant and of the same sign in both time periods. The sign on the import penetration variable coefficient changes to negative in the later time period. This is consistent with the hypothesis that mark-ups are forced down by the presence of import competition. The coefficient of the five-firm concentration ratio variable was insignificantly different from zero in the 1985–90 sample. It becomes statistically significant in the 1992–97 sample, although with a negative sign. Given the limitations of the data, we feel it is reasonable to conclude that our results for the period 1992–97 give further support to the results we report above for the period 1985–90.

THE RATIO OF MATERIALS TO WAGES (*j*)

The other factor Kalecki thought to be important in determining the share of wages in national income as well as the mark up, *k*, is the ratio of materials to wages, *j*. As King and Regan (1976, p. 55) observe, Kalecki offered no empirical evidence in support of the behaviour of *j* apart from the unsupported assertion that, as the wage share tended to be stable over long periods of time, then *k* and *j* would tend to move in opposite directions. The critical question posed by King and Regan is whether *k* and *j* are wholly independent of each other.

We test the relationship in the following way. For the UK for the period 1972 to 1997, we define k = gross output/(operatives wages + purchases) of the manufacturing sector (*Production and Construction Inquiries, PA1002*, Tables 1 and 2); and j = price index of imports (*Economic Trends Annual Supplement*, Table 1.21)/index of unit labour costs (*Economic Trends Annual Supplement*, Table 1.22. We then regress *k* on *j* using an autoregressive distributed lag procedure to determine the lag structure. Using the Schwarz Bayesian criterion to select the lag structure, as we report in Table 13.3, the coefficient of *j* is statistically insignificant.

We examine the relationship further by plotting Δk minus Δj in Figure 13.1. As the figure shows there is a clear cyclical pattern. The sum of the positive and negative deviations of Δk minus Δj is –0.04, which is very close to zero. This suggests that there has been no systematic long run effect of *j* on *k* in the UK for the 25 years from 1972 to 1997. We conclude, therefore, that movements in *j* have had no systematic impact on *k* during the 1970s, 1980s and well into the 1990s. Changes in the distribution of income over that period have come about solely as a result of changes in *k*.

Table 13.3 Autoregressive distributed lag estimates: ARDL (1,0) selected based on Schwarz Bayesian criterion

Regressor	Coefficient	Standard error	T-ratio [prob]
$k(-1)$	.83757	.13839	6.0522 [.000]
j	−.0076152	.063626	−.11969 [.906]
Constant	.26208	.26850	.97611 [.343]

Notes:

R-squared	.90391
SE of regression	.019117
Mean of dependent variable	1.5185
Residual sum of squares	.0062126
Akaike info. criterion	49.3904
DW-statistic	2.2104
R-bar-squared	.89261
F-stat. F(2, 17)	79.9606 [.000]
SD of dependent variable	.058334
Equation log-likelihood	52.3904
Schwarz Bayesian criterion	47.8968
Durbin's h-statistic	−.59900 [.549]

Dependent variable is k

20 observations used for estimation from 1977 to 1996

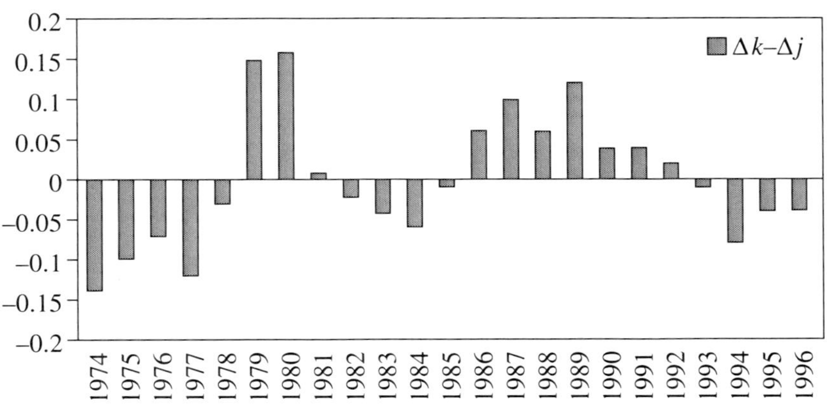

Figure 13.1 $\Delta k - \Delta j$ *in the UK from 1972–97*

CONCLUSION

In this chapter, we have re-examined Kalecki's degree of monopoly theory of income distribution. While some of the criticisms of it have been misplaced,

Kalecki's formulation does suffer from shortcomings. Whilst it is to Kalecki's credit that he recognized that his theory of income distribution must have both microeconomic and macroeconomic dimensions which, in a sense, lie side by side, he failed to provide a satisfactory explanation of how the two might be bridged. A solution to this problem can be found by linking Kalecki's concept of the 'degree of monopoly' with Olsen's 'selective incentives', to their mutual advantage. Once this link is made, then the factors that Kalecki thought might influence the 'degree of monopoly' can be seen as a subset of a wider set of collective activities undertaken by businesses in pursuit of an enhanced share of national income.

From two samples of UK manufacturing industries, we have produced evidence that such factors as product differentiation, entry barriers, exposure to foreign competition do influence firms' ability to determine the size of their mark-up over prime cost and, therefore, to influence the distribution of income. We do not find evidence to suggest that, in the UK at least, j, the ratio of material to wages costs has had any systematic influence on income distribution since the mid-1970s. Mair and Laramie (forthcoming) identify a significant shift in income distribution in the UK since 1975 in favour of profits' share. This suggests that the Kalecki-Olsen nexus has indeed been at work.

NOTES

1. We wish to thank Heriot-Watt and Staffordshire Universities for financial support in the preparation of this chapter. We wish to thank Anne Miller for econometric advice and Valerie Dickie for computational assistance.
2. In a number of models, reputedly in the Kaleckian tradition, this is captured by a 'conjectural variation' term. However, a problem with these approaches is that the 'conjectural variation' term is treated as a constant.

REFERENCES

Bronfenbrenner, M. (1971), *Income Distribution Theory*, London: Macmillan.

Conyon, M., and S. Machin (1991), 'The determination of profit margins in UK manufacturing', *Journal of Industrial Economics*, **39** (4), 369–82.

Domowitz, I.R., R.G. Hubbard, and B.C. Petersen (1986), 'The inter-temporal stability of the concentration-margin relationship', *Journal of Industrial Economics*, **35** (1), 13–34.

Kalecki, M. (1943), 'Political aspects of full employment', *Political Quarterly*, **14**, 322–31.

Kalecki, M. (1954), *Theory of Economic Dynamics*, London: Unwin University Books.

Kalecki, M. (1971), 'The class struggle and the determination of national income', in *Selected Essays on the Dynamics of the Capitalist Economy, 1933–1970*, Cambridge: Cambridge University Press.

King, J.E., and P. Regan (1976), *Income Shares*, London: Macmillan.
Mair, D., and A.J. Laramie (forthcoming), 'Full employment: gift horse or Trojan horse?', *Review of Social Economy*.
Mitchell, W.C. (1988), 'Inflation and politics: six theories in search of reality', in T.D. Willett (ed.), *Political Business Cycles*, Durham, NC: Duke University Press.
Olson, M. (1965), *The Logic of Collective Action*, Cambridge, MA: Harvard University Press.
Olson, M. (1982), *The Rise and Decline of Nations*, New Haven, CT: Yale University Press.
Reynolds, P.J. (1983), 'An empirical analysis of the degree of monopoly theory of income distribution', *Bulletin of Economic Research*, **36**, 59–84.
Reynolds, P.J. (1996), 'Kalecki's theory of prices and distribution', in J.E. King (ed.), *An Alternative Economic Theory: The Kaleckian Model and Post Keynesian Economics*, Boston, MA: Kluwer Academic.
Sawyer, M.C. (1999), *The Legacy of Michal Kalecki, Vol 1*, Cheltenham, UK and Northampton, MA, USA: Edward Elgar.

APPENDIX

Sample of Manufacturing Industries, 1985–90

MLH 346 Domestic-type electric appliances; MLH 412 Slaughtering of animals and production of meat and by-products; MLH 413 Preparation of milk and milk products; MLH 414 Processing of fruit and vegetables; MLH 415 Fish processing; MLH 419 Bread, biscuits and flour confectionery; MLH 421 Ice cream, cocoa, chocolate and sugar confectionery; MLH 423 Starch and miscellaneous foods; MLH 424 Spirit distilling and compounding; MLH 426 Wines, cider and perry; MLH 427 Brewing and malting; MLH 428 Soft drinks; MLH 429 Tobacco; MLH 451 Footwear; MLH 453 Clothing, hats and gloves.

Sample of Manufacturing Industries, 1992–96

MLH 151 Production, processing and preserving of meat and meat products; MLH 152 Processing and preserving of fish and fish products; MLH 155 Manufacture of dairy products; MLH 157 Manufacture of prepared animal feeds; MLH 159 Manufacture of beverages; MLH 174 Manufacture of made-up textile articles, except apparel; MLH 193 Manufacture of footwear; MLH 232 Manufacture of refined petroleum products; MLH 241 Manufacture of basic chemicals; MLH 243 Manufacture of paints, varnishes and similar coatings, printing ink and mastics; MLH 244 Manufacture of pharmaceuticals, medicinal chemicals and botanical products; MLH 245 Manufacture of soap and detergents, cleaning and polishing preparations, perfumes and toilet preparations; MLH 252 Manufacture of plastic products; MLH 286 Manufacture of cutlery, tools and general hardware; MLH 293 Manufacture of agricultural and forestry machinery; MLH 295 Manufacture of other special purpose machinery; MLH 297 Manufacture of domestic appliances; MLH 300 Manufacture of office machinery and computers; MLH 315 Manufacture of lighting equipment and lamps; MLH 323 Manufacture of television and radio receivers, sound or video recording or reproducing apparatus and associated goods; MLH 334 Manufacture of optical instruments and photographic equipment; MLH 335 Manufacture of watches and clocks; MLH 341 Manufacture of motor vehicles; MLH 354 Manufacture of motor cycles and bicycles; MLH 361 Manufacture of furniture; MLH 362 Manufacture of jewellery and related articles; MLH 363 Manufacture of musical instruments; MLH 364 Manufacture of sports goods; MLH 365 Manufacture of games and toys; MLH 366 Miscellaneous manufacturing.

PART V

Methodology

14. On the relation between individual and collective beliefs: a comparison between Keynes's and Hayek's economic theories

Richard Arena

Many articles and meetings have been dedicated to the relationship between Keynes's and Hayek's contributions to economic theory. Not surprisingly, most of them focus on monetary and business cycle theories: both topics were extensively discussed by the authors in the *Economic Journal* as well as in a famous private correspondence. This is why we will not consider these topics once again (see, for example, Arena, 1999a) but rather compare Keynes's and Hayek's contributions to a different issue: the relation between knowledge and beliefs, on the one hand, and economics, on the other hand. More precisely, we will consider what is the role given by both authors to individual and, possibly, collective beliefs in the analysis of the working of the global economic system and, more particularly, of markets.

Our project could be considered a rather strange attempt: Keynes and Hayek devoted their respective contributions to the present topic within very different historical and intellectual contexts, so that the comparison between their perspectives might appear illegitimate at first sight. Most of Keynes's ideas were developed in the *Treatise on Probability* (published in 1921), in Keynes's *Lectures, 1932–1935* (1989), in the *General Theory* (Keynes, 1936) as well as in 'The general theory of employment' (Keynes, 1937), namely during the 1920s and the 1930s. By contrast, Hayek began his reflections on these subjects at the end of the 1930s, even if he had already written the first draft of the *Sensory Order* during the 1920s. His entry in the field was his famous article on 'Economics and knowledge' (Hayek, 1937). Then, after the publication of a series of articles in the late 1930s and 1940s (collected in *Individualism and Economic Order*, Hayek, 1948), he never ceased to come back to the topic of knowledge and beliefs in economics till the end of his life. The only decade in which the reflections of both authors overlapped within the topic was therefore the 1920s, when Keynes published the *Treatise on Probability* he had written before the First World War and Hayek wrote the first draft of the *Sensory Order*. However, these contributions never generated a debate between both authors, especially because it is only in the 1950s that Hayek published the final draft of his *Sensory Order* (Hayek, 1952a).

This temporal gap does not mean that Keynes's and Hayek's contributions have nothing in common. Quite the contrary, a comparison makes sense since both analogies and differences between these contributions reveal important issues which are now being seriously reconsidered by a part of modem economic theory.

1 KEYNES'S AND HAYEK'S CONCEPTIONS OF KNOWLEDGE

According to Keynes, it is possible to define three types of cognitive factors which determine individual decisions. Keynes first refers to irrational beliefs:

> There is first of all the distinction between that part of our belief which is rational and that part which is not. If a man believes something for a reason which is preposterous or for no reason at all, and what he believes turns out to be true for some reason not known to him, he cannot be said to believe it rationally, although he believes it and it is in fact true.
>
> (Keynes, 1973, vol. VII, p. 10)

This quotation does not imply that 'irrational beliefs' have no essential role to play as a factor of individual decisions. Quite the contrary, there are specific cases in which this type of beliefs is the main determinant of economic behaviours. This is especially true in the case of long-term expectations when, according to Keynes's own words, the 'basis' of a 'strictly mathematical forecasting' 'does not exist' (Keynes, 1973, vol. VIII).

In this case, men behave according to what they think to be the best possible solution but obviously, very often, rational arguments are replaced by 'whim, feeling or luck' (Keynes, 1973, vol. VIII). Other types of motifs appear which contribute to the substitution of rationality by 'habit, instinct, preference, desire, will, etc …' (Keynes, 1979, vol. XXIX, p. 294).

Keynes also refers to 'rational beliefs'. These beliefs are not really proved or demonstrated to be true but we can refer to some type of ground to think that they are probable. From this point of view, according to Keynes, probability relations only express 'the degree of our *rational belief* in the conclusion' (Keynes, 1973, vol. VIII, p. 5). These rational beliefs cannot be characterized as proper *knowledge* since knowledge is not defined as a *probable* but as a *certain* rational belief (pp. 10–11): for Keynes, knowledge only corresponds to 'the highest degree of rational belief' (p. 10). On the other hand, if probable rational beliefs are not strict knowledge, however, they arise out of knowledge, namely, out of some certain knowledge basis which permits agents to carry out probability calculus (p. 11).

From this standpoint, it is possible to define three types of knowledge. The first type corresponds to what Keynes called 'direct knowledge' or 'direct acquaintance with things' (p. 13). Here, 'direct acquaintance' includes 'experience, understanding, and perceptions' (p. 12).

When this direct knowledge has been acquired: 'by some mental process of which it is difficult to give an account, we are able to pass from direct acquaintance with things to a knowledge of propositions about the things of which we have sensations or understand the meaning' (p. 13). This knowledge of propositions is called 'indirect knowledge' by Keynes (p. 12). This is a knowledge which we cannot acquire directly but only 'by argument' (p. 12). Indirect knowledge can be certain; in this case, Keynes, calls it indirect 'knowledge of the proposition' (p. 13). Indirect knowledge can also be probable; in this alternative case, Keynes calls it indirect 'knowledge about the proposition' (p. 13). From this standpoint, rational beliefs are nothing but this third type of knowledge. However, strictly speaking these beliefs cannot be assimilated to knowledge of things or of propositions about things (p. 13). They only are knowledge about propositions about things.

Keynes also seems to accept a fourth type of knowledge when he refers to 'vague knowledge' (pp. 17–18). He stressed the 'importance' of this type (p. 18) but argued that he did not know 'how to deal with it' (p. 17). This is why it is uneasy to characterize this fourth type of knowledge as the set of irrational beliefs or even, perhaps, as an intermediary form between irrational and rational beliefs.

Keynes's conception of knowledge does not exclude some form of subjectivism but it draws very precisely its limits. Thus, Keynes accepts the idea that direct knowledge 'is clearly relative to individual experience', even if men do not differ radically (Keynes, 1973, vol. VIII, p. 18). Keynes also accepts the idea of some subjectivity of indirect knowledge since, according to his view, intuitive capacities and cognitive habilities differ from man to man. Here again, however, Keynes' stresses the limits of this possible subjectivity:

> what we know and what probability we can attribute to our rational beliefs is, ... subjective in the sense of being relative to the individual. But, given the body of premisses which are subjective powers and circumstances supplied to us, and given the kinds of logical relations, upon which arguments can be based and which we have the capacity to perceive, the conclusions, which it is rational for us to draw, stand to these premisses in an objective and wholly logical relation.
>
> (Keynes, 1973, vol. VIII, p. 19)

This standpoint is perfectly compatible with Keynes's critique of subjective probabilities:

> But in the sense important to logic, probability is not subjective. It is not, that is to say, subject to human caprice. A proposition is not probable because we think it so. When once the facts are given which determined our knowledge, what is probable or improbable in these circumstances has been fixed objectively, and is independent of our opinion. The theory of probability is logical, therefore, because it is concerned with the degree of belief which it is *rational* to entertain in given conditions and not merely with the actual beliefs of particular individuals, which may or may not be rational
>
> (Keynes, 1973, vol. VIII, p. 4)

According to this conception, uncertainty offers two aspects which Keynes carefully distinguishes:

> The magnitude of the probability of an argument ... depends upon a balance between what may be termed the favourable and the unfavourable evidence; a new piece of evidence which leaves the balance unchanged, also leaves the probability of the argument unchanged. But it seems that there may be another respect in which some kind of quantitative comparison between arguments is possible. This comparison turns upon a balance, not between the favourable and the unfavourable evidence, but between the *absolute* amounts of relevant knowledge and of relevant ignorance respectively.
>
> As the relevant evidence at our disposal increases, the magnitude of the probability of the argument may either decrease or increase, according as the new knowledge strengthens the unfavourable or the favourable evidence; but *something* seems to have increased in either case, we have a more substantial basis upon which to rest our conclusion. I express this by saying that an accession of new evidence increases the *weight* of an argument. New evidence will sometimes decreases the probability of an argument, but it will always increase its 'weight'.
>
> (Keynes, 1973, vol. VIII, p. 77)

The introduction of this notion of weight contributes to a more tractable treatment of knowledge basis interpreted as a prerequisite for individual decisions. Thus, when this weight can be measured but tends to zero, it is more and more uneasy to trust the use of probabilities and irrational beliefs tend to prevail. By contrast, when the weight tends to be very high, Keynes considers it might be counter-productive to try to increase the volume of information beyond a certain point. This is the reason why he clearly excluded the existence of a maximal weight and noted: 'But there clearly comes a point when it is no longer worth while to spend trouble, before acting, in the acquisition of further information, and there is no evident principle by which to determine *how far* we ought to carry our maxim of strengthening the weight of our argument' (Keynes, 1973, vol. VII, p. 83).

These views are obviously very far from the modern ones according to which rational behaviour implies the necessity of collecting all available information. They do not mean, however, that Keynes rejected instrumental rationality as Simon did later. We know that, in chapter 2 of the *General Theory*, he accepted the 'first postulate' of the 'classical theory of employment' and that, in chapter 3, he also admitted the profit maximization assumption. We also know that, in his *Quarterly Journal of Economics* 1937 article, Keynes noted that, even confronted with radical uncertainty, agents will 'do their best', that is, will behave as 'benthamian' deciders (Keynes, 1973, vol. XIV, p. 214). This means that, agents can be placed in a situation where their cognitive rational basis tends to zero but where they yet use their instrumental rationality *as if* they were taking decisions, facing a probable or a certain future.

Hayek's conception of knowledge is clearly different from Keynes's. His definition of knowledge appears to include cases which could be considered as vague knowledge or irrational beliefs according to Keynes's terminology. Hayek's *Constitution of Liberty* offers a clear characterization of this conception of knowledge:

> The growth of knowledge and the growth of civilization are the same only if we interpret knowledge to include all the human adaptations to environment in which past experience has been incorporated. Not all knowledge in this sense is part of our intellect, nor is our intellect the whole of our knowledge. Our habits and skills, our emotional attitudes, our tools, and our institutions – all are in this sense adaptations to past experience which have grown up by selective elimination of less suitable conduct. They are as much an indispensable foundation of successful action as is our conscious knowledge.
>
> (Hayek, 1960, p. 26)

This quotation of Hayek shows that, in his view, individual knowledge cannot be reduced to 'explicit and conscious knowledge' (p. 25). Fleetwood perfectly describes this broad conception of knowledge when he stresses that it includes three main forms of knowledge.

The first form corresponds to *general explicit* knowledge. General explicit knowledge includes scientific, cultural or technical knowledge which can be transmitted from man to man according to universal means of communication. Hayek characterizes this first form, noting that this kind of knowledge is expressed through 'formulated generic rules that can be communicated by language from person to person' (Hayek, 1960, p. 33).

The second form of knowledge is *local explicit* knowledge. This form can be codified as the first one, but it only concerns the professional, cultural or sociological neighbourhood of the individual agent. The reasons which explain that these two first forms of knowledge can only be acquired *indirectly* are different. Explicit general knowledge is essentially acquired through the educative system and the information medias. Explicit local knowledge requires some more voluntary learning effort from the agent, namely the resort to 'formal institution' as specialized libraries, specific medias, professional meetings. Hayek refers to explicit local knowledge when he considers 'the knowledge of facts related to the close environment of agents' (Hayek, 1945, p. 525) or 'the knowledge of circumstances', when they are 'observable' or 'tangible' (Hayek, 1988, p. 89). For Hayek, explicit knowledge, either general or local, does *not necessarily* imply dealing with the individual specificity of agents. It can be transfered from man to man and the process of transfer is not *dependent* on the personalities of the sender and the receiver of the information.

The third form of knowledge that Hayek refers to differs entirely from the previous ones because it is always and at least partially *tacit* and *unconscious*. Hayek's inclusion of tacit and unconscious knowledge within general knowledge clearly differs from Keynes's view. For Keynes, strictly speaking, knowledge only includes logically justified beliefs, and logic implies consciousness. On the contrary, for Hayek, there is a difference between rule-following which he assimilates to 'knowing how' and the knowledge of a thing which he assimilates to 'knowing that' (Hayek, 1988, p. 78). Tacit and unconscious knowledge corresponds to what Hayek calls the knowledge of particular circumstances in a particular moment and in a particular place. By contrast with the two first forms of knowledge, this third form can be only acquired *directly* because he does not necessarily imply the preliminary definition of an objective of voluntary learning. Day after day, it is absorbed through social interaction. It is not acquired with the help of formal institutions but by the constant resort to rules of social behaviour the meaning of which is not necessarily understood by individual agents. Therefore, generally, individual agents are not conscious to use and to implement particular rules in order to face specific daily circumstances. Thus, tacit knowledge cannot be explicitly transfered with the help of a codified language. Its very existence is intimately related to the subjective personality of the agent. Moreover, what is interesting with Hayek's conception of tacit knowledge is its extensibility. Behavioural rules which found tacit knowledge in Hayek are not only concrete and basic rules as bicycle-riding or crossing a street safely. They also overlap the preservation of some complex traditions or the implementation of sophisticated professional routines.

If Hayek distinguishes these three forms of knowledge, he does not claim, however, that they are strictly independent. Thus, the development of tacit knowledge can help to the development of explicit knowledge (Hayek, 1960, p. 33): social knowledge can be founded on repeated observation of some behavioural rules by agents. As Hayek pointed out in several of his contributions, the observation of different people performing the same tasks or activities can be considered as a means of acquiring knowledge.

More generally, however, Hayek's conception of knowledge must be related to his subjectivist methodological choices. As Hayek (1952b) stressed in *The Counter-Revolution*, most of the objects of human or social action are not 'objective facts' in the sense of natural science. They cannot be defined physically. As far as human actions are concerned, things are what acting people think they are. This subjectivism which substantially differs from Keynes's moderate subjectivism is based on two main grounds.

The first justification of Hayek's subjectivism is cognitive. It is specifically developed in *The Sensory Order*. In this book, Hayek argues in favour of a connectionist approach to the working of the human mind according to which the starting point of mental representations is not the physical order of things – in contrast to the claims of 'scientist objectivism' (see Hayek, 1952a, ch. 5) – but the product of a large range of abstractions which are available to allow human mind to experience and understand specific realities (Hayek, 1952a, p. 67). For Hayek, therefore, individuals attribute qualities to physical objects which they experience. However, these qualities are not intrinsic properties of these things but relations created by our nervous system when we need to classify these properties. This means that there are as many subjective forms of knowledge as there are individual 'nervous systems', namely, heterogeneous agents.

The second justification of Hayek's subjectivism is related to what is called by Hayek the 'social division of knowledge'. For Hayek, the more developed civilization is, the more complex and specialized knowledge becomes in the society. Now, no individual agent can acquire alone the whole knowledge of society. Social knowledge is assumed to be *dispersed* among the various individuals who form the society. Each individual can only have access to a very small part of social knowledge, especially of the knowledge of the processes which permit the global reproduction and the regulation of social and economic activity.

2 INDIVIDUAL BELIEFS AND KNOWLEDGE IN KEYNES AND HAYEK

The subjectivist methodological choice favoured by Hayek leads to the analysis of individual cognitive rationality. As we just pointed out, referring to *The Sensory Order*, the cognitive capacities of each individual agent can be summed up by a kind of personal mental map, namely, this 'semi-permanent apparatus of classification' which offers the different generic elements that permit to build the 'models' of some particular situations

(Hayek, 1952a, p. 69). This mental map expresses the cognitive limits which constrain individual mental deliberations. It does not offer to the individual a 'picture of the world' but rather a kind of theory which explains how the world is working (Hayek, 1952a, p. 70). This approach might appear to be incompatible with the description of economic agents which is developed by neoclassical microeconomics, namely, with what Hayek called the 'pure logic of choice'. This is not, however, the case. Hayek's view is that microeconomic tools might be useful to analyse individual economic behaviour if they are first adapted to a subjectivist perspective. For instance, during the debate on 'socialist calculation', Hayek noted that it was misleading to consider a given list of goods and a given catalogue of productive techniques, namely, to assume the existence of given 'fundamentals', in accordance with the standpoint of general economic equilibrium. The same 'physical' goods or techniques might be perceived as distinct by different human minds and the consumption of a good or the use of a technique was fundamentally, for Hayek, a subjective activity (see Hayek, 1935). In the same way, Hayek was strongly opposed to any kind of economic aggregation since it implied the necessity of direct intersubjective comparisons.

The subjective theory of the working of the world which is available for each of us corresponds to what is called by some game theorists structural beliefs, even if, in a Hayekian world, information is obviously incomplete. These beliefs influence but cannot be assimilated to conjectural beliefs. Conjectural beliefs are those formed by agents when they are faced with particular situations and have to take specific decisions. These decisions entail actions and these actions produce results which are compared with expectations. The existence of a gap between expectations and results leads to revisions of conjectural beliefs and, less frequently, of structural beliefs. This 'feedback' process is therefore a process of *belief selection*. From this standpoint, it is easy to understand how permanent positive feedbacks may reinforce some structural beliefs and transform them into individual abstract rules or even into real routines (Garrouste, 1999, p. 891).

However, if agents only followed their individual beliefs or routines, it would not be easy to understand how a social order could result from a multitude of uncoordinated economic actions. Hayek clearly emphasized this problem which, according to his view, was related to the necessity of distinguishing 'the order of the actions of a group' from 'the behavioral rules of individuals' (Hayek, 1967, p. 67). The problem is, however, complex for two main reasons. First, inter-individual co-ordination is *context-dependent*. Thus, behavioural rules do not only change endogeneously but also in connection with what Hayek calls 'external circumstances' (Hayek, 1967). 'Fundamentals' are affected by permanent changes and cannot be considered as given (Arena, 1999b, p. 851). Now, different 'external circumstances' can produce various types of social order, even if they are combined to an unchanging set of individual rules.

Secondly, for Hayek, an unlimited pursuit of individual objectives does not necessarily produce an optimal social order, notably because no individual agent is able to understand the facts and mechanisms which underlie the existence of a social order. This is why, for Hayek, the 'knowledge of the society' cannot be equated to the sum of individual beliefs. This problem of a possible inadequacy between individual beliefs and social optimality was precisely pointed out by Vanberg when he showed that Hayek never gave a satisfactory solution to this problem. He stressed the incompatibilities between Hayek's methodological individualism and his evolutionary theory of cultural evolution. We indeed know today that two kinds of solutions are a priori possible to try to solve Hayek's problem.

The starting point of the first solution is the analogy developed by Hayek between the organization of the human mind and the organization of society. This analogy suggests that there exist limits to Hayek's subjectivism. If individual knowledge and beliefs are subjective, there are not however entirely heterogeneous; they have something in common, namely 'a common structure' which allows inter-individual communication (Hayek, 1952b, p. 45). From this standpoint, what is important is not that individual beliefs are objectively true or false, as is the case with Keynes's *rational* beliefs. What is important is the fact that agents might *agree* when they *think* that these beliefs are true or false. We may note here that this argument seems rather close to the case of Keynes's *irrational* beliefs. For Hayek, some beliefs or some rules will be followed by all the individuals belonging to the same society, because their environment is common and appears to be common to their various individual minds. Hayek, therefore accepts the idea that if individuals belong to the same historical and/or socio-cultural environment, they will tend to form what we could call *shared individual beliefs*. This standpoint seems to be confirmed by the importance attributed by Hayek to the role played by innovative and imitative individual choices in the process of emergence of behavioural patterns. This is, by the way, a permanent theme of the Austrian tradition: the convergence or the sharing of individual beliefs would be implied by the propensity of the majority of individuals to follow the rules invented by innovators when the adoption of these rules entails a positive feedback effect on the results of their actions. Vanberg, however, noted why this solution is not convincing: the process of convergence of individual beliefs towards new rules introduced by innovators has to be carefully distinguished from the process of selection among collective or shared beliefs. How is it possible to explain that some shared beliefs produce collective rules which appear to be socially superior to others? We know that, in the last part of his life, Hayek introduced a new analytical device in which *group interests* rather than individual interests offered a new explanatory scheme. Schemes, however, are not sufficient and it is therefore necessary to explain what is a group interest. Hayek's subjectivism obviously excludes the concept of group defined as an autonomous collective entity, independent from individual wills. As Vanberg noted, a solution might be the use of the notion of social convention defined as a co-ordinated set of shared individual beliefs. But this solution does not really solve the problem: no mechanism can secure that conventions will be socially optimal, in a sense which, however, has to be defined. There is no reason why self-organizing processes based on individual choices will necessarily generate optimal social states. This is, however, what Hayek assumes without proving it convincingly. His justifications are various: existence of an 'empirical tendency towards equilibrium'; characterization of a variant of pareto-optimality; existence of a predominant social group. They do not offer a real solution, but this did not prevent Hayek stressing the social superiority of the market order (see Arena, 1999b) by contrast with Keynes's view.

Keynes's treatment of individual beliefs and knowledge is substantially different from that of Hayek. As we already noted, Keynes's moderate subjectivism has little in common with Hayek's radical subjectivism. However, Hayek's problem is also a problem for Keynes but his solution is different.

If the prevailing situation corresponds to knowledge strictly speaking or to rational beliefs, decision processes imply some objective properties which, according to Keynes's views, are common to all men, namely what we might call shared logical abilities. In other words, if two agents have more or less the same knowledge basis, they will take the same decisions and, moreover, they will be able to understand their respective decisions. For Keynes, subjectivism does not prevent social communication.

To some extent, the case of short-term expectations might be interpreted as a situation in which rational beliefs are valid. In this context, the influence of the past, that is, of a knowledge basis which everybody can acquire easily, provides the main explanation of individual decisions. On the one hand, as Keynes stressed in the *General Theory*, changes in short-term expectations are slow and gradual. On the other hand, 'the most recent results' are the ones which 'usually play a prevailing role' in the determination of individual decisions (Keynes, 1936). Therefore, producers stand to favour an adaptive or an extrapolative behaviour since the reiteration of the past is the most probable possibility. As Keynes wrote, 'they have no definite reasons to expect a change' (Keynes, 1936). As Kregel (1976) showed, this adaptive conception of short-term expectation corresponds to what might be called the model of 'stationary equilibrium' of the *General Theory*. In this model, the state of long-term expectation is assumed to be constant or given. Short-term expectations can be deceived but expectation failure do not influence the state of long-term expectations. The temporal succession of adaptive expectations leads to a stationary equilibrium (Kregel, 1976, p. 215). In other terms, according to the model of 'stationary equilibrium', adaptive expectations are not only probable; they tend to become certain and the model of stationary equilibrium becomes a model in which expectations are always fulfilled (Kregel, 1976). This is the reason why 'effective demand always reflect the current expectations of the real demand' (Keynes, 1973, vol. XIII, p. 603). It is interesting to note that Keynes considers that the fulfilment of short-term expectations is the result either of a repeated method of trial and error or of a 'careful attempt' (ibid.) of the entrepreneurs to forecast the level of effective demand (Keynes, 1973, vol. XIII, p. 603). This interpretation is confirmed by a preliminary draft of the *General Theory* in which Keynes notes that he will only pay attention to the changes in short-term expectation which are 'perfectly founded' (Keynes, 1973, vol. XIII, p. 457). This is also why after the *General Theory* Keynes noted that if he had to write a new draft of the book, he would build his theory assuming first that long-term expectations are always fulfilled (Keynes, 1973, vol. XIV, p. 181).

Keynes models of static and stationary equilibria do not correspond to descriptions of the 'real world'. To use an expression of Davidson and Kregel (1980, p. 139), they only offer a 'logical exercise'. This exercise points out the contrast between short-term and long-term expectations. If the first can be dealt with, using rational beliefs, the second necessarily imply irrational beliefs and the introduction of the concept of 'moving equilibrium'.

Therefore, the context of long-term expectations does not allow the use of knowledge strictly speaking or even of rational beliefs. The main reason of this impossibility is the absence of an individual knowledge basis which could permit entrepreneurs to take decisions. In these situations, the weight of probability tends to zero and sometimes probabilities even cease to be measurable. The case of measurable probabilities is indeed characterized by Keynes as corresponding 'to those special cases, the existence of which will be demonstrated at a later stage, where algebraical representation is possible' (Keynes, 1973, vol. VIII, p. 22). However the problems which entrepreneurs confront when they have to take decisions are not always 'presented with a number of exclusive or exhaustive alternatives' (ibid., pp. 22–3). Now, it is obvious that, for Keynes, long-term decisions are associated with incomplete information. Therefore, they excluded the use of probability calculus. This is why in his *Quarterly Journal of Economics* 1937 article, Keynes noted that what he meant by 'uncertain' knowledge did not refer to the distinction between certainty and probability: there was simply no scientific basis on which to build any probability calculus. One might however think that, at least, probabilities could be ordered. Keynes, however, denies that this possibility is general. If the facts on which degrees of rational beliefs are founded, are entirely new, individuals cannot use frequencies and they are not always able to interpret these facts. If these facts are not homogeneous because the number of observations belonging to the same experimental field is not sufficiently large or because the variety of the experimental fields is not sufficiently high, individuals face the same situation and cannot form rational beliefs. The situation is even worse when these facts do not exist. The problem of the number of observations in the same field refers to what Keynes called the issue of 'induction'. The problem of the variety of the fields corresponds to what Keynes called the issue of 'analogy'. In the context of long-term expectations, it is perfectly possible that there is no sufficient inductive or analogical evidence to allow entrepreneurs to take decisions on the basis of rational beliefs. The tendency of the weight of probability to zero is also a prevailing possibility when entrepreneurs have to take long-run investment decisions. In all these cases, the use of the logical conception of probability becomes impossible (Kregel, 1987, pp. 525–8).

In such situations, agents adopt techniques or forecasting which are based on common sense or on the 'practical observation of markets and of business psychology' (Keynes, 1973, vol. XIV, p. 161). The first technique is founded on past results and based on the assumption that the 'state of confidence' will imply a continuation of the present state of business. The second technique leads agents to try to guess how mass psychology will evolve in order to conform permanently to the average opinion of the market. The last technique consists to assume that the actual behaviour of the market is the only one which has to be considered to be 'correct' (Keynes, 1973, vol. XIV, p. 114).

3 INDIVIDUAL, SOCIAL AND COLLECTIVE BELIEFS IN KEYNES AND HAYEK

It is easy to see that the technique of forecasting we just recalled corresponds to Keynes's irrational beliefs. Without any basis of knowledge, there is no logical a priori reason to follow these beliefs. However, these beliefs seem to be analogous to Hayek's behavioural rules, namely based on a kind of empirical, non-permanent and tacit knowledge. There is, however, an important difference between Keynes's techniques and Hayek's rules. Keynes's techniques correspond to *collective* and not to *shared individual* beliefs. This does not mean that the origin of collective beliefs is not rooted in the wills of the various individuals. However, after some time, these beliefs form a kind of autonomous entity which the agents consider as such and not as a result of their purely individual choice. In a context where indirect knowledge becomes impossible, the prevailing belief becomes a social belief, namely, the belief that social imitation is the only possible solution. This belief may take various forms. It may be extrapolative when agents believe that the past will continue to prevail and therefore imitate past behaviours. It may be mimetic when agents think that the actual state of opinion gives a right synthesis of the future perspective of the market and therefore try to imitate the average behaviour of the agents on the market. The behaviours of agents therefore correspond to *social conventions*, if we give to this word the meaning it has in Keynes's lecture of 1932–35 (see Keynes, 1989, pp. 119, 120, 128 and 153), in the *General Theory,* or in 'The general theory of employment'. When ignorance is prevailing, to some extent agents cease to have degrees of rational belief and they attempt to create together a substitute which is represented by collective beliefs about the future. In this situation, in accordance with Keynes's remark (Keynes, 1973, vol. XIV, p. 14), the psychology of the society is made by individuals who all tend to imitate each other. To be more precise, the point is that *all* agents imitate *all* agents. This means that none of them is independent from the others when he is elaborating his own beliefs. Nobody can impose a unique social convention which everybody would be obliged to accept. The creation of an agreement, of a 'convention' among agents takes the necessary form of a collective action. This process appears to be hard to perform. Moreover conventions are fragile and transitory since, at any moment, some agents can try to modify the prevailing collective beliefs. From this standpoint, market equilibrium is not predetermined but results from social interaction. It is easy to understand why, in this framework, according to Keynes's view, markets where long-term expectations are prevailing (as financial markets) are generally unstable.

Hayek's conception of the relationship between individual and social beliefs is completely different from Keynes's approach. We already noted that in Hayek, the use of the word 'belief' is always associated with the existence of *individual beliefs*. We recalled earlier how in Hayek, these beliefs could generate a self-reinforcing process and contribute to the emergence of individual behavioural rules. We also stressed how, through social communication and imitation, agents could *share* individual beliefs. The conclusion of these remarks might be that in Hayek, social behavioural rules namely, rules that explain the regularity and the coordination of individual behaviours could be defined as *shared individual rules*. Things are not however so simple.

As has already been noted by various commentators (Garrouste, 1999, pp. 887–91; Ioannides, 1999, pp. 874–6), the behavioural social rules which underlie in Hayek the existence of a spontaneous social order (as the market order) present specific features. They are first *tacit*, namely 'super-conscious' to use Hayek's significant expression. In other words, individuals do follow behavioural rules without knowing explicitly that they are doing it. These rules are also *abstract* and it is here interesting to note that Hayek characterizes abstraction as the result of *analogy* (Hayek, 1967, p. 32). As Keynes noted, it is through the observation of various particular actions and using the principle of analogy, that individuals are able to formulate abstract rules or what Keynes would call degrees of rational belief.

Now, tacit and abstract rules are necessarily *general*. If they are general, they are therefore valid for *all* individuals and can be applied to *all* particular cases. In other words, the nature of rules becomes independent from the specific individuals who adopted them or from the specific forms of action which generated their implementation. This does not mean that the origin of these rules is alien to the individual beliefs of the agent. However, rules are the result of a process which tends always to erase this origin. This is what Hayek means when he notes that these rules

> are the results of the experience of successive generations which are handed down. And, once a more efficient tool is available, it will be used without our knowing why it is better, or even what the alternatives are.
>
> These 'tools' which man has envolved and which constitute such an important part of his adaptation to his environment include much more than material implements. They consist in a large measure of forms of conduct which he habitually follows without knowing why; they consist of what we call 'traditions' and 'institutions', which he uses because they are available to him as a product of cumulative growth without ever having been designed by any one mind.
>
> (Hayek, 1960, p. 27)

This process of abstraction and generalization of individual behavioural rules is associated with their repeated use in time. This process and this use contribute to create a real autonomy of these rules as regards the individuals who invented and/or implemented them. If we consider a sufficiently long period, this autonomy creates the impression that individuals only adapt their individual beliefs to real pre-existing social rules without creating them. This is the way to understand what Hayek (1962, p. 51) calls the 'repertory of perceivable behavioral rules', that is the repertory inherited from tradition, culture or persistence of some institutions.

This interpretation is first confirmed by Hayek's analysis of the properties that rules must exhibit in order that independent individual action become able to generate a global order (see Hayek, 1967, p 50). These properties are devoted to the explanation of the transformation process, of *individual* (even shared) rules into *social* rules. Social rules are also 'normative' since they 'tell' individuals 'what they must do or what they must not do' (Hayek, 1967, p 57). This tendency to the social uniformity of rules is first related to the analogies between individual mental deliberations, namely, to the limits of subjectivism. Its origin might also be found in the existence of a common cultural tradition. It can also be imposed by the necessity of respecting the law, the decisions of the state, and by the fear of a sanction in case of violation of the rule. It can be noted that customs, convention, culture, law, and so on are elements which progressively acquired their autonomy as regards individuals. Therefore, they may appear to be completely external to them, generating real social norms.

These social norms are often founded on the existence of moral beliefs (as 'thou shall not kill') which are nothing but *social* beliefs since they govern individual rules (Hayek, 1960, p. 35). This example of moral beliefs shows that individuals do not only choose their individual behavioural rules in the repertory of available social rules but that shared individual beliefs are often analogous to social beliefs.

Hayek's remaining problem is however the working of the mechanisms which permit to select optimal social rules and beliefs. Hayek's solution is well-known: 'All that we can know is that the ultimate decision about what is good or bad will be made not by individual human wisdom but by the decline of the groups that have adhered to the "wrong" beliefs' (Hayek, 1960, p. 36). This reference to 'groups' obviously entails the question of the compatibility between Hayek's theory of social and cultural evolution and his methodological individualism. The answer to this question requires the introduction of the concept of 'knowledge of the society':

> Knowledge exists only as the knowledge of individuals. It is not much better than a metaphor to speak of the knowledge of society as a whole. The sum of the knowledge of all the individuals exists nowhere as an integrated whole. The great problem is how we can all profit from this knowledge, which exists only dispersed as the separate, partial, and sometimes conflicting beliefs of all men … .
>
> (Hayek, 1960, p. 24).

However, Hayek also notes:

> In other words, it is largely because civilization enables us constantly to profit from knowledge which we individually do not possess and because each individual's use of his particular knowledge may serve to assist others unknown to him in achieving their ends that men as members of civilized society can pursue their individual ends so much more succesfully than they could alone. We know little of the particular facts to which the whole of social activity continuously adjusts itself in order to provide what we have learned to expect.
>
> (Hayek, 1960, p. 25)

Therefore, Hayek defines a 'knowledge of the society' which is not directly accessible to any individual. However, for Hayek, if each individual implements his own knowledge, the interaction of all individuals will generate what we could consider to be positive externalities. Therefore, if the knowledge of the society is inaccessible to individuals and superior to the sum of their respective knowledge, yet they can *indirectly* benefit from this global knowledge. Hayek's answer is clear: tradition offers to agents a set of rules which is superior to human reason. It permits them to have access to 'collective wisdom'.

Finally, according to Hayek's view, the knowledge of the society is nothing but that which allows it to integrate consistently the various pieces of local and dispersed knowledge. It can only be considered as a characteristic of the social system and therefore be related to 'the impersonal process of society' (Hayek, 1960, p. 65). This means that, in Hayek, two levels of knowledge do exist (see, for instance, Hayek, 1960, p. 28). The first level is entirely ruled by subjectivist individualism; it corresponds to individual beliefs, either shared or not. The second level corresponds to the knowledge of the society. It defines another kind of knowledge, isolated from specific individuals and generated by their social interaction. This knowledge is the result of a process of social selection. This process permits the selection of those social rules which allow a global order to be built and to eliminate those which are not compatible with the reproduction of the society. This approach, however, is a weak point of Hayek's construction. His approach of social selection is indeed based on the evolutionary principle of self-organization but this principle does not ensure that the final social state will be optimal.

This problem does not prevent Hayek arguing in favour of the equilibrating character of market mechanisms. As in Keynes, these mechanisms are essentially founded on imitative behaviours. However, as Dupuy noted, these mechanisms do not have the same meaning in Keynes and in Hayek. In Keynes, there is no model, individual or group of individuals which is able to offer a social norm that behaviours will tend to imitate. As we stressed, in Keynes the existence of social conventions implies that all agents imitate all agents. In Hayek, things are different. No individual can impose his rule on others. However, the existence of social rules and of the knowledge of society creates a social norm which offers an implicit direction to follow. These rules and this knowledge indeed create the permanent conditions of market adjustments, even if no single individual is able to understand the contents and the meaning of these adjustments and, therefore, to influence them. From this standpoint and in contrast with Keynes, Hayekian agents do not generate collective beliefs through the emergence of social conventions. In Hayek, everything happens 'behind the backs' of the agents. The knowledge of society which is the result of social interaction acts as a real invisible hand and is so invisible that nobody can make it explicit.

4 CONCLUSIVE REMARKS

Our contribution points out the major differences which appear when we compare Keynes's and Hayek's conceptions of knowledge and beliefs, and their impact on the working of markets. These differences are certainly crucial. However, what is also crucial is the importance attributed by Hayek and Keynes to beliefs and knowledge in the analysis of individual behaviours and in the co-ordination of economic processes. This importance confirms the modernity of their contributions and contrasts with some of the developments of modem economic theory which purely and simply neglect these aspects. This is why the comparison between Keynes and Hayek we propose in this chapter is more an incentive to revive the approaches of both authors rather than an attempt to appraise their respective merits.

REFERENCES

Arena, R. (1999a), 'The Hayek/Keynes controversy in the light of modem business cycle theory', *History of Economic Ideas*, **7**, 1–2.

Arena, R. (1999), 'Hayek et l'équilibre économique: une autre interprétation', *Revue d'Economie Politique*, **109** (6), 851.

Davidson, P. and J. Kregel (1980), 'Keynes's paradigm: a theoretical framework for monetary analysis', in E. Nell (ed.), Growth, *Profits and Property*, Cambridge: Cambridge University Press.

Garrouste, P. (1999), 'La firme "hayekienne" entre institution et organisation', *Revue d'Economie Politique*, **109** (6), 885–902.

Hayek, F.A. (1935), *Collectivist Economic Planning: Critical Studies on the Possibilities of Socialism*, London: Routledge.

Hayek, F.A. (1937), 'Economics and knowledge', *Economica*.

Hayek, F.A. (1945), 'The use of knowledge in society', *American Economic Review*, **35** (5), 519–30.

Hayek, F.A. (1948), *Individualism and Economic Order (Essays)*, Chicago: University of Chicago Press.

Hayek, F.A. (1952a), *The Sensory Order: An Inquiry into the Foundations of Theoretical Psychology*, Chicago, IL: Chicago University Press.

Hayek, F.A. (1952b), *The Counter-Revolution of Science: Studies on the Abuse of Reason*, Glencoe, IL: Free Press.

Hayek, F.A. (1960), *The Constitution of Liberty*, Chicago, IL: University of Chicago Press.

Hayek, F.A. (1962), 'Rules, Perception and Intelligibility',

Hayek, F.A. (1967), *Studies in Philosophy, Politics and Economics*, Chicago, IL: University of Chicago Press.

Hayek, F.A. (1988), *The Fatal Conceit*, London: Routledge.

Ioannides, S. (1999), 'The market, the firm, and entrepreneurial leadership: some Hayekian insights', *Revue d'Economie Politique*, **109** (6), 874–6.

Keynes, J.M. (1921), *The Collected Writings of John Maynard Keynes, Vol. VIII, A Treatise on Probability*, New York and London: St Martin's Press and Macmillan.

Keynes, J.M. (1936), *The General Theory of Employment, Interest and Money*, London: Macmillan.

Keynes, J.M. (1937), 'The general theory of economics', *The Quarterly Journal of Economics*, February, added to *The Collected Writings of John Maynard Keynes, Vol. XIV*, p. 109.

Keynes, J.M. (1973), *Collected Writings of John Maynard Keynes, vol. XIII and XIV*, London: Macmillan.

Keynes, J.M. (1979), *The Collected Writings of John Maynard Keynes, Vol. XXIX, The General Theory and After: A Supplement*, New York and London: St Martin's Press and Macmillan.

Keynes, J.M. (1989), *Lectures, 1932–1933*, (ed. T. Rymes), London: Macmillan.

Kregel, J.A. (1976), 'Economic methodology in the face of uncertainty: the modelling methods of Keynes and the post-Keynesians', *The Economic Journal*, **86**, 342.

Kregel, J.A. (1987), 'The effective demand approach to employment and inflation analysis', *Journal of Post Keynesian Economics*, **10** (2), 133–45.

15. A Keynesian critique of recent applications of risk-sensitive control theory in macroeconomics

James Juniper*

INTRODUCTION

Recent decades of research in decision theory have witnessed a variety of departures from the constraints of expected utility theory. In part, these have been motivated by the desire to explain the finding that decision-makers routinely violate the independence axiom (Allais, 1953).[1] Typically, the abandonment of this axiom entails replacing the linear system of weighting expected utilities of each outcome in a lottery by their respective probabilities with a non-linear weighting system derived from a cumulative distribution defined over a partitioning of the state space (Chew, 1989; Dekel, 1986; Tversky and Wakker, 1995).[2]

Research on ambiguity or uncertainty aversion is also motivated by the Ellsberg paradoxes (Ellsberg, 1961), which are associated with lotteries over unknown probabilities. Consider bets over draws from an urn containing 30 red balls and 60 others that are black and yellow. Fishburn (1987, p. 782), in his summary of Ellsberg's findings, indicates that most people are observed to 'prefer to bet on *red* rather than *black*, and to bet on *black or yellow* rather than *red or yellow*'. In Savage's model, the first preference suggests that the probability measure over *red* is preferred to the probability measure over *black*, whereas the second preference suggests the opposite.

Under suitable conditions some of the generalizations of expected utility theory can accommodate uncertainty or ambiguity aversion. In Savage's (1954) subjective decision-making framework, the 'sure-thing' principle plays the same role as the independence axiom in the expected utility approach. Uncertainty aversion can be introduced by weakening the sure-thing principle (Gilboa and Schmeidler, 1989). Most mathematical formalizations are based on Choquet's expected utility theory: a generalization of probability theory grounded in the more general mathematical notion of capacities (Choquet, 1955). Gilboa and Schmeidler (1989) have established the mathematical equivalence between two capacity-based representations of uncertainty aversion: the first of these entailing the use of *sub-additive probabilities*, and the second, involving max-min optimization within a *multiple-priors* setting (see Basili, 2000, p. 6). Within a multiple-priors setting, ambiguity aversion arises when agent's relevant probabilistic beliefs are given by a *set* of probability measures rather than a singleton distribution.[3] To characterize the optimal rules in this context the researcher must therefore apply an intertemporal max-min expected utility approach. These rules are designed to protect the agent against unfavourable probabilistic structures in the financial environment.[4]

In this chapter I provide an overview of recent applications of risk-sensitive and robust control, which utilize a particular multiple-priors form of uncertainty aversion (Andersen, Hansen and Sargent, 1998a, 1998b; Hansen, Sargent and Tallarini, 1999; henceforth referred to as AHS and HST respectively). The authors of these papers have been motivated by justifiable concerns about the inadequacies of rational expectations (RATEXP) modelling.

In early versions of RATEXP, which employed the linear quadratic regulator, economic agents are presumed to have knowledge about the stochastic process but are unconcerned about the possibility of specification error. Under the certainty equivalence principle the optimal control is determined as if the agent was operating under conditions of perfect certainty with a deterministic system. In contrast, the econometrician must labour under conditions of relative ignorance, performing a battery of diagnostic tests that compare and evaluate alternative model specifications. HST argue that their robust control and filtering methodology enables them to overcome this asymmetry, which has plagued earlier efforts at rational expectations modelling. Now it is presumed that economic agents possess doubts about specification error that are similar to those held by the econometricians.

It is understandable that such a breakthrough would be profoundly satisfying for those who rank themselves amongst an intellectual elite in the economics profession. However, this is not the only reason why post Keynesian researchers need to pay close attention to these new theoretical and practical developments. From another angle, these theoretical developments can be interpreted as representing a systematic effort to incorporate uncertainty or ambiguity into economic thinking in a manner that appears to resolve certain paradoxes in the literature on decision-making (for example, the Ellsberg paradox) and also provide an explanation for well-known anomalies in the literature on asset pricing (for example, the equity premium puzzle).[5] As such this research, despite its neoclassical affiliations and generally conservative policy prescriptions, introduces a set of techniques that can be drawn upon to once again place concerns about liquidity preference at the centre of policy debate and empirical research. However, this objective can only be fully realized once existing models have been completely overhauled to eliminate their less tenable assumptions and constructions. In this chapter, I make some tentative suggestions about how this can be accomplished.

I begin by reviewing recent post Keynesian and orthodox research that relates to liquidity preference and turbulence in asset markets. I then suggest reasons why post Keynesians should be concerned about the techniques employed in the HST and AHT papers. My argument is that risk-sensitive control theory has a worthwhile contribution to make in the modelling of decision-making under uncertainty, but only after it has been extricated from its rational expectations, representative agent frame and the constraints of aggregative neoclassical capital theory. To justify this position, I next examine the approach adopted in the HST and AHT papers in an intuitive rather than a technical fashion, relating it to earlier research into certainty equivalence. Finally, I suggest ways that the techniques could be extended and applied in a post Keynesian modelling framework. However, I reach the provisional conclusion that the need to grapple with certain important aspects of real-world financial systems will inevitably limit future applications of these techniques in post Keynesian research.

A REVIEW OF POST KEYNESIAN AND RELATED RESEARCH IN FINANCIAL MACROECONOMICS

Paul Davidson (1994) has argued that the Keynesian revolution in economic theory and policy was firmly grounded in a rejection of the 'Euclidean axioms' of orthodox theory: the neutrality of money, gross substitution and ergodicity of the economic process influencing the prospective returns derived from investments in real and financial assets. Drawing on Camerer and Weber's definition of ambiguity (Camerer and Weber, 1992, p. 330), David Dequech (1999) has elaborated on Davidson's notion of non-ergodicity by drawing a distinction between risk (characterized by unique, additive and fully reliable probability distributions), ambiguity (created by missing information that is relevant and could, under different circumstances, be known), and fundamental uncertainty (reflecting the possibility of creativity, structural change, and surprise).

In *The General Theory* Keynes (1973) questioned the effectiveness of what are now conventionally labelled the Keynes and Pigou effects as equilibrating forces that could alleviate involuntary unemployment. Each of these effects supposedly comes into operation as the nominal wage and general prices begin to fall. The Keynes effect arises because falling prices raise the real value of money balances, lowering interest rates, in turn boosting investment and aggregate demand. The Pigou effect arises when falling prices raise the real value of household and firm wealth leading to wealth-induced increases in consumption and investment expenditure.

The Keynesian critique of the former effect implicitly drew on capital-theoretic arguments that questioned the existence of an inverse, monotonic relationship between the interest rate and investment (see Panico, 1993). Following the precedent in *The General Theory*, critics have essentially argued that, in a real-world economy where non-indexed, nominal contracting is ubiquitous, any (typically feeble) Pigou effects would be completely overwhelmed by adverse debt-deflation effects as falling prices shifted income from borrowers with a high propensity to consume to lenders with low propensities to consume (Palley, 1999).[6]

In a series of recent papers, Marc Lavoie and Wynn Godley have modified a Tobin-style macroeconomic model featuring a block of equations representing outcomes in asset market and a q-ratio model of investment to accommodate liquidity preference. Consistent double entry accounting for all monetary stocks and flows enables them to capture the impact of changes in liquidity preference on asset prices and real investment (Godley, 1999; Lavoie and Godley, 2000).

Hyman Minksy's (1985) research into financial instability goes beyond debt-deflation effects to emphasize the overall importance of financial position taking. Under conditions of stability and growth, banks, households and firms adopt more fragile financial positions, which require short-term borrowing to cover periods of increasing duration when cash flows become negative or fail to sustain interest payments on existing stocks of debt. A variety of researchers have constructed sophisticated dynamic models that incorporate various forms of Minsky-style financial instability (Foley, 1987; Taylor and O'Connell, 1985). Typically, these authors reject representative agent approaches to the modelling of economic processes preferring to model the outcomes of collective action using non-linear systems of differential equations.

Similarly, Chiarella and Flaschel (2000) have focused on the macro-foundations of microeconomics drawing on the Keynes-Goodwin-Metzler tradition of dynamic modelling. Goodwin-style Phillips curve dynamics are extended into goods and financial asset markets along with debt-deflation effects (see Keen, 1995). In combination, these elements give rise to complex and chaotic dynamic trajectories. Flaschel, Franke and Semmler (1996), construct a dynamic macroeconomic model in which real investment is sensitive to a 'state of confidence' variable. The state of confidence directly affects borrowings from the commercial banking sector, which provides discretionary funds for investment. In turn, the state of confidence is adversely affected by the ratio of debt to equity and is beneficially affected by the gap between net profits and the interest rate. The state of confidence is also influenced by changes in its own level to account for momentum in the cycles of optimism and pessimism.

In a similar vein, Trond Andresen (1999a; 1999b) has constructed models of monetary flows between rentier capitalists and agents in the 'real sector' who borrow to finance both consumption and investment. His ultimate intention is to integrate these prototype models of monetary hoarding with a model of stock market activity with feedback from booms and busts in equity prices influencing hoarding on the part of consumers and investors.

Another interesting research trajectory in the finance literature is embodied in the more orthodox work by Brock and Hommes (1997; 1998), Brock (1999), Brock, Lakonishok and LeBaron (1992), LeBaron, Arthur and Palmer (1999) and Arthur et al. (1994). The Brock and Hommes papers develop a family of models featuring what they prefer to call 'adaptive belief equilibria' (ABE). These models are characterized by deterministic chaos, an outcome that arises because representative investors can switch between differing camps – in the simplest version of these models there are two categories of investor: rational 'fundamentalists' and 'irrational', trend-chasing, chartists – based on some kind of performance criterion which takes into account the fact that fully rational expectations are far more costly to calculate. As such, the majority of investors resort to the formation of extrapolative or myopic expectations when the market position is close to the fixed point while more investors resort to the formation of rational expectations when the economy is far from the fixed point. To engage in optimal position taking the rational or 'fundamentalist' traders must therefore know the proportions of the investor population falling into each respective camp – their own and that of the irrational traders. In these models, it is this process of reflexivity that is responsible for introducing complexity (in the form of Hopf bifurcations) into the resulting dynamic trajectory of the market, in more sophisticated versions of these ABE models, additional categories of investor (for example, contrarian strategists) are introduced, which makes the dynamics even more complex.

In the latter two Sante Fe Institute papers that model artificial stock market dynamics, heterogeneous investors calculate optimal positions using genetic algorithms, which differ in their processes of coding and mutation. The simulated market can become unstable or turbulent with increases in choice intensity, decreases in the conditional variance of asset returns, or an increase in the diversity of beliefs. Brock and Hommes (1998, pp. 124–9) have established a close connection between their own work and that of researchers who investigate simulated stock markets. To accommodate a diversity of trading strategies and belief structures they introduce a large limit type – an ensemble limit analogous to thermodynamic limits in statistical mechanics.[7] In discussing their findings Brock and Hommes (1998, p. 132) caution against the notion that aggregation could 'wash-out' non-linearities across a sufficiently diverse population of agents because, in their models, heterogeneity is created through a process of evolutionary selection.

WHY SHOULD POST KEYNESIANS CONCERN THEMSELVES WITH THESE DEVELOPMENTS?

The above review of post Keynesian contributions to macro-financial research raises the question of whether there is any relationship between Keynesian notions of liquidity preference and orthodox developments in finance theory that are based on notions of uncertainty aversion.

On many occasions Keynes argued that irrational motives are a major driving force in human behaviour, not least in regard to the 'love of money'. In many of his writings he intimated that investors often acted on the basis of ignorance and irrational compulsion. Even in *The General Theory*, Keynes argued that it was often advantageous for more rational investors to direct their energies to anticipating what the outcome of such irrationality would be so that they could profit from the price movements resulting from irrational decisions rather than from those associated with the ultimate correction of any misperceptions arising in the market.

However, I would contend that a Keynesian critique of financial macroeconomics should not be predicated solely on these grounds. My reasons for arguing in this vein are that a critique based solely on an 'irrationalist' interpretation of the 'Beauty Contest' metaphor would have to explain how financial markets are structured to favour profit-taking based on the anticipation of irrationality over profit-taking based on the correction of misperceptions. Essentially, this is what noise-trading models do by imposing some kind of time constraint over the position taking of more rational investors (for example, through quarterly or annual reviews of their performance).

There is strong evidence to suggest that these short-term constraints could well be weakening as institutional factors and governance mechanisms adjust to reward longer-term position-taking on the part of fund managers. Does this weakening of 'short-termism' mean that asset markets will therefore become more orderly as a result, with less volatile bid-ask spreads, and less exposed to waves of pessimistic and optimistic sentiment? I would have serious concerns about such a sanguine conclusion. This is because I believe that 'short-termism' is more likely to be the product of liquidity preference or ambiguity aversion than of either some kind of irrationality or, perhaps, Pareto-constrained mispricing within incomplete asset markets.[8] I would go one step further in arguing that it ought to be conceived as varying in response to concrete changes in the ontological features of real-world asset markets (for example, increasing financial instability).

In their efforts to explain market volatility both the noise-trader and endogenous chaos models adopt a surprisingly traditional conception of uncertainty. A natural question to ask is whether we should simply replace these orthodox conceptions with a more modern notion – albeit, one that can be traced back to the nineteenth-century works of Hegel, Nietzsche and Freud – that some monstrous irrationality lurks beneath the calm, banal surface of everyday existence, occasionally erupting in a manner that completely evades any rational attempts at analysis? In an age of powerful financial software, parallel processing supercomputers and advances in financial mathematics, this prospect of irrationality must always be examined in the company of an equally rational and highly sophisticated machinery of stochastic optimal feedback and control: one designed for the sole purpose of supporting informed trading activity within closely observed financial markets. In this context I would suggest that any simplistic notion that the ripple of rational trading activity could somehow be swamped by a tidal wave of irrational, myopic trend-chasing or noise-trading must be replaced by a more sophisticated conception.

The casual links Keynes described in Book Five of *The General Theory*, which undermined the neoclassical adjustment process espoused by the UK Treasury, encompass both Fisherian debt-deflation effects and adverse movements in the marginal efficiency of capital (MEC) and speculative demand for money schedules. However, a purely irrational shift in sentiment could drive liquidity preference or the MEC schedule in either direction. Pure irrationality is not susceptible to any kind of causal analysis. It elides any theoretical efforts to articulate the relationship between real world phenomena such as non-indexed, nominal contracting and increasing financial instability and adverse shifts in liquidity preference.

At a time when theorists located in mathematical finance departments of universities in Taiwan, China, Norway and parts of the USA, routinely adopt continuous-time white-noise analysis for characterizing multi-fractal and Levy diffusion processes, it is all too easy to respond by claiming 'non-ergodicity' to be a feature of asset markets when it is this very characteristic that requires further explication.[9] I'm sure post Keynesians would agree – in opposition to the respective camp followers of Mandelbrot or Fama – that the real issue in finance theory is not the generality of the stochastic process that is being modelled. Rather, it is a question of the endogeneity of the return process as it responds to fluctuations in liquidity preference: it is this endogeneity that undermines any notion of fundamental value! Another issue that I examine in more detail below is what could motivate changes in the level of liquidity preference itself. Here, Keynes pointed to turbulence in the system of nominal wages and prices, while Minsky focused on financial instability.

AN APPLICATION OF RISK-SENSITIVE AND ROBUST CONTROL THEORY

To illustrate the potential of these techniques, and the limitations of most of the current applications, I have chosen to focus on Hansen, Sargent and Tallarini's (1999) (HST) analysis of a permanent income model. My review will avoid technical details in focusing on an intuitive understanding of how the techniques work in determining the final outcomes.

Hansen, Sargent and Tallarini examine the behaviour of a representative consumer who must choose between precautionary savings and consumption based on his or her expected future income. The latter is derived from two sources: the returns derived from financial wealth and that from labour income. Both income streams are discounted at the same risk-free rate of return earned on the consumer's financial assets. Under a preference for robustness, the consumer doubts the probability model used to form forecasts of future labour income. As such, these forecasts are derived using a probability distribution that is twisted or slanted relative to an approximating model that is initially used to represent the endowment process.

Hansen, Sargent and Tallarini show that a form of certainty equivalence applies to the robust decision-making process, allowing the optimal control decision to be decomposed into two stages. In the conventional, non-robust control case, the first stage of decision-making requires the consumer to solve a non-stochastic problem by maximizing the expected sum of discounted future one-period returns, conditional on the initial period state vector, and subject to both a given transition function and a sequence – presumed to be known – which describes the evolution of the exogenous component of the state vector. The transition function describes how the state variable adjusts endogenously given the previous state (comprising both an endogenous and an exogenous component) and the chosen value for the consumer's control variable (in this instance representing the choice between current consumption and current period savings). The control decision feeds back on the endogenous state vector and feeds forward on the future of the state vector in total (one that includes both exogenous and endogenous components). In the second stage, the mathematical expectation of exogenous component of the state variable vector is calculated conditioned on the history of this variable up to the current time period. This calculation is performed with full knowledge of both (1) the transition function describing how the exogenous component evolves – subject to the previous period's state and an independent identically distributed (iid) error term – and, (2) the cumulative distribution function for the error or perturbation term.

In the robust control case, the consumer assumes that the transition function governing the evolution of the exogenous components of the state vector is now subject to a further distortion represented by an additional 'slanting' variable with bounded volatility, which is itself a function of the history of the total state variable vector. The expectation of future returns is now taken with respect to the distribution generated by the distorted exogenous component of the state variable vector. The bound over the volatility of the distortion is an expression of the maximal specification error. The resultant slanting of probabilities leads the consumer to engage in a form of precautionary savings that shifts his or her consumption profile towards the future relative to the non-robust case. In practice, this shift is equivalent to the outcome that would be realized under an assumption that the consumer had become more patient. However, an increasing preference for robustness would still be manifest in the form of a difference in resulting vector of asset prices in comparison with the non-robust but more patient case. By modifying the discount rate to achieve an equivalence in consumption and savings patterns across both the robust and non-robust cases, HST are able to calculate the additional contribution that robustness to uncertainty makes to asset prices.[10]

In solving the optimal control law HST take advantage of an equivalence holding between different versions of a two-player zero-sum game. They commence with a so-called *multiplier problem* under which the decision-maker computes a Markov perfect equilibrium taking the other player's decision-rule as given. The first player, nature, chooses a worst-case distortion in full knowledge of the consumer's robust control law (that is one that minimizes the expected sum of discounted future returns). The consumer simultaneously chooses a control to maximize the expected return in a manner that is robust to the worst-case perturbation. Technically, robustness is achieved by penalizing the volatility of the distortion using a Legrange multiplier whose value reflects the consumer's robustness or aversion to ambiguity (hence the name *multiplier problem*). Thus, the decision rule is robust in the sense that it affords a lower maximal rate at which the expected rate of return would deteriorate with an increase in the degree of misspecification.

However, certainty equivalence in the form of a two-stage decision-making process is only revealed in a second Stackelberg-leader, recursive version of the game. In this version, nature – the minimizing player – chooses a worst-case distortion in each period based on information current in the previous period, and taking into account the best sequential response of the consumer – the maximizing player – who, in each period, continues to view the distortion as an exogenous process. Once again, the evolution of the endogenous component of the state variable vector is given by the unchanged transition function whereas the transition equation for the exogenous component incorporates the additive distortion.

Hansen, Sargent and Tallarini rely on the proof set out in Basar and Bernhard (1995) to the effect that the same decision rule for the maximizing player emerges from both the Markov perfect and Stackelberg versions of the game, providing a justification for the presumption of certainty equivalence. This equivalence allows HST to characterize equilibrium as comprising the minimizing player's solution for the worst-case disturbance taking the maximizing player's control law derived from the Markov perfect game as given, and the maximizing player's decision rule, which takes the worst-case disturbance as given, under the assumption that each of the players is exposed to the same initial conditions for the state variable.

In a variety of asset-pricing models, agent heterogeneity is the culprit responsible for market turbulence. This raises the question of how such agent heterogeneity can be incorporated into what are essentially representative agent models. Although this matter is not formally treated in the HST or AHS papers, Hansen and Sargent (2000), in a paper on robust optimal monetary intervention, show how this can be accomplished. They construct a robust version of a linear quadratic regulator problem that was originally conceived in non-robust form by Currie and Levine (1987). In their model both the government and private agents share a common model of the economy, but the government must find a sequence of rules that expresses the time t control as a function of the history of the relevant state variable vector y_t, up to that point in time. As the decisions of private agents are forward-looking, they are influenced by their anticipation of future policy interventions so that the government must take these influences into account in planning its decisions.

Hansen and Sargent show how this seemingly complex problem can easily be incorporated into the much simpler framework of a single-agent linear regulator problem. Initially, the problem is set up as a robust version of the standard Lagrangian problem. They derive first-order conditions for the control variable vector (combining both private agent and government decisions), the state variable vector x_t, and the vector of specification error shocks w_t. This yields a pair of feedback rules for both the government and the private agents. In each case, the solution represents a planned strategy for dealing with the worst possible vector of conceivable shocks that could be imposed on the given model. The elements of the state variable vector that expresses the agents' optimal control x_t, are all jump variables determined by the model at time t.

In addition, the stabilizing solution to the Ricatti equation yields a matrix P that gives a recursive representation for $\mu_t = Py_t$, for the shadow price μ_t of the state (that is, μ_t is the Lagrangian multiplier on the constraint that represents the stochastic equation of motion for the evolving system and its shadow price reflects the marginal effect that an 'easing' of this constraint has on the quadratic objective function). Hansen and Sargent demonstrate how the original problem can be transformed through partitioning the multiplier into two parts: one μ_{zt}, for the government and the other μ_{xt}, for the private agents, where each of the multiplier components is matched by the relevant component z_t and x_t, respectively, in a congruent decomposition of the state variable vector, y_t. Replacing the jump variables x_t that appear in the original robust version of the optimal linear regulator problem by the multiplier variables μ_{xt}, Hansen and Sargent (2000, s. 5.1) argue that these multiplier variables now play the role of *implementability constraints* over the government's choice of sequences for the relevant component of the control variable vector u_t. Hansen and Sargent (2000) partition the P matrix conformably, so that the agents' choice of the jump variable vector x_t, can be expressed as a function of the government's state variable vector z_t, and the implementation multiplier μ_{xt}. Using similar techniques, therefore, it would be quite straightforward to introduce agent heterogeneity into a representative agent, risk-sensitive control setting. In principle, it ought to be possible to introduce heterogeneity in the form of variations in the degree of uncertainty aversion or uncertainty perception on the part of other agents with whom the decision-maker must interact.

However, I would suggest that heterogeneity is not the most important weakness in existing applications of these techniques. To this end, I focus on the implications of generalizing Hansen and Sargent's analysis so that it can adequately account for interactions between the real and the financial components of the economy. To be completely consistent, Hansen and Sargent should apply their modelling framework of risk-sensitive control to investment modelled as a contingent claim or real option. But this would necessarily imply that levels of investment are now the endogenous outcome of shifts in the level of uncertainty aversion and uncertainty perception, with fluctuations in investment, via the point of effective demand driving overall economic activity (and the returns on financial assets) in a typically Keynesian fashion.

HOW THESE TECHNIQUES COULD BE MODIFIED TO REFLECT A KEYNESIAN WORLD

In risk-sensitive control theory 'uncertainty perception' and 'uncertainty aversion' can be related, respectively, to the magnitude of the stochastic uncertainty constraint and the risk-sensitivity parameter. In this case, time-varying liquidity preference of the form expressed in the models of Trond Andresen and Flaschel, Franke and Semmler would be analogous to changes to either the stochastic uncertainty constraint and/or the risk-sensitivity parameter that appears within the value or penalty function. Although risk-sensitive control theory – much like its LQG predecessor – has been applied to systems with time-varying system parameters – for obvious reasons it has not evolved to accommodate time-variation in either the penalty function or uncertainty constraint. While in economic theory the penalty function represents a utility function, in engineering applications it merely reflects a concern on the part of the system designer for controlling the given system robustly, in the absence of knowledge about the precise characterization of perturbation, observation error and model uncertainty. Whereas engineers have no concerns about whether changes in the penalty function could somehow influence the system under control, economists do not (or perhaps should not) possess that same confidence.

However, I would argue that three vital ingredients must be added to existing macro-financial models to accommodate Keynesian concerns about the nature of real-world economies. First, the equilibrating role played by the marginal productivity of capital as an ultimate driver of the real interest rate must be rejected. This critical role has clearly been identified by Sargent in his first book on macroeconomics (see Duménil and Lévy, 1985; Hahn, 1982; Harcourt, 1972; Sargent, 1986). Sargent (1986) established the block recursive structure of aggregative neoclassical macroeconomic models – a feature which comes to the fore in stochastic growth models (Brock, 1982), which extend the pure exchange asset-pricing model of Lucas (1978) to include savings and investment.

Second, the multiple heterogeneous-agent principle must be invoked, but not in the conventional form of a Gorman-style critique of aggregation (for example, inappropriately applied to consumers with different levels of income and non-homothetic preferences).[11] Instead, it must be pointed out that in a real-world economy rather than a Robinson Crusoe one, different groups of agents undertake acts of real investment, consumption and savings, or act as financial intermediaries between borrowers and lenders. Otherwise, consumption activity on the part of representative agents would simply rise as a counterpart of reduced savings, thereby taking into account (and fully offsetting the effects of) any downward shift in the conditional expectation about prospective excess returns to be derived from investment. In fact, an increase in uncertainty aversion would generally result in an increase in long-term interest rates, reflecting the adverse movement in liquidity preference.

Finally, debt-deflation effects should be incorporated if modellers are to account for an important aspect of the real macroeconomy – a requirement reflecting the absence of a widespread indexation of future and forward contracts. Magill and Quinzii have shown how this can be accomplished by drawing a formal distinction between nominal, indexed, and real contracts within financial models (Magill and Quinzii, 1998, ch. 7).

CONCLUDING COMMENTS

Once it has been acknowledged that the stochastic process driving dividends and other real or financial returns must become an endogeneous product of changes in uncertainty aversion, the inescapable implication is that Hansen and Sargent's systems framework becomes difficult to sustain. With the existence of mutual feedback between processes of cognition, prediction, and choice, existing techniques of risk-sensitive control are simply inapplicable in their conventional forms (see Vercelli, 1991, s. 9.2, pp. 143–8).

At this stage, an astute observer familiar with the machinery of modern finance theory could observe that all that is required to maintain the fiction of a representative agent fiction is the notion that each agent correctly perceives that he or she is unable to influence asset prices in equilibrium through their own actions when these are considered in isolation from those of other agents. For example, this assumption has been captured, in a formal sense, by Hansen and Sargent's use of 'implementability constraints' that account mathematically for the risk-sensitive decisions of other agents. However, what I am proposing here is that the imposition of structures such as this prevents us from 'seeing the wood for the trees'. If the Keynesian narrative of the beauty contest is reinterpreted from an uncertainty aversion point of view, in determining their forecast of the spectrum of asset prices each agent can be viewed as making some kind of assumption about the level of uncertainty aversion held by other agents (Keynes, 1973, pp. 156–7). A shift in the overall level of liquidity preference or uncertainty aversion would therefore seem to imply some kind of contagion effect. However, it would be the degree of uncertainty aversion that becomes the vector of contagion rather than some kind of irrationality or misperception. I have argued above that an increase in the vulnerability of the economy as a whole to an adverse movement in uncertainty aversion would become the trigger both for the initial outbreak and the subsequent and at times, surprisingly rapid, contagion. Whether this sort of contagion can be represented mathematically by an interdependency of utility between agents is a moot point, when the object of that interdependency is not the vector of returns or attributes of those returns but, rather, a key parameter within the utility or penalty function itself.

One likely response would be for Hansen and Sargent to suggest that I am attempting to account for the beliefs that agents hold about other agent's beliefs. And because there is no conceivable way of adequately representing changes in the pattern of 'beliefs about beliefs', they could just as well be represented by, say, a diffusion process. Effectively, this would allow conventional control thinking to be 'smuggled in through the back door'.

My counter-response to this kind of argument would be to return to the Minskyian analysis that I reviewed at the beginning of this chapter. I would strongly oppose the notion that changes in the pattern of 'belief about beliefs' could themselves be represented as a stochastic process because, as Keynes and Minsky have pointed out, they do not vary at random, but through the workings of a dialectical process of mutual conditioning and interaction between the uncertainty aversion of the majority of economic agents and actual conditions in the institutional world of banking and credit provision, household borrowing and corporate investment. It is wage-price instability and an increasing vulnerability of financial positions on the part of banks, households and firms to adverse movements in interest rates and resultant aggregate demand conditions, which actually determine fluctuations in the preference for money or near-money assets. The inevitable consequence of the fact that investment fluctuates in response to changes in uncertainty aversion is that activist policy interventions continue to play a vital role in efforts to influence or compensate for the undesirable cognitive aspects of decision-making on the part of private agents.

NOTES

* I wish to thank John van der Hoek for his assistance, although I take full responsibility for any errors of fact or opinion.

1. Some authors have chosen to focus on other axioms of Expected Utility Theory, including the axiom of continuity (as in the work of Bewley, 1986) and transitivity, while others have grounded their research in the notion that agents impose a lexicographic ordering over a hierarchy of feasible probability distributions.
2. For example, in cumulative prospect theory (CPT), a generalization of rank-dependent utility, the non-linear weighting function implies that, on one hand, individuals are risk-seeking for gains and risk averse for losses of *low* probability, while on the other hand, they are risk averse for gains and risk seeking for losses of *high* probability (Tversky and Wakker, 1995). In a recent paper (Juniper, 2001), I have provided an intuitive demonstration of the relationship between this *s*-shaped weighting function and relative entropy measures. Another approach to ambiguity that is based on fuzzy control theory (Cherubini, 1997), exploits the relationship between Choquet integration and fuzzy measures (on this see Mirofushi and Sugeno, 1989).
3. See Cagliarini and Heath (2000) for a simple but elegant diagrammatic explanation of uncertainty aversion for the case of a binary lottery defined over two states of nature.
4. Marinacci (1999) outlines a set of behavioural considerations that might motivate an approach to decision-making predicated on uncertainty aversion, while in Epstein and Schneider (2001), an axiomatic basis for uncertainty aversion has been constructed deploying a discrete-time, multiple-priors, recursive utility framework. A continuous-time variant is discussed in Chen and Epstein (2000). Also, see the debate between Epstein and Schneider (2001) and Hansen et al. (2001) over the precise nature of the relationship holding between risk-sensitive penalty functions and multiple-priors forms of generalized utility. Significantly, Grant and Quiggin have shown how Epstein and Zhang's (2001) definition of ambiguous events can be used to define ambiguity aversion over preference relations in 'a solely preference-based and model-free manner' (Grant and Quiggin, 2001, p. 2).
5. On the former see Ellsberg (1961), and on the latter see Weil (1989) who shows that the use of a more general Kreps and Porteus (1978) specification for recursive utility still fails

to explain the coexistence of a large premium on equity over fixed-interest securities under reasonable parameterizations for both the elasticity of inter-temporal substitution and the coefficient of constant relative risk-aversion. Hansen, Sargent and Tallarini note the correspondence between their risk-sensitive penalty function and a class of recursive utility functions explicated in Epstein and Zin (1989).

6. For a lucid and detailed articulation of these and other liquidity preference-related influences over macroeconomic adjustment see Vercelli (1991).
7. To some extent, this research mirrors that of Duncan Foley who has recently argued that statistical mechanics provides a more credible framework for modelling the outcomes of market trading than Walrasian tatônnement amongst heterogenous, representative, utility-maximizing agents (Foley, 2002).
8. Some theoretical support for this contention is provided in a paper by Veronesi (2001) who confirms the existence of long-term uncertainty premia in a pure-exchange, state-dependent utility-based model of uncertainty aversion.
9. For example, drawing on white-noise analysis and the Bochner-Minlos theorem within a continuous time setting, however, Elliott and van der Hoek (2000) show that conventional techniques of financial stochastics can be generalized and applied over Hilbert spaces which can accommodate infinitely dimensional distributions, including fractal Brownian motion and Levy processes.
10. Under two separate limiting conditions associated with different parameters within the risk-sensitive penalty function, the solution to the dynamic programming problem would either revert to that of LQG control and the Kalman-Bucy H_2-filter, or alternatively, to that of a deterministic H -control and filtering problem (Petersen, James and Dupuis, 2000). In general terms, the H -norm minimizes the worst-case root mean squared (*rms*) value of the regulated variables when the disturbances have unknown spectra, whereas the H_2-norm minimizes the *rms* values of the regulated variables when the disturbances are unit intensity white-noise processes (Shahian and Hassul, 1993, pp. 442–3).
11. Of course, the related results of the Sonnenschien-Mantel-Debreu lemma still serve as a valuable reminder that income effects render questionable any attempt to ground macroeconomic behaviour on microeconomic foundations. This lemma establishes that the only features of individual consumption behaviour that carry over to Walrasian excess demand functions are the symmetry conditions over the Slutsky matrix.

REFERENCES

Allais, M. (1953), 'Le comportment de l'homme rationnel devant le risque postulats et axiomes de l'ecole Amercaine', *Econometrica*, **21**, 503–46.

Andersen, E.W., L.P. Hansen and T.J. Sargent (1998a), 'Risk and robustness in general equilibrium', accessed at www.stanford.edu/sargent/research.html.

Andersen, E.W., L.P. Hansen and T.J. Sargent (1998b), 'Robustness, detection and the price of risk', accessed at www.stanford.edu/sargent/research.html.

Andresen, Trond (1999a), 'The macroeconomy as a network of money-flow transfer functions', Post-Keynesian Thought Archive website, accessed at http://csf.colorado.edu/authors/Andersen.Trond.

Andresen, Trond (1999b), 'The dynamics of long-range financial accumulation and crisis', Post-Keynesian Thought Archive website, accessed at http://csf.colorado.edu/authors/Andresen.Trond; forthcoming in *Non-Linear Dynamics, Psychology, and the Life-Sciences*, New York: Human Sciences Press.

Arthur, B., J. Holland, B. LeBaron, P. Palmer, and P. Taylor (1994), 'An artificial stock market', Sante Fe Institute working paper, September.

Basar, Tamar, and Pierre Bernhard (1995), *H – Optimal Control and Related Minimax Design Problems: A Dynamic Game Approach*, Boston, Basel and Berlin: Birkäuser.

Basili, Marcello (2000), 'Knightian uncertainty in financial markets: an assessment', Dipartimento di Economia Politica, Universitã degli Studi di Siena working paper no. 281, February.

Bewley, T. (1986), 'Knightian decision theory: part 1', Cowles Commission discussion paper no. 807, Yale University.

Brock, William, A. (1982), 'Asset-prices in a production economy' in John McCall (ed.), *The Economics of Information and Uncertainty*, including comment by Edward C. Prescott, Chicago:University of Chicago Press, pp. 1–46.

Brock, William, A. (1999), 'Rational animal spirits', in P.J.J. Herings, G. van der Laan and A.J.J. Talman (eds), *The Theory of Markets*, Amsterdam: North Holland, pp. 109–37.

Brock, William A., and Cars H. Hommes (1997) 'A rational route to randomness', *Econometrica*, **65** (5), 1059–95.

Brock, William A., and Cars H. Hommes (1998), 'Heterogenous beliefs and routes to chaos in a simple asset-pricing model', *Journal of Economic Dynamics and Control*, **22**, 1235–74.

Brock W.A., J. Lakonishok, and B. LeBaron (1992), 'Simple technical trading rules and the stochastic properties of stock returns', *Journal of Finance*, **47**, 1731–64.

Cagliarini, Adam, and Alexandra Heath (2000), 'Monetary policy-making in the presence of Knightian uncertainty', Reserve Bank of Australia research discussion paper RDP2000–10, December accessed at www.rba.gov.au/rdp/index.html.

Camerer, C., and M. Weber (1992), 'Recent developments in modelling preferences: uncertainty and ambiguity', *Journal of Risk and Uncertainty*, **5**(4), 325–70.

Chen, Zengjing, and Larry Epstein (2000), 'Ambiguity, risk and asset returns in continuous time', July, accessed at www.econ.rochester.edu/Faculty/Epstein.html.

Cherubini, Umberto (1997), 'Fuzzy measures and asset prices: accounting for information ambiguity', *Applied Mathematical Finance*, **4**, 135–49.

Chew, S. (1989), 'Axiomatic utility theories with the betweeness property', *Annals of Operations Research*, **19**, 273–98.

Chiarella, C., and P. Flaschel (2000), *The Dynamics of Keynesian Monetary Growth: Macrofoundations*, Cambridge: Cambridge University Press.

Choquet, G. (1955), 'Theory of capacities', *Annales Institute Fourier*, **5**, 131–295.

Currie, David, and Paul Levine (1987), 'The design of feedback rules in linear stochastic rational expectations models', *Journal of Economic Dynamics and Control*, **11** (1), 1–28.

Davidson, Paul (1994), 'Uncertainty in economics', in Sheila Dow and John Hilliard (eds), *Keynes, Knowledge and Uncertainty*, Aldershot: Edward Elgar, pp. 107–16.

Dekel, E. (1986), 'An axiomatic characterisation of preferences under uncertainty', *Journal of Economic Theory*, **40**, 304–18.

Dequech, David (1999), 'Expectations and confidence under uncertainty', *Journal of Post-Keynesian Economics*, **21** (3), 479–508.

Duménil, G., and D. Lévy (1985), 'The classical and the neoclassicals: a rejoinder to Frank Hahn', *Cambridge Journal of Economics*, **9**, 327–45.

Elliott, Robert J., and John van der Hoek (2000), 'A general fractional white noise theory and applications to finance', University of Adelaide Department of Applied Mathematics working paper,

Ellsberg, D. (1961), 'Risk, ambiguity and the savage axioms', *Quarterly Journal of Economics*, **75**, 643–69.

Epstein, L.G., and M. Schneider (2001), 'Recursive multiple priors', mimeo, University of Rochester, forthcoming in *Journal of Economic Theory*, accessed at www.econ.rochester.edu/Faculty/Epstein.html.

Epstein, L.G., and J. Zhang (2001), 'Subjective probabilities on subjectively unambiguous events', *Econometrica*, **69** (2), 265–306.

Epstein, L.G., and S.E. Zin (1989), 'Substitution, risk aversion and the temporal behaviour of consumption and asset returns: a theoretical framework', *Econometrica*, **57** (4), 937–69.

Fishburn, P.F. (1987), 'Utility and decision theory', entry in J. Eatwell, M. Milgate and P. Newman (eds), *The New Palgrave Dictionary of Economics, Vol IV*, London: Macmillan Reference Books.

Flaschel, P., R. Franke and W. Semmler (1996), *Instability, Fluctuation and Growth in Monetary Economies*, Cambridge, MA: MIT Press.

Foley, D.K. (2002), 'Maximum entropy exchange equilibrium', mimeo, Barnard College, Columbia University, May.

Foley, D.K. (1987), 'Liquidity-profit rate cycles in a capitalist economy', *Journal of Economic Behaviour*, **8**, 363–76.

Gilboa, I., and D. Schmeidler (1989), 'Maximin expected utility with non-unique prior', *Journal of Mathematical Economics*, **18**, 141–53.

Godley, W. (1999), 'Money and credit in a Keynesian model of income determination', *Cambridge Journal of Economics*, **23**, 393–411.

Grant, S., and J. Quiggin (2001), 'A model-free definition of increasing uncertainty', mimeo, 22 August, accessed at www.uq.edu.au/economics/johnquiggin/WorkingPapers/IncreasingUncertaintyWP.pdf.

Hahn, Frank H. (1982), 'The neo-Ricardians', *Cambridge Journal of Economics*, **9** (December), 327–45.

Hansen, Lars P., and Thomas J. Sargent (2000), 'Robust control and filtering of forward-looking models', draft 5 October, Thomas Sargent's personal website, accessed at www-econ.stanford.edu/faculty/sargent.html, Department of Economics, Stanford University.

Hansen, Lars P., Thomas J. Sargent and Thomas D. Tallarini, Jr (1999), 'Robust permanent income and pricing', *Review of Economic Studies*, **66**, 873–907.

Hansen, Lars P., Thomas J. Sargent , A. Gauhar Turmuhambetova and Noah Williams (2001), 'Robustness and uncertainty aversion', Thomas Sargent's personal website, accessed at www-econ.stanford.edu/faculty/sargent.html, Department of Economics, Stanford University.

Harcourt, Geoffrey, C. (1972), *Some Cambridge Controversies in the Theory of Capital*, Cambridge: Cambridge University Press.

Juniper, A. James (2001), 'Statistical entropy and recursive filtering in an uncertain business environment', paper presented at the British Academy of Management Conference, September, Cardiff, Wales.

Keen, S. (1995), 'Finance and economic breakdown: modeling Minsky's financial instability hypothesis', *Journal of Post-Keynesian Economics*, **17** (4), 607–35.

Keynes, John Maynard (1973), *Collected Writings of John Maynard Keynes, Vol 7, The General Theory of Employment, Interest and Money*, London: Macmillan.

Kreps, D., and E. Porteus (1978), 'Temporal resolution of uncertainty and dynamic choice theory', *Econometrica*, **46**, 185–200.

Lavoie, M., and W. Godley (2000), 'Kaleckian models of growth in a stock-flow monetary framework: a new Kaldorian model', Jerome Lévy Economics Institute working paper series, no. 302, June.

LeBaron, B., W.B. Arthur, and R. Palmer (1999), 'Time series properties of an artificial stock market', *Journal of Economic Dynamics and Control*, **23**, 1487–516.

Lucas, Robert E. Jr (1978), 'Asset-prices in an exchange economy', *Econometrica*, **46** (6), 1429–45.

Magill, Michael, and Martine Quinzii (1998), *Theory of Incomplete Markets: Volume 1*, Cambridge, MA: MIT Press.

Marinacci, M. (1999), 'Limit laws for non-additive probabilities and their frequentist interpretation', *Journal of Economic Theory*, **84**, 145–95.

Minsky, H.P. (1985), 'The financial instability hypothesis: a restatement', in P. Arestis and T. Skouras (eds), *Post-Keynesian Economic Theory: A Challenge to Neo-Classical Economics*, Hemel Hempstead: Wheatsheaf Books.

Mirofushi, T., and M. Sugeno (1989), 'An interpretation of fuzzy measures and the Choquet integral with respect to a fuzzy measure', *Fuzzy Sets and Systems*, **29**, 201–27.

Palley, Thomas I. (1999), 'General disequilibrium analysis with inside debt', *Journal of Macroeconomics*, **21** (4), 785–803.

Panico, Carlo (1993), 'Two alternative approaches to financial model building', *Metroeconomica*, **44** (2), 93–133.

Petersen, I.R., M.R. James, and P. Dupuis (2000), 'Minimax optimal control of stochastic uncertain systems with relative entropy constraints', *IEEE Transactions on Automatic Control*, **45**, 398–412.

Sargent, Thomas J. (1986), *Macroeconomic Theory*, 2nd edn, New York: Academic Press.

Savage, L.J. (1954), *The Foundations of Statistics*, New York: John Wiley.

Shahian, Bahram, and Michael Hassul (1993), *Control System Design Using MATLAB®*, Englewood Cliffs, NJ: Prentice Hall.

Taylor, L., and S. O'Connell (1985), 'A Minsky crisis', *Quarterly Journal of Economics*, **100**, 871–85.

Tversky, Amos, and Peter Wakker (1995), 'Risk attitudes and decision weights', *Econometrica*, **63** (6), 1255–80.

Vercelli, Alessandro (1991), *Methodological Foundations of Macroeconomics: Keynes and Lucas*, Cambridge: Cambridge University Press.

Veronesi, P. (2001), 'Belief-dependent utilities, aversion to state-uncertainty and asset prices', CRSP working paper no. 529, University of Chicago, August, accessed at gsbwww.uchicago.edu/fac/finance/papers.

Weil, Philippe (1989), 'The equity premium puzzle and the risk-free rate puzzle', *Journal of Monetary Economics*, **24**, 401–21.

16. Presenting 'demi-regularities' of pricing behaviour: the need for triangulation

Paul Downward and Andrew Mearman

INTRODUCTION

This chapter addresses one of the most contentious issues in post Keynesian economics and in heterodox economics more widely: the use of econometric methods. Econometrics is of course a major tool in orthodox economics; however, heterodox economists have long viewed it with caution. For instance, Keynes (1973) and Kalecki (1964) both wrote specifically about the necessary conditions for the use of econometrics. Authors informed by the increasingly important philosophy of Critical Realism are also skeptical (see Lawson, 1997). However, post Keynesianism is somewhat ambivalent about econometrics. While there is suspicion, there is also prominent use of econometrics in certain areas – for instance, on money supply endogeneity (Pollin, 1991) – and more generally, Mitchell (1991). Paul Davidson's work exemplifies this ambivalence: his own work implies many objections to econometrics, yet as editor of the *Journal of Post Keynesian Economics*, he publishes many articles that use econometrics. Sheila Dow (2002) advances a methodological pluralism, which entails the possible use of econometrics. Elsewhere, Downward (1999) and Downward and Mearman (2002a; 2002b) have argued that the use of econometrics is compatible with post Keynesianism and Critical Realism. This chapter aims to build on the methodological arguments of that work, which argued that econometrics could play a role as part of a strategy of methodological triangulation. The chapter illustrates this argument by presenting empirical work on pricing.

The structure of the chapter is as follows. First, econometrics is defined. It is argued that econometrics inherently possesses descriptive and inferential aspects, which allow econometrics to be used in various ways, for example in the codification of the empirical. Second, following Downward and Mearman (1999; 2002a; 2002b) it is argued that such methods do involve what Critical Realists describe as assumptions of closure; however, it is held that this criticism also applies to so-called 'descriptive' and 'qualitative' work. Thus, practitioners using empirical data must confront and accommodate implicit closure if they are to proceed. This closure creates a need to triangulate techniques in the act of inference. The third section illustrates the above arguments by the examination of empirical work on pricing behavior: this work uses insights from more than one empirical investigative method. The evidence presented is argued to offer support for post Keynesian theories of pricing.

ECONOMETRICS DEFINED

Econometrics is difficult to define. It encompasses a wide set of statistical techniques. These techniques are also nested implicitly or explicitly in particular inferential frameworks. Following Lawson (1989), which is arguably the seminal contribution from Critical Realism on the subject of econometrics, and Downward and Mearman (2002a; 2002b), this chapter focuses on the 'textbook' linear 'average economic regression' (AER), particularly associated with Haavelmo (1944), to illustrate the main characteristics of econometrics. However, as in Downward and Mearman, it is held that the arguments concerning the AER approach apply equally to the newer approaches to econometrics associated with Hendry (1995), Leamer (1983) and Sims (1980), to innovations in limited dependent variable and other essentially cross-section techniques, and to non-parametric econometrics (see Siegel and Castellan, 1988).

The essence of the AER approach is that a linear equation linking a stochastic dependent variable to a set of non-stochastic independent variables is put forward as a representation of an equilibrium relationship specified by theory. Typically, Ordinary Least Squares (OLS) is employed to estimate partial slope coefficients that identify both the sign and the magnitude of the influence of a particular independent variable upon the dependent variable. As it stands, the regression model can be viewed as producing purely sample-specific descriptive insights; OLS can be understood as simply a partitioning of the dependent variable into explained and residual components according to the Analysis of Variance identity.

Therefore, the AER approach implies a sharp distinction between estimation and inference. Additional assumptions are employed to make inferences. Thus, it is assumed that the mean of the random disturbance that affects the dependent variable is zero and that the variance and covariance of the disturbances are, respectively, constant and zero across observations. This produces a 'Best Linear Unbiased Estimator'. Thus in this approach most attention is paid to ensuring that the residuals of the regression, as estimates of the random influences, meet assumptions of normality, no serial correlation and homoskedasticity. At this point the statistical significance of the regression overall as well as particular coefficients is tested. The equation can then be used to predict the average value of the dependent variable conditional on values of the independent variables either within the existing sample, or beyond the sample.

However, several problems arose with the AER approach, mainly associated with identification and its ability to discriminate between theories. As Pagan (1987) and Downward (1999) note, three broad strategies associated with Hendry (1995), Leamer (1983) and Sims (1980) emerged in econometrics to address these fundamental problems. The three approaches challenged the duality of classically defined econometric inference and estimation, and they addressed issues of theory estimation, discrimination and adequate statistical representation in a more fluid manner. To varying degrees, each approach draws upon the interplay of theory and data to postulate an adequate econometric model.[1] Downward and Mearman (2002a; 2002b) discuss these approaches at length.

Therefore, the current state of applied econometrics is one of development and change in emphasis. However, as Downward and Mearman (2002a; 2002b) argue, the various contemporary approaches reflect a number of common themes. The first is that there is an increased recognition of the inability of econometrics to discriminate between theories, though it remains an aspiration. Second, it is clear that prior data analysis is much more important in the approaches that superseded the AER approach. This is either in terms of modeling through testing or in a priori consideration of the distribution of, say, the dependent variable.[2] Third, the emphasis on 'event regularities' is reinforced because *probabilistic* factors naturally become much more prevalent in the generation of econometric results.[3] Fourth, predictions are still treated as the mirror image of explanations, and vice versa. Finally, as Downward and Mearman (2002a; 2002b) argue, econometrics has a range of uses; one of these is the codification of the empirical level.

ECONOMETRICS AND CLOSURE

Critical Realism has recently become increasingly influential in Post Keynesianism. This is evidenced by the symposium of fall 1999 in the *Journal of Post Keynesian Economics*. Downward (1999), Mearman (2002a) and Downward and Mearman (2002a) discuss at length the relationship between Critical Realism and econometrics. Critical Realism places a central emphasis on empirical evidence. For example, the essence of the Critical-Realist approach is that science involves claims about causal mechanisms, deduced from empirical data via the logic of retroduction (see Lawson, 1997, p. 24).[4] Therefore, the process of research is said to begin at the empirical level, where rough and ready patterns, or 'demi-regularities' (see Lawson, 1997, p. 219)[5] are the genesis of the causal claims. Yet, despite this, Critical Realism tends to reject econometrics, the most powerful empirical tool available to economists. Critical-Realist objections tend to maintain that econometrics is only applicable in 'closed-systems', usually defined as situations in which event regularities hold. Critical Realists focus on the two main assumptions of closure implicit and explicit in regression techniques: the Intrinsic Condition of Closure (ICC) (see Lawson, 1997, pp. 78–9), roughly stated as 'every cause has the same effect'; and the Extrinsic Condition of Closure (ECC) (see Lawson, pp. 77–8), which can be understood as 'every effect has the same cause'.

A brief sketch illustrates the prevalence of closure within the AER approach. That approach, as outlined above, entails the specification of a linear equation relating a dependent variable with reference to a (set of) independent (that is, assumed fixed) variable(s). The uniform (partial) slope coefficient of the independent variable implies that the (in this case, linear) relationship holds over the entire period. As Keynes (1973) noted of Tinbergen's method, it would perhaps be more reasonable for the coefficient to vary for every one of the time periods involved. Therefore, the AER approach has made an assumption of underlying homogeneity (the ICC). Moreover, not only is the interaction of the variables assumed constant, but also the nature of the variables themselves is assumed constant (the ICC). As noted above, in the AER approach, the independent variables are assumed not to interact in practice. This is in itself an act of closure, since the act of the regression closes off the model from other variables, assuming them constant (the ECC). Furthermore, the AER approach, as it has been developed, makes various auxiliary assumptions, such as zero serial correlation, which flows from Keynes's 'technical' criticisms of Tinbergen (Lawson, 1985). One other such assumption is that of the normality of the error term in the regression.[6] Downward and Mearman (2002a) argue that essentially the same criticisms can be made of the developments of econometrics, discussed above, which superseded the AER approach.

These objections have led Critical Realists to specific conclusions about econometrics. First, they advise practitioners to establish *a priori* that closed systems exist and that therefore econometrics is appropriate. For instance, Lawson (1989, p. 247) advocates the use of techniques such as martingales that take into account non-homogeneity of economic material. Dow (1999) shares this approach. Second, they argue that in the absence of pure closed systems, econometric methods should be abandoned. This conclusion would also seem to be the logical inference from Davidson's (1991) arguments about non-ergodicity and the inappropriateness of a range of methods used by the orthodoxy. Third, they redefine econometrics:

> The measuring and recording of states of affairs, the collection, tabulation, transformation and graphing of statistics about the economy, all have an essential (if usually non-straightforward) role to play. So do detailed case studies, oral reporting, including interviews, biographies, and so on. Indeed, I suggest it is precisely to such indispensable activities that the heading of econometrics is properly attributed.
>
> (Lawson, 1997, p. 221)

However, Downward (1999), Downward and Mearman (2002a; 2002b) and Mearman (2002a) argue that such methods of descriptive statistics still involve closure assumptions. Specifically, all such methods presuppose that the conditions for quantification – which are not insignificant in the stringency of their requirements – are assumed to exist. This includes an abstraction from other aspects of the object. This involves tacit closure. Sayer (1992), for example, questions the legitimacy of quantifying units of labor, given the abstraction from the qualitative aspects of each laborer. Given this, the use by Lawson (1997, p. 206), as empirical examples, of the relatively low pay of women, or of unemployment rates, seems illegitimate; or at least it seems to involve several unexamined assumptions. More generally, Downward (1999) argues that all acts of theorizing involve the tacit invocation of the ICC.

The ultimate conclusion to be drawn from this analysis is that all empirical analysis involves closure, which might not be justified ontologically. This presents the economist with a problem if they are concerned with open systems but wish to use empirical evidence: if they cannot prove that their data has come from a perfectly closed system, they must either abandon the empirical evidence or adopt some other inferential strategy. Downward and Mearman (2002a) argue that this licenses a strategy of triangulating empirical insights. This naturally implies that, to a degree, triangulation involves methodological positions as much as specific empirical claims – for example combining ontological claims of open and closed systems. As Mearman (2002a) argues, this might involve the use of non-economic data and methods of analysis. It should be made clear, as Downward and Mearman (2002a) argue, that this triangulation strategy is distinct from merely counting cases of the same technique and inferring according to the law of large numbers or asymptotic properties. Moreover, as Downward, Finch and Ramsay (2002), Downward and Mearman (2002a) and Mearman (2002a; 2002b) argue, the triangulation of empirical insights can be linked to the concept of a refined ontology comprising a 'quasi-closed' system in which institutional and conventional behavior helps to produce regularity in social behavior. Indeed, Mearman (2002b) argues that because of the revealed human desire for stability and predictability, such institutional mechanisms are pervasive and that as such, 'quasi-closures' are more likely to be found in social settings than in natural settings.

Thus, a set of techniques and pieces of evidence, none of which can be presumed in isolation to yield reliable inferences, should be 'triangulated' to increase the power of the inference. Downward and Mearman (2002a; 2002b) argue that this approach is consistent with Keynes's theory of probability, in particular his concept of negative analogy. Under negative analogy, the degree of rational belief (in Keynes's terminology) in a hypothesis is increased by the collection of pieces of supporting evidence from *different* contexts. Also, the strategy implies something akin to Keynes' concept of 'weight', under which the strength of a rational belief based on a piece of evidence is affected by the total relevant evidence (see Runde, 1990). In using different techniques in different contexts, arguably the 'weight' of the inference is being increased. Moreover, as Downward and Mearman (2002a; 2002b; 2002c) and Mearman (2002a) argue, such an approach is consistent with post Keynesian methodology more generally: for example, the fallibility of knowledge in Dow's (*passim*) methodology makes the reliance on one technique flawed and inevitably implies a strategy of triangulation. Thus, the main aim of this chapter is to illustrate this principle of triangulation in terms of pricing literature.

EMPIRICAL EXAMPLES FROM UK MANUFACTURING

For two reasons, pricing has been a productive area of research for post Keynesian economics. First, post Keynesians have attacked the assumption of flexible price adjustment in response to excess demand, which lays at the core of neoclassical economics in general equilibrium theory and its core propositions about welfare. Second, development of a price theory has been a major contribution to a coherent post Keynesian alternative. Post Keynesian pricing theory draws together seminal elements of research that challenges neoclassical economics, including the work of Means (1935), Hall and Hitch (1939), Andrews (1949a; 1949b; 1964) and Kalecki (1954), and emphasizes that in manufacturing, prices are set by a mark-up on some measure of average costs with no explicit role for demand (see also Downward, 1999; Lee, 1998). Given the centrality of this issue in the orthodox-post Keynesian debate, it is not surprising that a considerable literature has developed.

In econometric terms, debate over pricing behavior has concerned three key issues.[7] These are the extent to which prices are related to full/normal or actual unit costs (full/normal costs refers to some measure of trend or long run costs), the extent to which demand exerts a direct effect on mark ups and prices and the extent to which excess demand influences prices. These issues have been usually addressed in the form of the following general linear model.

$$\text{Price}_i = \alpha_i + \beta\text{Cost}_i + \chi\text{Demand}_i + u_i$$

where i = index of observation and u = random error term.

Precise measures of variables have differed. Prices have been measured as wholesale or producer price indices. Average costs ('Cost') have been restricted to indices measuring labor costs and/or material, fuel and other costs. Further, either their current, or current and lagged, values have been included to capture, respectively, actual costs or full/normal costs – those associated with a longer period of production. In the latter case, some contrived measure of full/normal costs has also been used whereby the researcher recalculates average costs based on some trend measure of output rather than its actual value per period. Demand has also been measured in different ways. Some authors have argued for an essentially monopolistic view of price determination. In this case, levels of/changes in demand have been associated with levels of/changes in prices. Typically, output is used to measure demand here. Some authors have used a perfectly competitive market-price determination model that relates price *changes* to the *level* of excess demand. Others have combined some form of cost variable with an excess demand proxy for demand pressure.

Updating Downward (1999; 2002), Table 16.1 presents a summary of the main studies for the UK grouped broadly according to the way in which costs were measured, although the third column reports the only study adopting a pure excess demand investigation into pricing.

An examination of Table 16.1 reveals some interesting features. First, the studies do not provide definitive evidence that prices are set according to a mark-up rule. The evidence has not produced the 'covering law' aspired to in neoclassical methodology. There is evidence in favor of all of the specifications. This is most apparent in the studies by Neild (1963), Rushdy and Lund (1967) and McCallum (1970). Radically different conclusions are generated using the *same* data set.

Therefore, it would appear at first hand that overall the econometric evidence is not decisive and that one can defend any hypothesis from the data. This might justify the skepticism of those, including Critical Realists, who argue that statistical methods are inherently flawed and that their application is a rather futile exercise that artificially forces open-system reality through a closed-system lens to produce results that demonstrate little agreement. Moreover, Critical Realists would argue that the econometric evidence vindicates their claim that in open systems, universal regularities will not be found.

However, closer examination reveals that the 'qualitative' emphasis of the research clearly suggests that the *balance of the evidence* seems to support the post Keynesian theory of a version of mark-up pricing with weak direct effects of demand on pricing. It might be argued that this claim is somewhat

Table 16.1 A selective summary of econometric studies of UK pricing

Normal cost specification[1]	Actual cost specification	Neoclassical specification[2]
Neild (1963)[3] excess demand no effect (excess demand for labor used to proxy excess demand for output)	Neild (1963) excess demand – no effect	McCallum (1970)[4] 'accords well with the evidence', McCallum comments on Rushdy and Lund that price change is a function of excess demand only
Rushdy and Lund (1967)[4] current and lagged excess demand – no effect	Rushdy and Lund (1967)[3] current and lagged excess demand – significant effect	
Coutts, Godley and Nordhaus (1978) excess demand a small but insignificant effect (deviations of output around trend used to proxy excess demand)	Sawyer (1983)[5] weak effects of demand (the level of demand proxied by output)	
Sylos-Labini (1979) no effect of demand on prices (capacity utilization used to proxy demand)		
Smith (1982) respecifies Coutts, Godley and Nordhaus's normal costs and finds demand now significant	Geroski (1992)[5] supports Sawyer	
Downward (2002a) reconfirms Neild	Downward (1995) supports Sawyer	

Notes:

1. Normal cost transformations are applied to labor costs only, except for Sylos-Labini. The distinction between normal costs and actual costs may be weak in that lagged (that is, averaged) values of the latter, used, for example, by Sawyer and Geroski, may be an indication of the former hypothesis. However, as Rushdy and Lund argue, transformations of costs *prior* to regressions may effectively rule out demand effects.
2. This is termed 'neoclassical' because it adopts a specification where price levels/changes are a function of cumulative levels/current levels of excess demand only.
3. The preferred specification when a number were utilized.
4. These studies used Neild's data – hence basis of excess demand proxy.
5. These were disaggregated studies and noted important heterogeneities in behavior, though generally weak and insignificant demand effects.

bold; however, this hypothesis is supported under a number of criteria. The number of studies reaching this conclusion is persuasive, as is the fact that the supportive studies used more than one specification. Further, the hypothesis holds over data sets, thus reducing the possibility that the hypothesis is highly historically specific. Moreover, Downward (2002) revisited Neild's data using modern time-series econometric methods incorporating cointegration and structural breaks and reached the conclusion that Neild's original findings were supported. Thus, the post Keynesian hypothesis is also supported across a range of techniques.

Thus while no universal regular relationship can be shown to exist – and in open systems, this is to be expected – it is argued that what has been produced by the econometric studies is a rough pattern suggesting that mark-up pricing is used most of the time. In Critical-Realist terms, the econometric work has presented a 'demi-regularity'. Therefore, in contrast to the critics of econometrics, the evidence suggests that econometrics should not be abandoned; rather, econometrics can play a useful role in codifying the empirical level. This codification is essential to the act of making claims about the causal factors that are held by Critical-Realists to exist beneath the empirical level. Econometrics can be seen as increasing the effectiveness of 'retroduction' to the deep, causal mechanisms.

However, as argued in Downward and Mearman (2002a; 2002b), this may require more than the appeal to one isolated study or technique. At this point, the skeptic about econometrics might advocate that, given the inability of econometrics to provide decisive evidence, case studies and other 'qualitative' techniques should *replace* econometrics as the investigative tool. Indeed, the econometric work discussed above was originally motivated by a desire to evaluate the full-cost process of pricing first postulated by qualitative investigation, namely, Hall and Hitch's (1939) work. It is also true that 'qualitative' data requires less closure – but, as argued above, and by Downward and Mearman (2002a; 2002b), it does not avoid closure – and it does not seek out universal regularities. Therefore, in both ways it would appear more appropriate in an open-systems world. However, as Downward (1994; 1999) notes, such 'qualitative' causal research in itself is not straightforward to interpret, and is characterized by terminological and methodological imprecision. For example, three broad clusters can be established from the case study literature. First, many studies consider how firms pursue single or multiple pecuniary goals, such as profits or market share, through a process of personal or institutional adjustment to initial full cost prices in the light of demand pressure. A second group contains studies that recognize that firms also have non-pecuniary objectives. They address, as a general issue, the pursuit of multiple goals by firms. As with the first cluster, the pursuit of firms' goals through price adjustment is described as stemming from personal and informal considerations as well as 'objective' institutional procedures. Third, there are studies which are concerned primarily with the pursuit of pecuniary goals such as profits, but which emphasize 'objective' or institutionally based incremental decision-making processes for adjusting prices. Therefore, the case study literature has performed little better than the econometric evidence in producing a clear picture of firms' pricing. At a general level, it can only be said that there is agreement on the pricing processes that firms follow. Specifically, it is agreed that firms price using a mark-up on full costs, but that mark-ups may change via a variety of organizational mechanisms; however, they are less likely to do so if demand changes.

As argued by Downward and Mearman (2002a; 2002b), in the case above, econometric work can act as a check on the reliability of the attempts to distil a causal analysis from qualitative data. Therefore, the econometric analysis provides a means of adding legitimacy to those claims and (passively) provides a basis from which causal research can begin. The case illustrates that 'retroduction' can be enhanced by the use of econometrics. More importantly, it can be shown that the purported validity of conclusions can be enhanced by analysing data in a number of ways using a number of techniques. As Downward and Mearman (2002a) argue, that approach is in sharp contrast with neoclassical economics, in which 'triangulation' merely involves using the same technique of analysis on different data sets. In the neoclassical case, the aspiration seems to be to count enough cases as to construct a regular relationship, which can be considered universal.

The above analysis applies triangulation to a broad literature. Of course, it is also possible to illustrate the value of triangulation and of econometrics in a particular context, that is, one piece of research. This is the case in Lee and Downward (2000), who re-examine Means's work on administered prices, and Downward (2001), who analyses UK manufacturing using primary survey data. Downward and Mearman (2002c) combine new econometric estimation with Downward's (2001) results and argue for post Keynesian pricing theory. This illustrates triangulation in a single study. However, it should be remembered that in the limit, no research project is conducted in isolation and will be embedded in a wider literature, which will influence the inferences that are drawn.

CONCLUSION

This chapter has three main arguments, two of which are methodological. First, the chapter contributes further to the debate on Critical Realism and empirical methods, and demonstrates the argument that econometrics can play an epistemological role in economic enquiry from a Critical-Realist perspective. Second, and most significantly, the chapter develops and illustrates the argument of Downward and Mearman (2002a; 2002b) that empirical enquiry informed by Critical Realism can and should be based around a pluralist triangulation strategy, in which a range of research methods, including quantitative techniques, are drawn upon, in order to legitimize causal claims from retroduction. Reiterating the claim of Downward and Mearman (2002a), it is held that such a strategy is clearly distinguished from contemporary orthodox approaches, which either perform isolated case studies, or offer repeated trials with the same empirical technique. In contrast, a triangulation strategy places different techniques and investigative contexts at the heart of the act of inference. Ontologically, triangulation reflects an ontology of 'quasi-closed' systems, which deal with the lack of real experimental closure tempered by human attempts to construct institutional and conventional checks on uncertainty. This contrasts with orthodox literature, which either imposes a closure on reality, or engages in eclecticism without ontological license. Epistemologically, triangulation suggests clearly that all techniques are fallible and should not be relied upon in isolation. Moreover, it is held that such a strategy is broadly representative of post Keynesian methodology, as expressed by others such as Sheila Dow.

Third, the chapter illustrates these methodological arguments by drawing upon applied work in post Keynesian pricing. The chapter then concludes by briefly discussing a contemporary example of triangulation (discussed fully in Downward and Mearman, 2002c), which draws broadly on applied work from both an econometric and non-econometric nature. Based on the research reported above one can argue that both the process of price-setting and the behavior of prices that follows can be understood in post Keynesian terms. In this sense the traditional post Keynesian emphasis on – or, in Critical-Realist terms, the retroduction of – mark-up models has some legitimacy: manufacturing pricing behavior can be understood in terms of mark-up pricing processes where mark-ups are adjusted in line with competition.

NOTES

1. It should be noted that these approaches are not particularly mutually exclusive. Thus Hendry's 'general to specific' modeling strategy is employed in Vector-autoregression and cointegration analysis. Likewise, Bayesian ideas have been employed in these contexts.
2. This is perhaps most clear in cointegration analysis which has become wedded to Hendry's approach. Here much pre-analysis of the statistical characteristics of the data precedes any attempt to test economic relationships.
3. Lawson (*passim*) defines an event regularity as being, 'if event (of type) X, then event (of type) Y'. X and Y can be scalars, vectors, or matrices. Lawson (1997, p. 76) expands this original definition to encompass situations in which events are in regular succession within some 'well-behaved' probability distribution.

4. Lawson (1997, p. 24) defines retroduction as, 'the movement, on the basis of analogy and metaphor amongst other things, from a conception of some phenomenon of interest to a conception of some totally different type of thing, mechanism, structure or condition that, at least in part, is responsible for the given phenomenon'.
5. Lawson (1997, p. 219) defines a demi-regularity as, 'a special situation of the open world [... in which ...] certain mechanisms (whether natural or social) reveal themselves in rough and ready patterns ... it is a *special case of this special situation* that the patterns produced correspond to strict event regularities ... ' (emphasis in original).
6. However, as Siegel and Castellan (1988) note, regression and other 'parametric' tests assume the data is distributed across a Normal distribution, prior to testing.
7. There have of course been many other studies of pricing in the UK associated with industrial organization. The studies referred to here focus specifically on the pricing process and not influences from variables measuring the wider market structure.

REFERENCES

Andrews, P.W.S. (1949a), 'A reconsideration of the theory of the individual business', *Oxford Economic Papers*, **1** (January), 54–89.

Andrews, P.W.S. (1949b), *Manufacturing Business*, London: Macmillan.

Andrews, P.W.S. (1964), *On Competition in Economic Theory*, London: Macmillan.

Coutts, K., W. Godley and W. Nordhaus (1978), *Industrial Pricing in the United Kingdom*, Cambridge: Cambridge University Press.

Davidson, P. (1991), 'Is probability theory relevant for uncertainty? A post Keynesian perspective', *Journal of Economic Perspectives*, **5**, 29–43.

Dow, S.C. (1999), 'Post Keynesianism and critical realism: what is the connection?', *Journal of Post Keynesian Economics*, **22**, 15–33.

Dow, S.C. (2002), *Economic Methodology: An Inquiry*, Oxford: Oxford University Press.

Downward, P.M. (1994), 'A reappraisal of case study evidence on business pricing: neoclassical and post Keynesian perspectives', *British Review of Economic Issues*, **16** (39), 23–43.

Downward, P.M. (1995), 'A post Keynesian perspective of UK manufacturing pricing', *Journal of Post Keynesian Economics*, **17** (3), 403–26.

Downward, P.M. (1999), *Post Keynesian Pricing Theory: A Realist Approach*, Cheltenham, UK and Lyme, USA: Edward Elgar.

Downward, P.M. (2001), 'A post Keynesian microeconomic exposition of price stickiness', *Eastern Economic Journal*, **27** (2), 165–82.

Downward, P.M. (2002), 'Revisiting a historical debate on pricing dynamics in the UK: further confirmation of post Keynesian pricing theory', *Journal of Post Keynesian Economics*, **24** (2), 329–44.

Downward, P.M., and A. Mearman (1999), 'Realism and econometrics: alternative perspectives', paper presented to conference of the Association of Heterodox Economics, Nottingham, March.

Downward, P.M., and A. Mearman (2002a), 'Critical realism and econometrics: a constructive dialogue with post Keynesian economics', *Metroeconomica*, **53** (4), 391–415.

Downward, P.M., and A. Mearman (2002b), 'Critical realism and econometrics: interaction between philosophy and post Keynesian practice,' in P.M. Downward (ed.), *Applied Economics and the Critical Realist Critique*, London: Routledge.

Downward, P.M., and A. Mearman (2002c), 'Presenting demi-regularities: the case of

post Keynesian pricing,' in P.M. Downward (ed.), *Applied Economics and the Critical Realist Critique*, London: Routledge.
Downward, P.M., J. Finch and J. Ramsey (2002), 'Critical realism, empirical methods and inference: a critical discussion', *Cambridge Journal of Economics*, **26** (4), 481–500.
Geroski, P.A. (1992), 'Price dynamics in U.K. manufacturing: a microeconomic view', *Economica*, **59**, 403–19.
Hall, R.F., and C.J. Hitch, (1939), 'Price theory and business behavior', *Oxford Economic Papers*, **2**, 13–33.
Haavelmo, T. (1944), 'The probability approach in econometrics', *Econometrica*, **12** (Supplement), 1–118.
Hendry, D. (1995), *Dynamic Econometrics*, Oxford: Oxford University Press.
Kalecki, M. (1954), *Theory of Economic Dynamics*, London: Allen and Unwin.
Kalecki, M. (1964), 'Econometric models and historical materialism', in *Political Economy and Econometrics: Essays in Honour of Oskar Lange*, Warsaw: Polish Scientific Publishers.
Keynes, J.M. (1973), *The Collected Works of John Maynard Keynes*, vol. XIV, London: Macmillan.
Lawson, T. (1985), 'Keynes, prediction and econometrics', in T. Lawson and M.H. Pesaran (eds), *Keynes' Economics: Methodological Issues*, London: Croom Helm.
Lawson, T. (1989), 'Realism and instrumentalism in the development of econometrics', *Oxford Economic Papers* **41** (Supplement), 236–48.
Lawson, T. (1997), *Economics and Reality*, London: Routledge.
Learner, E. (1983), 'Let's take the con out of econometrics', *American Economic Review*, **73** (1), 31–44.
Lee, F.S. (1998), *The Foundations of Post Keynesian Price Theory*, Cambridge: Cambridge University Press.
Lee, F.S., and P.M. Downward (2000), 'Retesting Gardiner Means' evidence on administered prices', *Journal of Economic Issues*, **33** (4), 861–86.
McCallum, B.T. (1970), 'The effect of demand on prices in British manufacturing: another view', *Review of Economic Studies*, **37**, 47–156.
Means, G.C. (1935), 'Industrial prices and their relative inflexibility', US Senate Document 13, 74th Congress, 1st Session, Washington, DC.
Mearman, A. (2002a), *A Contribution to the Methodology of Post Keynesian Economics*, unpublished PhD thesis, University of Leeds.
Mearman, A. (2002b), 'To what extent was Veblen an open systems theorist?', *Journal of Economic Issues*, **36** (2), 573–80.
Mitchell, W. (1991), 'The role of econometrics in a post-Keynesian research programme', unpublished monograph.
Neild, R. (1963), *Pricing and Employment in the Trade Cycle*, Cambridge: Cambridge University Press.
Pagan, A. (1987), 'Three econometric methodologies: a critical appraisal', *Journal of Economic Surveys*, **1**, 3–24.
Pollin, R. (1991), 'Two theories of money supply process: theory and evidence', *Journal of Post Keynesian Economics*, **13** (3) (Spring), 366–96.
Runde, J. (1990), 'Keynesian uncertainty and the weight of arguments', *Economics and Philosophy*, **6**, 275–92.
Rushdy, F., and P.J. Lund (1967), 'The effect of demand on prices in British manufacturing', *Review of Economic Studies*, **33**, 361–74.
Sawyer, M.C. (1983), *Business Pricing and Inflation*, London: Macmillan.

Sayer, A. (1992), *Method and Social Science: A Realist Approach*, London: Routledge.
Siegel, S., and N. Castellan (1988), *Nonparametric Statistics for the Behavioural Sciences*, New York: McGraw-Hill.
Sims, C. (1980), 'Macroeconomics and reality', *Econometrica*, **48**, 1–47.
Smith, G.W (1982), 'The normal cost hypothesis: a reappraisal', in M.J. Artis, C.J. Green, D.L. Leslie and G.W. Smith (eds), *Demand Management, Supply Constraints and Inflation*, Manchester: Manchester University Press.
Sylos-Labini, P. (1979), 'Prices and income distribution in manufacturing industry', *Journal of Post Keynesian Economics*, **11** (1), 3–25.

PART VI

Issues in the History of Thought

17. Analysing and fighting recession with reference to Keynes

Claude Gnos[1]

In recent years New Keynesian writers have commanded the attention of economists and policy-makers by renewing the arguments for government action in favor of demand management. By the same token, they have been credited with restoring the aura of Keynes's economics. This chapter is aimed at challenging this point of view. It is meant to constitute a first stage in a research program the objective of which is to examine just how relevant and effective Keynes's theory of a 'monetary economy of production' – which post Keynesians and Circuitists currently set against the various strands of the neoclassical synthesis – is when it comes to analysing and combating the causes of present-day unemployment.

The first section is dedicated to showing that the New Keynesian approach to employment is not consistent with Keynes's theory of employment as characterized by the principle of effective demand.[2] The second section focuses on the originality of Keynes's view on unemployment and the way to cure it. In conclusion, the final section insists on the contrast between the two approaches.

NEW KEYNESIAN ECONOMICS INCONSISTENT WITH KEYNES'S PRINCIPLE OF EFFECTIVE DEMAND

To make our point, we need consider just two main characteristics of New Keynesian economics (NKE) and contrast them with Keynes's principle of effective demand.

First, it should be remembered that NKE appeared in the 1970s in opposition to the emergence of the New Classical economics which assumed continuous market clearing. New Keynesians hold that price and wage stickiness prevents markets from clearing and so allows shocks in demand (or supply, since employment is supposed to be dependent on the adjustment of supply and demand on market) to divert output and employment from their equilibrium values. They argue that this reasoning is representative of

Keynesian thought, and so makes their own approach consistent with the line laid down by the Old Keynesians. The whole thing may be put into a nutshell in this way:

> To many economists the hallmark of Keynesian economics is the absence of continuous market clearing. In both the old (neoclassical synthesis) and new versions of Keynesian models the failure of prices to change quickly enough to clear markets implies that demand and supply shocks will lead to substantial real effects on the economy's output and employment.
>
> (Snowdon, Vane and Wynarczyk, 1994, p. 288)

Secondly, the difference between Old and New Keynesian economics consists in the fact that the latter version criticizes the former for merely assuming fixed or sticky prices and wages. NKE sets out instead to explain wage and price stickiness with reference to microeconomic behaviors:

> The essential difference between the old and new versions of Keynesian economics is that the models associated with the neoclassical synthesis tended to *assume* a fixed nominal wage, while the attraction of the new Keynesian approach is that it attempts to provide acceptable micro foundations to explain the phenomena of wage and price stickiness.
>
> (Snowdon, Vane and Wynarczyk, 1994, p. 289)[3]

Let us now focus on the principle of effective demand. According to common interpretations underlying both the old and the new versions of what is deemed Keynesian economics, the principle of effective demand consists in a process of adjusting aggregate supply and demand by means of variations in quantities instead of prices and wages. Hence the role assigned in the corresponding models to price and wage fixity or, at least, to their stickiness. With reference to the standard theory of supply and demand it is argued that a decrease in nominal demand would have no substantial effect on the level of employment, and thence on the level of output if prices and wages could adjust rapidly enough. However, this interpretation may be challenged especially if we read the *General Theory* with reference to the 1937 articles on the theory of the rate of interest that Keynes published in the *Economic Journal*.

For one thing, we observe that the principle of effective demand is not a process adjusting supply and demand in the way depicted by the standard theory of supply and demand. In direct relation with what he terms the 'finance motive', Keynes argues that at the very moment when entrepreneurs make their decisions as to the amount of goods they are going to produce (and so as to the amount of employment they are going to provide), individuals have not yet received the money income they will expend in purchases or save and supply for financing the purchase of investment goods by firms. Moreover, he stresses, individuals do not know what their money income will be, especially when it arises out of profit, the latter being dependent on the actual proceeds of the sale of the goods produced (see Keynes, 1936, p. 23):

> There is, however, no such necessity for individuals to decide, contemporaneously with the investment decisions of the entrepreneurs, how much of their future income they are going to save. To begin with, they do not know what their incomes are going to be, especially if they arise out of profit. But even if they form some preliminary opinion on the matter, in the first place they are under no necessity to make a definite decision (as the investors have to do), in the second place they do not make it at the same time, and in the third place they most undoubtedly do not, as a rule, deplete their existing cash well ahead of their receiving the incomes out of which they propose to save …
>
> (Keynes, 1937c, pp. 216–17)

So, Keynes argues that there are no separate *ex ante* supply and demand forces encompassing the behavior of entrepreneurs and individuals, adjusting to each other, and determining the level of employment (and thence of income and output). As he puts it: '*Ex ante* decisions in their influence on effective demand relate solely to *entrepreneurs*' decisions' (Keynes, 1937a, pp. 182–3). Entrepreneurs have to make decisions that take into account decisions by consumers at a time when consumers are unable to make any decisions. In price theory, on the contrary, the demand schedule is not simply anticipated by sellers of goods: it depicts purchase decisions that buyers are prepared to make depending on prices. Thus, in total contrast to NKE, Keynes eschewed all reference to the standard theory of supply and demand. This is notably a justification of the emphasis post Keynesian literature famously places on the role of entrepreneurs' expectations in a world of radical uncertainty and historical time. According to the principle of effective demand, entrepreneurs, who have to decide on their scale of production, are condemned to forecast demand which will enter the equation only later on, that is after wages have been paid and goods produced.

For another thing, Keynes states that the payment of factor costs does not absorb any pre-existent resources but on the contrary forms the income that is going to be spent on the goods produced. With reference to common practice which shows that banks are able to finance firms' spending by creating money *ex nihilo*, he argues that '"finance" has nothing to do with saving … It does not absorb or exhaust any resource' (Keynes, 1937b, p. 209). This confirms that the reference to the standard theory of supply and demand, and thence the reference to price and wage fixity or stickiness, is irrelevant here. If wages are cut by, say, one half, then the income that individuals can spend is cut proportionately. Wage flexibility would in no way improve employment.

However, at this point, one may object that low wages mean high profits, so that cutting wages would improve profits and thus encourage entrepreneurs to step up their scale of production (or at least not to diminish it when nominal demand decreases). It is true that the level of prices being given, low wages mean high profits. But to assume that the level of prices remains fixed when wages are cut is to beg the question. This is so because demand is fueled by income. We explained above that the principle of effective demand does not draw on the standard theory of supply and demand. This does not mean, however, that this latter theory is irrelevant as regards the determination of prices on goods markets. There is no doubt then that prices cannot be maintained at their previous level when the amount of money buyers dispose of decreases. Or, if prices could be maintained, quantities sold would decline, as would overall nominal sales. Moreover, in keeping with the logic of the principle of effective demand, profits are incomes transferred from factors' income to firms:[4] entrepreneurs earn them at the expense of buyers on the market when prices exceed factor costs (profits are derived from the excess of the proceeds of sales over factor costs, cf. Keynes, 1936, pp. 23–5). Thus, profits are not a source of demand determined independently of wages. They cannot replace reduced money wages in fueling demand on the market, and consequently we can safely confirm that cutting wages does nothing to improve employment.

All things considered, we now better understand why Keynes ignored the possible effect of wage and price flexibility on employment when he stated the principle of effective demand. In fact, this principle can in no way be reduced to the process of adjustment of supply and demand on markets. Keynes's theory stands in sharp contrast to the New Keynesian models based on the neoclassical synthesis. In a 'monetary economy of production', as Keynes puts it, the actual sequence starts with unilateral decisions made by entrepreneurs in accordance with their expected costs and proceeds. Moreover, costs and proceeds are directly related to each other because the payment of factor costs forms the income which is going to be spent on goods markets. Contrary to what NKE argues, then, wage flexibility is irrelevant: to cut wages is to cut spending on the market.

The prevalence of the mainstream view that confines Keynes's originality to adjusting quantities instead of prices is all the more surprising because Keynes put his case very plainly. In chapter 19 in the *General Theory*, he highlights the role that money–wage flexibility plays in classical theory:

> The argument simply is that a reduction in money-wages will *cet. par.* stimulate demand by diminishing the price of the finished product, and will therefore increase output and employment up to the point where the reduction which labour has agreed to accept in its money-wages is just offset by the diminishing marginal efficiency of labour as output (from a given equipment) is increased.
>
> (Keynes, 1936, p. 257)

Keynes then undertakes to rebut this theory. His main point is that the above argument is 'tantamount to assuming that the reduction in money-wages will leave demand unaffected' (ibid., p. 258), which is a highly questionable assumption in his view. He had already concluded, in chapter 8, that 'if the wage-unit changes, the expenditure on consumption corresponding to a given level of employment will, like prices, change in the same proportion' (ibid., p. 92). He acknowledges, however, that in certain circumstances a reduction in money-wages can stimulate production but he comes to this conclusion with reference to his own analysis, that is the principle of effective demand and its determining factors (notably the propensity to consume), which he in no way shares with the classics: 'A reduction in money-wages is quite capable in certain circumstances of affording a stimulus to output, as the classical theory supposes. My difference from this theory is primarily a difference of analysis' (ibid., p. 257). Keynes could hardly more explicitly exhibit his dismissal of the Classical framework by which employment is supposed to be determined through the adjustment of supply and demand on markets.[5] By the same token, he also refutes in advance the Old and the New Keynesian interpretations of his theory.

THE ORIGINALITY OF KEYNES'S VIEW ON UNEMPLOYMENT AND ITS CURE

The fact that the payment of wages fuels demand does not imply that the proceeds from sales are necessarily equal to the costs paid. As we briefly mentioned above, the principle of effective demand is tied in with a theory of income distribution whereby profits are a redistributed share of wages, this share being transferred from purchasers to firms when prices exceed factor costs. So, entrepreneurs offer the output at a supply price which exceeds their factor cost, and determine the employment they provide in such a way that, according to their expectations, their profit is at a maximum: 'entrepreneurs will endeavour to fix the amount of employment at the level which they expect to maximize the excess of the proceeds over the factor cost' (Keynes, 1936, p. 25). The proceeds of sales may also be lower than factor costs, in which case entrepreneurs are unable to recoup in full the outlays spent to start production: they experience losses. This means that their expectations were wrong and that they have to cut the scale of their production.

How does demand deficiency fit into the picture? To examine this issue, let us suppose that entrepreneurs are mistaken in their expectations about proceeds. This means that they were wrong when estimating in advance the amount of the different goods that would be demanded at the prevailing supply prices, and they presently offer goods in excess of demand. One way to find additional buyers, then, although not, of course, to prevent the proceeds of sales from decreasing, is to cut prices. New Keynesians concentrate on this point arguing that a simultaneous cut in wages and prices would allow entrepreneurs to maintain their present scale of production with lower costs allowing lower supply prices and so boosting demand. As emphasized earlier, this is not Keynes's view: the principle of effective demand is alien to price determination on markets. This divergence between the two approaches has important consequences for the analysis of the causes of unemployment and the ways to cure it.

New Keynesians, as Stiglitz (1993) points out, are not much interested in examining why demand may be deficient: they just need to assume that some exogenous 'shock' in demand occurs. As said above, their point is that price and wage stickiness allows shocks in demand to effect the economy's output and employment. It is true, however, that some writers consider that wage and price rigidities are not essential. For instance, Greenwald and Stiglitz (1993) explain that, on the contrary, price flexibility may have a negative impact on firms' output during recession periods because it increases the risk of bankruptcy at a time when many firms are being denied access to equity finance because of asymmetric information and so are unable to diversify their way out of the risks they face. However, the method remains unchanged: market imperfections are supposed to allow shocks to have an impact on production.[6] What matters, here, is the way the economy responds to shocks in demand or, as mentioned earlier, in supply.

In Keynes's theory of employment, on the contrary, the very source of demand insufficiency deserves careful attention, irrespective of the way markets function and even irrespective of the fact that entrepreneurs may accurately forecast sales proceeds.[7] The formulation of the principle of effective demand is tied in with a possible discrepancy between what Keynes terms 'the propensity to consume' and 'the inducement to invest'. As said above, the payment of factor costs by entrepreneurs forms money incomes (wages and also profits that are derived from the former) which fuel demand on the goods markets. Naturally, part of these money incomes are going to be saved by their recipients (in greater proportion as real income is increasing). Nonetheless, saving does not necessarily mean low demand if the income saved is borrowed by entrepreneurs who spend it in buying investment goods. This is Keynes's point: demand may be deficient if the current amount of investment is not sufficient to absorb the excess of money income available (or output, that is, real income) over consumption:

> The outline of our theory can be expressed as follows. When employment increases, aggregate real income is increased. The psychology of the community is such that when aggregate real income is increased aggregate consumption is

> increased, but not by so much as income. Hence employers would make a loss if the whole of the increased employment were to be devoted to satisfying the increased demand for immediate consumption. Thus, to justify any given amount of employment there must be an amount of current investment sufficient to absorb the excess of total output over what the community chooses to consume when employment is at the given level. For unless there is this amount of investment, the receipts of the entrepreneurs will be less than is required to induce them to offer the given amount of employment.
>
> (Keynes, 1936, p. 27)

All things considered, the originality of Keynes's view on unemployment is very clear. Unemployment has nothing to do with market imperfections. As Keynes puts it: 'The essential character of the argument is precisely the same whether or not money-wages, etc., are liable to change' (ibid., p. 27). According to Keynes, the payment of factor costs by firms generates incomes which, contrary to what Say's law asserts, are not necessarily spent on goods, whether consumption goods or investment goods. The level of aggregate demand is therefore likely to be an obstacle to full employment (cf. Keynes, 1936, pp. 25–32). This view leads Keynes, notably in his concluding notes to the *General Theory* (Keynes, 1936, pp. 372–84), to carefully distinguish between intervention by the state, which should be involved in determining effective demand, and the free play of economic forces, which should be left to determine the other economic variables. All this is undoubtedly in sharp contrast to the New Keynesian approach, according to which government demand management policies are needed because market imperfections allow shocks in demand or supply to reduce employment, and which advocates institutional reforms destined to improve markets' workings.

CONCLUSION

Emphasis here has been on the contrast between Keynes's own theory of employment and the general framework of NKE, which claims to be representative of Keynesian economics. What is really at issue is nothing less than the interpretation of Keynes's principle of effective demand.

Contrary to common interpretations underlying both the old and the new versions of the standard Keynesian models, we have argued that the principle of effective demand is alien to the process of adjustment of supply and demand on markets. This is why, in Keynes's view, the state of demand deserves attention in its own right and calls for demand management policies regardless of the regime characterizing markets (perfect or imperfect competition, wages and prices flexibility or stickiness). For New Keynesians, on the contrary, a decrease in nominal demand (a 'shock' in demand) only matters in so far as wage and price stickiness on markets prevents the economy from returning to equilibrium, and so demand management policies are a means to make up for market shortcomings. Thus, clarifying the contrast between Keynes's theory of employment and the way it is commonly interpreted cannot fail to constitute a crucial step towards a reappraisal of Keynes's proposals on economic policy.

NOTES

1. I thank L. Randall Wray and participants to The Seventh International Post Keynesian Conference for helpful comments. The usual disclaimer applies.
2. On this issue, see also P. Davidson (1998).
3. See also Mankiw (1990) and Mankiw and Romer (1991, p. 149): 'According to Keynesian economics, fluctuations in employment and output arise largely from fluctuations in nominal aggregate demand. The reason that nominal shocks matter is that nominal wages and prices are not fully flexible … The research program described here is modest in the sense that it seeks to strengthen the foundations of this conventional thinking, not to provide a new theory of fluctuations. In particular, its goal is to answer the theoretical question of how nominal rigidities arise from optimizing behavior, since the absence of an answer in the 1970s was largely responsible for the decline of Keynesian economics.'
4. See Gnos (1998).
5. 'At the heart of Keynes's economics is a theoretical critique of both the theories of value and distribution underlying the traditional macroeconomic programme – the language of markets is theoretically invalid at the macroeconomic level' (Rotheim, 1998, p. 68).
6. This is also the case in the 'Strong New Keynesian Economics', which focuses on coordination failures (cf. Rotheim, 1998, p. 52).
7. As Keynes puts it: 'the theory of effective demand is substantially the same if we assume that short-term expectations are always fulfilled' (1937a, p. 181).

REFERENCES

Davidson, P. (1998), 'Setting the record straight', in Roy J. Rotheim (ed.), *New Keynesian Economics/Post Keynesian Alternatives*, London and New York: Routledge, pp. 15–38.

Gnos, C. (1998), 'The Keynesian identity of income and output', in Albert Jolink and Philippe Fontaine (eds), *Historical Perspectives on Macroeconomics: 60 Years After the General Theory*, London and New York: Routledge.

Greenwald, B.C., and J.E. Stiglitz (1993), 'Financial markets imperfections and business cycles', *Quarterly Journal of Economics*, **108**, 77–114.

Keynes, J.M. (1936), *The General Theory of Employment, Interest and Money*, reprinted in Donald Moggridge (ed.) (1971), *The Collected Writings of John Maynard Keynes*, London: Macmillan.

Keynes, J.M. (1937a), 'Ex post and ex ante', reprinted in Donald Moggridge (ed.) (1973), 'The General Theory and After', Part II, 'Defence and Development', *The Collected Writings of John Maynard Keynes*, London: Macmillan.

Keynes, J.M. (1937b), 'Alternative theories of the rate of interest', *Economic Journal*, June, reprinted in Donald Moggridge (ed.) (1973), 'The General Theory and after',

Part II, 'Defence and development', *The Collected Writings of John Maynard Keynes*, London: Macmillan.

Keynes, J.M. (1937c), 'The "ex ante" theory of the rate of interest', *Economic Journal*, December, reprinted in Donald Moggridge (ed.) (1973), 'The General Theory and after', Part II, 'Defence and development', *The Collected Writings of John Maynard Keynes*, London: Macmillan.

Mankiw, N.G. (1990), 'A quick refresher course in macroeconomics', *Journal of Economic Literature*, **28**, 1645–60.

Mankiw, N.G., and D. Romer (eds) (1991), *New Keynesian Economics*, Cambridge, MA: MIT Press.

Rotheim, Roy J. (1998), 'New Keynesian macroeconomics and markets', in Roy J. Rotheim (ed.), *New Keynesian Economics/Post Keynesian Alternatives*, London and New York: Routledge, pp. 51–70.

Snowdon, B., H. Vane, and P. Wynarczyk (1994), *A Modern Guide to Macroeconomics*, Aldershot, UK and Brookfield, US: Edward Elgar.

Stiglitz, Joseph E. (1993), *Economics*, New York: W.W. Norton.

18. From Say's law to Keynes, from Keynes to Walras's law: some ironies in the history of economic thought

Antonio Carlos Macedo e Silva[1]

Produce, supply, sell, buy: the inflection of a few verbs is sufficient to express the essential phenomena of a mercantile economy. This simplicity is, however, illusory. Even though these actions are carried out self-confidently by individuals, the conjugation of the verbs, in the discourse of economists, is far from being a trivial task. Impasses and controversies surround issues which can only be deemed basic.

There is, for instance, an insuperable disagreement regarding the definition of the essential properties of a mercantile economy. Mercantile, and *therefore* monetary, according to Marxists, Institutionalists and post Keynesians (monetary and therefore non-ergodic, the latter would add; see Davidson, 1982). Nevertheless, the hegemonic tradition intrepidly proceeds, clinging to the conception of the mercantile economy as being essentially an economy of direct exchanges (see, for instance, the assessment by Hahn, 1982).

The law of markets is one of the recurrent themes in economic debate. Over the past decades, a large number of interpreters have sought to establish the 'final truth' regarding it. The debate carried out by the mainstream proceeded, essentially, to rehabilitate the law, exempting it from the criticism of Keynes. In Schumpeter (1954), it becomes a precursor of Keynesian macroeconomics. In Becker and Baumol (1952/60) it coincides with the notion, essential to the neoclassical synthesis, of the existence of a price level compatible with general equilibrium. It is '*the beginning of sound thinking in macroeconomics*', for Blaug (1962, p. 149) and, in the opinion of Clower and Leijonhufuvd (1973), it is an essential proposition for the elaboration of any economic theory. In its more recent transmutation, it is seen as a predecessor to the New Keynesian theories on economic fluctuations or as a full-fledged classical theory of recession and involuntary unemployment, perversely disfigured by Keynes's interpretation (see Jonsson, 1997; Kates, 1997; 1998).

The aim of this chapter is to carry out a criticism of this criticism, from a Keynesian point of view. The interest of the theme greatly exceeds that of mere exegesis. After all, the debate surrounding the law and its interpretation by Keynes has never lost sight of its possible implications for theory. Criticism of Keynes as an interpreter is, in most cases, inseparable from criticism of Keynes as a theorist.

The main proposition presented in this chapter is that Keynes's thesis that Say's law is equivalent to the identity between aggregate supply and demand seems consistent with a careful reading of Say, James Mill and Ricardo (which does not imply that it is the only sustainable interpretation of the law, or that it encompasses all the propositions in some way related to it). It is suggested, however, that it is doubtful that the dichotomy between the law and the principle of effective demand was in fact able, in Keynes's time (and even more so today) to draw the line between 'orthodox' and 'heterodox' economists. Maybe the law of markets should be seen merely as a particular example (and of the less brilliant kind) of 'equilibrism' (to borrow the term from Hicks, 1975).[2]

The interpretation of the law by the mainstream is the object of the first two sections.[3] The third and fourth items resort to the classical texts in order to found the interpretation of the law as an identity between aggregate supply and demand. The fifth item formulates some hypotheses that may help to explain the profusion of propositions related to the law, a fact that has contributed to the persistence and the confusion in the debate surrounding the law. This is followed by a brief conclusion, containing some considerations on the opposition between Say's law and the principle of effective demand.

1 SAY AS A PRECURSOR OF KEYNES

In 1954, in the *History of Economic Analysis*, Schumpeter (1954, p. 617) wrote that 'Say's law is obviously true. Nevertheless, it is neither trivial nor unimportant'. From the point of view of studies in the history of economic thought, this was an important turning point. Paradoxically, in Schumpeter's interpretation, Say becomes a precursor of Keynes and of macroeconomic analysis.

According to Schumpeter (1954, p. 617) the law is the direct result of the interrelations between the producers who act in an economy distinguished by the *vertical* division of labour. The perception that production determines the generation of income flows would have permitted a triumph of logic against the simplistic and irrational underconsumption thesis diffuse among non-economists. Schumpeter's argument was subsequently taken up by Blaug (1962: 149):

> Production increases not only the supply of goods, but, by virtue of the requisite cost payments to the factors of production, also creates the demand to purchase

> these goods ... The demand for the output of any one industry must increase in real terms when the supplies of all industries increase, since these are precisely what generates demand for that industry's products. Say's law, therefore, warns us not to apply to macroeconomic variables propositions derived from microeconomic analysis.

There could be no greater irony than the transformation of Say into the pioneer of criticism of the fallacies of composition (Schumpeter, 1954, pp. 623–4). The privileged object of Keynesian demonology is converted into the patron saint of macroeconomic theory!

Baumol's article of 1977 is one of the perpetuators of the imbroglio initiated by Schumpeter. Baumol identifies (at least, he writes) eight Say's laws. According to the first, 'a community's purchasing power is limited by and is equal to its output, because production provides the means by which outputs can be purchased' (Baumol, 1977, p. 147)'. Baumol adds that this proposition just 'tells us, as Keynes did, that output is the source of effective demand – that output is purchasing power. But it does *not* say that all of that purchasing power will always be used to buy goods'.[4]

The hypothesis that Say's aims were so modest is simply astonishing. The concepts of the increase of wealth through the flow of production (and not through the accumulation of the stock of precious metals) and of the identity between production and income precede Say and Ricardo, and even Smith. It is hard to understand how the law of markets, in this minimalist form, could have deserved the enthusiastic allusion by Ricardo in the preface of the *Principles*, and have aroused such a polemic.

Leaving exegesis aside, this interpretation is also debatable from a strictly theoretical point of view. The positions of Baumol, Becker and Blaug are evidence that, even today, the meaning of the accounting identity between production and income can give rise to great confusion, when propositions of theoretical nature are introduced in a somewhat unthinking and tacit manner.

Such is the case of the propositions according to which purchasing power is limited by income and additional production instantaneously generates the exact purchasing power with which it can be purchased. Besides being unnecessary for the solution of the underconsumptionist challenge, they may be inconsistent with a Keynesian view of capitalism as a monetary economy.

The concept of income must be understood as the *monetary* flow derived by an agent as a result of his participation in the production of wealth. Considering the Keynesian period of production as a unit of time, we find that some of the flows of income generated by the decision of production are generated *ex ante*, such as wages and payments to the producers of inputs. On the other hand, part of the capitalists' profit is necessarily of an *ex post* nature, for it cannot be calculated before the proceeds from the sales are known. Therefore, the mere act of production *never* generates by itself an amount of income equivalent to the total proceeds expected by the capitalist. For the same reasons, it cannot be affirmed that production generates purchasing power equal to its expected value (at least, not *immediate* purchasing power; see Possas, 1987).[5]

To avoid the conclusions above, we would have to redefine the concept of income, in order to incorporate the concept of expected profit, calculated according to the present value attributed by the capitalist to his stocks of goods, both finished and undergoing processing. (In this case, however, we would also have to ascribe to an unemployed worker an income equivalent to the value he attributes to his labor.) Along the same line, we would have to affirm that a good is purchasing power owing to its *potential* of conversion into money. However, these solutions seek to bypass what is essential to mercantile production: the fact that only the sale can confirm whether – and in what measure – the production 'contains' new wealth (and, therefore, income); the fact that only money is immediate purchasing power. In this sense they are equivalent to the concept of the capitalist economy essentially as a barter economy with low transaction costs.

Clearly, the proposition that the increase in production does not, by itself, generate the income necessary to buy it does not bring us back to the universe of underconsumptionism – to the concept that the reproduction of the capitalist system faces, at each step, the 'problem of realization'. On the one hand, because the income effectively generated by the expenditure – for instance, the expenditure created by the decision of production – is gained in the form of money that can return to circulation (generating more income) an indefinite number of times. On the other, for the simple reason that purchasing power is a stock (augmentable through credit creation and capital gains) and therefore does not necessarily derive from current income. There is no realization problem intrinsic to capitalism. There always exists enough purchasing power to buy production, however large it may be (which does not imply that production will effectively be bought). But the fact that productive activity triggers off flows of income is only responsible for part of the explanation.[6] Production is only one of the sources of effective demand.[7]

In any case, neither Say nor the other defenders of the law contented themselves with the affirmation that, after all, capitalism is not impossible. The preoccupation in describing the nature of possible unbalances between supply and demand and in establishing the adjustment mechanisms between them pervades the polemic around the 'general glut'. However, before discussing this point, we will see how another interpretative line evolved, preoccupied with the relation between the law of markets and Walras' law.

2 SAY'S LAW AND WALRAS'S LAW

In 1944, an article by Lange defined the terms of the modern debate. He employed a small apparatus of general equilibrium in order to compare what he called Walras's law to his interpretation of Say's law, and to explore the implications of the latter.

Walras's law affirms that the aggregate demand for all goods (including the one used as money) is identical to aggregate supply. Lange observes that 'Walras' law does not require that the demand and supply of each commodity, or any of them, be in equilibrium' (Lange, 1944, p. 150). That is, Walras's law is defined as an *ex ante* identity between aggregate supply and demand.

In turn, Say's law is taken as a (stronger) proposition in which the aggregate demand for all the n-1 goods (goods and services, excluding money) is identical to the aggregate supply of these goods. This implies that the supply and demand for nth good – 'money' – are identical.

In my opinion, the proposition according to which the sum of the excesses of demand in the different markets of goods and services is necessarily equal to zero only transposes into modern language the proposition frequently and forcefully stated by Say, Ricardo and others, according to which there is no general glut. In the article, Lange is not preoccupied with the possible dynamic implications resulting from the existence of excess demand different from zero in one or more markets, except in the terms in which these implications are treated by the classical supporters of the law of markets.[8]

Lange's interpretation, developed by Patinkin, was rejected by Becker and Baumol (1952/60). With this article, Becker and Baumol founded a new line of interpretation of Say's law that would be continued in works such as those of Clower (1963/65), Baumol (1977) and Clower and Leijonhufvud (1973). Common to all these authors is the greater or lesser assimilation of the law of markets to Walras's law, with the latter understood in similar terms to those used by Lange.

According to Becker and Baumol, the interpretation of the law of markets as an identity ('Say's identity') does not find support in the classical texts. 'Say's Equality' – that is, the law itself, correctly interpreted – would be limited to establishing that

> 'supply will create its own demand' not despite the behavior of the price level but because of it ... The Cambridge equation implies that for every relative price structure there exists a unique absolute price level at which the money market will be in equilibrium (Say's equality). This is equivalent to stating that for every set of relative prices there exists a price level which brings about *over-all* equilibrium in the commodity markets, i.e., the total quantity of money offered for commodities is equal to the total value of commodities supplied.
>
> (Becker and Baumol, 1952/60, p. 758)

The law (or equality) of Say, in this interpretation, corresponds to a particular case of Walras's law, that in which in the goods markets, taken as a whole, the excess demand is equal to zero (as in the money market). It is a particular case because Walras's law does not exclude the possibility of disequilibrium in two, several or, even, in all markets. It does not exclude, in particular, the possibility of general overproduction, understood as a situation in which the excess supply of goods corresponds to an excess demand for money. In a situation such as this one, the fall of the prices of goods would generate a wealth-effect (Becker and Baumol, 1952/60, p. 758), re-establishing the general equilibrium (and, therefore, Say's equality).

This reasoning leads to a conclusion that, although not explicit, is obvious: Say's law, already in the nineteenth century, established the theoretical defeat (and *avant la lettre*!) of Keynes by the Neoclassical Synthesis (see Blaug, 1962, p. 157). The contribution of the *General Theory* would have consisted of arousing a debate through which, endowed with the instruments created by Keynes himself, the 'classical' economists (in the Keynesian sense) affirm the continuity of their tradition regarding the essential points of the doctrine.[9]

In the works of Clower and Leijonhufvud, the relation between Say's law and Walras's law is even stronger. They formulate 'Say's principle', based on which they intend to 'resolve all issues of substance associated with earlier discussions of Say's Law (Clover and Leijonhufvud, 1973, p. 146). The principle establishes that 'the net value of an individual's planned trades is identically zero' (Clower and Leijonhufvud, 1973, p. 146). This means simply that the agent intends to realize transactions compatible with his budget restriction – he does not steal, donate money or err in his budget calculations.

The aggregate version of the principle is, according to the authors, formally equal to Walras's law: 'the money value of the sum of all aggregate EDs [excess demand] is identically equal to zero' (Clower and Leijonhufvud, 1973, p. 152). Because it is omissive regarding the issues of the existence (of a price vector compatible with general equilibrium) and stability (Clower and Leijonhufvud, 1973, p. 158), the principle is 'consistent with indefinite persistence of unemployment on a large scale, for it involves no assumptions and yields no implications about the dynamic adjustment behavior of the economic system' (Clower and Leijonhufvud, 1973, p. 156). One of the few implications of the principle would be the impossibility of general overproduction, if this is defined as an excess supply of all goods and assets, including money (Clower and Leijonhufvud, 1973, p. 153)

To sum up, this brief history of the metamorphoses of the law of markets shows us how it was successively interpreted as an identity consistent with a non-monetary interpretation of a mercantile economy (Lange), as a specific case of Walras's law in which there is equilibrium in both goods and money markets (Becker and Baumol) and as a purely logical statement, necessary to the construction of any economic theory and independent of the formulation of any equilibrium condition (Clower and Leijonhufvud)

It is time to let the classical economists take the stand.

3 THE LAW OF MARKETS AND THE REPRODUCTION OF THE SYSTEM

For authors such as Say and James Mill, the law of markets is much more than an affirmation that there is always sufficient purchasing power to buy production (so that there would be no obstacles to the long-run growth of the economy). Their concern undoubtedly encompasses the problem of the reproducibility of the capitalist economy, but it goes well beyond this;[10] for them, this reproducibility is founded in a non-monetary theory of production (which, in turn, has as one of its possible implications the theory of the impossibility of a general glut, a point to be dealt with in the next item).

It is interesting to observe how Say, in one of his letters to Malthus, presents his law of markets:

> All those who, since Adam Smith, have turned their attention to Political Economy, agree that in reality we do not buy articles of consumption with money, the circulating medium with which we pay for them. We must in the first instance have bought this money itself by the sale of our produce ... From these premises I have drawn a conclusion ... the consequences of which appear to have alarmed you. I had said: As no one can purchase the produce of another except with his own produce; as the amount for which we can buy is equal to that which we can produce, the more we produce the more we will purchase. From whence proceeds this other conclusion, which you refuse to admit, that if certain commodities do not sell, it is because others are not produced, and that it is the raising produce alone which opens a market for the sale of produce.
>
> (Say, 1820, pp. 440–41; revised translation, based on Say, 1821)

Say is evidently referring to a mercantile economy, characterized by private production and by the social division of labor. In this economy, goods are produced for sale; the goods produced privately must be exchanged for money. Given this starting point, there are many possible questions. To one of them Say replies in a very particular way and, thus establishes the law of markets: what explains the decisions to produce?

The first step consists of emphasizing his affiliation to the Smithian theory of money. Wealth is not treasure, rather production that is continually renewed. Money is merely 'the agent of the transfer of values', performing 'but a momentary function' (Say, 1819, pp. 56–7). The monetary veil merely disguises what is in essence a barter economy.[11] The relevant – *real* – process is that by which each producer aggregates new wealth to the social product, giving himself credentials to obtain from others those goods he wants to make use of.

'From these premises', he extracts two assertions that, in my view, define the law and are aptly synthesized by the formula 'supply creates its own demand'. The first of them – 'the more we can produce the more we can purchase' – posits that the producer's purchasing power comes solely from the sale of the production (thus, it is equivalent to his income flow). The second – 'the more we produce the more we will purchase' – refers to the aim of the producer in a mercantile economy.[12] Production is not geared to selling (so as to obtain money),[13] but to buying.

In various passages, James Mill does indeed seem to cut out the selling stage, identifying production and purchasing power:

> We have already seen, that every man, who produces, has a wish for other commodities, than those which he has produced, to the extent of all that he brings to market ... His will, therefore, to purchase, and his means of purchasing, in other words, his demand, is exactly equal to the amount of what he has produced and does not mean to consume.
>
> (Mill, 1844, p. 231)[14]

Leaving Mill's imprecision aside,[15] the value each producer *hopes* to obtain with the *commodities* he produces corresponds to a given basket of *commodities* that he *desires*. The definition of this basket precedes and determines the decision to produce. The acquisitive desire of the collectivity determines the total volume of production, in any given period. Now, if for each producer the expected value of his production is equivalent to the value of the demand for other goods that *he hopes to effectuate*, on aggregate, each 'increase in supply will inevitably be a sign of an increase in demand of equal value.[16]

Say's law thus establishes an *ex ante identity* between the expected values of aggregate supply and demand.[17] To achieve this, it seems to dispense with any temporal clause: the identity between supply and demand is created with the decisions to produce, necessarily and instantaneously (see Mill, 1844, p. 237). However, up , to this point the law constitutes only an aprioristic and non-verifiable declaration as to the producers' motivation, consistent with *any* empirical result. Today's production represents a demand – whose temporality is not specified – for other goods. It does not matter that one or many sell and do not buy; they will buy 'tomorrow' or bequeath the money to their heirs for them to do so.

In fact, the law of markets calls for a more ample scope. For this reason, it must inevitably make a pronouncement on the question of time and offer a proposition, *ex post* in character, on the nature of the adjustment between supply and demand. It is only possible to do it by means of a more precise specification of the role of money and of the temporality of the demand for goods that is made explicit by the very decision to produce.

As will be seen below, the law of markets is saved from innocuousness by the inclusion of a temporal clause that is equivalent to restricting money to its function of means of circulation. This amounts to positing that the general glut is a logical impossibility. Additional conjectures, of an equilibristic nature, imply an in-built mechanism to prevent partial gluts from becoming generalized. The last sentence in Say's quotation – 'if certain commodities do not sell ... ' – announces the theme.

4 THE LAW OF MARKETS, MONEY AND PARTIAL DISEQUILIBRIUM

It is worthwhile noting that in Smith there is some ambiguity in the recognition of the liquidity premium of money.[18] In Say, the conceptual knot is unceremoniously undone:

> It is worthwhile to remark, that a product is no sooner created, than it, from that instant, affords a market for other products to the full extent of its own value. When the producer has put the finishing hand to his product, he is most anxious to sell it immediately, lest its value should diminish in his hands. Nor is he less anxious to dispose of the money he may get for it; for the value of money is also perishable.[19] But the only way of getting rid of money is in the purchase of some product or other. Thus, the mere circumstance of the creation of one product immediately opens a vent for other products.
>
> (Say, 1819, p. 57)

The issue of the convenience of carrying money disappears. The period of retention of money in its active function of means of circulation seems to tend to zero.[20] If every supplier of goods intends to immediately convert 'the money he may get for' his product into another product, the general glut is really inconceivable. Once again, it is worth resorting to James Mill. Supply must convert itself into demand within the 'annual' cycle of production and consumption:[21]

> In speaking here of demand and supply, it is evident that we speak of aggregates. When we say of any particular nation, at any particular time, that its supply is equal to its demand (...) [w]e mean, that the amount of its demand, in all commodities taken together, is equal to the amount of its supply in all commodities taken together.
>
> (Mill, 1844, p. 230)

> What is it that we mean, when we say the demand of a nation, speaking of the aggregate, and including a definite circle of production and consumption, such as

> that of a year? Do we, or can we, mean any thing but its power of purchasing? And what is its power of purchasing? Of course, the goods which come to markets. What, on the other hand, is it we mean, when, speaking in like manner aggregately, and including the same circle, we say the supply of the nation? Do we, or can we mean any thing, but the goods which come to market?
>
> (Mill, 1844, p. 238)[22]

In these extracts, as in many others, the understanding of the law of markets as an *ex ante* identity between the supply and demand of goods is clearly evident[23] (and one begins to discern the existence of important *ex post* implications). There is little need to highlight the similarity with the interpretations of Keynes and Lange. Strangely enough, the interpreters discussed in section 2 of this text flatly refuse to admit the plausibility of this interpretation (not even included by Baumol as one of his many Say's laws). Nevertheless, the central argument employed by Say, James Mill and Ricardo in the polemic of the general glut – certainly one of the most important economic controversy of the nineteenth century – is precisely that of the identity between supply and demand!

According to Say and James Mill, production is geared towards sale.[24] A sale should be followed almost immediately by a purchase. What happens, then, when the sale does not take place? For the law to be 'effective' – in the sense of allowing inference with regard to *ex post* variables – it is necessary to show the existence and efficiency of some kind of adjustment mechanism.

Undoubtedly, the law does not intend to determine the results of each producer's decision to produce, or of whole segments of the economy, taken individually. There is no mechanism that guarantees, *ex ante*, the consistence between the composition of supply and the composition of aggregate demand. Sectoral disequilibria between supply and demand – partial glut – are perfectly admissible.[25] In fact, the law is intended to dispute the possibility of general overproduction: 'Inability to sell, therefore, arises not from overabundance but from misallocation of the factors of production' (Say, 1803, *apud* Baumol, 1977: 156).[26]

The affirmation is presented as a corollary of the basic hypothesis of production geared towards buying. If the purchasing power that the producers expect to be contained in the produced goods is equal to the demand they intend to effectuate, if the set of decisions of production is related to a certain composition of demand, disequilibria between supply and demand imply an excess of some products and scarcity of others: 'It is observable ... that precisely at the same time that one commodity makes a loss, another commodity is making excessive profit' (Say, 1819, p. 57).

James Mill, far from criticizing Say, was happy to paraphrase his reasoning.[27] In the case of a partial glut, caused by the increase in the production of some goods,

> [t]hese goods would fall in exchangeable value as compared with others, others would rise in exchangeable value as compared with them. But there is a new demand created; for the owner of the new produce, as he has come into the market to sell goods of some kinds, so he has come to buy goods of some other kinds. As the supply, which he brought, of certain kinds of goods tended to reduce their value, so the demand, which he brings, for other kinds tends to increase their value. The result is, that now there are certain kinds of goods, which it is less profitable than usual to produce; others, which it is more profitable than usual to produce: and this is an inequality, which tends immediately to correct itself.
>
> (Mill, 1844, p. 241)[28]

Should this reasoning make sense, overproduction (always partial in the start of the process) might never become generalized, because, with each disequilibrium, the price system would produce an instantaneous signal: prices would fall where there is excess and would increase where there is scarcity. I would like to call attention to the fact that here, the reasoning *does not refer to a hypothetical 'long run' situation*; it tries to show how the system reacts in the concrete situations in which the disequilibria occur.

It is not by chance that Malthus's definition of general overproduction is in direct opposition to this conception of compensatory disequilibrium. He considers general overproduction to be 'a fall [in the prices] in a great mass of commodities below the costs of production, *not counterbalanced* by a proportionate rise of some other equally large mass of commodities above the costs of production' (Malthus, 1827, pp. 66–7, my emphasis).[29]

One may wonder whether what makes this definition unacceptable to Say is precisely the absence of the adjustment mechanism he postulates. The guarantees that overproduction is *temporary* – therefore not affecting the reproducibility of the system – would be precisely the fact of its being *partial*.[30]

Say does not demonstrate that the price system behaves in the way described (neither does James Mill). The acceptance of the initial conjecture that production is geared towards buying *is insufficient*. The definition of the level and composition of supply and demand is simultaneous; in (expected) value, supply and demand are identical, even though their compositions may differ. However, while the composition of supply is a 'real' phenomenon derived from the decisions of production, the initial composition of demand is purely virtual and *ex ante*[31] – resulting from a sum of the acquisitive desires of all the agents. With disparities between the compositions of supply and demand, there would certainly be opposite variations in prices *provided that*, in the real world of the markets, it were possible to confront *that same virtual demand* with supply; in the attempt to purchase the desired goods – in function of which the decisions to produce were taken – the producers would make the prices increase in some markets and fall in others.

However, it so happens that the initial hypotheses of the law are hardly compatible with the initial magnitude and composition of demand. If the objective of production is purchase, the actual income will be spent in buying the desired products, *provided that* the purchase is carried out in the terms foreseen by the producer. If, however, the producer's expectations are frustrated, the effectuation of his *ex ante* demand for goods could be partially or totally impossible – since, we are told, in order to buy, it is necessary to have sold first. The frustration of the expectations of the producers, when the expected income differs from the effective one, must alter unpredictably the individual decisions of expenditure and, as a consequence, the composition of aggregate demand in an unpredictable manner. The price system – flexible by hypothesis – will doubtlessly react to this state. However, this may not necessarily be in a 'virtuous' way, giving the different capitals a clear indication of the path to be taken. A cumulative process of fall in income and demand can make a fall in prices or in the profit rate become more or less generalized. In other words, there could be a general overproduction (see Possas, 1987, p. 60),[32] which would seriously disturb the regulating function of the price system.

The exclusion of the possibility of general overproduction presupposes the existence of a sufficiently efficient *adjustment mechanism*. Apparently, the search for such a mechanism in Say is a futile enterprise. Even more than in Ricardo, the adjustment is little more than an equilibristic conjecture.[33] In some passages, Say appeals to the reasoning of the entrepreneur (see Tapinos, 1972) – a truism also employed by Ricardo – while, in others, he just restricts himself to making an inventory of factors, of natural and political nature, which can delay the process.[34]

Curiously enough, in the most recent anti-Keynesian revision of the debate on the law of markets, Jonsson (1997) and Kates (1997; 1998) attribute to Say the pioneering role in the formulation of a Clowerian theory of recession. Yet another paradox and another supposed irony of history: the supporters of the law of markets could be the true creators of the New Keynesian theory of recession as a cumulative result of errors in the decision to produce, that is, of coordination failure.[35]

It is certainly true that Say's law can be made consistent with the occurrence of recessions and unemployment. However, as far as Say and James Mill are concerned, the evidence of a theory of recessions based on the generalization of partial gluts is rather weak (see Baumol, 1997). Jonsson and Kates stress some passages in which Say (1819, pp. 59, 137) and James Mill (1808, pp. 87–8) in fact deal with stagnation, impoverishment and unemployment. This proves that they did not deny the possibility of such phenomena, but not that they believed in the predominance of definite economic causes (see Béraud, 1992, p. 488) and, specifically, in the generalization of the partial glut as a primary explanation for recessions. In my opinion, the absence of macroeconomic treatment of the adjustment mechanisms sparked off by a situation of frustration of short-term expectations is precisely what makes the laws of markets, at least as presented by Say and James Mill, one of the meanest equilibristic theories in the history of economic thought.[36]

Kates does make the point that the connection between Say's law and a cumulative theory of recessions was accomplished by Torrens and developed by other classical and neoclassical economists.[37] But there is a great deal of arbitrariness in the contention that this would be the 'true meaning' of Say's Law. Moreover, such a cumulative theory can also be found … in Malthus.[38] This should not be surprising: there seems to be no theoretical incompatibility between such a theory and Malthus's approach, and, for that matter, with Keynes's principle of effective demand.[39]

5 AN ATTEMPT AT SYNTHESIS

The evolution of economic science has continually frustrated all the (millennialist) expectations that have been betting on the advent of an era without controversies. Even exegetic debates, like this one, instigated around a limited corpus of texts, find it difficult to reach a resting place. This need not be seen as frustrating, for as modern historians well know, we must accept with resignation and humility the fact that the interpretation of the past is inevitably rewritten from the viewpoint of present experience.

Therefore, the orthodox debate on the law of markets is punctuated over time by the state of the art in macroeconomic theory. The motives and the degree to which economists more closely linked to the mainstream appropriate, at a given moment, aspects of Keynesian thought – or simply reject it – are revealed with each reinterpretation of the law of markets.

On the other hand, it must be recognized that the persistence of the theme on the agenda of the historians of economic thought is equally due to certain peculiarities of the law of markets. As Baumol points out, it is useless to seek a clear and precise definition among those responsible for the formulation and divulgation of the law of markets. They never intended doing that.

The implications of the fact that we are dealing with a science which was still developing should never be underestimated. As Sowell (1972) pointed out, the debate on the general glut was greatly clouded by methodological, terminological and conceptual differences, some of which were only clarified after many years of discussion. Neither can we exclude the possibility that important authors have been inconsistent, or have simply changed their opinion over time.

Among the peculiarities of the classical debate is the illuminist conception of scientific knowledge. Natural law, in the classical economists, is not an evident empirical truth. In many cases, it is up to the scholar to deduce it, to make explicit the conditions under which it becomes valid and show why it is advantageous to institute such conditions (Ingrao and Israel, 1990, p. 43). Until the enlightened principles are established, arbitrariness flourishes and the natural laws do not fully conduct the business of men.

Thus it is not surprising to find, in the classical authors, a great number of passages in which the author identifies and discusses a phenomenon that, to judge from the reading of other extracts, should simply not exist. There is a difference between the theoretical discourse, when it presupposes a society under the auspices of natural laws, and the allusions to circumstances in which the institutional conditions present a very different character.

An obvious example is the Smithian treatment of hoarding. Yes, 'a man must be perfectly crazy who ... does not employ all the stock which he commands' in 'procuring either present enjoyment or future profit'. However, this is only valid 'where there is tolerable security'. To admit that hoarding is a rational attitude in 'unfortunate countries ... where men are continually afraid of the violence of their superiors' (Smith, 1776, vol. 1, p. 285) is neither proof of inconsistency nor a demonstration of the 'wealth' of the author's theoretical conception, for if there are no institutions compatible with the natural laws, everything is permitted. The theory of capitalism in suitable institutional conditions continues to lack a more encompassing conception of the role of money.[40]

In the texts defending the law of markets, the denial of the possibility of general glut coexists with frequent mentions of phenomena whose compatibility with the law is problematic, to say the least. In chapter XIX of the *Principles*, Ricardo eloquently describes causes and effects of 'sudden changes in the channels of trade'. The adjustment process can be long and costly and there will be idle capital and labor in a proportion directly related to the agents' incapacity to become aware of the situation and adapt to it (giving new uses to their productive resources) and to the impediments imposed by the authority. According to Sowell (1972, p. 32), Ricardo was aware that 'a sharp contraction of money and credit' would have '"the most disastrous consequences to the trade and commerce of the country", causing "much ruin and distress" in the economy'. Ricardo's final recognition of the possibility of persistent unemployment as a result of the advent of machinery is well known. Say (1819, p. 60), in turn, describes the impact of a strong contraction in circulation, in function of the expectations which lead the owners of goods and money to individually retain a substantial amount of their assets. To sum up, we have here Ricardo and Say talking of recessions, of 'goods' whose supply does not generate demand (labor) and of alterations in the velocity of money.

At no time in the *General Theory* does Keynes dare to delve into this embarrassment of propositions. Indeed, he opts for too partial a rendition of

Say's Law (although it preserves one of its constitutive elements, the identity of aggregate supply and demand). If taken too literally, Keynes's interpretation would imply that references to the above-mentioned phenomena should be outrightly discarded as inconsistencies committed by the authors.

Mainstream economists offer interpretations that, in my view, are similar to the Keynesian one in the way they abstract certain 'uncomfortable' elements from the classical texts. Except that here, the abstracted elements are precisely those stressed by Keynes. Curiously enough, the main argument against the general glut, as well as some possible short term implications of the law (clearly explained by Say and James Mill), are omitted.

A less partial and less preconceived interpretation should be simultaneously capable of recognizing, among the central propositions of the law, the identity between aggregate supply and demand and of classifying in different categories the 'deviant' phenomena identified by the authors. There are those consistent with the law, inasmuch as they are derived from institutional contexts quite distinct from the natural order. There are others, derived from semantic problems, as the difference (correctly stressed by Kates) between general glut and distress or stagnation. There are possible inconsistencies, maybe such as those that Ricardo criticizes in Say (see Kates, 1998, p. 31), or the former's admission of technological unemployment (on both of these, see Baumol, 1997). And there is the evolution of the authors' thought, an example of which are Say's last manifestations[41] on the law.[42]

6 CONCLUSION: A BRIEF NOTE ON THE OPPOSITION BETWEEN SAY'S LAW AND THE PRINCIPLE OF EFFECTIVE DEMAND

According to Keynes, the opposition between Say's law and the principle of effective demand marks a basic dichotomy, from which the orthodox vein and the Babel of heterodoxies differentiated themselves (Keynes, 1933, p. 97). As I hope to have shown, Keynes's interpretation of the meaning of the law as an identity between aggregate supply and demand is basically correct.[43] The thesis that there is an opposition between the law and the principle is fairly arguable too. According to the principle of effective demand, as formulated by Keynes (1936), supply does not create its own demand, and although variations in supply determine variations in demand, the balance between the two is fundamentally determined by decisions to invest that are independent of the level of production.

It is more complicated to accept the thesis that this opposition adequately describes the watershed between orthodoxy and heterodoxy, between the specific theory of the allocation of given resources and the 'general' theory.

This thesis, of indisputable rhetorical efficiency in the years that followed the publication of *The General Theory*, incurs the very dangerous error of underestimating the opponent. This is because the law of markets, despite its being conducive (when properly connected to other equilibristic propositions) to most of the propositions commonly defended by the mainstream – such as the ideas of the neutrality of money and of the tendency to full-employment equilibrium in the long run – is not in any way a *necessary* condition. The law of markets was just a minor (and quickly outdated) example of equilibrism, founded on hypotheses which are too restrictive and whose compatibility with evidently important phenomena is problematic.

The identity between aggregate supply and demand, albeit correctly related by Keynes to Say and Ricardo, is not necessary to obtain any of the fundamental theses defended by the modern mainstream, from the neoclassical synthesis to the New Classical authors, passing through monetarism.

So it is that, after the controversy of the general glut, the law of markets, as formulated by James Mill and Say, only reappears sporadically in the economic debate. As Keynes (1936, pp. 18–20) pointed out, the virtual disappearance of references to Say's law after John Stuart Mill is not in itself definitive evidence that the law had become irrelevant.[44] For him, the absence of the law in the orthodox argumentation signaled the fact that it had become such an obvious postulate as to no longer warrant naming.[45] However, there is another hypothesis, which I consider more plausible, and it is that equilibrism, after the contribution of John Stuart Mill, opts for less vulnerable paths, even before leaning clearly towards the Walrasian conception.

So it is that, from the 1940s onwards, orthodoxy elegantly and painlessly recovers from the Keynesian attack, by means of an operation that is completely independent of the recourse to the law of markets. The strength of the argument lies precisely in its simplicity (seductive and, in my view, deceptive). Walras's law is at the base of everything (see, for instance, Modigliani, 1944). The irony of history – here, indeed, the expression seems pertinent – consisted in performing the transition from the original truism to the thesis of convergence towards general equilibrium by using Keynesian instruments, as formalized by Hicks in 1937 (but also suggested in chapter 18 of *The General Theory*). Supply does not in fact create its own demand; it is recognized that demand can establish limits on production below the level of full employment ... for a *given* absolute level of prices. If, with unemployment, wages and unemployment fall, aggregate demand will tend to expand, due to the so-called Keynes and/or Pigou wealth effects.

This result – as with the long-run neutrality of money, reaffirmed emphatically by the monetarists – does not depend on the heroic hypothesis that the agents supply goods with a view to purchasing goods.[46] Nevertheless, it depends, inasmuch as its credibility as a foundation of economic theory and policy is concerned, on the presumption that it is reasonable to assume as a hypothesis the predominance of the endogenous tendencies of the markets towards a state of equilibrium; in other words, it depends on an equilibristic avowal of faith.

In *The General Theory*, the criticism of the equilibrism of Say's law and fertile examples of what could be a dynamic non-equilibrist analysis (as in Chapter 19) can be found. There is not, nevertheless, a *general* methodological criticism of equilibrism. The result of this, as I suggest in another text (Macedo e Silva, 1995), has been of simultaneously facilitating the acceptance of Keynesian policies *and* the maintenance of the hegemony of neoclassical thought.

NOTES

1. The author would like to thank an anonymous referee, as well as Susan Pyne, for the translation of a previous version of this chapter.
2. Equilibristic, in my point of view, are all the economic theories based on the hypothesis that markets are always in equilibrium or tending towards it. The equilibristic procedure – common to several economic schools – consists of eliminating the dynamics (adopting only statics or comparative statics) or in carrying out dynamics of a teleological nature, in which the changes admitted are those strictly necessary to the attainment of a predefined result (the final state of equilibrium). Criticism of equilibrism does not imply rejection of the possibility of (or the interest in) specifying states of equilibrium (for a contribution to the development of non-equilibristic macroeconomics, see Macedo e Silva, 2000).
3. More exhaustive renditions of the literature can be found, of course, in Sowell (1972) and Kates (1998).
4. Further ahead, Baumol (1977, p. 154) refers to the 'Keynesian point that effective demand is a rising function of *real* output, and that money merely facilitates the working of that relationship'. See also Becker and Baumol (1952/60, p. 764) and Blaug (1962, p. 156).
5. These propositions are related to what Carvalho (1992, p. 46) calls the 'temporality principle'.
6. Therefore, the 'profound observation ... that demand is constituted by supply' (Kates, 1998, p. 2) is in fact a simplistic proposition, obviously unsuitable for the analysis of capitalist economies. It is preferable to say, with Keynes, that 'expenditure creates its own income, i.e. an income just sufficient to meet the expenditure' (Keynes, 1973, vol. XXIX: 81), and that 'spending is constrained only by liquidity and/or timidity considerations' (Davidson, 1984, pp. 566–7).
7. It should be clear that 'effective demand' here means *actual expenditure*, and thus has to do with the *ex post*, 'expenditure version' of the principle of effective demand (see Amadeo, 1989).
8. And, for this reason, I think that the sarcasm with which Clower and Leijonhufvud (1973) and Jonsson (1997) refer to him is quite unfair.
9. This conclusion seems to reverberate in Samuelson (1946), when he suggests that the *General Theory* provides the instruments which would have made it possible for Say, Mill and Ricardo to understand and defend their own opinions.
10. Besides, according to Sowell (1974, p. 41), 'the general glut economists were as zealous in refuting these popular notions' – that 'some absolute limit to economic growth had been reached' – 'as were the supporters of Say's law'.
11. The same holds for James Mill (1808, p. 82).
12. There is a clear non sequitur here – the rejection of mercantilism does not imply any

specific declaration with regard to the motivation of the producers and the role of money. This was clearly noticed by Malthus (1827, p. 60n): 'It is quite astonishing that political economists of reputation should be inclined to resort to any kind of illustration ... rather than refer to money. I suppose they are afraid of the imputation of thinking that wealth consists in money. But though it is certainly true that wealth does not consist in money, it is equally true that money is a most powerful agent in the distribution of wealth; and those who, in a country where all exchanges are practically effected by money, continue the attempt to explain the principles of demand and supply, and the variations of wages and profits, by referring chiefly to hats, shoes, corn, suits of clothing, &c., must of necessity fail.'

13. As Keynes (1973, vol. XXIX, p. 81) would state, based on Marx.
14. Becker and Baumol (1952/60) state that it is not possible to discard the possibility that Mill considered money as one of the goods coveted by the producer in exchange for his surplus production. This proposition seems unwarranted to me. According to Mill. 'It makes no difference to say, that perhaps he ['every man'] only wanted money; for money is itself goods; and, besides, no man wants money but in order to lay it out, either in articles of productive, or articles of unproductive consumption' (Mill, 1844, pp. 233–44). Money is introduced only to be immediately discarded.
15. In macroeconomic terms, the proposition amounts to saying that the 'power of purchasing' of the nation 'is always equivalent to its power of producing, or at least to its actual produce; and that as it never can be greater, so it never can be less' (Mill, 1808, p. 86).
16. For Say, here lies the proof of the ultimate harmony between men and nations (see Say, 1828, pp. 213–15, 360; 1841, p. 51).
17. 'Although the equality of supply and demand was sometimes expressed as an *ex post* identity of purchases and sales, it was essentially a behavioral theory of an *ex ante* equality of supply and demand (Sowell, 1974, p. 36; see also Sowell, 1987, p. 250). It should be stressed that this interpretation of Say's Law as an *ex ante* identity is quite consistent with its presentation in chapter 3 of the *General Theory*.
18. 'And though goods do not always draw money so readily as money draw goods, in the long-run they draw it more necessarily than even it draws them' (Smith, 1776, IV, 1, p. 439).
19. The second edition is even clearer with respect to the 'perishability' of money (Say, 1814, *apud* Baumol, 1977, p. 158).
20. 'The money that individuals receive for what they sell, is immediately laid out by themselves, or by those to whom they lend it, on purchases' (McCulloch, 1864, p. 157).
21. The use of the metaphor of the annual cycle of production and consumption embeds the equilibrium hypothesis in the theory of income determination, forging a link between them that not even Keynes dared to question. In this respect, see Macedo e Silva (2002).
22. A careful reading of the item from which the two quotations were taken shows clearly that Mill is interested in the consequences of his behavioral theory of producers on the economy as a whole, and not in the development of the macroeconomic accounting identities.
23. It is worthwhile emphasizing that the proposition is stronger than the simple idea that 'anything that is sold must also be bought, and nothing can be bought without proper means to purchase it' (Jonsson, 1997, p. 205).
24. This hypothesis implies – I repeat – what I have been calling the *ex ante* identity of supply and demand. See, in this respect, Mill (1808, pp. 84–5; 1844, pp. 234–5) and McCulloch (1864, p. 145).
25. By the way, Kates's affirmation that, in the Keynesian interpretation of the law, 'everything produced would be bought' and 'unsold goods and services are a theoretical impossibility' (Kates, 1998, p. 222; see also p. 169), seems to be completely groundless.
26. This reasoning is repeated by Ricardo in many extracts (see, for instance, Ricardo, 1951–73, vol. II, pp. 305–6).
27. This weakens Kates's depiction of Say's approach ('clearly wrong', he writes) as idiosyncratic and his opinion that 'the more logical approach adopted by James Mill ... ultimately came to dominate' (Mates, 1998, p. 31).

28. 'It is, therefore, impossible, that there should ever be in any country a commodity or commodities in quantity greater than the demand, without there being, to an equal amount, some other commodity or commodities in quantity less than the demand ... The commodity, which happens to be in superabundance, declines in price; the commodity, which is defective in quantity, rises' (Mill, 1844, p. 235).
29. Ricardo warns Trower not to commit 'the great and fundamental error of Mr. Malthus, who contends that there may be at one and the same time a glut of all commodities, and that it may arise from a want of demand for all – he indeed argues that this is the specific evil under which we are at present suffering' (Ricardo, 1951–73, vol. VIII, pp. 256–7; see also McCulloch, 1864, p. 156).
30. This may have been the most important reason why partisans of Say's law have mistakenly and systematically attributed to their opponents the thesis that the glut could be general *and* permanent (see Sowell, 1972).
31. At least, partially. Obviously, there is a quantity of intermediary goods (and services) whose purchase was determined by the decision to produce.
32. The same can happen to an economy based on barter. I agree with Hahn (1977, p. 38), for whom 'the idea that there would be no unemployment in a barter economy is grotesque' (as is grotesque the idea of a mercantile economy without money; cf. Possas, 1987, pp. 62–4).
33. Ratified by Mises (1950, p. 316) many years later, and without qualification: 'To the overproduction of shoes corresponds an underproduction of shirts. Consequently the result can not be a general depression of all branches of business. The outcome is a change in the exchange ration between shoes and shirts ... What the seller wants ultimately to receive in exchange for the commodities sold is other commodities. Every commodity produced is therefore a price, as it were, for other commodities produced.'
34. According to Say (1819, p. 57), 'there must needs [*sic*] be some violent means, or some extraordinary cause, a political or natural convulsion, or the avarice or ignorance of authority, to perpetuate this *scarcity on the one hand, and consequent glut on the other*. No sooner is the cause of this political disease removed, than the means of production feel a natural impulse towards the vacant channels, the replenishment of which restores activity to all the others. One kind of production would seldom outstrip every other, and its products be disproportionately cheapened, were production left entirely free' [my emphasis].
35. 'But once errors were made in the production process ... then some goods, in what was referred to as a "partial glut", would remain unsold. Incomes would then fall bellow expectations, employment numbers would be reduced and the demand for other products would decrease. The consequences of partial glut in some parts of the economy could thus reverberate through the economy as a whole and would often end in recession. Recessions were thus conceived as structural' (Kates, 1997, p. 197).
36. The evidence is more favorable in the case of Ricardo, who tried to cope with the problem of economic distress in the oft-quoted chapter XIX of the *Principles*. Significantly, while Ricardo (1951–73, vol. I, p. 263) mentions the effects of changes in 'the tastes and caprice of the purchasers', the emphasis is placed on factors such as the 'commencement of war after a long peace, or of peace after a long war' (ibid., p. 265). There is no clear description of a cumulative process. In a letter to Malthus, Ricardo (1951–73, vol. VIII, p. 278) writes that he 'cannot conceive it possible, without the grossest miscalculation, that there should be a redundancy of capital, and of labour, at the same time'. Is it really reasonable to consider 'grossest miscalculations' as a basis for a 'structural' (in Kates', words) theory of recessions?
37. Sowell (1972, pp. 129–31) had already suggested that Torrens was the first to conceive the possibility of generalization of a partial glut. Nevertheless, he (as Béraud, 1992, p. 478) placed Torrens in the side of the critics of Say's law. According to Sowell (1972, p. 176), similar reasoning would be employed later by John Stuart Mill and Marx.
38. See Malthus (1820, pp. 317–18, 438). According to Béraud (1992, p. 483), the idea of a cumulative process of crisis, present in Sismondi, was 'frequently evoked the classics, by Malthus, by Torrens and by Say as well'.

39. It is convenient to add that Keynes's theory is *not* based on the assumption that a contraction of aggregate demand is the *only* conceivable cause of unemployment, and that it does *not* require the occurrence of any type of glut (partial or general) to deflagrate a recession process.
40. Similar arguments to these can be found in other classical economists, such as Say (1819, p. 59).
41. In several of his last texts (see Sowell, 1972, pp. 121, 139–41), Say explicitly reconciles himself with Malthus and Sismondi, finally accepting the existence restrictions on the demand side (see 1841, pp. 146–7, a 1827 letter to Malthus in 1848, p. 513 and 1828, pp. 345–7). These excerpts include what Baumol (1977, p. 159) called a 'rather curious tautological version of Say's Law'. See Béraud (1992, p. 488) and Kates (1998) for a different interpretation.
42. A careful interpretation should also deal specifically with John Stuart Mill's intervention, which was both late and peculiar. As Sowell (1972) shows, on the one hand Stuart Mill transforms the propositions of the critics of the law of markets into a crude caricature, in which it is possible that the relative prices all fall at the same time and the general glut becomes a permanent state (Mill, 1844, p. 74). On the other hand, Mill himself (1844, pp. 70–71) admits the fact that the monetary revenue derived from sale cannot generate an immediate purchase, which gives rise to a fairly clear formulation of what will later be called Walras's law (Sowell, 1972, emphasizes the similarity with the argumentation employed by Marx).
43. On the same theme – that of the lack of substance of the Keynesian interpretation (and/or of criticism) of Say's law – a greater number of variations than those described here were developed. According to Ackley (1961), there was never a Jean-Baptiste Say – at least, nobody with this name played a minimally significant role. The law attributed to this 'mythical scholar' should be seen as a modern creation, a 'straw man' sewn by Keynes (Ackley, 1961, p. 109; see Miglioli, 1981, chs 1 and 2).
44. Klein (1968) emphasizes the importance of Fred M. Taylor's textbook. Taylor (1913, p. 148) presents an interpretation of the law of markets that in my view is faithful to the originals (and totally compatible with Keynes's interpretation). Similarly, Mises (1950, p. 319), based on what we saw above to be less of an interpretation than a paraphrase of Say and Ricardo, fiercely defends the validity of the law: 'Keynes did not refute Say's law. He rejected it emotionally, but he did not advance a single tenable argument to invalidate its rationale'. For Mises (1950, p. 317), 'the acknowledgement of the truth contained in Say's Law' became in the nineteenth century (and presumably also in the twentieth century) 'the distinctive mark of an economist'.
45. This, by the way, is the opinion of Kates (1998).
46. This point was clearly perceived by Patinkin, according to whom, by acknowledging the Pigou effect, the 'classical' conception of a 'consistent' economy does not need Say's law. Thus, the Keynesian attack should be concentrated not on the law, but on the 'dynamic instability of our economic system – on its inability to restore full employment within a reasonable time after being subjected to a shock of one type or another' (Patinkin, 1949, p. 378).

REFERENCES

Ackley, G. (1961), *Macroeconomic Theory*, New York: Macmillan.

Amadeo, E.J. (1989), *Keynes's Principle of Effective Demand*, Aldershot: Edward Elgar.

Baumol, W.J. (1977), 'Say's (at least) eight laws, or what Say and James Mill may really have meant', *Economica*, **44** (174), 145–62.

Baumol, W.J. (1997), 'J.B. Say on unemployment and public works', *Eastern Economic Journal*, **23** (2), 219–30.

Becker, G., and W.J. Baumol (1952/60), 'The classical monetary theory: the outcome of the discussion', in J.J. Spengler, and W.R. Allen (eds), *Essays in Economic Thought*, Chicago, IL: Rand McNally.

Béraud, A. (1992), 'Ricardo, Malthus, Say et les controverses de la "seconde génération"', in A. Béraud and G Faccarello (eds), *Nouvelle Histoire de la Pensée Économique*, Paris: La Découverte.

Blaug, M. (1962), *Economic Theory in Retrospect*, 4th edn 1985, Cambridge: Cambridge University Press.

Carvalho, F.C. (1992), *Mr. Keynes and the Post Keynesians – Principles of Macroeconomics for a Monetary Production Economy*, Aldershot, UK and Brookfield, US: Edward Elgar.

Clower, R.W. (1963/65), 'The Keynesian counter-revolution: a theoretical appraisal', in D.A. Walker (ed.) (1984), *Money and Markets*, Cambridge: Cambridge University Press.

Clower, R.W., and A. Leijonhufvud (1973), 'Say's Principle, what it means and doesn't mean', in D.A. Walker (1984), *Money and Markets*, Cambridge: Cambridge University Press.

Davidson, P. (1982), *International Money and the Real World*, 2nd edn, 1992, London: Macmillan.

Davidson, P. (1984), 'Reviving Keynes's revolution', *Journal of Post Keynesian Economics*, **6** (4), 560–75.

Hahn, F.H. (1977), 'Keynesian economics and general equilibrium theory: reflections on some current debates', in G.C. Harcourt (ed.), *The Microeconomic Foundations of Macroeconomics*, Boulder, CO: Westview Press.

Hahn, F.H. (1982), *Money and Inflation*, Oxford: Basil Blackwell.

Hicks, J. (1937), 'Mr. Keynes and the classics', in J. Hicks (1982), *Money, Interest and Wages*, Oxford: Basil Blackwell.

Hicks, J. (1975), 'Time in economics', in *Money, Interest and Prices – Collected Essays on Economic Theory*, vol II, reprinted 1982, Oxford: Basil Blackwell.

Ingrao, B., and G. Israel (1990), *The Invisible Hand – Economic Equilibrium in the History of Science*, Cambridge, MA: MIT Press.

Jonsson, P.O. (1997), 'On gluts, effective demand, and the true meaning of Say's Law', *Eastern Economic Journal*, **23** (2), 203–19.

Kates, S. (1997), 'On the true meaning of Say's Law', *Eastern Economic Journal*, **23** (2), 191–203.

Kates, S. (1998), *Say's Law and the Keynesian Revolution – How Macroeconomic Theory Lost its Way*, Cheltenham, UK and Lyme, USA: Edward Elgar.

Keynes, J.M. (1933), *Essays in Biography. The Collected Writings of John Maynard Keynes*, Vol. X, reprinted 1972, London: Macmillan.

Keynes, J.M. (1936), *The General Theory of Employment, Interest and Money*, London: Macmillan.

Keynes, J.M. (1973), *The Collected Writings of John Maynard Keynes*, London: Macmillan.

Klein, L.R. (1968), *The Keynesian Revolution*, 2nd edn, first published 1947, London: Macmillan.

Lange, O. (1944), 'Say's Law: a restatement and criticism', in O. Lange, *Price Flexibility and Employment*, Bloomington, IN: Principia Press.

Macedo e Silva, A.C. (2002), 'O *homo economicus*, o tempo da economia e a lei dos mercados: um outro fio da meada', *Revista da Sociedade Brasileira de Economia Politica*, **10**, (June), 5–28.

Macedo e Silva, A.C. (2000), *Macroeconomia sem equilibrio*, Petrópolis: Vozes.
Macedo c Silva, A.C. (1995), 'A economia de Keynes, a busca de uma nova teoria econômica e a "armadilha do equilibrio"', *Economia e Sociedade*, **5**, 111–58 (a slightly modified version, 'Keynes' economics and the search for a new economic theory: the "Equilibrium Trap"', was published in *Textos para Discussão*, no. 22, Institute, de Economia, Unicamp).
Malthus, T.R. (1820), *Principles of Political Economy – Considered with a View to their Practical Application*, in D. Ricardo (1951–73), *The Works and Correspondence of David Ricardo*, P. Sraffa (ed.), vol. II, Cambridge: Cambridge University Press.
Malthus, T.R. (1827), *Definitions in Political Economy*, reprinted 1971, New York: Kelley.
McCulloch, J.R. (1864), *Principles of Political Economy*, reprinted 1965, New York: Kelley.
Miglioli, J. (1981), *Acumulação de Capital e Demanda Efetiva*, São Paulo: Taq.
Mill, J. (1808), *Commerce Defended*, reprinted 1964, New York: Kelley.
Mill, J. (1844), *Elements of Political Economy*, reprinted 1965, New York: Kelley.
Mises, L.V. (1950), 'Lord Keynes and Say's Law', in H. Hazlitt (1977), *The Critics of Keynesian Economics*, Princeton, NJ: Van Nostrand.
Modigliani, F. (1944), 'Liquidity preference and the theory of interest and money', in F.A. Lutz and L.W. Mints (eds), *Readings in Monetary Theory*, reprinted 1951, Homewood, IL: Irwin.
Patinkin, D. (1949), 'Involuntary unemployment and the Keynesian supply function', *Economic Journal*, **59** (235), 360–83.
Possas, M.L. (1987), *Dinâmica da Economia Capitalista: uma abordagem teórica*, São Paulo: Brasiliense.
Ricardo, D. (1951–73), *The Works and Correspondence of David Ricardo*, P. Sraffa (ed.), Cambridge: Cambridge University Press.
Samuelson, P. (1946), 'The *General Theory*', reprinted 1964 in R. Lekachman, *Keynes' General Theory: Reports of Three Decades*, New York: Macmillan.
Say, J.B. (1803) and Say J.B. (1814), first and second editions of the *Traité*, excerpts published in W.J. Baumol (1977), 'Say's (at least) eight laws, or what Say and James Mill may really have meant', *Economica*, **44** (174), 145–62.
Say, J.B. (1819), *A Treatise on Political Economy; or the Production, Distribution, and Consumption of Wealth*, translated from the 4th edn of the French, Philadelphia, PA: Claxton, Remsen and Haffelfinger, 1880 edn; Kitchener: Batoche.
Say, J.B. (1820), 'Lettres à M. Malthus sur différents sujets d'économie politique, notamment sur les causes de la stagnation générale du commerce', in J.B. Say (1848), 'Oeuvres diverse de John Say: exitenant "Catéchisme d'économie politique, Fragments et opuscules inédits ..."/Précedées d'une notice historique su la vie et les travaux de l'auteur, avec des notes par Ch. Comte, E. Daire et Horace Say', repr. 1966, Osnabrück: O. Zeller.
Say, J.B. (1821), Letters to Thomas Robert Malthus on Political Economy and Stagnation of Commerce, accessed at www.digital.library.upenn.edu/books/.
Say, J.B. (1824), *Traité d'Économie Politique, ou simple exposition de la manière dont se forment, se distribuent et se consomment les richesses*, 16th edn (1966), Osnabrück: Zeller.
Say, J.B. (1828), *Cours Complet d'Économie Politique Pratique*, excerpts published in Reynaud (1953), *Jean-Baptiste Say – Textes Choisis*, Paris: Dalloz.
Say, J.B. (1848), 'Oeuvres diverses de J.-B. Say: contenant "Catéchisme d'économie

politique, Fragments et opuscules inédits ..."/Précédées d'une notice historique sur la vie et les travaux de l'auteur, avec des notes par Ch. Comte, E. Daire et Horace Say', reprinted 1966, Osnabrück: O. Zeller.

Schumpeter, J.A. (1954), *History of Economic Analysis*, London: Allen and Unwin.

Smith, A. (1776), *An Inquiry into the Nature and Causes of the Wealth of Nations*, reprinted 1976, Oxford: Clarendon Press.

Sowell, T. (1972), *Say's Law: an Historical Analysis*, Princeton, NJ: Princeton University Press.

Sowell, T. (1974), *Classical Economics Reconsidered*, Princeton, NJ: Princeton University Press.

Sowell, T. (1987), 'Say's Law', in J. Eatwell, M. Milgate and P. Newman (eds), *The New Palgrave: a Dictionary of Economics*, London: Macmillan.

Tapinos, G. (1972), Préface, in J.B. Say, Traité d'Économiè Politique (1826), Paris: Calman Lévy.

Taylor, F.M. (1913), *Principles of Economics*, 2nd edn, Ann Arbor, MI: University of Michigan Press.

19. Power of the firm and new mercantilism: an analysis based on Joan Robinson's thought

Dimitri Uzunidis and Blandine Laperche

The critical method adopted by Joan Robinson to present the partisan content of the neoclassical approach often refers to international economic relations in her vision of economy. But this post Keynesian conquest of the enrichment (or impoverishment) process of an economy due to international trade (or finance, or cross-border investment) materialized brutally in the face of liberal orthodoxy, which, in turn, reduced international facts to mere flows or utilization of goods. It is important to underline the fact that in Joan Robinson's science, history and politics shape economic players' choices, functions and activities. Without spelling it out, the national state – a political organization, an economic agent and a regulator – is omnipresent in international economics. Through her long flashbacks to historical facts, Joan Robinson stands up for the argument of the evolution of international relations by confronting diverging and unequally powerful national interests, both political and economic. She also emphasizes the particular and unavoidable part played by one nation's economic power on the economic development and positioning in the international relations of other nations.

As early as 1965, the British author clearly questioned many issues regarding the economic power of certain countries based on the economic power of their firms; so far, international economists have not been able (or willing) to answer such questions. 'As long as the overall market does not grow fast enough to make room for all, each government considers that increasing its own share of the global activity for the benefit of its own country is both a valid and desirable objective' (Robinson, 1965, p. 227). Or, even later: 'The principle of labour division is useful for justifying policies which go against the effort produced by the periphery to develop their industry' (Robinson, 1979, p. 142). The consequence of unequal economic relations is that while some are becoming richer, others are becoming poorer, even if the global demand is increasing. This old economic law has its roots in the political sphere of the constitution of national economies.

If the growth of international markets is not sufficient to absorb global exports, each economic power will attempt to achieve an excess balance of payments. Such is the 'new mercantilism' which brings the USA face to face with Europe and Japan, and resembles the seventeenth century when England (poor in labour and land) became richer thanks to trade (notably sea trade) and state intervention. Joan Robinson simply showed, using a didactic method, how 'One man's good fortune is another man's bad fortune'. It is easier for powerful economies to defend their own interests and impose an 'international division of labour'. Means of defence are evolving, but the principles are still the same. It is true that in order to understand the subtlety of new mercantilism, today's economists have to abandon their usual tools for a moment (free-trade hypotheses and models). They must also accept seeing the world through the prism of its history.

NEW MERCANTILISM AND MONOPOLIES: NATURAL TRENDS OF CAPITALISM

For Joan Robinson, mercantilism is the natural trend of capitalism because an economy of market and private enterprise is most of the time an economy of buyers. Such an economy comes up against the insufficiency of effective demand. Excess in the supply capacity in terms of capital, money and goods with respect to the solvent demand, as Marx and Schumpeter cleverly demonstrated, means that firms have continuously to renew their production process (renovate the supply, reduce costs and open new markets); therefore, they must export. Joan Robinson shows without difficulty that the capitalist world is always, in a way, this market of buyers, within which the production capacity exceeds what can be sold for a profit (1965, p. 227).

A situation in which demand exceeds what firms can physically produce and sell is often a precarious one. The resulting investment and recruitment increase production capacities to the point where they achieve excess production. Since the evolution of the capitalist society is conditioned by the forecasts made by the entrepreneurs, new investors enter profitable areas in large numbers and rapidly saturate them. Competition and the short-sightedness of entrepreneurs, together with opaque markets and the retention of information, lead as much to excess production as to monopoly.

The development of the firm to a monopolistic or quasi-monopolistic position also represents a natural trend of capitalism to Joan Robinson. In 1971, Joan Robinson wrote, 'A firm's desire to grow has characterised capitalism from the beginning; to tell the truth, had it been otherwise, capitalism would never have existed' (1976, p. 170). This statement results from the long methodological progression of the author's thinking from her early days with

Marshall and Pigou to her ideas on imperfect competition (Robinson, 1933) to her questioning of each individual assumption underlying the liberal analysis of competition. The interest she takes in economic reality and in 'historic time', as opposed to logical time, draws her towards the Marxist and Schumpeterian analysis of the concentration/centralization process of capital. 'Where competition is fierce, there has to be a tendency towards monopoly, which often stops at the oligopoly stage when a small number of firms prefer armed neutrality to the final fight for hegemony' (Robinson, 1976, p. 170). Joan Robinson also explains that 'Marshall's dilemma' should have been solved by the coexistence of increasing returns in industry with the lasting assumptions of pure and perfect competition. The right way to avoid Marshall's dilemma, according to Joan Robinson, consisted in doing the exact opposite of Pigou's proposition (that is, revealing an 'optimum size' of the firm – note of the authors). 'Successful firms accumulate capital and swallow up unsuccessful ones. Most corporations keep growing and many competitive branches tend to a situation in which the market is dominated by one company or a small number of companies' (1977a, p. 39). Foreign economies represent opportunities that need to be seized rapidly in order to maintain and increase profits.

In spite of the criticism and the limits which came to light, Joan Robinson (1951) acknowledged Rosa Luxembourg's work on economic imperialism as a significant improvement on economic orthodoxy. The expansion of capitalism to new territories makes it possible to form capital partly funded by the value (note that Robinson would not accept this term!) produced there and partly by loans granted by the investing capitalist countries. The incitement to invest comes from the fact that those new territories are, in a way, stocks of goods, which either do not exist in the established countries or can be produced at lower costs. In the pre-capitalistic stage, foreign countries identified as potential markets or investment opportunities, offer new outlets to established, domestic industries and save them from the complications arising from insufficient demand. By adjusting this approach to the facts of her era, our author defines, describes and analyses new mercantilism.

As soon as a buyers' economy is in place, the closing down of borders worldwide is not only reprehensible but, above all, unbearable. That policy is bad, not from the point of view of the assumed superiority of free trade, but because gaining market share in the export of goods and capital is as beneficial to the capitalists as to the workers. In order to understand the difference between free trade and new mercantilism, Joan Robinson notes that, although full employment is not guaranteed, profit and employment levels could be higher at all times in a capitalist country if exports increased more rapidly than imports. 'The trading nations have always been mercantilist at heart.' To champion the adoption of free trade policies, one must mention that the advantage of abolishing foreign trade barriers is, for the national exporters, greater than the disadvantage of lifting their own national trade barriers (Robinson, 1979, p. 92).

New mercantilism, therefore, is only favourable to the industrialized countries and their big monopoly or quasi-monopoly corporations, due in part to the favourable policies implemented by those states. New mercantilism is one of the more obvious policies, as it facilitates the expansion of companies and stimulates their activity. In fact, in an industrialized country, a trade balance surplus facilitates productive investment, further improving the country's position in overall international trade. Competitive monopolies and new mercantilism, therefore, necessarily go hand in hand:

> In a country which is in a strong position, investment brings about technical progress which improves its competitive position and further strengthens its trade balance, whereas a country in a fragile situation drifts towards stagnation or is hit by prejudicial jolts.
>
> (Robinson, 1965, p. 231)

New mercantilism, like the traditional form before it, is a system, which impoverishes debtors. At all times, the most powerful economies (the ones with foreign accounts showing a surplus and/or with a common currency used as legal tender for international transactions) pour their surpluses (goods and capital) into other countries, while carefully selecting their purchases from those countries. Thus, they further their own national economies and levels of employment. And then, once their savings surpluses have irrigated economies in need of capital, they take no further interest in their debtors' long-term solvency. In contrast, the logical solution would be to increase their own imports and improve the terms of the transactions for basic products, while helping to develop an industrial and processing base within the foreign country aimed at exporting, and so on. Nothing of the kind, however, actually occurs, except if under pressure the Organization of Petroleum Exporting Countries. The mercantilist paradox precludes that creditors should make a profit from their loans; and thus, they demand repayment while not really wanting it. Competitive market laws are imposed upon raw material producing (and exporting), and they must face the substitution products of the rich countries which are imported with prices determined under the law of monopoly (the price of manufactured goods is determined based on their total cost price plus a mark-up). This paradox leads debtors into the spiral of debt and the crisis of getting back out of the red. In order to be able to maintain their access to funding sources and eventually reduce the yearly and overall burden of their debt, bankrupt economies must conform to their lenders' financial and political conditions. If rich countries really wanted to develop poor economies, they would try to encourage alternative activities and promote imports. This policy, however, would create friction within new mercantilism, because 'the rules of international economic relations are aimed at favouring the most powerful countries' (Robinson, 1965, p. 235).

This tendency towards impoverishment is aggravated by two factors, which structure international exchanges: international pricing and the demand for imports by developing countries. Here again, imperfect competition, and therefore complementarity, is the rule. The prices of manufactured products exported by rich countries or sold by multinational corporations on international markets are determined by the monopolies so that all costs are covered and a substantial net profit is made; prices and sales are regulated by the volumes introduced into the market (the volume sold is whatever quantities that can be absorbed by the market providing the anticipated profit is achieved). On the other hand, the rural populations in developing countries sell their produce to intermediaries who take advantage of the seasonal fluctuations in the supply and the sticky demand (inflexibility) from industrialized countries. In contrast, the import of manufactured products, especially arms, by Third World countries leads to incompressible expenses, which, in turn, increases the need for funds, strengthens the grip of multinational corporations on the trade and production activities of the developing countries, diverts part of the national demand, creates inflationary pressures and reduces the capacity to export. It is obvious that there is no economic machinery to achieve market equilibrium. The economic machinery attempts to work itself out in the political arena with political relations becoming very antagonistic in nature (this is demonstrated by the deteriorating terms of exchange for basic products).

We can state with R. Harrod that trade between developed and developing countries may only be profitable to both parties if the unused savings of the former are transferred to the latter and used for financing internal investment or for buying capital goods and technologies from industrialized countries. But, the multiplying effects in developing countries may be distorted if the investors who profit by the savings surplus are, in fact, the giant internationalized monopolistic corporations. The latter 'only show their patriotism towards capitalism globally speaking and make no distinction at all between domestic and foreign production' (Robinson, 1979, p. 92). They use their profits as they see fit, by repatriating them, reinvesting them, or even investing them elsewhere. It is therefore obvious that 'new mercantilism' is shortsighted, just like investors and capitalism in general. Instead of helping other countries to produce and export, to meet the basic needs of their populations and to improve their standard of living and their incomes in an environment of growth in the solvent demand, the rich countries prefer to compete in shrinking, fluctuating and uncertain markets. They even adjusted international law to match the immediate interests of multinational corporations (both firms and banks) at the expense of their own employment levels and standards of living for their fellow citizens.

BIG CORPORATIONS AND NEW MERCANTILISM

Joan Robinson's 'new mercantilism' was limited by the restraints of the 1960s and 1970s: governments then were concerned about levels of employment and maintaining growth in a buyers' economy, so they tried to achieve a positive balance of trade. As a good Keynesian or post Keynesian economist, the author progressively developed her argument on the strategic and economic impact of big corporations while taking care not to depart from the essential (that is, the role of the states and international organizations in the management and evolution of neo-mercantilist relations). The over-accumulation of capital in rich countries, generated by the foreseeable developments of the buyers' economy, was the reason why the crisis of the 1970s 'restored the pre-Keynesian orthodoxy as the conventional wisdom concerning economic policy both national and international' (Robinson, 1977, p. 252). The 'opening of borders' was therefore regarded as being one of the remedies for the inflation of the 1960s, which was caused by a sharp decrease in the reinvestment of profits and by rising costs. This arguable theory regarding the causes of inflation should not distort our neo-Robinsonian perception of mercantilism. *If* in a monopolistic environment, compensation of the workforce increases more rapidly than productivity, industrialists will be prompted to increase selling prices, on the condition that trade unions are powerful, the labour disputes aimed at protecting purchasing power will bring about further wage increases.

The remedial measure, recommended by the world monetary authorities for avoiding recession, consists of credit cuts: an old cure, which causes sufficient activity shrinkage to reduce imports and sufficient unemployment to frustrate wage claims. This method maintains the power of financial authorities over industry. 'In addition, in the days of free-trade, we used to make deficit nations swallow that pill, but today there is some irony in swallowing it ourselves' (Robinson, 1965, p. 232). The pre-eminence of financial matters over production growth worldwide, will later induce Joan Robinson to say that in the 1960s 'uncontrolled movement of capital became a major destabilising factor' and to stress that the IMF was totally inadequate for its specific task of protecting national economies against external shocks (Robinson, 1977, p. 252).

If we follow the author's reasoning, the nature, the extent, and the strengths and weaknesses of new mercantilism cannot be understood outside the global framework of international relations. As a matter of fact, after the Second

World War, the growth of new mercantilism started with the expansion of the commercial and monetary forms of American capitalism. During the nineteenth century and until the beginning of the twentieth century, Britain was the warehouse, the workshop and the bank of the then expanding colonial capitalism. Her balance of payments, her technology and her money were the organizers of international activity and spread capitalism to the remotest parts of the world. The economic and political globe would continue to evolve, however, because the free-trade hypotheses were, indeed, not yet confirmed. The American opposition to British power caused a strong questioning of the commercial, institutional and military organizations throughout the world.

Are the Great Depression and the Second World War, then, the consequences of the economic and political oppositions between the old and the new mercantilist nations? The possibility that a powerful nation directs and organizes international relations (even each country's internal relations) is worth thinking over. Joan Robinson emphasizes the fact that from the 1950s until the mid-1960s the political and economic power of the USA was such that the country funded a major part of the world in the form of 'butter and guns'.

If globalization is defined as meeting the needs and aspirations of large market and high profit firms through global commercial relations, then, Joan Robinson's thesis leads us to hold the opinion that globalization, as we see it today, is only the relative metamorphosis of 'new mercantilism'. 'Sadistic' deflationary policies (*dixit* Keynes) have been combined with policies focused on reducing customs duties, relaxing foreign exchange controls and increasing foreign trade. In this highly competitive international environment, globalization seems to solidify established inequalities among both countries and individuals for the benefit of the multinational corporations (MNCs), which 'are forced to make profits taking only their own interest into account' (Robinson, 1979, p. 143). These MNCs have thus become the secular arm of the superpowers in their fight to capture the greater market share and greater access to the production resources feeding their industries.

The power of the MNCs derives not only from their capacity to differentiate prices and take advantage of production factors, as was shown by Joan Robinson in *The Economics of Imperfect Competition* (1933), but also from their financial power:

> Marshall explained that growth is due to the scale economies which give a company a competitive edge by reducing its production costs. This is important where technology requires substantial and indivisible investment, but, in general, the advantage the firm takes of its size lies in the size itself – i.e. the financial power. In the days of Marshall, every single firm operated within a specific industry and had the required related know-how and commercial networks. But nowadays big corporations can switch from one industry to the other using their own experts or

> by taking over a smaller company already in that industry. The modem development of conglomerates clearly shows that what makes it possible for firms, which are already significant, to expand is the financial power rather than the technical dimension.
>
> (Robinson, 1972, pp. 171–2)

Later, Joan Robinson added:

> The abundance of financial resources, on the one hand, allows them to take advantage of the specific assets of the various national economies; the big firms create subsidiaries in many countries and employ workers and managers of many nationalities. They have developed into independent entities, and some are even larger and more powerful than many nations, but the large capitalist firms consider it their duty to 'maximise their profits' by looking for cheap labour wherever they can find it.
>
> (Robinson, 1977b, p. 53)

Moreover, it facilitates stronger potential innovation and thus the imposition of barriers into markets: 'Designing new goods is very important for innovation. In this field, big firms, which have abundant capital, have a big advantage. They can fund research teams and test large numbers of innovations in the hope that one of them will eventually stand out as the best' (ibid., p. 51). This analysis by Joan Robinson seems very modern even if some aspects should be adjusted to account for the current strategies of the big firms.

The increase in the size of firms is still highly dependent today on their financial power. The implementation of policies, such as open markets and liberalization, by the industrialized countries in the 1970s and 1980s were then extended to the group of less developed countries. This extension led to fierce competition and the expansion of the particular markets in which big firms compete. The former national monopolies whose size had greatly increased over the years of growth in the aftermath of the Second World War had to change their strategies and structures. Since sophistication and fast renewal of supply are now the pillars of competition, conglomerate diversification, which was intended to take advantage of the excess production capacities of the big firms, gave way to refocusing on key activities by firms in the 1980s and 1990s. The financial power of firms today is no longer used for extending their activities but for strengthening their basic functions (design, research and development, marketing) through takeovers, mergers and strategic alliances and thus obtaining the 'critical' size required for global markets. The activities of the multinational corporations are then localized according to the double principle of production rationalization (production units are localized in low-salary countries) and of scientific and technological specialization (research laboratories are set up in countries rich in scientific, human, financial and technical resources) (Uzunidis and Boutillier, 1997). At the same time, in order to reduce the costs related to oversized 'management' or 'bureaucratic costs', according to the modern expression (E.O. Williamson), big firms give legal autonomy to larger and larger numbers of functions (production, technical and organizational services). Signing contracts (subcontracting, licensing agreements, franchises, and so on) with independent entities makes it possible for the parent company to maintain its economic control over the devolved activities.

NEO-MERCANTILIST REASON

After 1945, the USA had become, by far, the strongest competitor, and exercised its influence to promote agreements on customs tariffs: General Agreement on Tariffs and Trade (GATT), International Monetary Fund (IMF), among others. But they did not object at all to tariff walls when their own industries were facing Japan's strong competition (Robinson, 1977b, p. 56). In prolongation of this perception, we cannot believe what the 'gnomes' in the State Departments of Trade and international trade and financial institutions (not to mention the media experts) want to instil into us: global markets decide, judge and sanction. With Joan Robinson's permission, we will say that the World Trade Organization (WTO) and the IMF impose a set of rules to ensure the international activities of firms, banks and other financial and trade institutions. This set of rules is certainly at the source of a transnational legal framework for accumulation and profit. But this legal framework, which is essential for the organization of the world, has been produced by tensions and political compromise between influential states, in their own interrelations and in their relations with poorer countries. The aim is to create, somehow or another, the required conditions (measured in terms of return on capital invested) for using the excess capital accumulated for more than 30 years by the North American, European and Far-Eastern economies (Uzunidis, 1999, p. 153).

The application of this legal, liberal and transnational accumulation framework illustrates the prime objective of a big mercantilist country through international institutions: to preserve the economic power of its big industrial and financial firms and to ensure, in return, its own legitimacy as a global power. In 1979, our author wrote that a 'multinational corporation has its head office in one of the very developed countries … and expects some form of protection from its government while it is not really part of a national economy' (Robinson, 1979, p. 8). Thus, a powerful national economy has to expand worldwide, by appropriating, through butter and guns, new regulatory spaces for the profit of its MNCs. Western powers, especially the USA, exercise a considerable influence over Third World governmental policies, either directly or through international institutions such as the World Bank and the International Monetary Fund in which they have a majority, as well as through the countless branches of international finance (ibid.).

Today, more than ever, the financial results of big international firms prevail over the Keynesian and national action engaged by the states. Economic integration, especially between countries industrialized by the mechanisms identified above, has made it possible for the big firms to have access to solvent private and public demand and to react quickly with diversification and renewal, as well as with abundant savings and exceptionally abundant scientific and technical resources. Third World countries (and also the industrially devastated areas in northern countries), on the other hand, appear as resource reserves (standardized labour, raw materials, and so on) and economic crisis absorbers (cost reductions, securitization of local industrial assets). According to the United Nations (UN) and the World Bank, at the end of the twentieth century, the richest 20 per cent of countries of the world (all of them member states of the Organisation for Economic Co-operation and Development (OECD!)) monopolized 86 per cent of the world's negotiable wealth, and the 20 per cent poorest countries only 1 per cent. One and a half billion people in the world live on less than US$1 per day. As Joan Robinson had predicted, unequal development among countries has been perfectly achieved and institutionalized.

The two main features of present neo-mercantilism are that international economic relations are dealt with by financiers and that disputes between national economies are settled within the international organizations. 'The confusion between financial wealth and means of production has never been elicited' and, further, 'the form of accumulation depends on the identity of those who control the capital intended for its funding' (Robinson, 1979, pp. 16–17). The financial deregulation produced by the external and internal policies of the powerful countries and propagated worldwide by the IMF directives, combined with the reduction of tariff barriers, allows the unceasing flow of capital both ways, thus making the investment and growth process more fragile. In this context, global production and trade strategies cannot be dissociated from the fluctuations of capital markets. The confusion and panic, which often seize financial circles, cause crises that immediately have repercussions throughout the production and employment sphere. Derivative instruments (futures, swaps, options, and so on), which were in theory supposed to protect speculators from the risk of brutal fluctuations in interest and exchange rates, have themselves become an object of speculation. Finance is therefore becoming dangerous for the whole structure of accumulation since it is difficult to master, and especially because it must not be retained. The ghost of substantial deflation hangs over economies, and as the buyers' economy is on its last legs it must adapt even if it means undermining its own foundations (those built by substantial solvent demand).

Starting from the principle revealed by Joan Robinson that the nature of capitalist accumulation allows the futile desires of some to prevail over the urgent needs of the masses (1977a, p. 58), the diktats of the finance sector increase the risk taken by firms in markets with minimal expansion. Tied-up capital is very costly for two reasons: the growing need for innovation to renew the supply for a well-defined solvency of global markets increases the cost of investment, and stock exchange and monetary fluctuations make it impossible to foresee the results of production and marketing activities for necessarily new and diversified goods and services. The result of this situation is the global concentration of the ownership of capital (mergers, acquisitions, reciprocal shareholding). In order to protect themselves and increase their market power, big firms implement portfolio diversification strategies and agree as much as they can to pool and share the risks of investing in technological research and development, production and even the capture of more substantial market shares.

Neo-mercantilist reason is prompted by the choice to uphold accumulation in open economies (and then it will only be a question of applying supply policies: of cost reductions and of privatizing procedures for the appropriation of productive resources – Laperche, 1998). But, reasonably, this choice primarily benefits big firms with a global scope. Thus, it is normal that intervention by industrialized states should extend beyond national borders and include the imposition of tariffs on other economies (especially the weakest ones).

THE NEO-MERCANTILIST FRAMEWORK

The financial management of international economic relations and the preservation of the profit potential of big firms have shaped new mercantilism in the context where each powerful country tries to increase its exports (including through its MNCs) while protecting its own market. The developments of GATT reveal how much the US economy presses heavily on the world. This country joined the World Trade Organization because it could maintain its legislation making it possible unilaterally to sanction the countries whose trade practices are considered unfair (Articles 301 and Super 301). And yet, provisions had been laid down in the 1986–93 period of negotiation for a progressive liberalization and organization of agriculture, textile, services and patents worldwide. Today the same sectors, and others, are shaken by neo-mercantilist conflicts. The WTO's Dispute Settlement System (DSS) has to hear dozens of complaints lodged by the USA against the whole world (and sometimes vice versa). Whether the sectors under dispute are strategic ones (some Third World countries do not comply with patents), of national interest (the arms industry is well protected by states through government subsidies and orders – Bellais, 2000), highly competitive (agricultural products), or with a very strong impact on health and the environment (biotechnology, hormones, genetically modified organisms), the superpowers fight with regulations and lawsuits.

The free investment agreement (known as the Multilateral Agreement on Investment) did not mobilize its energies during the 1990s in defence of either the free-trade cause or the nationalist cause against a global neo-mercantilist shift. This treaty was supposed to apply to OECD member states first, and then spread to all WTO member states. It was intended to make up a multilateral legal framework ensuring 'national processing' of foreign investment all over the world. The US Administration has convinced the majority of the country's population of the advantages of free trade and foreign free-investment for US corporations; however, it chooses to give up neither its extra-territorial legislation (Helms and D'Amato Acts) nor the prohibition of foreign investment in sectors that give the USA its full power (military technology). On the other hand, Europe (and France in the first place) has used public opinion to denounce the US 'cultural imperialism' and to save its rural population, which accumulates debts and subsidies. This agreement has failed due to the mercantile and political divergence between the superpowers. It has also failed because many Third World countries are against the implementation of social standards (minimum subsistence wages and benefits, prohibition of child labour, and so on) that would increase their wage costs, which are regarded as their only remaining comparative advantage.

Again, the situation is a paradox: in the name of free-trade, neo-mercantilist powers protect themselves and attempt to impose their rules worldwide, while the economies poor in savings and skilled labour are engulfed in the downward spiral of inequalities, poverty and dependence. The issue of the globalization of poverty is indeed an economic one, but the integration of poor countries into the neo-mercantilist regime is secured by making national political regimes compatible with the economic imperatives of industrial states, as illustrated by the association of the concept of democracy with the free-trade ideology (Petras, 2000). The legal, liberal and global framework of accumulation should emerge from these considerations: it should be liberal for the others; global for big firms, expanding markets and finance; and legal and protective for the powerful neo-mercantilist states.

Behind this free-trade rhetoric and behind the international regulations, neo-mercantilist powers structure the world economic domain in a unilateral or bilateral way where they then give battle. The dialectics of competition – where co-operation does not only apply to multinationals – is above all the results of the political will expressing the economic requirements of powerful national economies. A huge country with a vast home market within its control has some economic advantages that a small country does not have. The latter has to optimize its revenue prospects in connection with specialization and the security of its national production, whereas the big country may benefit from the two aspects (Robinson, 1965, p. 228). Here, Joan Robinson takes the example of the European Union to emphasize, with some scepticism, how difficult it is for mature national economies to make mutual concessions in order to create a common market. And yet, European countries are on the verge of achieving this integration. In addition, the North American Free-Trade Agreement (NAFTA), the Mercado Commón del Sur (MERCOSUR) in Latin America or the Association of South East Asia (ASEAN) in Asia are international co-operation areas aimed at increasing the size of national markets.

The word 'regionalization' conveys free trade and enterprise in a multinational area, and is often measured in terms of the ratio of inter-regional exchanges to the international trade of the countries making up the area. According to WTO data, the ratio is 52 per cent for NAFTA, 63 per cent for the European Union, but only slightly over 20 per cent for the MERCOSUR and the ASEAN. The maturity, and also the solvency, of North American and Western European economies may account for the pre-eminence of its area over the rest of the world. The dependence of Latin America and South East Asia on the economies of rich countries (including Japan) deprives the MERCOSUR and the ASEAN of the protective and specializing functions of the activities of their member states. On the other hand, regionalization offers the neo-mercantilist superpowers wider commercial and monetary spaces as backup and safety elements for their main firms (hence their disputes concerning international treaties). Another function of these areas is to facilitate the commercial and political expansion of the main economies composing them. What would become of Africa, the Baltic area, the Black Sea area, the economic co-operation between Asian and Pacific countries, the ASEAN or the MERCOSUR without the active and often protective presence of the USA, Germany and its European allies or Japan?

But, the economic and political competition between superpowers also tends towards systematic non-aggression pacts. Such is the case of the transatlantic economic partnership signed by the European Union and the USA at the London Summit in May 1998. The objective is to issue liberal and harmonized rules for their economic relations: the reduction of trade barriers, the opening of public markets, national processing of investment on each side, and compliance with patent rights. Does this transatlantic alliance which already covers about 50 per cent of world production, 40 per cent of international trade and more than 50 per cent of the world mergers and acquisitions reflect what the world economy will be like in the future? – that is, a kind of organization of international economic and political relations in line with the growth and prosperity objectives of the superpowers, public and private, on both sides of the Atlantic.

CONCLUSION

Economists should show gratitude to Joan Robinson for her fine analysis of new mercantilism. The author's pessimism (or realism) proved correct on many occasions, and the future is still uncertain! 'Free-trade for the *others* favours the strongest competitor's interests in global markets, and a competitor which is strong enough does not care at all about trade barriers' (Robinson, 1977a, p. 56). European mercantilist countries fear the American economy. The systematic charges made against US policy are much appreciated by many European intellectuals and political activists. The rhetoric has it that international institutions are an extension of the American law and power. But what should we think of the leverage and spinoff effect of the US economy on the rest of the world? With a $250 billion plus foreign trade deficit and a $300 billion plus balance of payments deficit in 1999, the USA only accounts for 13 per cent of world exports compared with 47 per cent for Western Europe and 18 per cent for Japan and Asia's newly industrialized countries. The US imports 17 per cent of all goods and services sold worldwide. Reserves in US dollars amount to 60 per cent of the world's monetary reserves; half of all financial and commercial transactions in the world are carried out in US dollars. We could say that it is logical that the US Administration should want to set the trade balance on its feet again and impose rules that would be favourable to the USA. But it is also more logical to see the natural trend of new mercantilism in the clashes of interests opposing the USA to the other industrialized nations: 'each nation wants to have a surplus'. In addition, we can appreciate a tremendous subtlety of new mercantilism: the central player of the world economy (the USA) may concurrently have a large share of world activity (through its MNCs, its finance and its currency) while having a foreign trade deficit.

The rising political competition comes from unstable, international economic relations and develops the spirit of invention of the states in terms of protectionism. In a situation of open economy, the decision to produce and the act of producing are sanctioned by financing; the states then use regulations to justify the expansion or relative drop effects. The fact that economic activity is conditioned by politics prompted Joan Robinson to say, on several occasions, that international law is the law of the mightiest. America wants to maintain, in the short term, its superpower status and to evolve, in the long term, towards an institutionalized world co-operation. On the other hand, the

European Union has endowed itself with a currency (the euro) aimed at countering the American mercantilism; but we have doubts about its success. The multinationalism and historical divergences have not, so far, provided the EU with the political tools required for giving a social and political destiny to the economic integration through market and currency.

As the states give up power in their home territories, they extend their action of organizing space for the capital of their national big firms and wealthy individuals through international institutions, treaties and agreements. Thus, we can outline new mercantilism and correctly understand 'globalization'. As Joan Robinson had foreseen, the national and international 'sadistic' policies have intensified inequalities, multiplied military conflicts and broken the social solidarity established by the Keynesian revolution. 'We can note with irony that after the substantial technical progress brought about by the period of growth, all we are offered now is the return to massive unemployment and poverty amidst affluence' (Robinson, 1977a, p. 253).

REFERENCES

Bellais, R. (2000), *Production d'armes et puissance des Nations*, Paris: L'Harmattan.

Laperche, B. (1998), *La firme et l'information*, Paris: L'Harmattan.

Michiels, J-P., and D. Uzunidis (1999), *Mondialisation et Citoyenneté*, Paris: L'Harmattan.

Petras, J. (2000), 'Capitalisme et démocratie, conflit, compatibilité et instrumentation', *Innovations. Cahiers d'économie de l'innovation*, Paris, no. 11.

Robinson, J. (1933), *L'économie de la concurrence imparfaite*, reprinted 1975, Paris: Dunod.

Robinson, J. (1951), *Collected Economic Papers*, Oxford: Basil Blackwell.

Robinson, J. (1965), 'Le nouveau mercantilisme', in *Contributions à l'économie contemporaine*, reprinted 1984, Paris: Economica.

Robinson, J. (1972), *L'accumulation du capital*, Paris: Dunod.

Robinson, J. (1976), *Hérésies économiques*, Calman Levy: Paris (first published 1971 by Basic Books).

Robinson, J. (1977a), 'Qu'est devenue la politique de l'emploi?', in *Contributions à l'économie contemporaine*, reprinted 1984, Paris: Economica.

Robinson, J. (1977b), 'Quelles sont les questions?', in *Contributions à l'économie contemporaine*, reprinted 1984; Paris: Economica.

Robinson, J. (1979), *Développement et sous-développement*, Paris: Economica.

Uzunidis, D., and S. Boutillier (1997), *Le travail bradé*, Paris: coll. Economie et Innovation.

Uzunidis, D. (1999), 'Firme mondiale et Etat national. Le libéralisme en cause', in J.P. Michiels, D. Uzunidis (eds) (1999), *Mondialisation et Citoyenneté*, col. *Economie et Innovation*, Paris: L'harmattan.

Williamson, E.O. (1975), *Markets and Hierarchies: Analysis and Antitrust Implications*, New York: Free Press.

Index

Account
money as a unit of 72, 77, 89, 90, 95, 101
Advertising Statistics Yearbook 238
Alami, T. 92
Allais, M. 267
Amadeo, E. 176
Ambiguity 269
Analogy 260, 262
negative 290
Andersen, E. 268, 276
Andrade, J. and Silva, F.M.L. 150
Andresen, T. 271, 277
Anderson, B. 89
Andrews, P. 290
Annual Census of Production (ACOP) 234–5, 240–41
Anti-inflationary policy 121–37, 139–56
Arena, R. 249, 256, 258
Arestis, P. 16, 19
Arestis, P. and Sawyer, M. 106
Arestis, P. McCauley and Sawyer 20
Arida, P. and Lara-Resende, A. 175
Argitis, G. and Pitelis C. 19
Arthur, B. 271
Arthur, W.B. 271
Artis, M. 14
Asset Prices 44, 61
Auer, M.R., Reuveny, R. and Adler, L. 167
Australia
Bond rates 196
Exchange rate equation 188
Inflation 187, 195
Interest rates 196
Monetary commodity prices 187–8, 195, 199–200
Parsimonious model 196
Primary commodity markets 188, 193
World business cycles 199
Bahmani O. and Techaratananchai, A. 92
Balance of payments 34–5, 48, 172
Surplus 334
Bank money 103, 104
Banking system
reserves 73, 79
Barter 316
Basar, T. 276
Basili, M. 268
Baumol, W. 310, 312, 314, 315
Bean, C. 3
Becker, G. 310, 314, 315
Behavioral rules 254, 256, 260, 261, 262
Abstract 261, 262
Tacit 261, 262
Bell, S. 113, 114
Belief
Collective 260, 264
Conjectural 256
Individual 257, 258, 260, 261, 262
Irrational 250, 257, 259, 260
Rational 250, 257, 258, 259, 260
Structural 256
Berger, P. and Luckmann, T. 86–8, 91, 93, 94
Bernhard, P. 276
Bewley, T. 280
Bibow, J. 3, 16, 20
Blandchard, O. 192–8
Blaug, M. 310, 312, 315
Blecker, R. 153
Blinder, A. 81, 123, 124, 137
Bloch, H. 187–8, 190–91, 194
Blunder-Wignall, A. 190–92
Bonds, government 32, 36–7
Bresciani-Turroni, C. 173, 174
Bresser Pereira, L.C. and Nakano, Y. 182
Brock, W. 271, 278
Brown, L.R. 163

Business Monitor 238

Cadette, W., Levy, D. and Thiruvadanthai, S. 53
Cagan, P. 173
Cagliarini, A. 280
Câmara, A. 182
Câmara, A. and Vernengo, M. 182
Cambridge tradition ix
Camerer, C. 269
Cancian, F. 92
Capacity utilization 5, 19, 46
Capital mobility 139–56
Carbaugh, R.J. 110
Cardim de Carvalho, F., Pieres de Souza, F.E., Sicsu, J., Rodriguez de Paula, L.F., and Studart, R. 143
Cardim de Carvalho, F. 182
Castellan, N. 286, 296
Central bank 36–7
Central bank independence 3–4, 10, 11, 17, 19
Cesarano, F. 81
Chartalism 32
  Neo-chartalism 33
Chen, Z. 280
Cherubini, U. 280
Chew, S. 267
China 92
Circuit 30
  monetary circuit 303
Chiarella, C. 270
Choquet, G. 267
  Expected utility theory 267
Clark, J. 212
Clower, R. 231, 310, 314, 315
Clower-Olson approach 231
Colander, D. 85–6
Collective action 261
Collective wisdom 264
Commodities 316
Confidence, state of 270
Contractionary policies 140–56
Convention 261
Conyon, M. 234
Cornford, A. and Kregel, J.A. 131, 137
Costa, C. and De Grauwe, P. 74
Council for Mutual Economic Assistance (COMECON) 157, 159, 169
Courvisanos, J. 205, 208, 215
Coutts, K. 292
Credibility 3
Credit 4–5, 60, 63
Credit rationing 338
Creditworthiness 35
Critical realism 287
Currency boards 109–12
  Bulgaria 111–12
Currie, D. 276

Davidson, Paul 19, 125, 137, 172, 259, 269, 285, 288
Dawes Plan 175
Dean, J. 92
Debreu 281
Debt 29
  Private 35, 44, 45, 49, 60, 64
Debt deflation 45, 60, 62 64, 113
Debt load 58–61, 66
Decision making process 274
Deficits 29, 31, 33, 173
Deflation 7, 17, 121
Debt deflation 45
DeGrawe, P. 106
Dekel, E. 267
Dequech, D. 269
Desmonde, W. 93
Dickey-Foller Test 193
Disequilibria 123–30
Distribution of income 227
Domowitz, I.R. 234
Dostaler, G. and Maris, B. 95
Dow, S. 285, 288, 290, 295
Dowd, K. and Greenaway, D. 71
Downward, P. 285, 286, 287, 288, 289, 290, 291, 292, 293, 294, 295
Duménil, G. 217–18, 278
Dupuis, P. 281
Dupuy 264

Eastern Europe 157–71
  Energy sector 160–64
  Environmental degradation, concern for 158–69
  Privitization 165–7
Eatwell, J. and Taylor, L. 147, 151
Econometrics 285, 286, 287, 289
  Critical realism and 285, 287, 288, 291, 293, 294
Economic growth and development 334

Economic imperialism 335
Economic Restructuring 159–71
Edwards, S. 123, 137
Effective demand 4–5, 128, 259, 302, 303, 324, 334
Eichengreen, B. and Von Hagen, J. 106
Electronic money 70, 71, 73–5, 79–81
Elliot, R. 281
Ellis, H. 174
Ellsberg, D. 267, 280
  Paradox 267, 268
Emerging market economies 139
Employment 5, 15, 16
  Employment, free trade and mercantilism 335
Epstein, L. 280, 281
Equilibrium 238
  Concept 3, 121, 276
  Market 261
  Markov perfect 275
Equity bubble 51, 54, 60, 64
Euphoria 44, 65
European Bank for Reconstruction and Development (EBRD) 164
European Investment Bank (EIB) 164
European Union 3, 108
  Enlargement 167
  European Central Bank (ECB) 3, 12–18, 20, 70, 82, 106, 107
  Economic growth and development in 3, 334, 345
  Stability and Growth Pact 17, 18, 106
  International trade 344
  Labor productivity 5, 6, 17
  Monetary union 3, 11, 12, 16, 18, 20, 39, 106–108, 347
  Unemployment 12, 15
Exchange rates 44, 47, 122, 123, 133, 136, 173, 176
  Argentina 109, 135, 136
Exchange Rate Mechanism 240

Fanning, C. and O'Mahoney, D. 65
Fama, E.F. 72
Federal Reserve Bank 13, 18, 20
Feldstein, M. 137
Fiat money 32
Finance motive 302, 303
Financial crises 121, 135, 146, 147
Financial fragility 44, 50, 52, 64
Financial liberalization 132, 139–56
Finch, J. 289
Fiscal policies 106, 135
Fishburn, P. 267
Fisher, I. 61, 113
Flaschel, P. 270, 277
Fleetwood, S. 253
Foley, D. 270, 281
Forder, J. 3
Foreign direct investment (FDI) 165–8
Franke, R. 270, 277
France 214, 218–19
Freedman, C. 75, 76, 82
Friedman, B. 73, 74, 78–9, 81
Freeman, C. 212
Foley, D. 102, 103, 114
Foreign currency reserves 111, 112, 115
Full employment
  Political aspects of full employment (PAFE) 228
Functional finance 100, 108, 111
Furness, W.H. 96–7
Furtado, C. 175

Garagnani, P. ix
Garrouste 256, 261
General Agreement on Tariffs and Trade (GATT) 170
Generalized Instrumental Variable Estimation Technique (GIVE) 197–8
Germany 214, 218–19
Geroski, P. 292
Gilbert, M. 85, 93
Gilboa, I. 267
Ginsburg, J. 164
Globalization 339
  Destabilizing movements of capital 338, 342
  Export-led growth and 335
  Imports promotion 337
  Corporations' financial power 339, 340
Godley, W. 34, 66, 107, 270, 292
Goodhart, C. 71, 75, 82, 105, 113
Goodwin, R. 208
Grabel, I. 115
Graham, F. 174
Grant, S. 280
Great Britain 339

Great Depression 220
Greenfield, R.L. and Yeager, L.B. 72, 81
Greenspan, A. 35, 39
Gregory, R.G. 190, 192
Gruen, D. 190, 192, 198

Haavelmo, T. 286
Hahn, F. 278
Hahn, F. and Solow, R. 137
Hall, R. 290, 293
Hanke, S. and Schuler, K. 111
Hansen, L. 268, 274, 275, 276, 277, 278, 279, 280, 281
Harcourt, G. 278
Harrod R. 337
Hassul, M. 281
Haustein, H.-D. 219
Hawken, P., Lovins, A., and Lovins, L.H. 164
Hayek, F. 249, 250, 253, 254, 255, 256, 257, 258, 261, 262, 263, 264, 265
Heath, A. 280
Hefeker, C. 140
Hein, E. 10, 19, 20
Heine, M. and Herr, H. 14, 19
Helfferich, K. 174
Hendry, D. 286, 287, 295
Hicks, J. 104, 125, 325
Hitch, C. 290, 293
Hoarding 323
Hobbes, T. 93
Holland, J. 271
Hommes, C. 271
Hong Kong 92, 109
Hubbard, R.G. 234
Huerta, A. 142
Hyperinflation 172–84

Import penetration 234–5
Induction 260
Inequality 26, 38
Inflation 3–4, 7, 13, 15–16, 17, 29, 172–84
  Argentina 135
  Balance-of-payments theory 172, 176–81
  Conflict models 173
  German school theory 172, 174
  Latin American neo-structuralist view 172, 175
  Latin American structuralist theory 175
  Mexico 144
  Neo-classical interpretation 173
  Post Keynesian view 172
Infrastructure 38
Ingham, G. 85, 89, 91, 93, 94, 96
Innovation 205–207, 219, 222
  dynamics 206
  Radical vs. incremental 206–207
  Stages of lifecycle 207
Institutions 4, 86–7
Interest rates 4, 5, 15, 29, 36, 121–37, 172
  Exogenous 36
  Overnight rates 77
  Theoretical case for lower interest rates 37–8
International financial statistics 193
International Monetary Fund (IMF) 35, 57, 115, 121, 162, 188, 193, 341, 342
International trade 35
  New mercantilism 334
Investment 49, 54, 65, 125
  Two price model of 45, 49
  Transfer of developing countries' saving 337
Ioannides 261
Israel 92
IT revolution and central banking 69, 72–6, 78–80

James, M. 281
Japan 214, 218–19
  Economic growth and development in 334
Juniper, J. 280

Kaldor, N. 80, 82, 125, 175
Kalecki, M. 6, 49–50, 65, 187–207, 221, 227–44, 285, 290
  Degree of monopoly 227–8, 230–33, 244
  Endogenous innovations 206
  Extended reproduction model 207
  Investment activity 220
  Political aspects of full employment (PAFE) 228
  Theory of Economic Dynamics 227–8, 231

Theory of Income Distribution 227–8, 244
Pricing Analysis 187–8
Susceptibility cycle 213, 215
Katz, L. 192–8
Keen, S. 270
Kenen, P. 115
Keynes, J.M. ix, 3, 45, 47, 62, 85, 89, 90, 95, 101, 102, 113, 174, 222, 249, 250, 251, 252, 253, 257, 258, 259, 260, 261, 262, 264, 265, 269, 272, 273, 279, 280, 285, 288, 290, 301–307, 311, 323, 324
Effect 269, 270
King, J.E. 227, 243
King, M. 82
Kittel B. and Traxler F. 10
Kleinknecht, A. 213
Knapp, G.F. 103
Knowledge
Hayek and 253, 254, 263
Keynes and 250, 251, 254, 258
Social division of 255
Korean War 217
Kregel, J.A. ix, 105, 131, 258, 259, 260
Kreps, D. 280
Krueger, M. 81
Krugman, P. 123, 137
Kyoto Protocol 161

Labor productivity 5, 6, 17
Ladd, J. 92
Lakonishok, J. 271
Laramie, A. 227–8
Latin America
Debt problems 142
Inflation 121–37, 139–56
Stabilization programs 121–37
Lavoie, M. 19, 270
Lawson, M.L. 166
Lawson, T. 285, 286, 287, 288, 289, 295, 296
Layard, R. Nickell, S. and Jackman, R. 8, 19
Leaner, E. 286, 287
LeBaron, B. 271
Lee, F.S. 290, 294
Lehnert, D. 206
Leijonhufvud, A. 310, 314, 315
Lemmen, J. and Goodhart, C. 115
Lender of last resort 75, 76
Leontjeva, E. 110
Lerner, A. 100–102, 104, 105, 111, 113, 114
Levine, P. 276
Lévy, D. 217–18, 278
Lewis, D. 84–5, 92
Liquidity preference 31, 52
Locke, J. 93
Lucas, R. 278
Lund, P. 291, 292
Luxembourg R, 335

Machin, S. 234
Macroeconomic Stability 121, 136
Magill, M. 278
Mair, D. 227–8
Maizels, A. 188
Malthus T.R. 320
Marinacci, M. 280
Mark-up 233, 238, 244, 290, 291, 294
Estimation of 233–8
Market Economy, models of transition to 157–8
Market Failure 121
Marshall-Lerner condition 4
Marx, Karl 6, 334, 335
McCallum, B. 291, 292
McKinnon, R. and Huw, P. 132
Means, G. 290, 294
Means of payment 71, 102
Mearman, A. 285, 286, 287, 288, 289, 290, 293, 294, 295
Means of production 210–12
Medium of exchange 72, 85, 87, 88
MERCOSUR 345
Mexico 139–56
1995 crisis 121
Competitiveness with United States 145–8
Unemployment 143, 153
Mill, J.S. 316–21
Millier, J. 115
Minsky, H. 44–6, 49–50, 52, 61–2, 102, 113, 114, 270, 274, 280
Mirofushi, T. 280
Mises, L. von 114
Mitchell, W. 285
Monetarism 230, 325
Monetary policy 124–37, 139–56

Monetary policy and liquidity preference 31
Monetizing the debt 107, 121
Money
  As a creature of the state 32
  As social relationship/convention 84, 89, 91–7
  As a unit of account 72, 77, 89, 90, 95, 101
  Conventional 72–5, 79–81
  Chartal means of payment 102
  Creation of 30, 32
  Electronic money 70
  Fiat money 32
  Hierarchy 101–105, 107, 114
  Means of circulation 318
  Non-neutrality 124, 136
  Object 86, 94–5
  Origins 30
  State money approach 114
  Substitutes 80
  Taxes-drive-money approach 95–6, 102, 105
Money supply 110, 173
Monopoly 334, 335, 336, 340
  Degree of monopoly 227–8, 230–33, 244
Moore, B.J. 19, 144
Morck, R., Shleifer and Vishny R. 46
Morgan W. 188
Mosler, W. 107
Mundell, R. 123
Mundell-Fleming Model 123

National Income Identity 33–4
Needlman, J. 95
Neild, R. 291, 292, 293
Neo-Chartalists 95–7
Neuwirth, E. 219
New Keynesians 7, 301, 302, 321
New mercantilism 334, 335, 339, 341, 343, 344
Newton-Raphsen interactive method 194
Network effect 71
New Monetary Economics 73, 81
Non-accelerating-inflation-rate-of-unemployment (NAIRU) 7–11, 13, 15, 17–18, 19
Nordhaus, W. 292
Noyola, J. 175

O'Connell, S. 270
Olekalns, N. 196
Olive, M. 191
Olivera, J. 182
Olsen, M. 228–31, 236
  The Logic of Collective Action 228
  The Rise and Decline of Nations 228
  Selective incentives 228–9, 231, 244
Operatives wages 240
Ordinary least squares 286
Organisation for Economic Co-operation and Development (OECD) 161, 162, 188, 193, 224
Orthodox approach 121–37, 149, 153
Ortiz, E. 123, 125
Ortiz, E. and Motamen, S. 123

Pagan, A. 191, 198, 287
Palley, T. 270
Panico, C. 270
Parguez, A. 115
Parrinello, S. ix
Pasinetti, L.L. 106
Pentecost, E. 137
Petersen, I. 281
Peterson, B.C. 234
Phillips Curve 191–2
Pigou Effect 269, 270
Poisson distributed random process 206
Poisson regression 220
Pollin, R. 285
Porteus, E. 280
Prebish, R. 127
Presser, F.M. 150
Price stability 3, 14, 18
Prices 173
  Short run world pricing equation 189
Pricing behavior 290, 306, 336, 337
Prisoners' Dilemma problem 228
Probability 259
  Sub-additive 268
  Subjective 252
  Theory of 252
Product differentiation 244
Productivity 37–8
Profitability 125
Profits 44, 45, 49–52, 304, 305, 312, 335, 337, 341
Purchasing power 196
  Purchasing power parity index 223

Purchasing Power Parity Principle 141

Quantity Theory of Money (QTM) 113, 173, 181
Quiggin, J. 280
Quinzii, M. 278

Radford, R.A. 92
Ramsay, J. 289
Regan, P. 227, 242
Regression, average economic 286, 287, 288
Reynolds, P. 227, 236
Ricardo, D. 312, 323
Riccatti equation 276
Risk 269
Rochon, L.-P. 95
Robinson, J. 333–43, 345, 346
Ros, J. 123
Rosenberg, N. 213
Rowthorn, R. 173
Runde, J. 290
Rushdy, F. 291, 292

Sahal, G. 206
Santomero, A. and Seater, J. 81
Sapsford, D. 188, 194
Sardoni, C. and Verde, A. 81
Sargent, T. 268, 274, 275, 276, 277, 278, 279, 281
Savage, L. 267
Saving 47, 54, 125, 303, 306
Sawyer, M. 19, 107, 205, 227, 292
Say J.B.: 311, 316, 318, 319, 321, 323
  Say's Law 303, 311, 324
Sayer, A. 289
Schenk, C.R. 92
Schmeidler, D. 267
Schmidt-Bleek, F. 160
Schneider, M. 280
Schumpeter, J. 205–206, 208–209, 213, 310, 312, 334, 335
  Clust-Bun effect 208, 213, 224
  Evolutionary dynamics 205–206, 208–209
  Innovation dynamics 206, 224
  Schumpeterian Cycle 213
  Schumpeterian Dynamics 216,219
Semmler, W. 270, 271
Shalian, B. 281
Shock therapy 158
Short run world pricing equation 189
Siegel, S. 286, 296
Silverberg, G. 206, 213
Sims, C. 286, 287
Small open economy 122–37
Smith A. 312, 323
Smith, G. 292
Single internal market 240
Snowdon, B., Vane, H., and Wynarczyk, P. 137, 302
Social mobility 25
Soete, L. 212
Sonnenschien 281
Southeast Asian crisis (1997) 121
Specialization index 238, 241
Sraffa, P. ix
Stabilization programs 135
Stagflation 219
Standard Industrial Classification 240
Standard of value 89
State
  New mercantilism 336
  Sovereignty 347
State money 102, 103
Steindl, J. 210
Stevens, Ed 114
Stiglitz, Joseph 121
Store of value 91
Structural adjustment 219
Structural change 121–37
Structure-Conduct-Performance (S-C-P) paradigm 232
Subjectivism 255, 258
Sugden, R. 93
Sugeno, M. 280
Sunkel, O. 175
Sustainable development 159–71
Swanke, T. 85–6, 91, 92
Sylos-Labini, P. 292

Tainter, J. 171
Tallarini, T. 268, 274, 275, 276, 281
Tavares, M.C. 140, 144, 146, 147
Tax 39
  Death tax 27
  Estate tax 27, 28
  Inheritance tax 26–7, 28
Taxes-drive-money approach 102

Taylor, C. 115
Taylor, L. 182, 270
Taylor, P. 271
Terms of Trade 190
Tcherneva 85
Thompson, C. 192, 198
Tobin, J. and Galub, S. 104
Trade unions 233
Tversky, A. 267, 280
Two-price theory 46–7

Uncertainty 252
  Aversion 267, 268
  Fundamental 269
Unemployment 8, 12, 15, 30, 121, 301–308
Unions 6–7
Unit prime cost 191
United Kingdom 214, 218–19, 240
United Nations 342
United Nations Conference on Trade and Development (UNCTAD) 140, 145
United States of America 214, 217–19, 220
  Dollar determination 94
  Federal Reserve System 13, 18, 20
  International trade and 344
  Patent system 223
Uribe, M. 92

van der Hoek, J. 281
Van Duijn, J.J. 219
Vanberg 257, 258
Vercelli, A. 213, 279, 281
Veronesi, P. 281
Vernengo, M. 182
Versailles Treaty 174
Verspagen, B. 205, 213, 215
Vietnam War 217

Wages 177–8
  Wage and price stickiness 301, 303, 306
  Wage curve 192
Wakker, P. 267, 280
Wallstrom, M. 168
Walras L. 314
Wealth 24–43, 47
  Defined 24
  Democratization of 25
  Distribution 25–6
Weatherford, J. 90
Weber, M. 269
Weil, P. 280
Wilkinson, J. 190
Williamson E.O. 341
Williamson, J. 110
Wilson, T. 90
Winters, L.A. 194, 196
Woodford, M. 76–8
World Bank 121, 164, 167, 342
World Trade Organization (WTO) 35, 170, 341, 343, 344
World War I 217
World War II 217, 220
Wray. L.R. 95, 96, 102, 103, 104, 105, 113, 114, 137, 182

Zhang, J. 280
Zin, S. 281
Zelizer, V. 91, 94